W9-CNR-087

MONTGOMERY COLLEGE LIBRARY
RUCKVILLE CAMPUS

WITHDRAWN FROM LIBRARY

Journey with Genius

Caricature of D. H. Lawrence, made from memory by Miguel Covarrubias (Courtesy of the artist)

Journey with Genius

RECOLLECTIONS AND REFLECTIONS

CONCERNING THE D. H. LAWRENCES

by Witter Bynner

ILLUSTRATED

OCTAGON BOOKS

A DIVISION OF FARRAR, STRAUS AND GIROUX

New York   1974

Copyright, 1951, by Witter Bynner

Reprinted 1974
by arrangement with the original publisher, The John Day Co.

OCTAGON BOOKS
A DIVISION OF FARRAR, STRAUS & GIROUX, INC.
19 Union Square West
New York, N. Y. 10003

Library of Congress Cataloging in Publication Data

Brynner, Witter, 1881-1968.
　　Journey with genius.

　　Reprint of the ed. published by the J. Day Co., New York.

　　1. Lawrence, David Herbert, 1883-1930.　2. Lawrence, Frieda
　　(von Richthofen) 1879-1956.　I. Title.
[PR6023.A93Z58　1974]　　　　　823'.9'12 [B]　　　　　73-21674
ISBN 0-374-91137-1

Printed in USA by
Thomson-Shore, Inc.
Dexter, Michigan

TO

FRED AND JUANITA LEIGHTON

Acknowledgments

FOR permission to quote from books by D. H. Lawrence, I acknowledge the courtesy of The Viking Press in the United States and of William Heinemann, Ltd., in England as to excerpts from: *Aaron's Rod, Apocalypse, The Captain's Doll, Etruscan Places, Fantasia of the Unconscious, Kangaroo, Lady Chatterley's Lover, Last Poems, Letters of D. H. Lawrence, The Lost Girl, The Lovely Lady, Phoenix, Psychoanalysis and the Unconscious, The Rainbow, Sea and Sardinia, Sons and Lovers, Studies in Classic American Literature, The Trespasser,* and *Women in Love*. Acknowledgment is hereby given like courtesy extended by Alfred A. Knopf, Inc., and by William Heinemann, Ltd., as to excerpts from: *Assorted Articles, Mornings in Mexico, The Plumed Serpent, Short Stories, Tales of D. H. Lawrence,* and *The Woman Who Rode Away;* to Duffield and to William Heinemann, Ltd., as to *The White Peacock;* and to The Gotham Book Mart as to *Letters of D. H. Lawrence to Bertrand Russell*.

I am grateful to Mrs. Lawrence for permitting quotation from her husband's letters, from her own, from his books, and from her own book, *Not I but the Wind;* to Mrs. Remington Stone (Idella Purnell) for Lawrence's letters to her, hitherto unpublished, and her own letters to me; to Willard Johnson for quotation from *The Laughing Horse* and himself; to Frederic W. Leighton for his recollections of the Lawrences in Mexico City and Chapala; to Roy Chanslor for his letter concerning Lawrence's review of *Fantazius Mallare;* to Miguel Covarrubias for use of his Lawrence caricature; to Knud Merrild for use of his Lawrence portrait, and to custodians of the Louise and Walter C. Arensberg Collection at the Philadelphia Museum of Art; to Robert Hunt for many sessions of detailed advice concerning this book and for indexing it; and to Dorothy Wendland for painstaking assistance with the manuscript.

For the right to quote passages from books about Lawrence, I appreciatively acknowledge permission from the author and University of Washington Chapbooks as to *D. H. Lawrence, An Indiscretion* by Richard Aldington, whose biography, *D. H. Lawrence,* was not issued in time for me to make use of it in these chapters; from the author and J. B. Lippincott Company as to *Lawrence and Brett, A Friendship,* by Dorothy Brett; from John Carswell as to *The Savage Pilgrimage* by Catherine Carswell; from Jonathan Cape as to *D. H. Lawrence, A Personal Record by E. T.* (Jessie Chambers); from Dodge Publishing Company as to *The Life of D. H. Lawrence* by Hugh Kingsmill; from The Viking Press as to *Not I but the Wind* by Frieda Lawrence; from the author as to *A Poet and Two Painters* by Knud Merrild; from the author and Jonathan Cape as to two books, *Reminiscences of D. H. Lawrence* and *Son of Woman* by J. Middleton Murry; and from the author and Columbia University Press as to *D. H. Lawrence and Susan His Cow* by William York Tindall.

For other quoted passages, I appreciate permission from the author and The John Day Company as to *The Good Earth* by Pearl Buck; from the author and Duell, Sloan and Pearce as to *God's Little Acre* by Erskine Caldwell; from Norman Douglas as to *D. H. Lawrence and Maurice Magnus—A Plea for Better Manners,* privately printed; from Harcourt, Brace and Company as to *Looking Back* by Norman Douglas and *Aspects of the Novel* by E. M. Forster; from the author's agents, Mary Pritchett–Barbara Brandt as to Graham Greene's *Another Mexico,* published by the Viking Press; from the New Mexico Quarterly Review as to articles by Eric Russell Bentley, Oliver La-Farge, and John C. Neff; from the Atlantic Monthly Press and Little, Brown and Company as to Sir Osbert Sitwell's *Laughter in the Next Room;* from the author and Harcourt, Brace and Company as to *World within World* by Stephen Spender; and from the author and *The New Yorker* as to an article by Edmund Wilson on the Shalako ceremony at Zuñi, New Mexico.

I also acknowledge brief quotations from Ernest Boyd, Bennett Cerf, William Gerhardi, A. E. Housman, Aldous Huxley, Melvin Lasky, Wyndham Lewis, Norman Mailer, John Masefield, Eugene O'Neill, V. S. Pritchett, George Santayana, Elizabeth Shepley Sergeant, Karl Shapiro, Bernard Shaw, Diana Trilling, Frank Waters, H. G. Wells, and Rebecca West. And I especially thank Kai Götzsche for the several notable letters of his which are here reprinted from Knud Merrild's *A Poet and Two Painters.*

WITTER BYNNER

Contents

Illustrations

Note

EXCEPT for *Sons and Lovers* and such by-the-way essays as *Sea and Sardinia,* I had not in 1922 found D. H. Lawrence an engaging or coercing writer. Magnetic, yes, because of testy fervors this way and that and impressive because of his individual, vigorous, imaginative use of English, the best refreshment of the idiom I had found since reading George Meredith in 1900. After the fine autobiographical novel, however, *Fantasia of the Unconscious* and *Psychoanalysis and the Unconscious* had alienated me.

Of Lawrence personally I knew very little. I had heard rumors that during the war he and his German wife, daughter of a Baron and cousin of the air ace, Von Richthofen, had been suspect of tepid allegiance to Britain's cause, and this had not surprised me, since Germany's cause had seemed to me in the large an imitation of Britain's, and the conflict, at least in the beginning, a grapple of two Empires with comparable aims. I had heard also a direct report from Amy Lowell of a call she had paid the Lawrences in London, where they occupied, she told me, a deplorably dingy, airless basement harmful not only to his spirit but to his health. She spoke of him as gaunt, frail, nervous, possibly tubercular. Though as a man he had seemed to her opinionated and willful, she greatly admired his work. Handing me a letter to him, she bade me give assistance in any way I might if he should come to New York, a move she had encouraged. Later, after my own westward move to New Mexico, I had seen some of his letters to Mabel Dodge Sterne and felt behind them a man whom I should well like to meet, and so I was glad that Mrs. Sterne had induced the Lawrences to swing from Australia to San Francisco and thence to pay her a visit at Taos in 1922.

In 1950, a young Sicilian poet showed me, outside Taormina, Fontana Vecchia, the hillside villa where Lawrence wrote his famous snake poem and much else. "The landlord, Ciccio Cacópardo," explained the poet on our walk, "owns three houses now and rents them and is very rich." "A friend of David Lawrence is here" he called across high terraces. A sturdy middle-aged man clambered from the garden where he was working, greeted us warmly in good English, and led us up to the house, overlooking rural slopes and blue sea. "It then had only lamps and water which was carried, but now is electricity, and we have a bathroom where their little kitchen used to be." He and his wife had in the old days lived on the ground floor and the Lawrences in the two upper stories, "where now lives a Swedish girl, a painter," said the poet, bright eyed. His eyes glistened still more when she opened the door for us. We were all bound by Lawrence. "I have copied his Taormina poems into a book," she beamed, "and set my water colors round them. It is beautiful to be where he was and to hear the feet of the goats go by in the morning as he heard them, like leaves blown in the wind. I read him once when I was unhappy," she continued, "and he comforted me, and I am translating these poems into Swedish." Then Ciccio remembered "David H. Lawrence's early mistakes in Italian. It was in 1920. *'Avete del latte di capro?'* 'Have you he-goat's milk?' It has been ever since in the community a laughing memory. He used to put his head back when he spoke and close his eyes, and his face was thin with a beard." Ciccio compressed his own face between his palms. "And is Frieda still large and light-haired?" Then Emma, Ciccio's wife, put in, "There was a bench here outside my mother-in-law's room and he would sit on it and talk with her and everyone said she had a new beau!" "My mother died twelve years ago," mused Ciccio. "Frieda will remember Grazia."

Then he poked among dead leaves and petals on the ground near the front of the house and exposed a metal plaque. "Look up there where it was," he said, pointing to an oblong blotch on the wall, "but it was not accurate, I had to pull it out. See, it says 'D. K. Lawrence.' I would not have that. So I took it down." And he prodded it under leaves again with his foot. "But the other plaque is still on the wall at the rear by the lane where the goats passed." We went and looked. And it read:

D. H. LAWRENCE
ENGLISH AUTHOR

1 9 1885 · 2 3 1930

LIVED HERE

1920 – 1923

"Three years!" he gloated.

At Taormina in 1922 and 1923?

Perhaps the western months recorded in this book are a dream.

W. B.

Chapala, Jalisco, Mexico

Journey with Genius

1. Santa Fe

IN 1922 the road from Santa Fe to Taos was formidable—rough, narrow, and through a steep canyon, by no means the easy hour's drive it is today; and Mrs. Sterne, meeting her guests in the capital, had decided to postpone motoring them north until the morrow. She had neglected, however, to arrange lodgings for them. Hotel accommodations were few then; and having found a room for herself elsewhere, she happened to hit upon me as their host for the night. The adobe house which my secretary, Willard (Spud) Johnson, shared with me, had not yet grown beyond three rooms; but, persuaded by Mrs. Sterne that the Lawrences would prefer its native roughness to somebody else's more capacious, more modern dwelling, I eagerly assented to the suggestion. Paul Burlin, the painter, had added a kitchen to the original two rooms of the house which I now own but was then renting from him; so it was possible, through use of couches in the living room, for the Lawrences to be given the bedroom—next to the tub and toilet which at that time Spanish-American neighbors used to come and view as curiosities—and for William Penhallow Henderson, with his wife, Alice Corbin, and their fourteen-year-old daughter, Little Alice, as well as Mrs. Sterne and Tony Lujan, the silently impressive Taos Indian who was driving for her, to join us and share a kitchen supper.

Presently the car arrived in my bleak little yard, where I had been assiduously watering downy tufts of green, still ignorant that they were tumbleweed. A red-bearded man started out of the car just as Tony decided to back it a bit, whereupon I heard my first Lawrencian explosion. He had been in Taormina, before continuing eastward round the world, and had bought there a Sicilian peasant-painting: the back panel of a cart vividly decorated with two scenes of medieval jousting. He had carried his trophy, some five feet long and two feet high, from place to place for months, his wife thinking that perhaps he would decide to settle in Taos and that there at last the panel too would rest. It never reached Taos. In my yard the panel and his mind were settled with one savage flash. The board had been under his arm as he was alighting and one end of it, being on the ground when Tony backed, had buckled and split, giving him a shove as it did so. Lawrence's thin shape cleaved air like the Eiffel Tower, his beard flamed, his eyes narrowed into hard turquoise, he dashed the panel to the earth, and his voice, rising in a fierce falsetto, concentrated on the ample woman behind him, "It's your fault, Frieda! You've made me carry that vile thing round the world, but I'm done with it. Take it, Mr. Bynner, keep it, it's yours! Put it out of my sight! Tony, you're a fool!" Mrs. Lawrence maintained a smile toward us; the Indian stirred no eyelash. Mrs. Sterne, pleased with the show, took command of it by introducing us in her pleasant, innocent voice, and Lawrence shook hands with us as affably as though the outburst had not occurred. But despite Frieda's *"jas"* and noddings that she would like to keep the panel even with its crack, nobody's plea could move him to let her have it, though I believe he would have liked to keep it, too. After these many years, Mrs. Lawrence still sees it on occasion in my study and laughs over its connection with our stormy first meeting.

Lawrence's appearance struck me from the outset as that of a bad baby masquerading as a good Mephistopheles. I did not feel in him the beauty which many women have felt. I have since read—in *The Savage Pilgrimage*—Catherine Carswell's impressions at her first meeting with him nine years before mine. "The immediately distinguishing thing," she says, "was his swift and flamelike quality. . . . I was sensible of a fine, rare beauty in Lawrence, with his deep-set jewel-like eyes, thick, dust-coloured hair, pointed underlip of notable sweetness, fine hands, and rapid but never restless movements." Four months after that, in October, 1914, he had written her: "I was seedy and have grown a beard. I think I look hideous, but it is so warm and complete, and such a clothing to one's nakedness, that I like it and shall keep it." She describes it as "a beard quite different from the hair of his head, of a deep glowing red in the sun and in the shade the colour of strong tea." Richard Aldington records, as of 1914, ". . . the head looks moulded of some queer-coloured stone, the beard gives the right touch of Mohammedan 'touch-me-not-ye-unclean.' " I remember quickly wondering at Santa Fe in 1922 what Lawrence would look like under the beard, which gave somewhat the effect of a mask with the turquoise eyes peering from it. The beard and the hair, too, seemed like covers he was cuddling under—a weasel face hiding under the warm fur of its mother and peeking out. Mrs. Carswell was accurate as to the colors. The beard, which he retained through the rest of his life, appeared to me more like a connected part of him than did his mat of hair, with its forward sidelong bang, which looked detachable, like a wig or a cap. In his writings, he forever removed that cap, exposed his cranium and its cerebral contents in all nakedness; but physically the beard clung close over his face as if he wished there the darkness into which his whole nakedness was always striving to return, or to progress. How he would have enjoyed classic proportions and a clean-cut Greek visage instead of the look of a semistarved viking! The Hon. Dorothy Brett, the Taos painter from England, relates of their first meeting, "I look up, realizing with surprise the eyes are blue, not black, as I had thought." Mrs. Carswell, too, had originally thought the eyes another color and then found them blue. Aldington recalls from his own first meeting in 1914, ". . . you were immediately impressed by his fiery blue eyes" which "seemed to exist independent of their owner," whereas John Galsworthy could not like the "provincial novelist" because of his "dead eyes." Perhaps Lawrence could shift their color for women. He himself, however, knew well what hue they were and how they could change in mood and temper. In *The Rainbow* he says of the Brangwens, his own clan, "One could watch the change in their eyes from laughter to anger, blue-lit-up laughter, to a hard blue-staring anger." Although he was to say later that all the gods have blue eyes, he had confided to Jessie Chambers ("E. T."), his early intimate: "For me, a brown skin is the only beautiful one." His own skin was too white, and I do not think he enjoyed it. Somewhere he quotes the Greeks as having said that "a white, unsunned body was fishy and unhealthy."

He occasionally vented in his writings his reluctant distaste for the physique he was born to carry and he tried to put the fault outside himself. Mrs. Lawrence records in *Not I but the Wind* his pathetic remark to the doctors when his end was near: "I have had bronchitis since I was a fortnight old." He had come through pneumonia twice in his twenties. And so when he tells, in *Kangaroo,* the bitter story of his examination and rejection for British army service, he almost blames the official for his own humiliated and unbelieving distress in not being of more heroic mold: "The chemist-assistant puppy looked him up and down with a small grin as if to say, 'Law-lummy, what a sight of a human scarecrow!'" He appeared anything but a scarecrow that evening in Santa Fe, though he was a bit gangling, and his voice was occasionally like whistlings of the wind. "His voice," says Aldington, "such a pleasant devil's voice, with its shrill little titters and sharp mockeries and even more insulting flatteries. . . . I welcome his 'tee-hees' and 'too-hoos,' which puff away a deal of silly cant and affectation." "A high tinkling laugh," contributes Dorothy Brett, "the ever-ready amused jeer." Norman Douglas, less kindly, in a comment on Lawrence's satirical writing about recognizable persons, is undoubtedly describing and disliking the physical voice: "that squeaky suburban chuckle which is characteristic of an age of eunuchs."

We had heard the shrillness of the Lawrence voice over the broken wagon board and we heard its variations later that evening in satirical comments on persons and places.

Mrs. Lawrence's presence, meantime, had been easy to take. Her smile from the first had meant, "I'll like you till I find a reason not to and I'll be all of myself whether you like it or not." Her body had German breadth and stature; she was a household Brunhilde; her fine profile was helmeted with spirit; her smile beamed and her voice boomed. In her were none of the physical timidities and reservations which made one questioningly aware of her husband's personality. With her there was no question. On the other hand, she did not intrude her strong presence, did not interrupt with it. It would assent or dissent firmly but with deferent timing. She never had to insist that she was there.

The homing instinct was at that time, probably always, more alive in Mrs. Lawrence than in her husband. He was always seeking a farm, a ranch; but by his own reports it was more because it might be the headquarters of a group he could head and because it would afford him growing vegetable life around him than because it would house him and his wife and give them a hearthstone. And then he would flee each harbor. For Mrs. Lawrence the search was now different. Flight from the first husband, an uncongenial, pedantic mate, had been the important break, and she did not need all the subsequent little escapes from escape.

On that first night in Santa Fe, after the one outbreak over the Sicilian cart-painting, Lawrence, the excitable fugitive, became Lawrence, the domestic expert. His wife said that when he broke an egg it never drooled and that he never set a dish too near the edge of a table. Deftly he joined the two Alice Hendersons and my awed maid in preparing supper, over which we sat long—quickened with the Lawrences' tales of world voyaging and world figures, with memorable mimicry of some of the latter, including Middleton Murry and Norman Douglas, and with tales from us about our local Spanish-Americans and Indians. I remember Lawrence being specially amused by a current New Mexico anecdote told by Johnson. Elizabeth Shepley Sergeant had just published in *Harper's Magazine* her *Story of a Mud House,* an account of life in an adobe dwelling at Tesuque and had spoken of her pretty maid as "the belle of Santa Fe." Someone had shown the passage to the maid who, reading English but scantily, had made vigorous protest, "I am *not* the belly of Santa Fe!" They liked also my own maid's assurance to us that she was not a backbiter. "I speak everything in people's faces—not in their behinds." And Frieda chuckled over Mrs. Sterne's enjoyment of the fact that earlier settlers in Santa Fe, those who had built more or less conventional, nostalgically Eastern-style houses on Palace Avenue and could not understand the flair among painters and writers to acquire native adobe shacks, had taken to calling us "the mudhut nuts."

Henderson, or perhaps Mrs. Sterne, told a story well known locally about "Long John" Dunne who ran the stage to Taos from the Denver and Rio Grande station, still extant in those days, across the canyon. Annoyed by passengers who were nervous on the steep declivity or who pestered him with questions he had heard a thousand times, he once gave an aside to a friend: "Pity God didn't put fur on some people, so's you could shoot 'em." I decided long afterward that Lawrence's coldness toward the quip was because he was sorry not for the person but for the imagined animal.

His amusement revived, however, when Alice Corbin told of a well-known Santa Fe hostess who had imported a Scandinavian husband and wife from Denver as domestics and who, on finding that they had no religious affiliation, but would oblige her with one if she would arrange it for them, had gone to the Methodist minister and asked him to take them under his wing, "because the Methodist Church, I understand, makes a specialty of common people." Lawrence's enjoyment of the story seemed to rise less from our American slant of amused shock as democrats than from an English satisfaction in the convenience of a proper disposition of lesser breeds. It is recorded that his mother had considered Methodists "common." In his last work, *Apocalypse,* he says of the Primitive Methodist Chapel, "Even I thought it rather 'common.' "

It may be my afterthought or afterimagination that Lawrence's eyes and thoughts were back in Derbyshire a moment among Methodists, but returned to Santa Fe when young Alice told of old Mrs. Laughlin's comment on the artists there, among whom I, like many of the others, was a wearer of Navajo shirts and jewelry, "At first we respectable residents of Santa Fe hated the way you artists and writers went about in any old kind of clothes and no neckties, but you do afford interest and amusement to the tourists and if you can stand it, I guess we can." I wondered later if he remembered the remark and relished it anew, when he himself went about open throated in flannel shirt and cowboy hat.

Above all, in his response to us that night, I remember the jump of his eye when I told him a remark of another old resident, Mrs. Crist, a Scottish niece of Sir Richard Burton, affectionately known as "Lady Crist." She had said to me, apropos of I forget what, "I am a woman, but I never tell anything. Now I am going to tell *you* something. I have never made a confidant. As Christ is born, I am my own confidant." One of the greatest confiders of all time, one who tried through his books to confide everything to everybody, he turned toward the absent Mrs. Crist, as I see it now, a childlike gaze, a profoundly amused gaze, of envious respect. Her remark in our story was a lightly told touch of the solitude he wanted. On the other hand, he liked the fact that she gabbled too.

When the others had left, the Lawrences, though tired from their journey, sat late into the night; and Johnson and I were drawn and held by their magnetism. Quickly I knew that the reports I had heard as to Mrs. Lawrence being beneath her husband's stature, and something of an incubus, were either malicious or stupidly mistaken. I felt from the first a sense of their good fortune in union: in his having realized his particular need of her and in her having made her warm, wise, earthy womanhood an embracing Eden for this inquisitive, quick-fingering, lean animal of a man—this eager origin of a new species. For all his flares at her, usually over trifles, he knew that she

was his mate. Lion-chasers and neurotic women, who tried to dis-.
parage Frieda and to attract him by substituting their ambitions and
vanities for her fond, amused, understanding, creative patience found
presently that a real lion would have been tamer in drawing room or
boudoir than this odd simian cat whose interest in them was finally a
puzzled, tolerant curiosity. In a way he liked the flattery of their attentions and with almost Frieda's patience indulged their vagaries;
but often his purring would stop and a claw would come out. On that
first night, despite his extreme good humor and friendliness to all of
us, I felt the cat-nature in the man, as well as the monkey-nature,
and with a respect for cats I was attracted by it. At least he was no
dog, hopping and fawning. He was in a house, moving sleekly; but
he would never be properly domesticated.

On September 18, 1922, I wrote Arthur Davison Ficke: "On their
way to Mabel Sterne's the other night, the D. H. Lawrences rested
in my 'dark bed.'" He must have called it that, "dark," without my
yet realizing the respect in his use of the word.

Lawrence's talk that night quickly made clear the fact that Tony's
clumsiness in the car had not dulled the Red Indian lure which has
been felt by many an Englishman. John Masefield wrote me later: "I
envy you your life among the Indians. Even after all these centuries
of fire-water, they must be the most interesting of all the peoples now
alive."

Lawrence had already indicated his sense of the "Red Indian" spell
by the runes of his mimic Indian troupe in *The Lost Girl*. He was now
actually present in the neighborhood of his noble savage. Let Tony
be clumsy with a car. Motor cars were not Indian business.

In the morning I was up ahead of the alarm clock for once, to make
sure that the guests should have a decent breakfast before Mrs. Sterne's
arrival to drive them north. Supper dishes were still to be washed in
the kitchen. I went quietly around the house to the back door; but
Lawrence opened it for me. Every dish had been washed. The table
was laid with an ample breakfast. The bed had been neatly made in
the room beyond. They had been about to call us. Just then my maid
appeared from across the street where she lived; but the Lawrences
had finished a complete job. The maid looked ashamed; but the guests
were beaming as well as hungry. Frieda said that Lorenzo had done
all the cooking. Breakfast proceeded at a hearty pace, giving us another interval of talk before Mrs. Sterne walked in. The night had

been the Lawrences' first in an American house. For me it felt like a wholly good omen. It was in reality a mixed omen.

As far as we knew at the time, life in Taos advanced at an amiable pace for the Lawrences and their neighbors. This was not yet the Taos year which Mrs. Carswell has described as "a combat of python-esses." Mrs. Sterne gave the newcomers a house apart. Tony Lujan introduced them to the pueblo, its people, its ceremonies, and its thoughts. The Taos Indians soon named Lawrence "Red Wolf." Earlier, in villages as far apart as the Tewas' Santo Domingo and the Hopis' Hotevilla, Indian acquaintances of mine, without their knowing in any of the places that the same name had been given me in another, had christened me "Mountain Antelope." In Santo Domingo it sounded, varying, Go-tay-kerts or Go-tay-mot, in Hotevilla Cher-der-kwee, in Tesuque Dom-pin; but in each case it meant Mountain Antelope; and I should have taken warning that there might be hazard in an antelope's association with a wolf.

Dorothy Brett says in her book that the Indians called him "Red Fox." My own memory, from what they and he have told me, is that it was "Red Wolf," a memory corroborated by his poem of that name, from which I quote:

> And wolf, he calls me, and red . . .
> I'm the red wolf, says the dark old father.
> All right, the red-dawn-wolf I am.

Lawrence, of course, had to change it a little and make his prowl mean dawn. I wonder if Brett, with her ear trumpet, may not have been just as deafly inaccurate when she understood that the Indians called Mrs. Lawrence "Angry Winter." A winter with plenty of snow perhaps, to keep the soil green, a forceful winter.

Whatever was happening, there had been as yet no anger toward me from the wintry Frieda and no growls from the wolfish Lorenzo. Books written later about that period in Taos record growls in other directions, both from the wolf and from the wolf's mate. Why not, when alien she-wolves were determined to jostle her in his lair? But Taos was eighty miles away from Santa Fe and during that early period we heard few echoes of friction, except Alice Corbin's report of one sharp quarrel Lawrence had picked with her, when she was visiting Mabel Sterne, over some trifling difference of opinion.

He wrote me: "If we don't like Taos, or find neighbors here op-

D. H. Lawrence at Witter Bynner's house in Santa Fe, 1922

The D. H. Lawrences at Witter Bynner's house in Santa Fe, 1922

pressive, we can go to Mexico. Perhaps you and the Spoodle could come with us." He had already displaced Johnson's nickname, Spud, with Spoodle.

After these few months the wander-fever was in Lawrence again. His feet itched to be going somewhere—Mexico this time. Whatever preparations he could make in Taos were being made. His busy mind applied itself to Terry's Mexican guidebook and a Spanish grammar. Maps were studied and costs calculated, while he delegated to us and others the questionings at railway offices. When he was in Santa Fe one day and some information had come through, he stayed outside the office and let me gather the data. He always shunned official desks with a nervous dislike for them and for the power of the men behind them. He resented, with helpless fury and flurry, the fact that his own superior intelligence and efficiency should have to defer to officiousness. He might be the helm when they set sail, but Mrs. Lawrence was usually the prow that breasted the waters. On the other hand, her bold confusion was often less helpful than his timorous plunge might have been. At least he would scoldingly take the tickets from her once she had them; for she was always losing everything except her reason and sense of life and sense of humor. And he scolded less, she says, when she lost guineas than when she lost shillings. Neither of the pair was used to carrying much money. Loss of guineas was enough punishment.

2. *"The Laughing Horse"*

S EVERAL years before, while an undergraduate at the University
of California, Johnson had founded and edited, with his friend,
Roy Chanslor, a lively publication called *The Laughing Horse.*
On the Lawrences' first evening in Santa Fe, Johnson showed them
a copy of it, and the showing led to a momentarily sensational sequel.
Chanslor was continuing publication in California, with James Van
Renssalear helping on the spot and Johnson at long distance. Together
with the editors, the magazine was graduating. They had become
ambitious for it; and, joining the ranks of the little magazines which
then flourished, it attracted contributions from writers who enjoyed
expression less conventional than stuffily established journals could
present. The December, 1922, issue of *The Laughing Horse* was forth-
coming. I had given Johnson some lines for it, under the pseudonym,
Emanuel Morgan, which I had adopted seven years before, with
Arthur Davison Ficke as Anne Knish, in our disguised issuing of
Spectra, a hoax on what we thought pretentious and disingenuous
schools of poetry. The lines, "Little Fly," would hardly nowadays
seem shocking:

Little fly,
For making a marriage
    bed
Of my bald head,
You had to die.

The other one,
The one that escaped—
Was it Paolo
Or Francesca?

10

Shortly before this, Covici-McGee had published a private edition of a Ben Hecht satire in novel form on authors like Lawrence who had begun making fiction a blend of sex and psychoanalysis. Even its title, *Fantazius Mallare,* was derived from *Fantasia of the Unconscious.* It had fairly lewd illustrations by Wallace Smith. When Johnson read it, he jumped to the hope that Lawrence, whose novels were under criticism for outspokenness, might review it for *The Laughing Horse,* and Lawrence readily consented, the more readily since he found it smut for the sake of smut. Such bawdiness not only irked him personally but made more difficult for writers a free expression of decent candor. This book may especially have offended him because he felt the dig at himself to be unwarranted and cheap. His review, however, was too openly phrased for even *The Laughing Horse* to print.

Roy Chanslor writes me, *"Fantazius Mallare* annoyed hell out of D. H. L. His review was full of dark gods, etc., and practically all of the four letter words in the language. We had no intention of publishing it, since we knew we'd be tossed in the can. But Hecht and Smith were arrested in Chicago and D. H. sent us a frantic wire not to publish the review, ending with 'Heavens what a cause to be martyred for!' So, being annoyed by this, we decided to publish it. We craftily cut out every four letter word, leaving blanks, and then cut out a few innocent words, leaving blanks, and the whole thing, apparently, became more obscene than ever. We thought it all a joke, of course. But I was pinched and tossed out of the University, by President David Prescott Barrows, in person. My case was dismissed in the local court, when Paul Eliel, a lawyer friend, filled in the blanks with perfectly innocent words, which was quite a feat of imaginative writing."

I asked Chanslor about a story current at the time, that President Barrows, taking exception not only to the Lawrence review but to "Little Fly," stated that I was the sole offending author, since "everybody knows that Bynner writes under both pseudonyms, Emanuel Morgan and D. H. Lawrence." Chanslor dispelled the yarn: "As to the interview with Dr. Barrows, he denounced all of us as 'communists and decadents,' including you and Upton Sinclair. He did know that E. Morgan and W. Bynner were one and the same, but I'm afraid the story to the effect that he thought Morgan and D. H. Lawrence were both aliases of yours is slightly apocryphal. I've heard it until I almost believe it, and it may even be true! But if he was literate enough to know about *Spectra,* I doubt if he really believed you and D. H. L.

were one and the same scoundrel. He was a conservative man, to put it mildly, but no fool, simply biased. I will always be grateful to him for hurling me forth so spectacularly; I doubt if I'll ever rate eight-column banner lines again, unless I assassinate Stalin."

The review of the Hecht book was prefaced with an editorial note: "D. H. Lawrence, the famous English novelist, writes a letter to the readers of *The Laughing Horse,* reviewing Ben Hecht's new privately printed novel, *Fantazius Mallare;* and takes the opportunity to give them some sound advice. We were advised at the last moment to leave out words in this letter which might be considered objectionable. We hope that this censorship will in no way destroy the sense of the text."

And here, antedating the frank indulgences of Hemingway, Caldwell, Faulkner, and others, is the Lawrence review, in which I am italicizing words left blank in *The Laughing Horse:*

Chère Jeunesse:
  Many thanks for sending me the Ben Hecht book. I read it through. But I'm sorry, it didn't thrill me a bit, neither the pictures nor the text. It all seems to me so would-be. Think of the malice, the sheer malice of a Beardsley drawing, the wit, and the venom of the mockery. These drawings are so completely without irony, so crass, so strained, and so would-be. It isn't that they've got anything to reveal at all. The man's *coition* with a tree for example. There's nothing in it but the author's attempt to be startling. Whereas if he wanted to be really wicked he'd see that even a tree has its own daimon, and a man might *lie* with the daimon of a tree. Beardsley saw those things. But it takes imagination. The same with the text. Really, Fantazius Mallare might mutilate himself, like a devotee of one of the early Christian sects, and hang his *penis* on his nose-end and a *testicle* under each ear, and definitely testify that way that he had such appendages, it wouldn't affect me. The word *penis* or *testicle* or *vagina* doesn't shock me. Why should it? Surely I am enough a man to be able to think of my own *organs* with calm, even with indifference. It isn't the names of things that bother me; nor even ideas about them. I don't keep my passions, or reactions, or even sensations IN MY HEAD. They stay down where they belong. And really, Fantazius, with his head full of *copulation* and committing MENTAL *fornication* and *sodomy* every minute, is just as much a bore as any other tedious modern

individual with a dominant idea. One wants to say: 'Ah, dirty little boy, leave yourself alone.' Which after all isn't prudery. It's just because one has one's own genuine *sexual* experiences, and all these fingerings and naughty words and shocking little drawings only reveal the state of mind of a man who has NEVER had any sincere, vital experience in *sex;* just as a little boy never has, and can't have had; and so he's itching with a feeble curiosity and self-induced excitement. Which is principally tedious, because it shows a feeble, spunkless sort of state of things. If Fantazius wasn't a frightened *masturbator,* he'd know that *sex contact* with another individual meant a whole meeting, a contact between two natures, a grim rencontre, half battle and half delight, always, and sense of renewal and deeper being afterwards. Fantazius is too feeble and weak-kneed for the fight, he runs away and chews his fingers and tries to look important by posing as mad. Being too much of a *wet-leg,* as they say in England, nakedly to enter into the battle and *embrace with a woman.* The tragedy is, when you've got *sex* in your head, instead of down below where it belongs, and when you have to go on feebly *copulating* through your ears and your nose. It's such a confession of weakness, impotence. Poor Fantazius is sensually, if not technically, impotent, and the book should have for subtitle: 'Relaxations for the Impotent.' But there's the trouble: men have most of them got their *sex* in their heads nowadays, and nowhere else. They start all their deeper reactions in their heads, and work themselves from the top downwards. Which of course brings disgust, because you're only having yourself all the time. No matter what other individual you take as a *machine à plaiser,* you're only taking yourself all the time. Why can't you jeunesse let all the pus of festering *sex* out of your heads, and try to act from the original centres? The old, dark religions understood. 'God enters from below,' said the Egyptians. And that's right. Why can't you darken your minds, and know that the great gods pulse in the dark, and enter you as darkness through the lower gates. Not through the head. Why don't you seek again the unknown and invisible gods who step sometimes into our arteries, and down the blood vessels to the *phallos,* to the *vagina,* and have strange meetings there? There are different dark gods, different passions; Hermes Ithyphallos has more than one road. The god of gods is unknowable, unutterable, but all the more terrible: and from the unutterable god step forth the mysteries of our promptings, in different forms: call it Thoth or Hermes, or Bacchus or Horus or Apollo: different promptings, different mysterious forms. But why don't you leave off your old white festerings in the head, and let the mystery of life come back to you? Why don't you become silent into yourselves, and wait and be patient in silence, and let a night fall over your mind and heal you. And then turn again to the dark gods, which are the dark promptings and passion-motions inside you, and have reverence again, and be grateful for life. Fantazius Mallare seems to me such a poor, impoverished, self-conscious specimen. Why should one be self-conscious and impoverished when one is young and the dark gods are at the gate? You'll understand if you want to. Otherwise it's your own affair.

Whatever Lawrence understood, it seemed to me that in the latter part of this, he failed to convey it and that those "dark gods" of his were a convenient legerdemain for the disappearing act of lucidity. I could feel that he was right—bravely though somewhat confusedly—in his respect for the phallus and his insistence that its light should not be hidden under a bushel of prudery; but I could not feel that youth, however much it might wish to understand him, could interpret his symbology as any other advice than to give the passions headlong rein. It is interesting to note that a few years later André Gide was coming to a conclusion in his journal which goes exactly contrary to Lawrence's. "What we call impulses of the heart," writes Gide, "is but the unreasonable jostling of our thoughts; it is still in the head that the drama is enacted, and it is again the brain that man needs in order to love." Lawrence would have glared at Gide, or gone back to his pen.

It is possible that the letter about *Fantazius Mallare* was written rapidly to let off steam, to amuse Johnson and me and with no thought that the editors would dare to publish it. The telegram to Chanslor intimates Lawrence's realization that the review was not finally good enough to become the focus of attention which would be made of it by legal attack. California papers, as it happened, were more concerned with a university fuss between student and president than with an English author's obscenity; but Lawrence's name figured in both the Western and the Eastern press.

3. *"Poor Pipsy"*

WHILE the smoke from the *Laughing Horse* episode was still drifting, my mother decided that she would like to come from New York to see the wild sort of place in which her son had chosen to live and the actual caliber of such notorious and apparently wild associates as Lawrence and Johnson—also to see the Shalako Dance.

Every December tall mountain gods, escorted by cavorting fire gods and mudheads, come down from their caves to bless the people of Zuñi; and the ceremony is so eerily august a spectacle that I wonder the Lawrences were not prompted to see it with us.

After resting awhile in the comfortable guesthouse at Mrs. Sterne's, they had moved to an adobe ranch cabin fifteen miles beyond Taos, perched high on a mountainside over the village of Valdes.

The Del Monte ranch belonged to John Evans, Mrs. Sterne's son, and with its airy remoteness was an ideal retreat for a writer. It comprised several primitive buildings, a corral, a brook, some tall pine trees, and a breath-taking view over wide colorful plains far below, but no such conveniences as running water. A quarter of a mile away lived the only fixed neighbors, a congenial family named Hawk, who could on occasion provide milk and eggs; and in a cabin rented from the Hawks were two likable Danish painters. I believe that Mr. Hawk had long since found this high dry place because of troubled lungs. Amy Lowell would have been glad to see the Lawrences transferred here from the airless London basement she had told me about and would have been as impressed as we were by the resources and aplomb with which they faced simple, isolated living, especially later when a kitchen stove and a living-room fireplace were all they had against winter, and their mile of steep woods–road, off the highway was almost impassable with snow.

Despite forbidding weather in late November, my mother acquiesced in acceptance of an invitation from the Lawrences that we lunch with them on their hill. We felt sure that they would kindle to the idea of Zuñi with us. But after our climb, the idea was not broached. Something had gone wrong in the household. The personal air was black that day; it was no occasion for amiable planning.

When Mrs. Lawrence, for all her Wagnerian stature, submitted meekly to several savage onslaughts from her husband, my mother was startled and partly amused but, as a feminist, aroused. At one point, while he was cooking, he brandished a frying pan as if to brush to the floor a cigarette dangling from the corner of his wife's mouth and fuming into her eye, an indulgence of hers which often drove him to angry protest. Smoking by women did not please my mother, but she disapproved still more of their being browbeaten and cowed by men; and I had to remind her later that, while Brunhilde meeched a bit, the cigarette had remained firmly in place. It always did through similar attacks; and Lawrence's bile, as almost always, seemed shortly to have been purged by his outburst. "She should have hit back," declared my mother. "What's the matter with her? She looks strong. He's an odd duck, but he's worth hitting back at."

According to St. Augustine in his *Confessions,* his mother, Monica, "had learned that an angry husband should not be resisted, neither in deed nor even in word. But so soon as he was grown calm and tranquil, and she saw a fitting moment, she would give him a reason for her conduct, should he have been excited without cause." This example would, I am convinced, have appealed as little to Mrs. Lawrence as to my mother.

To Santa Fe about this time came Stephen Graham, the English writer on Russia, who was still trying to live down his repeatedly printed conviction that the Slavs would not reject their Little Father, the Czar. The Lawrences and I had met Graham previously and through him we now met his amiable, quiet friend, Wilfred Ewart, who had come from England to New Mexico for his health and with the thought that its calm might cure him of a stutter.

In December neither the Lawrences nor Graham accompanied us to Zuñi; but Ewart came along. During the trip, he told us that as soon as he returned to Santa Fe he was proceeding to Mexico, where Graham was to join him later; and he said that there had been talk of the Lawrences following in the spring.

Soon after our return to Santa Fe, we read in the *New Mexican* a letter from Stephen Graham which reported that Ewart, in a small Mexico City hotel, leaning against the iron railing of his balcony on a holiday, had been killed by a stray bullet. It was believed an accident, that the bullet had come from a drunken celebrant. "I don't think so," said Lawrence, when we discussed it. "I don't think so. I believe that it's an evil country down there."

Nevertheless, partly perhaps because there was evil also in the wintry rigor of Del Monte, the wander-fever was tugging at Lawrence still, and in the direction of Mexico. Perhaps, on this occasion as on others, he might have said with André Gide: "Never have I been able to settle in life. Always seated askew, as if on the arm of a chair; ready to get up to leave." Whatever it was, he wrote me on January 19, 1923:

> . . . I think we may really be coming by Santa Fe next month or in early March. I would like to go down to Old Mexico in spite of Wilfred Ewart. I read Stephen Graham's letter in the Santa Fe newspaper. Where is Graham now? I would like to find out from him just what conditions are in Old Mexico now. . . . It's awfully nice of you to offer us your hospitality; our first and last roof in America. One can't count hotels: they have only lids. . . . I'll write in plenty of time.

On March 8, he sent word again:

> . . . Did Johnson get my letter, written about twenty days ago, asking if you wouldn't like to come along to Mexico City with us? Anyhow I am fixing definitely to leave here on the 18th, and arrive in Santa Fe either on the 20th or 21st of this month. Stay just a night. Don't you bother about putting us up if you have things to do.

And again on March 14:

> I had your letter. Do come along with us. . . . I expect to catch the stage on Monday morning. In which case we need sleepers booked for Wednesday. I enclose my letter to the agent; will you

forward it? If Tuesday night is too soon for you to leave, let me know. I would like us all to go together. And alter the day on my letter to El Paso, booking the Pullman, if you wish a later day. . . . If you wish to wait a day or two longer, I will do so too, but let me know. I would awfully like to take the little black dog with us. Could we do it, do you think? How would she have to travel?

They did stay overnight with us. I fail to remember why his letter to Johnson had gone three weeks unanswered, unless because of irresolute delay in our decision to accompany them; nor do I remember why we had to defer our going.

Lawrence was unhappy that they had not brought "the little black dog." It was Pipsy, about whom much has been written by him and others. A few months earlier, angry at the animal because, in heat, she had broken loose to join an attentive male dog and jealous because, after his cuffing her for it, she had taken refuge in the Danes' cabin, he is said to have kicked her savagely and hurled her outdoors into the snow. A decade later, when this violence had been brought against him in print, Mrs. Lawrence wrote: "If Lawrence could lose his temper, he could also be patient and tender. I think that, after all, the story shows how much Lawrence cared for that small dog."

An hour after we had seen them off at the Santa Fe station for Lamy, Albuquerque, El Paso, and Mexico, we found in the hall of the house two umbrellas strapped together. We both remembered Lawrence's having said severely and solemnly at breakfast, "Your only lookout, Frieda, is the umbrellas."

We laughed for a moment.

"Poor Pipsy!" said Spud.

"But Frieda can take care of herself," said I. "She doesn't need to wield an umbrella." Little did I realize that before long I should be offering her a cudgel, whether she needed it or not.

4. Mexico City

WITHIN a week, we were ready to follow to Mexico. We knew very little Spanish at that time and had been relieved when Lawrence telegraphed us that he would meet our train. But the train was fourteen hours late. He had gone to the station on a false report of its arrival and on the next day, giving the hotel porter a description of us, had sent him to meet the train with a note to us which failed to reach us till he himself handed it to us several days later: "Don't know if you are coming. I met train yesterday, but give this note to the hotel courier on chance. It is a little Italian hotel, clean and good food, but *not* elegant: costs only four pesos a day, food and all [which meant then two dollars]. We tried the Regis—didn't care for that. The man speaks only Spanish—we speak Italian happily in the house. You take a taxi with hand luggage —the hotel will fetch your trunk in the morning. Taxi about two pesos. Perhaps best take the courier with you—he's nice really. Everything is quite easy."

Meantime, the day before, unmet, we had found in the station an English-speaking Mexican who kindly telephoned the Hotel Regis, where we had thought the Lawrences would be, only to be told that they were no longer there. Then when we called the British Consulate, we were told that there was no record of the new address. So we capitulated to the most aggressive of the hotel agents who were still plowing at us and found ourselves accompanying him in a taxi bound for some hotel with a German name which I have forgotten. The bell-boy showed us into a high-ceilinged room on the third floor and unfolded great shuttered windows which opened on an iron-railed balcony. By the flood of light he pointed to stains along the table under our bags. "We put him on this *mesa,*" he explained, half in English,

"a man from *Londres. Mira,*" he led us to the balcony and pointed to
the railing, "here he died from a *pistola.*"

We had been met not by Lawrence but by the ghost of Wilfred
Ewart. Too dazed to ask that we be moved, we quickly left his room
and went to a *cantina* to consider procedure. But we were at a loss.
For two days we retained our grim eyrie, staying in it as little as possible. Further inquiries at the Regis and the Consulate were of no
avail. All we could do was to walk up and down, back and forth,
hoping against hope that, even in a big city, somehow there would
be a meeting. And on the third day there was. Johnson brushed sleeves
with Lawrence at a crowded corner; and within an hour the four of
us were laughing and jabbering in the Hotel Monte Carlo, on Avenida
Uruguay next to the National Library.

For general comfort, it was high time. Lawrence had had enough
of Mexico City and its environs and was fretting to be off to other
parts of the country. I forget now what places he had already seen but
remember that he was disappointed in all of them and resolved, if the
country didn't do better by him, to sail back to Europe. Yet he would
shake his red beard slowly and say, "But Europe is dead, dead and
stinking."

˙ Poor man, he was ever between the devil and the deep sea. Where
should he go? I wondered if he thought of himself sometimes as a
Greek fugitive whose pursuing furies were the spirits of places. In
The Plumed Serpent he says of himself and Mexico City, through the
figure of his protagonist, Kate Leslie, that she "was afraid, she dreaded
the thought that anything might really touch her in this town, and
give her the contagion of its crawling sort of evil." Again: "She could
feel the demonish breath of evil moving on the air in waves."

To us newcomers Mexico City was still a magnet; and, whatever
Lawrence felt about it, he settled back to showing us round. He tried
to prevent our buying cheap loot in Frieda's paradise, the *Volador,*
the Thieves' Market, or even better stuff in the *Monte de Piedad,* the
government pawn-shop. He liked to lean against a low railing over a
street corner deeply excavated and to see ancient shadows below him
on Aztec pavements and stairways which the digging had exposed.
The capital's business section reminded me of Shanghai, its parks of
Brooklyn, its newer public buildings and residences of Paris and Los
Angeles, or a World's Fair. Its churches, palaces, and older dwellings,
Lawrence said, were better than buildings of the same period in

Spain because Mexico's wealth had attracted the ablest Spanish architects away from the motherland to the colony. The fine old Colonial mansions had not then been sacrificed to bald or tawdry modernism. Their size and right proportions, the placing of the tall windows looking out from tall rooms, the gay amplitude and Continental facades were impressive and exciting. No one seeing Mexico City a quarter century later can guess how harshly progress has dealt with its charm. Châteaux have been replaced by dismantled battleships. Morelia, by some grace, has preserved its architectural beauty better than any of the cities and is still Colonial Mexican. The capital, with a noble structure left here and there, grows now more and more mongrel, grows stark and hurried. The semimodernistic new buildings already have a hangdog look. But in 1923, though Lawrence did not like the spirit of the place and its people, he was moved to admiration by much of its architecture.

In some of the government edifices which he showed us, Mexican painters were beginning their now famous frescoes. Through Sr. José Vasconcelos, Minister of Education, the State was giving them, together with room and board and a pittance of pesos, lavish opportunity to whet their talents and beautify the capital. An American named Fred Leighton had contributed to *The Freeman* what was, I think, the first report of this project, the first appraisal of Diego Rivera and the others, to be printed in the United States. Through the American Embassy I met Leighton who, under Roberto Haberman, was in charge of the teaching of English in Mexico City schools. We soon found him an agreeable guide for all of us. He came often to the Monte Carlo, which was then less a hotel than a pension where Italian women used to sit at the dining table with their long damp black hair drying loose on towels across their shoulders, where sailors stored the bolts of English suiting they had professedly smuggled from Naples or Genoa, where a headquartering vaudeville troupe aired its trained apes and dogs and cockatoos under the washlines on the roof, where young Faustino Forte, son of the establishment, flitted and chirped helpfully in all places at once, where his placid mustachioed father moved benignly from kitchen to office to dining room, never once removing an old cuttle-colored cap, while his wife superintended perfectionism of minestrone, ravioli, and spaghetti which, with Chianti from straw-wrapped bottles or vermouth or Spanish wine, soothed our palates and sometimes soured our stomachs under blessings from a colored print of Garibaldi on the dining-room wall. It was a piece of the Italy Lawrence now thought he had loved, transplanted unspoiled from a ruined Europe and affording him homely refuge from the Mexican life surrounding it, a Mexican life which seemed to Lawrence raw, lifeless, and frightening. Through Kate, he refers in *The Plumed Serpent* to the fact that some of our new acquaintances were surprised by our choosing such humble quarters: "I don't think they like it that we stay in the Hotel San Remo. It is too poor and foreign. . . . It *is* small, and nearly all Italians. But we tried some of the big ones, and there is such a feeling of lowness about them, awful! I can't stand the feeling of prostitution. And then the cheap insolence of the servants. No, my little San Remo may be rough, but it's kindly and human, and it's not rotten. It is like Italy as I always knew it, decent, and with a bit of human generosity. I do think Mexico City is evil, underneath."

Though his Spanish had already become plentiful, Lawrence enjoyed using Italian with the family and with the guests, many of them permanent. We grew fond of the Fortes and were pleased that, unlike some of our other acquaintances, Fred Leighton approved our taste in hotels and hotelkeepers.

Fred's joining the group cheered Lawrence; and we met a few others whom we liked, so that we lingered contentedly in the capital. Leighton and Roberto Haberman took us through a broken old convent which the government had given the Communists for a hall and dwellings. Through the two we also met radical poets and other writers, and Luis Morones, who was head of the labor movement and who invited us to a dance in the gymnasium of some huge labor center. As far as I know, Lawrence has portrayed none of these figures in his writings, though he does say somewhere, in a letter, I think, "The Spanish-Mexican population just rots on top of the black savage mass, and Socialism here is a farce of farces, except very dangerous." But the second chapter of *The Plumed Serpent* records with extraordinary fidelity the persons and interchange at a tea party given us by Mrs. Zelia Nuttall, an English widow distinguished in Mexico City as archeologist, *grande dame,* and conservative hostess-owner of a historic house in Coyoacán built by Pedro de Alvaro in the time of Cortes.

A wing of this house had been offered him by Mrs. Nuttall. After his arrival in Mexico on March 23, he had written his Danish friend, Knud Merrild on April 11: ". . . I want to find a house. A rich Englishwoman offers us one in Coyoacán, a suburb here. . . . Spit on Taos for me." But he was already gathering spit for Coyoacán. In *The Plumed Serpent* he describes the offered house, the "ponderous" suburban house: "A certain dead, heavy strength and beauty seemed there, unable to pass away, unable to liberate itself and decompose. . . ."

However, I am grateful to him for having pilloried in the novel a stuffy, stubborn British judge whom we met in that house and whom I finally had to let decree, against my own knowledge as a collector of its many colors in China, that jade could be only green. "He trembled with irritation," writes Lawrence of the judge, "like an access of gout."

The novelist tries to scoff at Mrs. Norris, as he calls her in his book, at her life and her ways: "a lonely daughter of culture" with an expression of "tomb-like mockery." But she had a British dignity and authority which beat him down. Reflecting his subjection, he observes: "The world is made up of a mass of people and a few individuals. Mrs. Norris was one of the few individuals. True, she played her social game all the time. But she was an odd number; and all alone, she could give the even numbers a bad time," something he liked well to do himself. Again, she "always put her visitors uncomfortably at their ease, as if they were captives and she the chieftainess who had captured them." In spite of seeing through Mrs. Nuttall's role, he respected it as a role he himself would often have liked to play as successfully, an outworn European role few unimitative Americans would like to play at all.

We took occasional short trips to such places as Xochimilco and its canals, where Frieda, like an expanded Cleopatra, lolled on a flower-decked barge and relished the chicken *mole* served us hot from a dugout drawn alongside, or the ruined monastery, El Desierto de los Leones, in a drizzle as dreary as Lawrence's spirits were that day. On the way to San Juan Teotihuacan, we stopped at another old monastery, San Agustin Acolman, and here he was happy. The half-circle of chaired figures frescoed in sepia and gray in the choir won his full approval, and he beamed at the camera when I took his photograph in one of the cloisters. On that same road he was amused by another fresco, this one on the wall of a *pulqueria,* the kind of high-colored, witty, fantastic painting which then brightened such walls all over Mexico, bearing such names as "The Little House of the Magdalen," "The Devil's Bell," and "Remembrances of the Future." This one showed a group of erect and busy pigs dealing with human sinners as devils deal with them in theological pictures of hell: piercing them with spits, shoving them into hot cauldrons. Yes, I think it was on a pulque shop, though it might have been on a butcher shop. Whichever it was, Lawrence emphatically called it "much better than Diego Rivera."

Children in this settlement brought us small pottery images, insisting shyly that they were authentic. A ragged old fellow, carrying a heavy burlap bag, watched us while we bargained. Lawrence liked one nicely modeled clay torso but claimed that since the figure was cut in half, so should the price be. "There's no head," he pointed out. "Here's the head," gleamed the ragged bystander and lifted from among chunks of meat in his *bolsa,* a skinned sheep's head with dead teeth grinning. His jest cheated the children, for Lawrence moved quickly away. But they were paid with amusement.

We climbed the pyramids at Teotihuacan and like other tourists photographed one another on them. According to Catherine Carswell: "This Pyramid of the Sun . . . he found 'very impressive . . . far more than Pompeii . . . or the Forum.'" In the great quadrangle of Quetzalcoatl, we saw Lawrence stand looking and brooding. The colored stone heads of the feathered snakes in one of the temples were a match for him. The stone serpents and owls held something that he obviously feared. In *The Plumed Serpent* he mentions "the ponderous pyramids of San Juan Teotihuacan, the House of Quetzalcoatl with the snake of all snakes, his huge fangs white and pure today as in the lost centuries when his makers were alive. He has not died. He is not so dead as the Spanish churches, this all-enwreathing dragon of the horror of Mexico."

Perhaps the germ of the novel's theme came to him then, his half-fascinated, half-frightened impulse to banish from Mexico the gods in human image and replace them with an animal, with this animal of all animals, this "snake of all snakes," this creature part snake and part bird, Mexico's natural god and in many ways his own.

Though I think he was already planning his novel, I doubt if he was yet working on it. But he was by no means idle. In the evenings, after supper at the Monte Carlo, we would have coffee, cordials, and conversation in their room, while Lawrence, reclining on the bed with notebook and pencil, would be busy at essays, sketches, reviews, random writings, which went off in the mails. Jessie Chambers notes that in his boyhood "he would sit at the table doing his lessons, not in the least put out by the conversation going on round him." Here in Mexico we marveled constantly at his ability to be writing and talking at the same moment, but Frieda seemed used to it. He was like a man in a newspaper office, whose copy could come clear, through interruptive confusion. I wondered one Monte Carlo night if his pencil might be jotting points in a narrative from Fred Leighton concerning Carranza. His brow and eyes were alert to the story, while his fingers moved on the page. It seemed that the President, when his regime was tottering, had withdrawn bullion from the national treasury and loaded it on well-guarded freight cars ready for flight. He and his family and close official associates climbed aboard when the critical time came. The train pulled out for Vera Cruz. But the engineers, whom he trusted, were rebels and at the top of the steep grade downward from the plateau they opened the throttles, leaped from the engine and left the presidential caravan to a runaway plunge. At the foot of the descent, the train toppled and crashed. Lawrence liked especially hearing that peons, gathered around the broken freight cars which had spewed out fortunes of gold and silver coins, picked for their pockets only a few pesos each, so that the bulk of the treasure was recovered for a new officialdom. "Lucky peons," he said. Alive or dead, the story went, the body of Carranza had never been found. Perhaps Lawrence knew better. Wherever they were then, the remains of Carranza are supposed to rest now in the Monument to the Revolution at Mexico City, and I have found in Lawrence writings no trace of the train yarn. Perhaps, while he listened, he was ignoring Carranza and was garnering notes about unworldly, noble Indians who should become followers of a new Quetzalcoatl, a new Lawrence.

5. Alarums

INTERESTED in the Indian revival which was being encouraged by the Minister of Education, with men like Dr. Atl renouncing their Spanish names in favor of Aztec, Lawrence expressed one evening a desire to meet Sr. Vasconcelos; and Leighton arranged for us all to have lunch with the Minister and Carleton Beals.

When we had assembled in the waiting room, a sudden complication had arisen, and a polite request was sent us that our appointment might be postponed till the following day.

Lawrence went stiff. He blanched. Then he sprang to his feet, crying, "I'm busy too! I won't meet the man! Tell him I won't meet him!" Hysteria fed itself. He began denouncing not only Vasconcelos, but the government and finally the whole Mexican race.

His mate made matters worse by saying, "Men of importance have unforeseen interruptions, Lorenzo."

"I'm important too!" His voice cut the air like a saw. "But I don't break engagements at the last moment! Frieda, you're an imbecile!"

Leighton and Johnson were held quiet, bewildered; but I was irritated and put in another mistaken word, "What's one more day in Mexico? Besides, it was we who wanted to meet him, not he who wanted to meet us."

"I was a dolt to want to meet him," he shrilled, "and we'll have an end of it. Just tell him, Leighton, that I refuse to meet an impertinent political puppy!"

Leighton and Beals left in one direction, we in another.

On the walk back to the hotel, Lawrence, his temper vented, chuckled at us, "Before you joined us in Mexico, I was asked to meet one of President Obregon's secretaries at the British Consulate. The Secretary handed me a telegram that had been sent to the President: 'I am

America's most important author,' it said. 'I have come to your country to put it on the map, as I put Cuba on the map. But I wish co-operation. I wish at my disposal an automobile and chauffeur, a private railway car, and for companion and guide an official who speaks English.' 'Is he so important?' the Secretary asked me. 'No,' I said. 'He's a third-rate American novelist. Don't answer him.' And the fellow got no reply. But I wish now," snapped Lawrence, "that I'd suggested Vasconcelos for 'companion and guide.' They'd have deserved each other."

"It was Booth Tarkington," added Mrs. Lawrence brightly.

"Nothing of the sort, you silly gabbler," he retorted. "What do you ever get straight? It was Joseph Hergesheimer."

A bit in *Sons and Lovers* throws light on Lawrence's frenzy toward Vasconcelos. Of himself he says, "He was the sort of boy that becomes a clown and a lout as soon as he is not understood, or feels himself held cheap." In *The Lost Girl* he had written: "If a man is conscious of being a *gentleman,* he is bound to be a little less than a *man*. . . . If a man must loftily, by his manner, assert that he is *now* a gentleman, he shows himself a clown." It is odd that such self-knowledge did not more comfortably direct its possessor's conduct.

That night, from our room next door to theirs, Johnson and I could hear his voice scaling higher and higher as he berated his wife for the sins of Vasconcelos and the world. "Such a pleasant devil's voice," says Aldington. But the devil was not pleasant this night. It is an odd phenomenon in my experience that time and time again, a marked exception being Norman Douglas, English men of letters have these treble, almost soprano, voices. Lytton Strachey's and E. M. Forster's are famous. Lawrence's normal tone was high enough; but when he was agitated it would lift its pitch and then the sound of the rise would further excite it till it was as high as it could go. Wave after wave of fifelike fury dashed on Mrs. Lawrence. I myself by this time had been alternately fevered and chilled with anger toward Lawrence and was determined that, even though he changed his mind, he was not to be allowed a meeting with Vasconcelos but that we were to take her with us, come what may. It was not a question of allowing. He stood firm. He would not go. At least in our presence, he raised no objection to his wife's accompanying us and she made next day a plausible apology for his absence, pleading illness. Sr. Vasconcelos proved to be cordial, interesting, generous, anything but a "puppy."

"An unordinary man," nodded Frieda, "just the sort you should meet, Lorenzo." But they never met. It is recorded that to the inspector of the school at Croydon Lawrence in his youth had never said, "Sir."

Shortly after this episode the four of us went one evening to a now vanished Bohemian section of Mexico City. It extended hardly farther than one short street, on which were four or five eating places and cantinas where painters and writers met and where musicians, whetted with tequila, marihuana, or appreciation, would sing or play piano or violin. I remember in Greenwich Village long ago, at Romany Marie's, hearing similar piano playing by Carlos Chavez, now Mexico's famous conductor. This evening Johnson had tried to find again for us a haggard-faced violinist virtuoso whose playing had spellbound us several times before; but the man was in none of his haunts, and we were having coffee at a corner restaurant in the section, the *Monotes,* the Big Monkeys, belonging to a brother of the artist, Orozco, when our eyes were caught by a row of small, striking water colors hanging unframed on a back wall. They were mostly Mexican types, expertly painted in flat bright colors, children, vendors, bricklayers and such, in a style made widely familiar since by Rivera's small paintings. We went to the wall and studied them, exclaiming over them. We asked the woman at the counter who the artist was, and she answered, "The artist is a young man very much delighted. He is sitting at that table behind you." We turned and were met by a glowing smile from the young man, who quickly accepted our suggestion that he join us. He told us that he was an usher at a theater but that he was also a pupil of Rivera's, whom he much admired, and he happily gave each of us one of the water colors. Friendliness grew out of the meeting. He took us to see Rivera and the others at work on their scaffolds in the public buildings, and we have long remembered the companionable ardor with which the painters were developing their frescoes. As far as we could observe, there was none of the friction among some of them which has developed since. Where could one meet a jollier, heartier giant than Rivera, looking to me, who had seen Zuñi Indian dances, like a mudhead, or rough, half-formed, primeval being, grown Olympian. And what a joy to watch the delicate workmanship of his big hands!

Our young friend proved to be a son of the Director of the National Lottery and very eager to visit New York. I gave him a letter to Carl Van Vechten and have often been with him since in New York and in Mexico. Once, years later, he regretted not having known what a great man was with us and that he had failed to make sketches of him. Though he had not seen him again after the year of our meeting, this regret was no sooner spoken than he sat down and nimbly drew a caricature from memory, extraordinary not only as caricature but as likeness. He gave it to me, signed Covarrubias, and it has more Lawrence in it than most of the photographs.

Lawrence was always gentle with Miguel, even when they disagreed as to the quality of the Mexican painters whom Covarrubias revered. Lawrence found most of the paintings ugly.

"But they express ugly facts," Miguel would urge.

"Negatively, not constructively, not creatively," Lawrence insisted. "The propaganda swamps the art. And it's not propaganda in favor of what is fine and profound in the Indian. There's none of that. It's merely propaganda against what's obviously rotten in state and church, for violent overthrow of oppressors, not for encouragement of inherent nobility in the oppressed, never that. Nothing to indicate that Europeans are yielding supremacy to the spirit of the dark men." It was not often that Lawrence's chronic fear of these particular dark men changed in his talk to a sort of paean. But he was assailing Rivera and grasped for ammunition. He often liked a thing just because it was against something else, but he did enjoy watching well-to-do Spaniards with bloated shoulder padding trying still to conquer a country of firm, graceful poverty. On he went. "These painters just use the Indian to exploit imported ideas. You remember, Bynner, the factory town we were taken to, all modern and model? Those rows of new houses, each one neat and up-to-date, but each one like every other. Every new comfort but no old dignity. You should be proud, Covarrubias, of the Indians who wouldn't live in them, left them empty, set up their own shacks on the edge of town. Their benefactors might iron out of the houses all character, all individualism but not out of the Indians. And so those silly socialistic houses stood empty. That would have been a thing to paint. That would have been Mexican!" One might have thought Lawrence himself a Mexican at the moment, with proud defiance kindling flame in his eyes, a blue flame. "But no," he perorated, "these socialist painters' ideas are not Mexican. They are imported as Maximilian was. They are European, not Mexican. And the painting is caricature, not art, and just what one might expect under the patronage of a ninny like Vasconcelos and with the encouragement of foreign meddlers like Leighton and Bynner."

Covarrubias, hearing Leighton and me attacked as well as Rivera and Orozco, Americans as well as Mexicans, would smile and shrug his shoulders. And then Lawrence would smile too. And I would try to mediate. "For me, Lawrence, these Mexican artists, like other great artists before them, like Goya or El Greco, paint grotesque beings as human beings, whereas so many of our American moderns, like other poor artists before them, paint human beings as grotesque beings." Lawrence was not impressed by my neat differentiation, but I was. And Miguel was mollified.

It is interesting, in *The Plumed Serpent,* to come upon Lawrence's later, considered reflections as to the frescoes we had seen together in the public buildings, some finished, some not, when we had met Rivera, Orozco, Montenegro, Merida, and others. "The young Mexican who was accompanying the party" figures in the book as a composite of Covarrubias and a youthful professor. "There was something fresh and soft, petulant about him. Kate liked him. He could laugh with real hot young amusement, and he was no fool." Covarrubias, then a disciple of Rivera, was always stoutly defending his master and the others. Lawrence says through Kate in the book, "But they were men—or boys—whose very pigments seemed to exist only to *épater le bourgeois*. And Kate was weary of *épatisme,* just as much as of the bourgeois." About Rivera in particular the novel condenses what Lawrence said to us all, more than once: "The man knew his craft. But the impulse was the impulse of the artist's hate. In the many frescoes of the Indians, there was sympathy with the Indian, but always from the ideal, social point of view. Never the spontaneous answer of the blood. Those flat Indians were symbols in the great script of modern socialism; they were figures of the pathos of the victims of modern industry and capitalism. That was all they were used for: symbols in the weary script of socialism and anarchy."

As early as 1926, H. G. Wells, in a chapter headed *Psychoanalysis of Karl Marx,* part of his novel, *The World of William Clissold,* wrote: "Romantic Communism expresses itself by pictures, presenting indeed no sort of worker, but betraying very clearly in its vast biceps, its colossal proportions, its small head and the hammer of Thor in its mighty grip, the suppressed cravings of the restricted intellectual for an immense vitality."

These muscled miners struck no spark in Lawrence's imagination. He had seen enough of such in his boyhood. His visualized caveman strode forth instead with stalactites for a beard, became overnight a fine-limbed patrician in Etruria, dominating conjugal couch, judicial chair, martial chariot and vital tomb. And this should be the Indian of Rivera, or Orozco; not the bulge-muscled revolutionary oaf but the assured and shapely lord of life and death.

What awed and fascinated and frightened Lawrence most of all in Mexico was the Indians' deep-rootedness in the reality of death. "When you got these dark-faced people," he writes, "away from wrong contacts like agitators and socialism, they made one feel that life was vast, if fearsome, and death was fathomless." It was that sense in the people which he would have liked to see painted, and so he told Covarrubias.

"But I don't like death," protested the young painter.

"I don't altogether blame you," said his elder.

Lawrence had been gentle too long. It was time for another spasm. Underneath the gentleness he was restless. And his restlessness always, sooner or later, took toll of his wife.

I had noticed that his flare-ups were more likely to occur when we had had wine. One day, with the Monte Carlo meal ended but with a little Chianti left, he was still sipping while Frieda smoked. Her cigarette began to slant downward in the left corner of her mouth. I saw his attention light on it, saw him watch grimly fascinated till she gave a pull on the dangling stub and then tilted her head up to ease her eye from watering. Though the dining room was full, he stiffened suddenly, jerked himself to his feet and blared, "Take that thing out of your mouth!" She gazed at him, wide eyed, without answering. "Take it out, I say, you sniffing bitch!" And then, though she was seated behind a corner table, half hidden from everyone by the cloth, "There you sit with that thing in your mouth and your legs open to every man in the room! And you wonder why no decent woman in England would have anything to do with you!" Flinging the remaining drops of his Chianti at her, he darted past the other tables into the lobby and then out into the street.

Johnson looked away from both of us, fixing his eyes on the floor as though he were absent. He often did that. Frieda, with the cigarette still in place, breathed hard for a moment, looking straight at me, just as she had looked straight at Lawrence. There had been latterly none of that submission my mother had resented in Taos.

"*Ja,*" she said, sitting bolt still, "I have to put up with him but I do not answer him. I do not know what to do. Some women in England treated me badly because I am German. He knows that, and it was not fair of him."

If she had not been Frieda, I should have thought there was a tear in the eye. But it was a cigarette fume.

Not long after this outbreak, Fred Leighton had come for supper and we were sitting as usual in the Lawrences' room, watching him write while he talked, hearing him talk while he wrote, when all of a sudden he laid his open notebook upside down on the bed with an air of finality. We had had Chianti with supper and then a cordial; but there was no visible spite this time except in the hard blue chill of the eyes which he turned on Fred.

"Leighton," he announced as though an icicle spoke, "I have had enough of you."

"What—what do you mean?" stammered Fred.

"I do not need you any more," was the answer. "You have done all you can for me. So please leave."

"All I can do for you now is to leave, is that it?" Fred asked with groping dignity.

"Yes," decreed Lawrence.

It was not the nasty snarl of a dog. It was the neatly arched back and the paw stroke of a cat.

"Lorenzo!" exclaimed Frieda.

Leighton left the room, Johnson and I following him. After a first shock at the cold-blooded dismissal and then a moment's thought that it might be a poor joke, I had been flooded with a suffusion of hatred for Lawrence, akin to his own kind of suffusion.

"He goes his way from now on, and I go mine," I said to Fred on the sidewalk, my insides boiling again. "He knows that you're my friend, and his insult to you is an insult to me, is probably meant more for me than for you. You've done everything on earth for him, and he's been glad to accept it. He knows that I don't like him as well as you do. He wants to hit at me, but he's too cowardly, so he hits at me through you, that's what it is. Well, he's done with all of us, or, rather, we've done with him."

"He's a sick man," said Fred. "Don't say anything to him till tomorrow. If Frieda can take it, I can or you can."

"No," I insisted. "It's impossible." And I had every intention of taking off somewhere, anywhere, next day.

Fred lingered with us at a cantina and, over a few beers, continued his reasonableness. "I have had a great deal out of him, more than he's had out of me, and if he doesn't feel like giving me any more, that's his business and I'll stay satisfied with what I've got. He blames me for the Vasconcelos business. He has the faults of a sick man, and we must be patient with him. We've seen his tempers before."

"This wasn't temper, Fred—this was slow, mean calculation."

"Keep calm," said Fred, "and stick it out." Johnson agreed.

Next day Frieda gravely asked us to continue with them, for her sake if for no other reason. "I don't know what I'd do without you. He's growing worse."

So we stayed and resumed plans for trips; but I had misgivings.

Though Lawrence did not see Leighton again in Mexico City, the rest of us saw him often, and Fred held no grudge, cheerfully bore Lawrence as he had been and was. Later, at Chapala, Lawrence bore Fred with equal equanimity, as shall be told.

It was at this time that we made our trip to Cuernavaca, where the Lawrences particularly enjoyed a vista down a narrow street at the end of which stood a narrow church flanked by two narrow cypresses. "It's more like Italy," beamed Lawrence. "*Ja,*" glowed Frieda, who gave hearty romantic sighs in the Borda Gardens, where the ghosts of the guests, Maximilian and Carlota, still strolled. Lawrence was saddened by evidences of the Zapata uprising and depredation in Morelos: ". . . noble ruined haciendas with ruined avenues approaching their broken splendor," as he later recorded.

Johnson recalls this expedition better than I do, and with reason. "I remember the Cuernavaca trip," he reminds me, "because that's where I got my lumbago. We went on the train, getting there in the afternoon. And that night you and I did a sort of pub crawl from bar to bar, which as usual was my undoing. You found a bar where the barkeeper spoke English—had worked in Milwaukee. He fed us very potent absinthe cocktails and I was sick as a dog all night. Next afternoon we took the train back to Mexico City. The train was late—

it was very hot—I was exhausted from my night and, when the train finally wound up the cool mountainside, I fell asleep with my back to the open window. That apparently did it. Next morning when I walked down the long staircase at the Monte Carlo to breakfast, I got the stab of pain in my back that laid me flat and practically immovable until you *carried* me downstairs several days later, put me in a taxi, and took me to the American hospital."

Lawrence was sympathetic with Johnson and a kindly visitor at the hospital. He was firm, however, in his resolve that we had had enough of the capital and that longer trips must come now or he would take Frieda to Vera Cruz and sail for England, an alternative not then attractive to Frieda. Johnson, glad of prospective ease from pain and worry, urged our leaving him; and Lawrence, still hopeful, though both he and Frieda had caught bad colds, proposed Puebla. So the three of us took off on what should have been a short train trip.

6. *Excursions*

DURING our protracted trip from the border to Mexico City
we had seen with wondering interest that armed soldiers rode
on top of the cars. Disturbances had been reported in our
North American papers; but we had not realized that trains on the
main route were liable to attack. Ours had come through with no
interference, though we had more than once felt a premonition of
bullets piercing the window shades at night. Random shooting would
have been easy. Once more, between Mexico City and Puebla, we saw
armed guards perched on the car tops, like blackbirds on cattle. Nowadays in Mexico a train will come to a spastic stop in a village or in
a field, and the passengers will patiently accept half a day's wait with
no questions answered. The papers next day will explain that a country-
wide six- or eight-hour strike had been called—for all trains, wherever
they might be—to begin at a given hour. If passengers were told the
length of the interval, allowed to stretch legs, to explore the region,
there would be little tedium; but no, they may only wait in ignorance.
In 1923 it was different. It was not strikers but rebels or bandits, and
the railroad preferred pauses to clashes. One of those pauses had happened to us. We were stalled for hours. Then, as now, passengers'
questioning went unanswered; but, with all window shades drawn,
they could guess and be patient while the guards atop the cars, I have
no doubt, were equally content with delay.

For Frieda and me a different danger was imminent, was close by.
Lorenzo, weary of watching travelers and hearing their talk, of reading a novel in Spanish, of chatting or fuming with us and blowing
his nose, began to condemn and lacerate. It was the railway service
first, the government second, the Mexican race third, the human race
fourth. Hour after hour, in a car already hot enough, we scorched

35

under his diatribes. By the ninth hour we were not hearing what he said, not listening, but he was still scolding. Other travelers stared at him and whispered to one another about this foreigner. Finally the train grumbled into motion. Some miles ahead of us government troops and bandits had skirmished with a few casualties on each side. We saw bodies when we passed the spot. But we were safe, except for the glare in Lawrence's eyes. To him the whole episode had been a personal affront. His cold was growing markedly worse.

Puebla appeased us, first the view from the *azotea* of the Hotel Jardin over the city's roofs and tiled domes. As Graham Greene in *Another Mexico* has said of Puebla, "It had more than the usual wounded beauty: it had grace." There were fine tiles in the kitchen of an old convent. Then there were onyx trifles and Spanish jewelry to be bought, prettier and lower-priced pieces of the latter than we had seen in Mexico City's governmentally run pawnshop. Frieda writes me twenty-six years later: "Puebla I remember, and there were two big pear-shaped pearls I wanted. They were only seven pounds, cheap for what they were but too much for us." Buildings stood about solidly set in ornate Colonial stone. The cathedral had a stronger dignity than its brother in the capital. The mass of twisted lacquer in the Rosario chapel with its cherubs and foliage was the richest of its sort we had seen, though a little too much like a Laocoön statue with muscles and serpents of gold.

Apparently, from later comment, Lawrence was less impressed with the onyx interior of the cathedral and with the Rosario carvings than we were and than we thought he was. Perhaps his view was colored by remembrances of his cold. He notes the "dead interior" of "all Mexican churches, even the gorgeous Puebla cathedral. The interior of almost any Mexican church gives the impression of cynical barrenness, cynical, meaningless, an empty, cynical, mocking shell. The Italian churches are built much in the same style, and yet in them lingers a shadow and stillness of old, mysterious holiness. The hush. But not in Mexico. The churches outside are impressive. Inside, and it is curious to define it, they are blatant; void of sound and yet with no hush, simple, and yet completely vulgar, barren, sterile. More barren than a bank or a schoolroom or an empty concert hall, less mysterious than any of these. You get a sense of plaster, of mortar, of whitewash, of smeared bluewash or graywash, and of gilt laid on and ready to peel off. Even in the most gorgeous churches, the gilt is hatefully gilt, never golden. Nothing is soft or mellow."

I wish that he might have seen the partly ruined Dominican church and monastery at Yanhuilpan on the present highway to Oaxaca. He visited Oaxaca the following year; but I judge that the monastery was then inaccessible to even such pertinacious travelers as Lawrence. He would have found that, like San Agustin de Acolman through which he had prowled with reverent approval, it looms in memory high above all Mexican ecclesiastic architecture for grand-scale, austere, time-mellowed original beauty, untouched by latter-day monkeyshines. He would have lingered in its cloisters, and relaxed, and perhaps had quiet time to remember that in *The Lost Girl,* he had written of an Italian church at Casa Latina: "She went inside and was almost sick with repulsion. . . . The lousy-looking, dressed-up dolls; . . . the blood-streaked Jesus; . . . the mouldering, mumbling, filthy peasant women on their knees; all the sense of trashy, repulsive, degraded fetish-worship was too much for her."

It is apposite here to quote again from *Another Mexico,* by Graham Greene, concerning what, in Mexican churches, Lawrence still felt to be a degraded "fetish-worship": "There was no ignorance in this devotion," says Greene, "even old peasant women carried their books of devotion and knew how to contemplate the agony. Here, one felt, was a real religion in the continuous traffic of piety." Lawrence, on the other hand, felt that the bloody sacrifice of the single victim by the Jews or Romans was, to the old peasant women and their families, little different from the bloody sacrifice of multitudes by Aztecs. It was a blind devotion in either case and a continuous traffic for the priests.

After Puebla, we went to Orizaba. It seems to me that our trip was by night and that we arrived there not very well rested and pinched with an early morning chill. There was at any rate a definite chill in ourselves as soon as we set foot on the platform. Lorenzo, with his cold worse, with a hard face, and with nervous jerks of his head in this and that direction, waved porters aside and suddenly walking between them and us, ejaculated with the now too familiar high pitch of a nervous seizure: "We are not staying here, Frieda. We are leaving." He inquired the hour of the next train back. Frieda gave a sigh of relief when we learned that it was considerably later. She asked him what the matter was. "Don't you feel it?" he railed. "Don't you feel it through your feet? It exudes from the platform. The place is evil. I won't go to the town, I won't go to a hotel, I won't go anywhere. I can stay here at the station till train time. You can do as you like. The place is evil, the whole air is evil! The air creeps with it!" And he screamed at the finally intimidated porters to go away.

My patience broke. I tried hard to speak quietly and perhaps did. "Lorenzo, I am going to see the town. If I like it I am going to spend the night. There is no reason why I should give in to your whims. I knew from the way you treated Leighton that I ought not to come with you and I'm sorry now that I did. But you're not going to boss me. I'm going to the hotel. If Frieda wants to come along, you can indulge your nerves here by yourself." I don't know whether or not my voice shook from the shaking of my ganglion.

He looked extremely and childishly surprised, not as if my standing him off was a shock, but as if it was an unwarranted attack on him out of the blue. He was instantly docile and dumb. He followed us into the vehicle. He sank his beard into his breastbone. He was a deflated prophet.

And then came in my own history one of its most comic episodes. We reached a friendly old-fashioned Mexican hotel, built around a court, the two-story arched patio lined with potted plants and flowers, the walls hung with caged birds, the rooms sequestered in the old Mexican way so that when room doors were closed there would be darkness and no air, the dining room with its soiled tablecloths, and the kitchen with its charcoal stoves open amiably to the sociable pigskin chairs on the ground floor. All was as it should be for the native or the open-minded foreign guest. I liked it and was tired and was glad to see my suitcase at rest in a corner. But the devil entered me. I waited until the Lawrences might have unpacked some of their belongings and be relaxing. Then I knocked at their door. Frieda opened it. I stalked in. "It's impossible," said I. "There must be another hotel. I can't stay here."

"Why not?" asked Lorenzo, a pathetic martinet.

"Why not?" I yelled. "I couldn't close an eye here. The whole atmosphere is polluted. Evil seeps up from the ground under the whole building, nothing but evil. We must leave and leave now."

"You think the hotel is evil too? You think it's that bad?" asked Lawrence, with the eyes of an alarmed child.

"Think?" I stormed. "I know. Don't you feel it in your feet? It comes up from the floors. I'll find another hotel. Stay if you like, but I'm leaving."

"We'll go with you," peeped Lawrence. "Only a few minutes to pack." He was utterly meek.

We canceled our rooms. The hotel boys, thinking us maniacs because of my storming, carried our luggage to an inferior hotel two squares away. I went ahead, saw two rooms, chose for the Lawrences an airless enclosure alongside the noisome hotel privy, returned to the lobby and led them to their miserable quarters—mine were miserable too—orating, "This is better. We are away from that poison. This is safe. This is decent. We can sleep."

Before we slept, we toured the town and found it not much to our liking. Perhaps because of our personal vexation, the churches seemed to us gaunt, the market dirty, the houses not snug, the whole place uncomfortably different from Cuernavaca and Puebla. It was an industrial place. We saw tired-looking factories. "There was a strike here in Diaz' time," Lawrence informed us. He had been reading *The Mexican People: Their Struggle for Freedom,* by L. Gutierrez de Lara and Edgcumb Pinchon. "Diaz," he went on, "sent a commission to hear grievances, or to pretend to hear them. What they did do was to summon all the strikers for a meeting in some building and then lock the place and set it on fire." I wondered if that was the evil which Lawrence had sensed oozing up from the station platform. I felt more kindly toward him, with a wave of repentance that I had moved them out of the good hotel. And yet he needed the lesson. And it had seemed good for him.

At least on the surface we were an amiable trio when, studying Terry that night, we decided against further touring below the plateau. Vera Cruz would only be a point of departure for England. We should return to Puebla and thence, via Cholula and Atlixco, to the City.

That night he handed me as a present his copy of *The Mexican People: Their Struggle for Freedom.* On the title page he had written, "History is little else than a picture of human crimes and misfortunes. Voltaire."

Soon we were at church-filled Cholula, imagining how it had looked when an Aztec temple had stood in the place of every present church.

It was here, Lawrence reminded us from recent reading in Prescott, that Spanish Cortes had anticipated the similar cruelty of the Indian Diaz, by assembling a native contingent suspected of disaffection, by blocking them into a building, and by ending doubt with fire.

"It's all of one piece," he protested wearily, "what the Aztecs did, what Cortes did, what Diaz did—the wholesale, endless cruelty. The land itself does it to whoever lives here. The heart has been cut out of the land. That's why hearts had to be cut out of its people. It goes on and on and will always go on. It's a land of death. Look at this dead soil all around us—the dagger-fingered cactus—the knife-edged sun! It's all death."

"Then hadn't we better watch ourselves, Lorenzo," asked Frieda with her gleam of michief, "what Mexico might do to us if we stay too long? We don't want to grow bloodthirsty, do we? We bigger ones might kill the Spoodle."

"Why can't women be serious—except in love?" he snapped, turning to climb the long stone stairway to the church on the pyramidal hill.

The Plumed Serpent develops the ideas expressed in these talks: through the feelings of Kate, who "firmly believed that part of the horror of the Mexican people came from the unsoothed dryness of the land and the untempered crudity of the flat-edged sunshine. If only there could be a softening of water in the air, and a haze above trees, the unspoken and unspeakable malevolence would die out of the human hearts."

And then Kate (D.H.L.) goes on to a wider guess, one of those theoretical, melodramatic generalizations in which the novels are ever eloquent: an ordered summary of the frequent jabs which Lawrence in conversation had been thrusting at Americans and all their works. He had been maliciously pleased by a line he showed us in a Mexican newspaper: "The American man is a husky old maid with an overdeveloped sense of commerce"; but that was mild compared with his own sweeping appraisal of the Americas as a "death-continent" swallowing and destroying all the good that had come from the rest of the world. He delighted in shooting this doctrine at an American believer that the "melting pot" might become a cleansing away of the world's selfish, greedy animosities. "Yes," I would come back at him, "I do believe in it, I believe with Jefferson, Lincoln, Wilson that our democracy offers mankind life as against the death inherent in your old systems!" But like Kate he "wondered whether America really was the great death-continent, the great *No!* to the European and Asiatic and even African *Yes!* Was it really the great melting pot, where men from the creative continents were smelted back again, not to a new creation, but down into the homogeneity of death? Was it the great continent of the undoing, and all its peoples the agents of the mystic destruction? Plucking, plucking at the created soul in a man, till at last it plucked out the growing germ, and left him a creature of mechanism and automatic reaction, with only one inspiration, the desire to pluck the quick out of every living spontaneous creature. . . . Was that the clue to America? . . . Was it the great death-continent, the continent that destroyed again what the other continents had built up? The continent whose spirit of place fought purely to pick the eyes out of the face of God? Was that America?"

Wyndham Lewis, in *America and Cosmic Man,* pursues the theme with gusto, sees the United States as becoming "a great big promiscuous grave into which tumble, and there disintegrate, all that was formerly race, class, or nationhood." His predecessor had asked, "And all the people who went there, Europeans, negroes, Japanese, Chinese, all the colours and races, were they the spent people, in whom the God impulse had collapsed, so they crossed to the great continent of the negation, where the human will declares itself 'free,' to pull down the soul of the world? Was it so? And did this account for the great drift of spent souls passing over to the side of Godless democracy, energetic negation? The negation which is the life-breath of materialism. And would the great negative pull of the Americans at last break the heart of the world? . . . These handsome natives! Was it because they were death-worshippers, Moloch-worshippers, that they were so uncowed and handsome? Their pure acknowledgment of death, and their undaunted admission of nothingness kept so erect and careless."

He spoke more than once with repugnance of Mexican doings on November second, *El Dia de los Muertes,* The Day of the Dead, though he had not yet actually seen it, when with gay skulls and skeletons all over the place, death is brought alive and becomes prankishly intimate. The very pastries and candies are bones of the dead. The Mexican consumes death before death consumes him. This attitude disturbed Lawrence, made him physically as well as spiritually uncomfortable and was one of the pricks which induced his constant reference to the death-presence in Mexico. I reminded him of the Ko-share, amiable spirits of the dead, "sacred clowns," who in our Tewa Indian ceremonials at home, prance and prank, protectively colored and supposedly invisible, among the still living dancers and scatter blessings on both vegetable and animal crops. "That's different," he countered, "having death come back and bring blessings. Here it's man that's grimly playful and tries to belittle death, cannot see any light in it, only darkness and tries to fight off the darkness with ridicule. There's no hope or happiness in it, no real gaiety, only a black, crude cynicism. They need a new religion; it's the one thing that can help them. Your Indians around Santa Fe have a live religion. They have survived. They're different."

After Cholula we paused at a simple, comfortable hostelry in Atlixco, where we managed to stomach the hot milk vinegared with coffee-essence, the latter ever stored cold in cruets standing on the soiled tablecloths. Here too we sampled fresh pulque and liked its milkiness well enough to try the riper kind. But with that we had to hold our noses over the stench from the glasses, which was like a stench of vomit, and we had to spit out our samples. Lawrence and Frieda had been as American as I, trying anything once. But we liked *tepache,* a sort of May wine made of fermenting fruits.

During our several days at Atlixco Lawrence was as contented as I had seen him anywhere in Mexico. He was amused by remembering the jaunty names lettered on trucks, such as *Ponte Chango, No Besame, Cara Sucia, Yo Sufro Mucho* (Be On Your Monkey-Toes, Don't Kiss Me, Dirty Face, and I Suffer Much). He smiled over a sign he had seen in some restaurant: *Servimos con sonrisa,* accompanied by the English translation, We serve with smile. He led us on long walks through the town and around the countryside. We climbed the spiry shrine-crowned hill against which the town leans and were struck by the dramatic effect it presented with Popocateptl's huge massive symmetry behind it. We climbed the hill again one day at dawn and stood silent before the very Fujiyama which Hokusai had seen for his wood block, slopes aflame with sun as though with red lava.

"I wonder," mused Lawrence, "if the pyramids looked like that, running with blood." We others were troubled too by the image. The sight was too awesome, the image too remindful of Prescott. But the light soon changed and we relaxed again.

We photographed one another on burros. We read. We were at ease with ourselves and one another. We approved of Mexico. D. H. was at his genial best and, for that reason, so were we. His best was very good. Perhaps he wrote a little then. I think he did. He was enjoying Mme Calderon de la Barca's book of letters, *Life in Mexico,* and I recall his sharing with us the very Mexican story about her cook, whom she had trained to such culinary skill that diplomatic society was envious. Then the woman and her daughter had suddenly disappeared from the household with no explanation or word of farewell, and every quest for them was vain. One day when, driving in a suburb, Mme de la Barca saw the pair sitting by the roadside begging, she stopped the carriage to ask what it meant. Hadn't they been comfortable, happy, well treated, well paid? Yes, yes, all that, indeed yes— but "O Jesus, the joy of doing nothing!" "Just the nothing we are doing!" beamed the busy Lawrence, "and, O Jesus, the joy of it!" For once he felt in the Indian no omen of dark doom. He quoted from somewhere else, *"Que hermoso es no hacer nada y luego descanzar!"* ("How delightful it is to do nothing and then rest!") "But I can't continue doing nothing. We must go somewhere and settle. I must write. I want to write, and we've a living to make." There was very little income at that point from his books.

We decided to go back and make our plans with Johnson in Mexico City, where a Spanish troupe was presenting plays by such dramatists as Benavente and Lope de Vega, and where on Sunday a popular Mexican matador was to appear in the bull ring.

"We ought to see both these shows," he advised, "and then go seeking out a place in which to settle and be at work."

"Why not Atlixco?" I wondered. "We like it here." And I meant too that we liked one another in Atlixco.

"No. Though it's small, it's too urban. I want a place with water. Perhaps Mazatlan or Manzanillo on the Pacific. But there are also two lakes, Patzcuaro and Chapala. We'll see. And if there's nothing, we'll sail."

7. The Capital Again

W E were all four at the Monte Carlo again. Johnson was restored to health and ready for us. We told him of the endless hot train ride and of our disappointment in Orizaba, and he was forgivably glad that we had not been too content without him.

We attended the first night of the run of Spanish plays. It was talkative drama and conveyed very little to the three of us who lacked Spanish; but Lawrence watched and listened with sharp focus. Through half of the first act I was puzzled by a booing and hissing from the audience. Since the play was a drawing-room comedy, I could not believe that a villain was being harried as by provincials in early days at home. When the intermission came, Lawrence explained that the company was speaking Castilian and that Mexicans, by whom the lisping consonants had long since been repudiated, would have none of the foreign tongue, would have nothing but good, Mexican, original, pure Spanish. They had thrown off Spain and they had thrown off affected Spanish. Why should they tolerate mispronunciation just because a Spanish king had lisped and his court had flattered him by imitation? "The poor actors were sweating," he said. "They had a bad time twisting their tongues. But whenever one of them slipped, the house drowned him. It was so hard for them that of course none of them could act. I suppose all day tomorrow they'll be slaving to learn Spanish, poor devils!"

He feels this unusual tenderness, I conjectured, because they are Europeans. It is his chronic nostalgia to be somewhere else than where he is.

He told us during the second intermission about another Spanish occurrence, the origin of ecru lace. Some important dame—was it a queen during a crusade? I have forgotten—had vowed not to take off

44

her dress until her absent husband should return. It was a lace dress and became yellowed with wear. So the ladies about her flatteringly conformed by dyeing their own laces to resemble the soiled color of hers. He told about the Empress Josephine bringing dainty lace handkerchiefs into fashion because she was ever using one to hide her bad teeth. And that reminded him of how the elevated handshake had originated. Some French prince, I believe, had had to spare a carbuncle under his arm. Lawrence's memory was acutely retentive and accurate, not only for what he had read but for actual conversations, as illustrated in his recording of Mrs. Nuttall's tea party. He could often have put it to better use in fiction if he had not been determined that so many of his characters should talk Lawrence instead of themselves. In his own personal quoting of conversations, he did very little of this.

We stayed in the capital longer than we had planned, through that week and then another week. He had misread the date of the bullfight, which was to take place on Easter Sunday, a Sunday later than he had understood. He and I went to the town office to buy tickets. There was a waiting line. With his better idiom than mine, he joined the queue but, when he reached the window, shook his head, forfeited his place by dropping out of line and waving me to the far end of it. I wondered why he had not beckoned me to take his place before he dropped out. But he was suddenly confused, stricken again by his distaste for ticket windows, clerks, officialdom. He came to my elbow, though, when I reached the wicket and spoke for me in his fluent Italianate Spanish.

We decided now that there was no harm in his mistake as to the bullfight date, that events had turned out well, that it would be interesting for us to spend Holy Week in Mexico City, not knowing then that Holy Week is the great Mexican holiday that empties the capital of all who can afford to leave it. They throng to various fashionable or popular resorts, which are swollen-priced for the occasion and primed for gaiety. So we spent those days comparatively free from jostle and racket. There was enough population left to jam the churches; and on Good Friday we visited many of them. A memorable sight in Mexico is a throng of worshipers slowly inching forward on their knees, their arms held out like Christ's on the cross, their faces rapt with an absorption of His suffering. By this particular devotion, Lawrence might well have been as impressed as Graham Greene; but it alienated him.

In the massive cathedral, in the Sagraria alongside, its façade trickling thick with carven red stone, in every church on every street, we saw long, slow, lavalike streams of people entering at one door, emerging from another; thousands of kneeling figures: women with dark *rebozos* not quite hiding their wistfully wrinkled features, an occasional widow in smart weeds, men of the world in North American outfits, ragged peons and their trailing families with huaraches or even barefoot. And always that sound as though from somewhere else, that murmur of praying voices, with a faint treble dominant, like the one breath of an Eastern temple blown and blent from many small bells.

At the cinema next evening, in a silent film, *The Passion of Christ,* we watched Jesus loom forward with a lamb on His shoulder, nearer and larger, into the hearts of His audience, while marimbas played a gaily swinging tune to welcome Him. The fact that during the Crucifixion the tune was "Three O'Clock in the Morning" seemed in no way to lessen reverence. Frieda laughed about it, but Lawrence's emotions were mixed. The Church's hold on Mexico depressed him. He felt it a poor change from Quetzalcoatl.

"All this is unreal," he complained. "It's all done for the show. It's not real. One moment they're groveling in the churches. You would think they were agonized by the old tragedy. The next moment they're gadding in the streets, full of gaiety and pulque, as though they had never heard of Jesus. And the Judases they burn, that tells the story. That's when they show themselves the sadists they really are. They have no sense of the betrayal and what followed it. They rig up their papier-mâché Judases like clowns, like us as a matter of fact, like the foreigners they hate, tog us out in proud colored paper, paint our faces full of bloated complacency, and then light the fuse and off we explode, losing a leg, another leg, our arms, and then with a great bang our heads and our centers, all gone where they'd like us to go. They're not thinking about Christ at all," he grimaced, "except for a morbid pleasure in the fact that he was tortured and murdered. You know how they smear his image with blood. They're out for blood. They're out to kill. Not Christ's enemies but their own. And they think we're their enemies. Perhaps we are. Certainly you Americans have been their enemies, and they never forget it. They never forget their dying cadets at Chapultepec. And I doubt if they forget their obsequious Archbishop welcoming General Scott and suggesting that you annex Mexico. The Church is foreign here. They need their own religion, which used to let them kill *ad lib*. That was it."

He wanted Quetzalcoatl back again and yet was as afraid of the old gods as of the new. With brow clouded, he was once more becoming uneasy, distrustful, resentful of himself and of everybody.

8. The Bullfight

LAWRENCE had heard in Europe high praise of the famous Spanish matadors, Belmonte and Joselito, the latter killed in the ring only three years before; and we were told that the Mexicans, Rodolfo Gaona and Juan Silveti, were performers of comparable skill and prowess. Silveti was to be the star on Sunday.

On Easter morning, having been to churches Friday and to a sacred movie on Saturday, we were wakened by bells of resurrection and in the afternoon attended the bullfight. It was a first experience for all of us, and we approached it curious but apprehensive.

At the entrance to the arena Lawrence, Johnson, and I, like other males filing through, were frisked for firearms: it had been announced that President Obregón would be present. At the last moment, word spread that he could not attend; but other dignitaries entered the presidential box escorting three or four bright-fluttering women who wore flowered mantillas and high combs.

Since seats cost but half as much in the sun as in the shade, we were sitting in the sun, except that this day, to Lawrence's special pleasure, there was no sun. Our backless bench tier of concrete was within five rows of the ring. Below us, paralleling the wall of the ring was a circling five-foot wooden fence with here and there a gap and before each gap a small barrier, making safety boxes for performers when hard pressed. The crowd, now thickening and seeming less an assemblage than a single mass monster, was already—with its murmurs, growls, and yells—grinding our nerves a little.

"I begin to feel sick," whispered Lawrence. "Look at their faces. The eyes don't seem hard, or the mouths. It's that cruel dent of relish above the nostril."

Opposite us, rose a roar of voices. Somebody's hat had been tossed

48

across the tiers into a group which was scrambling for it. Other hats followed, on our side too. Orange peels began flying. A shoe landed in Lawrence's lap. He sat immobile while someone from behind him seized it and sent it scaling again.

"Shall we leave?" asked Lawrence, his head twitching upward like that of a horse.

Half an orange just missed my bald spot. A second half hit it. Other bare heads were being hit. A kindly Mexican motioned that I should put on my hat. Obeying him, I was spared further pelting. Apparently uncovered heads were permissible targets.

Three bands, one at a time, entered their sections near the President's box and were shouted at for *musica!* When a rousing Mexican march blared out, the vocal din was only accelerated. The crowd had not wanted music so much as a beat for their own noise.

What looked like a folded coat landed in the arena. It seemed a signal. Like water from a broken dam, the mass of men in unreserved seats swelled over the reserved section which in a trice was filled solid. Seatholders who came later were vain claimants.

On the exact moment advertised, a wide gate opened, a square colorful procession strutted with music into the arena toward the President's box to make bows, with waists and trim buttocks held tautly, shoulders back; two groups of fine-stepping *toreros* with bright cloaks above their embroidered boleros and half-length, skin-tight trousers and salmon-colored stockings; then mounted picadors; then *banderilleros* with silver embroidery; then matadors with gold and with red capes, all these men wearing berets over abbreviated pigtails; and finally, in red harness, two dingy teams of three mules each, ready to drag away carcasses. "The right symbol!" muttered Lawrence. "They're all jack-asses." The procession, after circling the ring and receiving a round of plaudits, dispersed.

Then, with no warning, no noise, a huge white bull swam into the arena and stood a moment, his tail waving, his head bewildered, apprehending foes. Lawrence's head rose and sank with the bull's. "The bull is beautiful, Lorenzo," said Frieda. The foes were there, the first of them: two stationary horsemen. When the lowered head made clumsily for a horse, the rider warded it off with a lance. The second rider did likewise. And then into the ring came the toreros, to nag him with scarlet mantles. He saw them one at a time. He snorted. He charged a cloak. It was whisked over his head. He curved quickly and charged again, cleaving the air with his horns under a swing of color. Now and then he would corner a torero who, amid jeers and whistlings, would either dodge into one of the safety boxes or vault the *barrera* into the shielded alley way. All of a sudden the bull too had heaved his pawing bulk over the fence. Attendants scurried to cut off a section of the gangway by closing gates. Commotion subsided. "He beat them," Lawrence said as though to himself. "They should let him go." A fluttered cape teased the bull out again into the ring, where he stood still, waving his tail. His belly lifting, falling with his heavy breath, he looked round and lowed; then once more he leaped the fence, this time breaking it. And once more the blocked exit, once more the flashing taunts, the deft weavings and wavings of five toreros; once more his return to the ring, his half-seeing eye, his wasted strength. "They're dastardly!" Lawrence exclaimed.

He turned to us. He had been shifting in his seat and looking sharply at us now and then as if to see what we thought of it all. We could tell that the teasing of the beast, the deliberate baiting and angering had made him as tense as the animal, with whom he was almost identifying himself. "They keep him starved and in the dark," he snapped, "so that when he comes into the ring he's angry but can't see. He's the only one among them with heart or brain. He despises them, but he knows what they are; he knows that he's done for. The toreador jumped the fence to get away from the bull; the bull jumped the fence to get away from the lot of them. They let the toreador get away. Why don't they let the bull get away?" he exhorted us. "Why don't they respect his intelligence and bow to him instead of to those nincompoops in the box? He's not the brute; they're the brutes. He abhors them and so do I. But he can't get away and I can. Let's get away." He was on his feet. None of us stirred to follow him. He sat down again.

"It sickens me too, Lorenzo," I agreed. "But hadn't we better see at least one round of it through, to know what we're talking about when we say we don't like it? I shan't want to see another bullfight any more than you will."

"Very well," he glared. "But I don't need to see a round through, as you call it. The trouble is that you're as bloodthirsty as the rest of them. You can't resist it. Frieda can't resist it. Spud can't. I could resist it, but I'll give in to you." He sulked back on the bench and looked away from us, away from everything.

But now came a change, a chance for the bull to vent his disgust, if not on a man, then on a decrepit, blindfolded horse. The rider spurred toward him. The picador, with armor under his trousers, urged the shivering mount to expose its belly. The crowd was hushed, expectant, on the edge of its seats. Lawrence was breathing hard and glaring. Suddenly, given a chance not so much by the rider as by the bull, the horse struck with his thin hind legs, fought free and stalked off with an air of doddering valor, only to postpone a next encounter not at the center of the ring where he had had clearance, but close to the barrera, with no room for him to dodge; and though the picador was supposed with his blunt lance to shunt the bull off, the crowd knew better. The bull pawed up earth, slowly bent his head. The lance was futile. The horse reared and floundered. In and up went the horn. While the picador tumbled against the fence and sheepishly found his feet, the bull shoved and gored and ripped; and while the crowd gave a sigh of relief, Lawrence groaned and shook. By the time the toreros had again drawn their prey toward the cloaks and the picador had remounted and forced his steed into motion toward the exit, the horse's bowels were bulging almost to the ground, like vines and gourds. But the bull had not had enough. "Stop it!" cried Lawrence to the bull, jumping out of his seat. But just before the picador reached the gate, horns were lowered again for another snorting plunge, and this time the entire covering of the horse's belly was ripped off. He fell dead, his contents out on the ground, with earth being shoveled over them by attendants. Lawrence had sat down again, dazed and dark with anger and shame. Frieda was watching him. The proud front of the bull—head, neck, chest, leg, hoof—shone crimson in a moment of sun. The crowd was throatily satisfied!

There had been something phallic, Lawrence might have noted, in this fierce penetration, this rape of entrails, this bloody glut. But his nerves exploded. Fortunately people were too intent on the ring to notice him, and only a few of them heard a red-bearded Englishman, risen from his seat, excoriating cowards and madmen. Frieda was as alarmed as Johnson and I, for he was denouncing the crowd in Spanish. But he sickened suddenly, plunged away from us, treading toes, and lurched down the row toward the exit.

"I'll go with him," exclaimed Frieda. "I'd better. There's no knowing. You stay. He'll be worse if you come. You stay. Leave him to me. *Ja!*" And she squeezed her way out.

"Yes, I think we'd better stay," said Johnson, with a drawn face. And we did stay, though we were as revolted by the performance as are most Europeans and Americans. I supposed the audience had more than once seen outraged foreigners bolt away, and learned to ignore them as barbarians. I dreaded what we were still to watch, felt my insides sift like ashes, was sorely tempted to follow the Lawrences. But we did stay.

Lawrence wrote Knud Merrild: "We saw a terrible bullfight and ran away after ten minutes." But he was wrong: the time had been triple that.

I noticed then that a rain had begun, with large drops. A shower fell quickly. It became a downpour. Many of the onlookers scattered for cover. But most of them, including Johnson and me, remained, huddling from the wet and not feeling it much. In spite of rain and mud, the show continued.

A banderillero advanced toward the bull, with no protective cloak, but holding up in each hand a pink-stemmed barb. He coaxed the brute, wheedled him, yelped at him, hopped in the air, with feet clicking together below him and darts clicking together above him. Lawrence might have admired the birdlike poise. Now on this side, now on that, he waited and watched till the bull gathered its puzzled wits again and charged. In a flash the man had leaped aside and in the same flash had planted the two barbs jiggling at a neat angle on the shoulders. He did it again with green *banderillos,* shorter ones—an alert and precarious performance; and though the deed seemed ignoble to us, we applauded, feeling at the same time relieved that Lawrence was gone and could not see us.

For a moment the animal shook his body and bellowed slightly. Then came the matador, his scarlet cape hung athwart a long sword. Here came a sudden, sure, personal authority. Lawrence would have liked this presence, this sureness, this motion of a bird with wings slow, then swift. This was different. Directly facing the bull, choosing a moment when the horns hung toward him at precisely the right slant, this lordly authority, this death-dealer, thrust the *espada* half to its hilt in the vulnerable spot exposed between lowered shoulder blades. There with the banderillos the sword joined a halo like a section of the nimbus around Our Lady of Guadalupe; I would tell that to Lawrence.

The bull stood stock still, seemed to be wondering how these pains could have reached him. For a last few moments before the end, he faced and followed his enemies, but with weaker and weaker lunges.

His knees crumbled. He sank. He was up, but only for a second, then down again, a grisly likeness to a bull at rest in a meadow. His eyes glazed. He acknowledged death. Thereupon, with one swift jab, an attendant dispatched him. In came the mules. Proud and stalwart until now, now flabby and ignominious, the bull's body was dragged out at one gate, and the horse's body and entrails out at another. The drenched crowd was ready for scene two. Now I could feel again the presence of Lawrence's thin, tortured face and Frieda's eyes, watching him. Perhaps we should have left with them.

Rain over, the wet people were gay again. There was more tossing of orange peel and this time soaked wads of newspaper.

By now Johnson and I knew that we were staying to the end. We felt ashamed but hypnotized, cataleptic. Later, we held our breath when Juan Silveti, in the very act of executing the firm, delicate master stroke, slipped and fell and might have been injured but that his huge victim at once drooped and stood quiet, stricken from within by a mortal vent of crimson, triply spilling with his breath from throat and nostrils. In a few moments he was dead from that one stroke, and the matador was gracefully acknowledging gusty applause, striding and bowing past section after section of the amphitheater. If Lawrence had stayed this long, he might have been hissing the hero—and might have been roughly handled.

In the fourth round one of the horses, receiving a horn in the chest, managed to walk all the way out with a steady spurt of blood from above his forelegs, like a jet from a wall fountain. In the fifth round Juan Silveti relinquished to one of his lesser fellows a bull not fierce enough or not foolish enough for heroes.

Then in the sixth and last round the banderilleros inserted their gay darts as neatly as ladies used to adjust hat pins; and Silveti kneeled to let the clumsy beast attack, as ever, the cloak instead of the man. By adroit passes, he attracted two or three charges in the customary time of one, then walked nonchalantly away with his back to the bull, dragging his cape at his heels. Finally he placed a handkerchief on the ground and succeeded in so directing his victim's attack that he could thrust the *espada* without budging from his small white foothold. The game needed these variations, these graces, this ballet precision; Johnson and I reluctantly confessed to each other that the crowd's enjoyment was not altogether blood lust, and wished that the Lawrences might have seen the artistry and considered it as something apart. At least Frieda would have granted it a reluctant but admiring *"ja!"* Experienced Mexican eyes could of course see far better than we the exact gaugings, manipulatings, side-steppings, balancings, and piercings. We vowed though, as we filed out, that it was our last bullfight.

In the corridor we came upon a middle-aged Polish professor of psychology, whom we had casually met at the Monte Carlo. He was vacationing from some American university, spoke fair Spanish, and was with a Mexican friend, both of them gesticulating with joy over the events of the afternoon. "Magnificent!" he exclaimed. We bowed, without assenting but without disturbing the ecstasy of chatter between the two. "We are going to Silveti's hotel," the Pole called out. "Why not come with us? My friend knows him well." "Thanks," I answered, "but I must join our own friends. They were shocked and left." "Yes, I saw them," he laughed. "They shouldn't be shocked. They are just new to it. But we'll see you later at the hotel, unless Mr. Johnson will come with us." "Go ahead," I urged. And Spud went.

Lawrence greeted me at the hotel with a hard look of contempt. "So you stayed through all of it. I thought you would. You Americans would run to any street accident to see blood. You are as bad as the dirty Mexicans. You would have held Frieda there in that slaughterhouse. You tried to keep her there."

"No, Lorenzo!" she protested.

"But they wanted you to stay. I know. They not only fooled themselves with their nonsense about 'seeing it through,' they wanted to fool you as well, but you were too fine for them."

"He compliments me," smiled Frieda. "How angry he must be with you!"

At supper, after Johnson's return from the bullfighter's hotel, Lawrence expatiated. "What we saw this afternoon," he snorted, "was the grandeur of Rome, soiling its breeches! You like scatological jokes, Bynner. No wonder you liked this dirt."

"He didn't like it," Spud defended me mildly, "any more than I did."

"You both stayed it through," flamed Lawrence. "The way not to enjoy it was not to stay it through."

The Pole was with his friend at a nearby table and, when they had finished eating, came over to ours and asked if they might join us. But before bringing the Mexican, he touched off the fuse. "It was my sixth bullfight," he gloated. "I was shocked at first, like you, Mrs. Lawrence. I saw that Mr. Lawrence had to take you out. But I've learned now.

Didn't you see how happy the bulls were?" He beckoned to the Mexican and continued, "I'd like to have you meet my—"

"No," said Lawrence firmly. "I do not wish to meet your friend, or anyone else in this loathsome country. And I have seen, as well, all that I wish to see of you."

"Ja!" nodded Frieda vigorously.

The Pole was silenced. But as most Mexicans react when bullfights are condemned, the friend was kindled and, more because Lawrence had left the ring than because of this rudeness, he came close and took up the cudgels. "You are English," he challenged in our tongue. "You run after animals, little foxes, tire them out and then let dogs tear them to pieces, while you ride your high horses. We Mexicans face big animals, stronger than we are, and we are not dogs. We face them as men and kill them with our hands. You English hunt little people too and make dogs of your soldiers to tear little people to pieces."

"I abominate fox hunts," sparred Lawrence, in confusion.

But the Mexican did not spare him. "You have judged all Mexico by one bullfight, but I will not judge all England by one Englishman." He bowed to Frieda, turned on his heel and conducted the Pole with him out of the dining room, out of the hotel.

By now Lawrence was seething, and I expected further outbursts against one or all of us. To my surprise the seething settled; and, with no more mention of Poles or Mexicans, we had a pacific session in their room, during which he opened one of those stores of information with which he frequently surprised us. He had been studying somewhere the history of bullfighting and had taken notes, in fact he produced a page of data and he half read, half remembered for us:

"In the sixteenth century the Vatican took a stand against the filthy business, which was going on here even then. Pope Pius V," he glanced at a note, "banned it. So did Sixtus V. But a great protest followed, led by poets," he gave me a look, "and by the whole faculty at Salamanca. With the next Pope," and here a final use of the paper, "yes, Clement VIII, the Church gave in, just as it had to give in to your Penitentes in New Mexico and to letting your Indians add their pagan rites to the Mass. That was different. I like that. I suppose a Church which murdered heretics shouldn't mind the murder of a few bulls." He dropped the sheet of notes into a wastebasket and smiled indulgently when I picked them out again.

I have been reminded of Lawrence's running away from the bullfight by a passage in Catherine Carswell's *Savage Pilgrimage* telling of his similar flight from a performance in 1920 of Tolstoy's *Living Corpse*: "It made him so unhappy," she says, "that before the performance was half through he found himself unable to endure it longer, even with his face buried in his hands. . . . There was nothing for it but for us to squeeze our way out . . . earning, as we did so, black looks from a long row of earnest Russophile playgoers."

But it was only five months after the Mexico City bullfight, when Lawrence had returned to Mexico with the Danish painter, Kai Götzsche, that the latter wrote Knud Merrild, October 15, 1923, concerning a village near Tepic: "As we came into a small town, a bullfight was to be staged, so we stopped to take that in. . . . Interesting, but how raw it was. We saw four bulls, of which two were killed. . . . The poor animal, he tried to lie down and die. But he was constantly aroused to make hopeless attacks at a red rag. . . . I got provoked and furious just to think of the yellow and dumb performance."

This time Götzsche was the outraged dissenter. Lawrence not only stayed and watched the show but wrote a short story later about a bullfighter and his cruelty to an enamored rich woman. The story was called *None of That* and reported the lady's initial experience at a bullfight: "At first she was very disgusted, and very contemptuous, a little bit frightened, you know, because a Mexican crowd at a bull ring is not very charming." Finally, because of the torero's vicious cruelty to her, the woman poisoned herself and left him half her property.

9. Echoes of the Bullfight

W HEN *The Plumed Serpent* was issued three years later,
Johnson and I discovered the use Lawrence had made of
our Mexican experiences together.

It at once became evident that the protagonist, Kate Leslie, was a
fusion of himself and Frieda, the hand the hand of Frieda but the
voice the voice of Lawrence, that Owen Rhys, her cousin, was I and
that Owen's friend, Bud Villiers, was Johnson. My belief then and
now is that he had intended our continuing to play rather ignominious
American roles throughout the novel but that, having come to know
and like us better, he mercifully let us out of it.

Kate, he wrote, "was really fond of Owen. But how could she respect
him? So empty, and waiting for circumstance to fill him up. Swept
with an American despair of having lived in vain, or of not having
really lived. Having missed something. Which fearful misgiving would
make him rush like mechanical steel filings to a magnet, towards any
crowd in the street. And then all his poetry and philosophy gone with
the cigarette end he threw away, he would stand craning his neck in
one more frantic effort to *see*—just to *see*. . . . And then after he'd seen
an old ragged woman run over by a motor car and bleeding on the
floor, he'd come back to Kate pale at the gills, sick, bewildered,
daunted, and yet, yes, glad he'd seen it. It was Life!" Spud, figuring as
Villiers, was similarly deprecated by Kate: "Everything he said, everything he did, reversed her real life-flow."

Lawrence in the book reversed his own life-flow sufficiently to transfer to the Frieda-half of Kate his own emotions and actions at the
bullfight. It is the woman, Kate, who cries out her disgust and rises
and leaves, with unchivalrous Owen failing to accompany her. Though
it had been Lawrence who initiated and arranged attendance at the

corrida, when Kate says in the book, "I'm not very keen on going," Owen replies, "Oh, but why not? I don't believe in them on principle, but we've never seen one, so we shall *have* to go."

"Owen," continues the novel, "was an American, Kate was Irish. 'Never having seen one' meant 'having to go.' But it was American logic rather than Irish, and Kate only let herself be overcome." It would have been a feat to overcome Lawrence. Then when Kate leaves in the rain, which I do not think had begun when Lawrence left the ring, but which in the book aggravates her plight, and when Owen asks, "Do you really think you'll be all right?" and when she answers, "Perfectly. You stay. Good-by. I can't smell any more of this stink," Owen turns, the book says, "like Orpheus looking back into hell, and waveringly made towards his seat again."

Later "Owen came back to the hotel at about half-past six, tired, excited, a little guilty, and a good deal distressed at having let Kate go alone. . . . She was really very angry with Owen. He was naturally so sensitive and so kind. But he had the insidious modern disease of tolerance. He must tolerate everything, even a thing which revolted him. He would call it Life! He would feel he had *lived* this afternoon. . . . Ah, men, men! They all had this soft rottenness of the soul, a strange perversity which made even the squalid, repulsive things seem part of *life* to them. Life! And what is life? A louse lying on its back and kicking? Ugh!"

Villiers, when he returns, a half-hour later, having followed a group to the hotel of the chief toreador and seen him "lying on the bed like Venus with a fat cigar, listening to her lovers," is as little spared. "At about seven o'clock Villiers came tapping. He looked wan, peaked, but like a bird that had successfully pecked a bellyful of garbage. 'Oh, it was GREAT!' he said. . . . 'They killed *seven* BULLS.' "

Then in the book comes part but not all of the episode with the Pole and his Mexican friend. The Pole says, " 'You missed the best part of it. You missed all the fun!' " and Kate retorts, " 'I don't want to hear. I don't want you to speak to me. I don't want to know you' "; but the Mexican's onslaught as to fox hunting, which followed in the actual incident, Lawrence omits altogether. Instead "the fellow went green, and stood a moment speechless. 'Oh, all right!' he said mechanically, turning away." And then Kate loftily leaves the room, departing not only from the Pole and the Mexican but from Johnson and myself as *canaille.* A fine frenzy!—though not so haughty in true occurrence.

And yet which of us does not spare himself and try to improve his own role in remembrance and record of events? Lawrence's sudden curt dismissing of people never, I believe, seemed a weakness to him but rather a genuine sign and resolute gesture of superiority. I could but think of his lordly orders to Leighton, and to the Pole and Mexican after the bullfight, when I read how Ramon in *The Plumed Serpent*—and Ramon was largely Lawrence—waved away Carlota, his first wife, with a lofty explosion, " 'Go away! I have smelt the smell of your spirit long enough.' "

Thirteen years later, six years after Lawrence's death, my mother joined Robert Hunt and me at the same Monte Carlo Hotel in Mexico City and was curious to see a bullfight. This time Hunt and I played the Lawrencian part and would not go. Faustino Forte found, as escort for her, a European guest in the hotel, an *aficionado* of much the same type as the Pole whom Lawrence excoriated long before. The American woman, unlike the fictitious Irishwoman, stayed through the rounds and returned to the hotel exhilarated with admiring excitement over men and bulls alike. "You are wrong," she said. "Lawrence was wrong. Such skill, poise, movement, grace, such exactness! With us at home, bulls are given no chance. They die in the slaughterhouse, but here they are given their last, glorious fling and how they love it!" To be sure, the goring of horses was in this later time prevented by wooden armor or sacks filled with sawdust, and lunges against flanks spilled no blood or bowels. But I should like to have heard a verbal duel as to bullfighting between the American woman and the English novelist. My mother could let fly too. I should like to have heard the two of them denouncing the smell of each other's spirits! How cordially they would have cleared their nostrils of each other!

After the bullfight, Lawrence's revulsion against Mexico returned with increase. Passage to England loomed again. We lingered at the Monte Carlo through another week while we read *Terry's Guide to Mexico* and debated. Yes, he would give the country one more chance: Chapala. It would have been two chances but for the likelihood of severe heat in Oaxaca. Besides, he had been told that the southern train trip was rough and wearing, perhaps the worst in Mexico, whereas the line to Guadalajara on the way to Chapala was good. Still smarting from experience on other trains, he relinquished Oaxaca that year. He reached it the following year. This time he set us reading Terry's long disquisition on the beauties and attractions of Lake Chapala and its little town of the same name. It was apparently all birds and flowers and friendly villagers. "But Terry's a fool," crackled Lawrence. "He's been a liar about the other places and why should we expect him to be anything else about this one? We'd be lunatics to believe him and all four of us risk it. I'll give the country one more chance. You two stay here with Frieda for May Day and I'll go and investigate. If the place is any good at all, I'll telegraph and we'll share a house and stay awhile. If it isn't, we two'll sail from Vera Cruz and you two can do what you like."

"On one condition," I agreed. "No sharing a house. In one hotel if you wish, or you two in a house and we in a hotel. I can't live in the same house with people. Your hours are different from ours. Besides, you want to work. So do I. And we'll be better off not under one another's feet."

"As you like," said he, vaguely.

So it was settled. He would be on the move again, with only himself to blame, and we for a few days at peace, with the May Day celebration to enjoy as we liked, uncriticized.

We saw him off at the train. Through the window he appeared wistful and forlorn.

"But it was his idea," said I.

"*Ja!*" assented Frieda, looking back along the platform.

10. Frieda

IT was the next day that Frieda opened her heart more fully to us concerning her problem with her husband's intemperate bursts. "When we are in a house," she explained, "like the place at Taormina, and there are no people close, I can suffer it. I know that it will pass and be as though it had not happened, until it happens again. And I know, as Fred Leighton said to you, that the irritability comes from illness. When Lorenzo feels ill, it infuriates him to have me feel well. When his nerves are carrying him too fast, he cannot bear to have me feel tired. When I wish I might see my children again, who have not even written me since I left their father, he shakes all over and vilifies me. He does not want me ever to mention them. Because he should not smoke, my cigarettes are red rags to him. Because I cannot do anything while he can write, he calls me a nincompoop. And I am. He has a right to complain about my uselessness."

Her shoulders suddenly rose. "And yet he never mentions how closely I watch his health and how usefully I take care of him. He shows that he knows I do when he gets rid of adoring disciples like Middleton Murry or people like your friend, Fred Leighton, or like the two last week, and then he turns back to me. In spite of all his criticisms, I am the one who satisfies him. There are two bonds. One of love, one of strangeness. In our hearts, it is well."

She relaxed for a moment and then resumed, "But in our lives, when we are with other people, he makes me absurd and makes me ashamed. He does not mean the things he says, like no decent women in England having anything to do with me, but he says them and I don't know what to do about it. If I answer him, it's worse. If I don't answer him, that's bad too but it's the best I can do. So I sit and stare at him like a silly dummy and people think that what he says is true or that I have no feelings, that I'm just a dumb beast as some of them say."

Her eyes studied the cigarette in her fingers, then her voice rose spiritedly, "I can't be so dumb when he quotes me all the time in his books. He may quote me just to attack me, but he quotes me and often what he quotes from me is attacking what he himself says and in the book he lets me have the best of it. He knows I'm not dumb. He knows that I'm useful. He likes to have me oppose him in ideas, even while he scolds me for it. I know all those things. Better impatient temper from him than any patient venom. And yet he makes me sad at heart so much of the time because of other people."

She studied the cigarette again. It was not drooping in her mouth now. It made a gesture. "I like people more than he does and he doesn't want me to like them more than he does. He does things for people, Hal, because he's soft in some ways. He writes interesting letters all the time to people he doesn't really like, which is not what I would do."

She raised her shoulders again and puffed her cigarette. "But he always comes back to me. Nobody else would be as comfortable for him as I am. I sometimes wonder if any other woman would live with him. He is bad tempered and never sorry. Even the kind of woman who mothers a man, tries to make of him more of a child than he is, doesn't like to have the child scratch her and kick her." She pondered. "I sometimes wonder if I myself can live with him. But what could I do if I left him? I have lost my own children; he has wanted me to lose them. I would not go back and be a burden on my family in Germany. No, I won't be a burden. But how could I earn a living? I was never taught anything which might earn me a living. Who would buy my foolish embroideries? I am helpless. I am caught." She took a deep breath. "And yet I wish to be caught. We love each other. It is just that I don't know how to treat him in public, how to manage him so that he won't all the time make a fool of me."

The results of what I answered made for dubious comedy later, but they might have made for worse. Being forty-one, I had, as often as anyone, heard complaints and appeals from wives with grievances, sometimes from husbands in similar strait, and I think that I had been as cautiously reticent as anyone in giving advice. "The quarrels of a man and wife are as sacred as their bed. Keep out" was an entry in my diary at this period. Perhaps I was right. Mates can be two claws of a lobster. If you try to bind a wound on one of the claws, both will close on you. Worse than that, many a woman is capable of extracting sympathy from an outsider only to excite her husband or make him jealous by quotation from the sympathizer. Men incline to the habit too. Let mates work out their own problems. On the whole they enjoy the process and delude themselves when they think they need assistance from outside. But this time I was rash. Prodded by my own irritations with Lawrence, I suggested to his wife use of the trick, or an improvement on it, by which I thought I had bettered him at Orizaba. Foreseeing likely tangles in Chapala, I had been making plans of my own. I knew that the day would come when I should be a handy victim for his spells of temper and in casting about for weapons of defense, I had remembered that offense is the best of them.

"Frieda," I said solemnly, "when you see that hardening in his eye, when those lids narrow toward you as they always do before he strikes, strike first. Get in the first blow and make it a good one. Knock him out with it. I bet it would work."

"Yes, I bet too," she beamed. "Oh, wait till I do that. Oh, I wish we didn't wait! I'll do it, Hal. I'll do it. *Danke schön.*"

Content came over both conspirators, mixed with anticipation.

We turned to other talk. Relieved of Lawrence's presence, she was relieved of nervous apprehension and flowered freely and fully into her own nature. She began on Lawrence's good points, his eventual kindnesses, his immense patience with people, especially with women, who wanted his help, "even when they hoodwink him," she said. "Then he takes it out on me, or on someone else. Just now, he's taking it out on you, on Mexico, on the Indians. He thinks he's jealous of you because you are fond of me, but he is really pleased. He does not dislike it here or the people. He just thinks some other place or some other people might be better. It's all inside him. And I wish it weren't. *Ach,* how I'd like to settle down somewhere, to stop this wandering. I want a home."

While I was listening to her, I was thinking that Lawrence was theater and Frieda was life, he shadow she substance, he calculation she spontaneity, he tentative she assured, he lightning she rainful thunder. I did not always trust what he said; but what she said, yes. Sometimes I had found myself listening to her to hear what he was meaning. And it is so in his books: his own many voices are confused, her one voice rings clear—comes out of his pages, alive. She needed no shift from country to country. She was herself country enough. As I presently wrote Barry Faulkner, she was herself the earth, the home, while he was the constant change of houses.

In *Sea and Sardinia,* when he had flown into a rage with an inn-keeper because the inn was dirtily Sardinian, when he had "cursed the dirty aborigines, the dirty-breasted host who *dared* to keep such an inn, the sordid villagers who had the baseness to squat their beastly human nastiness in this upland valley," he records—and I think with a degree of humility for once—Frieda's reprimand: "Why are you so indignant! Anyone would think your moral self had been outraged! Why take it morally? You petrify that man at the inn by the very way you speak to him—*such* condemnation! Why don't you take it as it comes? It's all life."

11. Letters and Notes

THE morrow, Saturday, was May Day, when there was to be a great labor parade. Consulting with the Fortes, we had engaged an open Ford, so that we might drive to the Zócalo and Frieda might watch the turnout from comfortable vantage a little above the crowd. But that night, instead of reading newspaper clippings concerning the celebration or instead of continuing with *Women in Love,* which was irritating me the more because of my irritation with its author, I pulled out notebooks and looked over a few records I had kept of the Lawrences from the time of our meeting, in fact from the time I had known we should be meeting.

On a flyleaf of *Fantasia of the Unconscious,* which I had reread before their arrival in Santa Fe, I had written: "Subconsciousness, like inner functions of the physical body, has been given a protective layer for the general good of the system. It plays its part under that layer just as the heart or lungs or intestines play theirs under the skin. The current practice of leaving insides exposed is about as bad for the subconscious as it would be for the bowels. Psychologically speaking, Lawrence and his ilk seem to me to be suffering from multitudinous hernia." On the back page I had written: "People read a book of this sort, as they might read a quack medical book, to find their own symptoms and to glory in them: to find some sickness to excuse their faults, some ailment that will allow them an air of mysterious and rather sinister initiation beyond the experience or understanding of their neighbor. Pshaw! It's a sick age, this new decade. Or, worse than that, it's a would-be sick age. In either case it needs less of the new-fashioned psychic and more of the old-fashioned physic. And a little humor would do no harm—to cure some of the wit."

It was easier to reread these notes with Lawrence not in the next room. I might otherwise have felt his eye gimleting through the wall between us. But it could not pierce all the way from the lake end where, we had been informed by wire in the afternoon, he had safely arrived.

Then I looked into my diary notes of our current days: "Lawrence's is an inversion of the usual process, the usual technique of so-called mysticism. Love-mysticism being out of fashion, enter hate-mysticism. Besides being new, it's easier to apply, easier both to preach and to practice, easier, anyhow, for Lawrence. The rules may be amended and adapted at any moment according to individual will. The technique is the same, however, as in other schools of mysticism, with a final resort and refuge, safely above reason, in vague and evasive intimations of personal superiority. The Christian has been selected and saved from sin. Lawrence, by the same token, inverted, has been selected and saved from love. At difficult moments in conversation, when somebody presses a little closely on his abrupt inconsistencies, a convenient Egyptian priest or a druid will whisper into his ear some incommunicable key word. He will thereupon agree with the druid, or lightly correct him, and all will be well again. Or, rather, ill again. For in this man's philosophy it is an unthinkable wind that blows no ill. And it blows good only in one direction. It spares Lawrence. It blows him above vulgar irritations. Behold how his fleas become scarabs!

"He has a way of flying about the world like a lightning bug" was another entry. "By his mere animal motion he gives a kind of light, but it is all light of the surface. Of inner light, of soul, or of whatever we may call the spark which gives men a happiness and an aspiration beyond mere animal ways—of this element Lawrence has nothing. To an acute animal sense of observation he has added, by virtue of his humanity, very little but malice. It is almost as if some feline creature, assuming mortal guise, were moving among men with a crafty and cruel gleam over their wants and wickednesses.

"Hating my faith in democracy, he bids me, 'Forget the fools, Bynner, withdraw into yourself.' He said the same thing to Leighton, who is hoping for democracy in Mexico. Looking at their two faces, I wondered into what sort of a recess Lawrence was advising this retreat. I wondered if he could mean into a self like his own, into such inner blankness as he himself contained. It is like the blankness at the center of a New England sewing circle. Neighbor after neighbor considered and picked clean. A druid ring of sharp ears and sharp tongues and at the heart of it an invisible altar of white bones.

"No wonder he sees in Mexico nothing but a momentary foothold! Whenever the ground anywhere becomes uncomfortable for the foot, he finds fault not with the foot or with the way he placed it, but with the ground, with the people round about him. Let him stub his toe on a stone in the road, a stone he might as well have stumbled over in England, India, France, or Kamchatka; he at once attributes to dwellers on the surrounding terrain a special spirit of evil, a malignant animal magnetism, an incurable diabolism. He at once thinks not in his head, not in his heart, but in his injured toe. And like a child he invests the humanity nearest him with the spite he himself feels toward the stone in the road. He sees in Mexico this or that individual, natural and picturesque or imitative and ugly, trespassing upon him with occult malice. He hates Leighton's reasonableness. Leighton sees, among Mexicans, in a thousand symptoms and against his own hopes, the fouling touches of greed and cynicism. Under Obregón, as under other presidents and rulers here or anywhere, political posts are being bought and sold, promises broken, ideals degraded: the power of money is again a paralysis upon the power of man. But through all the impediments, through all the complications and disappointments, Leighton can see the illuminated fact in Mexican history—the simple, dogged, persistent belief among a vital body of the people that they have the right to a reasonably comfortable existence in return for a reasonable application of toil. Deprivation is a thing which the ordinary Mexican has constantly suffered and resisted. However it has shadowed his life, whether in the shape of priests Aztec or Roman, of conquerors Spanish or French, of capitalists British or American, the outstanding fact in Mexico, the fact that magnetizes men like Leighton and baffles men like Lawrence, is that all the devils of Church, State, Army, and Plutocracy have not been able to overcome in Mexico the persistence of a simple Idea—the native's idea that his life is his own to lead or to mislead or to sacrifice in his own way and the accompanying idea that the land he lives on belongs to him by natural right and ought to yield him not profit, not the subjection of neighbors, but a simple and sufficient livelihood. Hence, his eternal insubordination, so disquieting to his masters and to Lawrence as a member of a 'master race.' "

I did not realize then as I do now, with more thorough reading of

Lawrence, the distemper which overtook him in any country, except finally in New Mexico. I was liking the Mexicans and resenting his disparagement of them. And yet, from being with him and hearing him talk, I must have recognized the fundament of his trouble, since I jotted down at the time, on a page of *Women in Love:* "Although Lawrence finds in his constant change of scene and company, stimulus and material for his writing, he is already in his own being quick with stimulus and stored with material. He would have found material anywhere, without his incessant quest. But perhaps, if he had continued long in one place, his impatience with the people in it would have mounted beyond endurance, or his impatience with himself, if he had not kept moving away from it. . . ."

Several friends have sent me letters which I wrote them at this period concerning the Lawrences, passages from which will expand or rectify what I am recording from memory after twenty-eight years.

Barry Faulkner, the painter, had been the first person to connect me with Lawrence's writing; he thought highly of *Sea and Sardinia;* and from Santa Fe in 1922 I had sent him a report of the writer's arrival at my house there: "D. H. Lawrence and his wife proved to be, in at least so brief a meeting, simple, human, jolly creatures. Like many of the writing Englishmen, he has that curious blond voice, that almost petulant treble. It is a petulance that whines into an ascendant chuckle. Apart from that and in spite of his gnomish beard, he was as likable and easy as a kid. His wife, a capacious and vibrant German, was even more magnetic, with the large and ready charm almost all German women have for me. It was as if she were the earth, the foundation, and he the house. The house of course gets the notice. Before long, mainly out of loyalty to you, I shall tackle another of his books. Since *Sons and Lovers,* I have read nothing but his absurd rubbish on *Psychoanalysis and the Unconscious.* I suspect he is more of an artist than he lets himself be, that he is, as it were, afreud of himself."

And from Cuernavaca there had been a letter to Porter Garnett, written a fortnight before the May Day that Frieda and Spud and I were now awaiting at the Monte Carlo: "I suppose Haniel Long has told you that we are in Mexico with the D. H. Lawrences. I had long been intending a trip here. They came down to Santa Fe from Taos and urged us to accompany them. I had a few misgivings, which have since been borne out. The man himself, and his wife, from a brief earlier meeting, I had liked well enough, but I had never liked the spirit of the man in his books. He had seemed to me a sort of Freudian prig—anything but immoral—and I still find him so. Give me a promiscuous lover any time instead of a promiscuous hater. Promiscuous hate is really a more degraded form of immorality than the other. Fortunately, there are two phases of Lawrence which one may easily and simply enjoy. By nature, and except as he has tampered with himself, he is an impulsive, boyish, gentle soul; and as a writer he is by nature eminently gifted. The trouble with him is that he has let his intellect and his more intemperate inclinations elaborate a code of thought and conduct which permit him all sorts of rather pretentious self-indulgence. I think I should like the man very much indeed if he were a real self instead of a fabricated self. What is left of the reality under the fabrication, together with a rather neat wit, makes him supportable. When his hearty German wife is with him and they take semiseriously their constant petty bickerings, I am amused and at ease. When I am alone with him, I have a hard time not to be bored. A contrast between the stature of this man and that of Meredith shows to what a degree the English novel and the spirit behind it has deteriorated. It has come down from generous genius to a bitter knack.

"We are probably due for a few more weeks together. This morning I thought I should have to contrive a pretext for escape; but this afternoon I feel better. The Lawrences' attitude toward Johnson and myself is genial and charming—with always a shadow lurking as to what he will say about us later. So far I have hardly heard him say a decent word about anyone—even those supposed to be his close friends. It is curious to think of literature falling into such clutches.

"Today we are in Cuernavaca, the capital of Morelos, a town about the size of Santa Fe. It has beautiful vistas and a rather oppressive magnetism. The peons here baffle me more than people I have met anywhere; seeming simple and amiable, they somehow fail to give one any current of connection—even one who has been prepared by gradual acquaintance among the Pueblos. Lawrence tells me that he has better hope for them than for any of the dark-skinned races; but I more than suspect him of fitting them into a prearranged edifice."

On April 25 I had written my mother: "Difficulties have cleared since my last." This previous letter—missing, perhaps, through her wise judgment—must have contained detailed complaint. "The Lawrences have both done with their colds, and Spud is up and around again, albeit a little rickety, much as I used to be after a spring attack of rheumatism. Lawrence is a strange fellow. The height of his enjoyment appears to be discontent. On the other hand he has been very genial to Spud and me; and on the whole the joint trip has so far been well worth while."

It surprises me that in these extant letters I made so light of Lawrence's violence toward his wife, which had been the main reason for my impulses to break away from him. They were written, to be sure, several weeks before Frieda's exposition of her dilemma; but I had not needed that colloquy to dislike and to resent her husband's conduct toward her and his general indulgence of a bad boy's temper. Probably at that time I was keeping those ignominious episodes out of my correspondence. But Frieda and I had now conferred. We were both on watch and I was hoping that the bad boy, caught with his pants down, might soon be given a good spanking, either by Frieda or perhaps by myself. Alternately enjoying him and spoiling to see him disciplined, I hoped that he would commend Chapala and summon us there.

12. May Day

M AY DAY dawned bright on the Monte Carlo. We had been wakened at six by the explosion of endless *cohetes,* rocket cannon-crackers, sent into the air all over town to signal the raising of red and black flags above headquarters of labor unions, syndicates, leagues of resistance, even above homes of workers. The celebration was beginning similarly, we had read, all over Mexico.

Newspapers had for days been full of the program and of controversy preceding it. Though I was still a deaf-mute as to hearing and uttering Spanish, I had studied enough to find that, with a dictionary, I could read the vocabulary of journalism. Though I could not hear meanings in Spanish, I could see them. Lawrence had done most of the general translating for us; but he had read us only headlines concerning the labor celebration. It had not seemed greatly to interest him. So now, relieved of his indifference, I brought clippings to the breakfast table, read aloud to the two others the calendar of the day's events and then spelled out rough résumés of the conflict between governmental and capitalistic interests.

Under President Obregón, Mexico, especially in the capital, was full of self-conscious socialism, with a considerable friendly leaning toward Russia. Not only was Luis N. Morones, the labor leader and head of the Confederación Regional Obrera Mexicana, an eager radical, the President himself, his cabinet, and the Camara de Diputados had marked leftist leanings. When the President had ordered all government offices to close on May First and the capitalist press had questioned his authority to do so, the Chamber of Deputies had supported him with a bill declaring May First a national holiday. A section of the Bill read: "It is true that the killing of the workers in Chicago for demanding the eight-hour day should not be a day of 'fiestas,' it should more appropriately be a day of sorrow. Considering, however, that social progress has always been paid for with blood, the First of May should be the cause of just pride for the proletariat not only of the United States but of the whole world and a holiday for labor." When Vasconcelos decided against closing the schools, it was not a move of opposition but on the contrary a decision to keep all students in their classrooms in order that the teachers might read them a manifesto explaining the significance of May First, a manifesto which he himself wrote to educate the young in proletarian sympathy and to help offset the reactionary influence of the Church. In the neighboring town of Tacuba a cornerstone was to be laid in the afternoon, following the parade in the capital, for a statue to "The Martyrs of Chicago."

"Who were the Martyrs of Chicago they're making all this fuss about?" asked Frieda.

Spud and I looked sheepish. Between us we guessed that they were the anarchists who had been executed in Cleveland's time for bombing in some strike. We vaguely recalled that there had been a good deal of public sympathy for them, as for Sacco and Vanzetti later, and that Governor Altgeld of Illinois had done his vigorous but vain best to save them. It did seem odd that years afterward there should be this furor over them in a foreign country when at home they were almost forgotten. We could not remember whether or not their names still figured in our own labor circles. Frieda was amused by our ignorance.

Later, when our open Ford was stationed in the Zócalo, among the milling throngs of celebrants, we bought a copy of a labor sheet, *Nueva Solidaridad Obrera,* and, under the big headline, "The Chicago Massacre," read in smaller heavy type, "Spies, Fisher, Engel, Lingg and Parsons: victims of the Government of the Country of 'liberty.' " We read further: "Much has been said about the crimes committed in Chicago in 1886 by the shameless and villainous procedure of the world-wide capitalistic rabble represented by the North American courts of Justice." And much more followed about the event which was stirring all Mexico to continued acute protest, thirty-seven years later. Frieda laughed at us again when we said that as Americans we were feeling not only conspicuous but in some way guilty.

"Now you know how I felt as a German," she said suddenly, with hurt, proud remembrance in her face.

All shops were closed. There were no streetcars. The colors and flags of the workers were everywhere. It was a red flag with a stripe of black running crosswise. Roberto Haberman came to the Ford and explained that black was a concession to anarchist sentiments still flickering among the workers, an inheritance from the first organizers of labor in Mexico about eighteen years before, "two of them from Barcelona and one from Italy." Ernest Gruening, now Governor of Alaska, then on the staff of *The Nation,* was with him. Haberman wore red in his lapel, like almost everyone around us. Hundreds of jitneys were wrapped in red. Even peddlers had red flags on their packs.

We looked at Frieda's yellow-flowered parasol and bought some red bunting for it. The spirit of the occasion was infectious. Russia at that time seemed to offer mankind liberation; and most of the Mexican painters and writers and politicos whom we had met, as well as youthful acquaintances of several nationalities, were ardent liberals, warmly sympathetic to the cause of labor.

Soon after Haberman and Gruening had wandered away, two young Dutch painters, brothers, whom we had met and liked for their exuberant spirits, joined us. A group, with many of the artists in it, they told us, had planned a stroke. The plotters were to congregate on the roof of the cathedral, as though for a good view, and then at a signal were to hoist the red banner with its sickle and hammer on the cathedral's flagpole and ring the great bells. The Hollanders asked Spud and me to join them.

"Yes, go," urged Frieda. "I shall be safe and happy here. And I brought a book. I shall wait exactly here till you return. What fun you'll have! And I shall have fun watching. Or could I go with you?"

"No women, Mrs. Lawrence," said the boys. "We don't know who else will be up there and we might have a scrap."

"What fun!" beamed Frieda. "Yes, have a good scrap and beat them! I'll be here watching. *Ja!*"

Contingents were hurrying across the Zócalo to join the Red Parade. Strains of a military march came around the corner, nearer and nearer. Spud and I ran toward it, leaving Frieda. Then with a band blaring at its head, the mile-long procession swung into the Zócalo now jammed with onlookers. Group after group came by, communist, trade unionist, syndicalist; and, borne between poles at the front of each group, stretched a breadth of cloth, lettered with the name of a union or with an incendiary slogan. Besides all the expected unions, there were icemen, seamstresses, bartenders, bullfighters, and even gravediggers from the Panteón de Dolores. The names of the Chicago martyrs ran across a number of the banners. A peasants' union, *La Union de Campesinos,* carried a banner, "We have suffered enough," and, farther back in their ranks, was a great revolutionary signal which warned in red letters, "Bourgeoisie, shave your heads and get ready for the guillotine." All the marchers wore red and black ribbons in their lapels and constantly along the route, with or without a band to lead them, broke into the "International."

The spectacle sent excitement up and down our spines, felt to us like an onrush in the French Revolution, as if some spark might at any moment set the people ablaze with riot, looting, that we might hear battered windows and see or feel crushed heads.

We hastened back to see how Frieda was taking it. She was standing up in the car, squealing and pointing. As we reached her, "Look, look!" she cried, brandishing her parasol toward the cathedral. We turned and looked up as if caught on a motion of water, for all those thousands of bodies in the Zócalo were turning, all those thousands of faces were looking up. A red flutter climbed the flagpole, and a swelling rumble rose from the multitude. People were applauding and cheering. A few here and there were dazed, sullen or angry. The rumble broke into a roar as the Russian flag climbed to the flagpole's top and flared out like a flame. Frieda, leaning toward it with eager excitement, nearly tipped out of the car but saved herself by a grasp of the grinning chauffeur's arm.

Spud and I flung our coats into Frieda's lap before darting across the square. Spud clung to my shirttail when we climbed the crowded stairs of the bell tower. In the great throng on the roof we found the Hollanders, and a few others whom we had met, tugging at the bell ropes and glad to let us relieve them. Every rope was busy. We felt tons of sound crushing through our ears along our nerves. The clangor was a pandemonium, and still we pulled, panted, laughed. The *obreros* were gleaming with sweat as they gave place to one another at the scores of bells, either pulling tongue ropes with a sharp knack or heaving a hunk of bronze slowly over and over by push after push on its thick rim. New recruits arrived, wiping their faces and stretching their bodies after the close dark climb. The clock tower at the center of the front railing bore, under the flagpole, a stone image of Christ. Three workmen, members perhaps of a carpenters' union, had perched themselves on his head and shoulders. Over the four heads hung and swayed the folds of the blood-colored flag, while not a bell died down.

Lawrence's lip would have curled at it all. Later, when we tried to make him feel the gusto of the occasion and of our share in it, he shook his head solemnly. "It's sheer folly," said he, "to take part in any of these movements. Leave it to the rascals who understand it and profit by it. Have nothing to do with mankind in the mass, with any political surge. Leave it aside. Let them do what they like in their filthy world. Reject it. Go about your own business." But there was no such pessimism that day on the cathedral roof. Though some there were not participants, none interfered or protested. My guess is that many of the bell ringers had had no part in the plot, were in fact good Catholics, but had been caught into the contagion.

Though we could not hear one another speak, gesticulation came to us from figures at the stone railing over the Zócalo. We crowded forward and saw, far below, a platoon of soldiers nearing the cathedral. The staircase was too jammed for them to enter; but they could block it. And after another half-hour of bell ringing our zest in the performance was over. After our cheers when someone threw the red flag to a sympathizer below, who escaped with it, we began to realize that the joke was now on us. We were caught.

"We should have thought of this before," said Spud when the last of the bells had hummed into silence and we could talk again. "What if we're arrested? What'll Frieda do?"

"She'll probably get us out," I hazarded and hoped, "through the Fortes or Fred Leighton. How Lorenzo will jeer at us! We Americans again having to be in on everything!"

We could see Frieda's red-wrapped parasol at the far end of the Zócalo, stationary and waiting, while fragments of the parade still sidled past her.

The file ended, petered out, the crowd falling in behind it; but our siege continued. Nothing happened. No soldiers forced the stairs; but they were still at the base of the cathedral. Acquaintances joined us for consultation. The Dutch boys suggested our crawling down the back of the cathedral into the courtyard of a house there. It looked feasible. We started over juts and slants of stone and stucco till we saw that with a final good jump we could make it. But out of the house below into the courtyard stalked five men who, with stern faces, raised their arms and aimed revolvers at us. Whether they were officially connected with the cathedral or were lay Catholics resenting impiety we never knew, but we did know at once that they were unfriendly and we scrambled up again.

Another hour passed. In the Zócalo only a few stragglers were left and at its far end the stationary car and the lone parasol. The Dutchmen, dispirited for once, advised, "Let's make a break for it. We might as well be in jail as here." Our group agreed and a score of us started down the narrow stairwell into darkness. Then, with one shouting, laughing move, hundreds of others plunged into it after us. A voice came up, "They've locked the door! We can't get out!" Those in the jam behind us could not hear, nor those behind them, but continued pouring down on us while the forward group tried to push us back from below. Our chests were squeezed. Spud, just behind me, lost his footing and, because other feet and legs closed in under him, could not regain it. Clutching me round my gullet, he was flattened on my back. We were all yelling. Feet were trodden, heads bruised, while, from above and below in the dark, downward and upward thrusts surged and swayed. No laughter was left in us, only groans, oaths, and panic. Suddenly a different sound broke out below, a cheering yell, and we could see a shaft of light. The door had given. Pressure ceased against ribs; but the lunges from behind tore Spud off my back sideways and the sleeve of my shirt with him. As we fell forward I could see, with increasing light in the maelstrom, that other shirts had been yanked apart, some of them entirely off. By twos and threes we fell panting through the door and pitched blinded across the sidewalk, where we expected arrest. Soldiers were there but, like the circle of civilians behind them, they only laughed at us. After the glorious flag raising, the triumphant bell ringing, these exhausted, bedraggled, ignominious demonstrants, limping, stumbling, staggering out of their stronghold! Emerging one after another, they looked sheepishly round and, when they saw that no arrests were being made, dribbled away through the crowd. Where was Spud? I had thought him close behind me on the stairs. After four or five minutes, I felt anxious. Spud was fragile and might easily have been trampled. But at the very end of the line he limped into view, a friendly big Mexican holding him up by the arm. My shirt sleeve was still dangling in his fist, his face was wan, his eyes very large. I grabbed him, thanking the Mexican, who shook hands and left. "Are you hurt?" I asked. Spud shook his head slowly.

When we reached the car, our driver was hunched asleep but Frieda was leaning toward us eagerly.

"And did you have great fun?"

"No," replied Spud. It was his first word.

"But poor Frieda?" I asked. "All these hours!"

"Oh, I had fun!" she boomed. "I loved the parade! And did you read about the guillotine? I could read that one! And then the Russian flag and the bells and all the people looking up! Some of them were shaking their fists at you. And the soldiers! I thought 'and now will Hal and Spud be the Martyrs of Mexico City! Will they shoot you and why did Lorenzo have to miss it!' And then two hours and nothing happened, but I never read my book at all. The chauffeur was asleep, but for me there was always something to watch and to think about. I did wish, though, that I'd brought a sandwich. Don't you think we can eat now?"

"And drink," said Spud.

"And you can tell me what happened. Did you ring a bell?"

"All of them," I nodded, beginning once more, though feebly, to enjoy the adventure.

"I saw the flag come down," she said, "and I thought the soldiers had got it, and got you too. It's a good thing Lorenzo wasn't here. He wouldn't have loved it as I did. He would have thought all of us great idiots."

We still had time, after a quick lunch with our reviving tequilas, to reach the cornerstone ceremony in Tacuba. We had read about the statue and seen a picture of it: a lifesize worker with one hand resting on a hammer and the other raising aloft a torch which was to hold a red light. The pedestal was to bear the names of the Martyrs of Chicago. "You can tell people when you go home," Frieda suggested with a mischievous glint, "how friendly Mexico is to the United States, how it is putting up monuments to famous Americans!"

After our experiences earlier in the day, the afternoon was an anti-climax. We had already seen enough union members; and the speeches of their leaders, though fiery, were unintelligible to us. We decided on the spot to forego hearing speeches at the Teatro Lirico that evening, even with music and poems and great presences.

But there came a highlight before we left Tacuba. Church bells, clanging close by, suddenly interrupted an address by the Presidente Municipal. Our eyes went quickly to the church roof, but we saw no red banner. The annoyed comrade checked his speech, summoned four policemen, and obviously gave them orders for this orthodox bell ringing to stop. The police trotted over to the Templo de San Gabriel. Presently the bells moaned down and the Presidente resumed. We left him to his oratory and peered into the church. Near the door the four policemen were together on their knees, with heads bowed.

13. The Telegram

NEXT afternoon a telegram came for Frieda: CHAPALA PARADISE. TAKE EVENING TRAIN. PURNELLS MEET YOU IN GUADALAJARA I IN CHAPALA. IF ANY CONFUSION GO TO HOTEL COSMOPOLITA ACROSS FROM STATION.

"We can't make it," said Spud.

"We must make it," said Frieda. "He was furious enough when he met the train here and you weren't on it. We can't do it again. No. I must pack."

"In two hours?" I wondered. "Tickets, packing, everything? How can we?"

"We must!" declared Frieda and went at her wardrobe like a walrus at fish.

Faustino telephoned the station for us. There was only one berth left.

"I'll take it," declared Frieda.

"You'll go alone?"

"Yes, I can. He'll see." And articles flew helter-skelter into trunks, into valises, into *bolsas,* stout Mexican handbags of colored twine. "I must have more bolsas," she panted in a flushed panic. We gave her ours.

Fred Leighton arrived at that moment to bring us an invitation for—

"Never mind for what! Don't tell me anything!" gasped Frieda. "Don't talk. Don't make me think."

Then Faustino arrived with word that, since his first telephone call, a section had been released and Manuel, the porter, had bought us three berths. "But there aren't any taxis," cried Faustino. "There must be a strike."

"Get packed," ordered Fred with authority. "I'll find something."

A Mexican flurry followed. Everything went wrong and then right.

We had given our bolsas to Frieda; but Carmen, the chambermaid, found us others. My suitcase was locked and the key lost; but Manuel scampered away with it to the house of a locksmith. We had forgotten our laundry; but Carmen rushed it to us unironed. Our trunk got packed. The suitcase came back, but no Fred and no Manuel. Suddenly Fred arrived winded, Manuel and a strange Mexican behind him. "Trunks ready?" he puffed.

"You have a taxi?"

"No, but the trunks and the big bags. I'll get them there in a push-cart and check them and maybe you can follow. It's a chance."

We remonstrated but he subdued us, while the pushcart man heaved our trunk on his back and started away with it. I ran to Frieda's room to tell her.

"*Gott in himmel!*" she cried. "*Ja! Ja!*"

And we bundled ourselves out, with the whole staff of the hotel in our wake, clattering down the circling concrete stairway. At the entrance of the hotel the pushcart, already piled with our luggage, was wobbling away from us with Fred trotting alongside it. But again no Manuel, only emptiness in the narrow avenue. Our watches warned us of a very slim interval. Our hearts sank. At the last possible moment Manuel came round the corner of Isabel la Católica in a taxi. We huddled aboard, reached the station three minutes before train time, grabbed the trunk checks from Fred, and fell into the car seats with hearts pumping under our sweat.

"Thanks, thanks!" to Fred, who left us with a tired laugh.

The train shuddered, heaved, and was off. But no. It heaved back and did not start again for half an hour.

After an interval, during which we all three slumped without speech, Frieda set a cigarette in her mouth, before realizing that she must not light it in the sleeper, and puffed at us, without smoke. "He will be writing again there. He will be happier."

14. Guadalajara

IT had been agreed earlier that, if we went to Chapala, Spud and I were to accept an invitation from the Purnells to spend a few days with them on the way through the city. Idella Purnell, former pupil of mine in poetry at the University of California, was living in Guadalajara with her father, an old-time dentist there. She was publishing a verse magazine called *Palms,* laboriously set up by printers who knew no English. She was eager for advice and help from her visiting teacher. She had arranged with Lawrence, moreover, to meet us at the station and, after breakfast, to head his wife toward Chapala by camion at a specified hour. This had saved him the necessity of spending the night in town. So, in good time, when we had breakfasted well and talked busily, we extricated our luggage from the baggage room, had it transferred to a truck, then put Frieda aboard her camion and waved her off.

Lawrence acknowledged receipt of her: "Thank you for looking after Frieda and the mountains of baggage. We are already in our house—pleasant—near lake but not looking on it, on our own little garden: the first corner after the Villa Carmen, house next the dark trees. It belongs to the Hotel Palmera. The Palmera is the smartest hotel—I stayed at the Arzapalo, which faces the lake—manager Winfield Scott, American. It's shabby but pleasant—both charge 4 pesos a day, cheaper for a long stay. There is a new hotel, Gran Hotel Chapala, charges 3 a day. Chapala very pleasant—just enough of a watering place to be *easy*. We can bathe from the house. There are camions to Guadalajara in 2 hours—several a day. I must come in soon to go to the bank. Face the unpacking. Greet the Spoodle. Walk about 4 minutes east from Arzapalo, along lake front."

Nothing in the note about our sharing the house with them. He had obviously acceded to my wish. Spud and I should be staying at one of the hotels.

Something, perhaps the nervous tension of our departure from the capital, had brought back a touch of Johnson's lumbago; and next morning I was cramped with a bowel complaint common among foreign visitors in Mexico. So our first uneaseful days with the Purnells—and they were hot days too—discolored our impressions of Guadalajara and occasioned a melancholy message to Lawrence. He answered from Zaragoza 4, Chapala: "I hope the fears, the pains, and the disgusts have all passed. If Guadalajara is worse than Orizaba, then alas! Damn all shops and markets, so nothing is left. Here too the middle of the day can be hot, but morning and evening beautiful, very cool. We intend to come to Guadalajara tomorrow, by the first camion, leaving here about 7. I will call at 150 Galeana to see how you are, also do the bank and a few things, then come back. We can discuss the choice of hotels here. Do hope you are well."

This second note confirmed my assumption, and relieved my mind further, as to our prospective mode of living. Idella telephoned a message to the Hotel Cosmopolita suggesting that he come to her house for supper and hoping that Mrs. Lawrence was with him. He sent an answer saying that they would both appear.

Never have I seen Lorenzo more amiable, more ingratiating than he was that evening. He listened to poems of Idella's and to some of her *Palms* material. He was full of saintly deference to everyone, including Frieda, whom I had heard call him, when he was in similar moods, "St. Francis" or "San Francisco." He was passing her a plate of napkin-wrapped *tortillas,* and cordiality in the room seemed as rounded as a full moon when, with no relevancy and no warning, she blazed at him, "Stop it, Lorenzo! You're impossible! I won't have it. You can hold your silly tongue and behave yourself. Had you been born to manners, you might have some!" The bolt stilled everyone. Had she perhaps thought him overattentive to Idella? Or had her mind wandered back to our conspiracy and was she ignoring a need of reason for experiment and just jumping in? Whatever it was, she lashed at him again: "I won't have you making an idiot of yourself with your nasty tongue and letting Hal's friends see what a poor fish you are." She liked the phrase "poor fish." There was a dead silence. Everyone was staggered—except me. Lawrence sat stunned, wordless, while Frieda stole at me a look of victory. She had done it. She held her stately bosom high and looked round at us all with superb content. It had worked.

Dr. Purnell quietly drawled conversation back to normal; but he and his daughter were convinced for a long while, even after my private explanation of what had happened, that Lawrence was a meek martyr and his wife a termagant. Frieda informed me later that Lorenzo made no query, never even referred to her onslaught. She was sure that she had seen the dangerous glint hardening in his eye and that she had done wisely to strike. And she was so fortified by what she thought the success of her blows that in Chapala she wielded them again and again, often—or so it seemed to me—when there was no provocation, no slightest portent in her husband of anything but considerateness and peace. As on that first occasion when she struck first, he would stare at her and sink into a blank silence similar to her own silences when she had been the one reduced.

"I may make mistakes now and then," she told me apart, "but I'd rather make a mistake than run a risk." Gradually Lawrence learned not to give her the warning of the glint. But she would see it anyway; and the battle of the sexes was no longer one-sided. Perhaps it had never been one-sided. Perhaps Frieda had dramatized her case a little with the natural sympathy anyone has for one's own side in a combat. There are many records of Lawrence quarrels, both before and after my days with them in Mexico. I believe, however, that Frieda's tactics, as employed that night in Guadalajara worked for a while.

Mabel Lujan's book, *Lorenzo in Taos,* records, with obvious sympathy for the male, an occasion when one of Frieda's attacks met plenty of counterattack, and in terms much like those I had heard Lawrence use at the Monte Carlo. Catherine Carswell describes a still stormier quarrel—over that taut issue of the place Frieda thought her children should occupy in her heart alongside her husband's place—a dispute which culminated in Frieda's cracking a stone dinner plate on his head, not during the row but because he sang in the scullery after it was over. I had had the impression that Mrs. Carswell was a witness of the scene; but recently, when I asked Frieda about it, she expostulated with a smile, "No, no, I would not have done it in public, it was in private." And true enough, when I reread the Carswell pages, I found "they told me in concert of a quarrel." Another Carswell page says that Mrs. Lujan "often fails in understanding the idiom used in talk both by Frieda and Lawrence—especially Frieda."

Idella Purnell, now Mrs. Remington Stone, has lately written me: "Of course there was a lot of talk by you and Spud about these two people we were soon to meet; but I recall nothing of it; to me they were just Names. I asked Spud please to tell me, was this the H. D. who contributed so much to *Poetry?* For at that time I confused D. H. L. and H. D. Even warned about the red beard, it was with a sense of shock that I met Mr. Lawrence, so thin, so fragile and nervous-quick, and with such a flaming red beard, and such intense, sparkling, large mischievous blue eyes, which he sometimes narrowed in a catlike manner. His rusty hair was always in disorder, as though it never knew a comb. But otherwise the man seemed neat almost to obsession and frail, as though all his energy went into producing the unruly mop on top and the energetic, stiff beard. Mrs. Lawrence, very large and motherly, seemed placid and soothing and relaxed, but when anything amused her, her laugh was as generous and violent as your own."

Mrs. Stone remembers an episode at tea with the Lawrences in Chapala: "We talked about a recipe for *tepache.* Mrs. Lawrence made some remark which irritated Mr. Lawrence, so that he turned apoplectic-looking and fairly shouted at her, 'Frieda, don't be so stupid! I should slap you for that!' and to my horror I heard my own voice saying, 'Shall I slap *him?*' At which a moment of astoundment filled the patio, and then you whooped and Spud did, and I was saved. After this I remember that Lawrence and Daddy used to go off for long long walks up and down the beach, talking of a thousand things. And I remember telling you I had asked him to give me some poems for *Palms* and you retorting, 'I know you did, and do you know what he said about you? "Impertinent, stupid little upstart, who does she think she is, to ask ME for poems? I shan't give her any." ' At that time Daddy was doing some canning as a sideline and it occurred to me that Lawrence, being English, might like some of the marmalade. So I filled a five-pound can and sent it to him by camion. To my amazement, by mail only a day or two later, there came a large group of L's poems, from which I was to select anything I liked for *Palms!* And when we saw Lawrence again, he was all smiles and affability and told us how good the marmalade was, with its correct proportion of bitter, so unlike most American marmalades which are only sweet."

Later Lawrence gave Idella other poems, and he was always ready with patient, painstaking criticism of material which came to her, as

The D. H. Lawrences and Witter Bynner at the latter's house in Santa Fe, 1923

D. H. Lawrence at Chapala, Mexico, 1923

well as of her own writing. Here again, as has often been noted, was his characteristic generosity with time, attention, and advice afforded to women. His weather toward outside females was almost always clement, while Frieda took the squalls.

Since Idella was busy with printers next morning and Dr. Purnell had a roomful of patients, Spud and I joined the Lawrences at their hotel. It was our last day in town before progressing to Chapala, and we had decided to tour the town in a *calandria*. Picture postcards called it a *carruaje en uso desde* 1900. It is still a city-wide Guadalajara feature—a bedraggled Victoria with an elderly driver on his high seat, demanding life from a horse too rickety even for use in a bullfight.

Though Spud and I were now recovered from illness, we were still not so impressed by Guadalajara as he had been by Cuernavaca and I by Puebla. Nor were the Lawrences. "But we must not tell Idella," cautioned Frieda. The streets were as dull and dingy as the forlorn brick railroad station had led us to expect, though now and then a door would be open and a glimpse would show us that life around the patio inside had more comfort and color and charm than we might guess from the exterior. The Zócalo was impressive, with its huge Indian laurel trees, the bizarre cathedral along one edge, the distinguished Municipal Palace along another and along the other two the busy *portales:* covered sidewalks lined with booths toward the curb and opening on the square through high arches.

"Yes, it has interest," commented Lawrence, "but you will really like Chapala. Chapala is really Mexico. It is the place we have been waiting for." From a catlook in his eyes I sensed that something stubborn was coming. It came. "You may inspect the hotels, if you like, but I think you will prefer sharing our capacious house."

So the letters had dissembled. Should I put my back up or wait? I said nothing. Frieda acted as though she had not heard. Johnson gave me a slow wink.

On the avenue to San Pedro Tlaquepaque we noted the tall wide trees that lined it; and in the village we admired the solid, deep-patioed residences. Though only a few miles from town and equally hot in summer, it had been a community of so-called country houses for rich Guadalajarans, and many of the buildings were more spacious, more established-looking and with better architectural heritage than those we had seen in the city. Later a busy center of pottery making and selling, Tlaquepaque had then only one *alfareria* worthy the modern term. Most of the work was still done as a family occupation at home; but Mrs. Percy Holmes, the wife of the British consul, had given native craftsmen a wing of an old mansion she rented, making of the other wings an airy, ample dwelling for her own household. She received us cordially as friends of the Purnells and showed us about. Designers with their pigments and brushes were seated on the ground in several courtyards, painting repetitive patterns which, even to our eye, were departure from the beauty of their native, spontaneous craftmanship. Mrs. Holmes was instructing them in the change. "I give them good English china for models—" she explained, "Spode, Davenport, even Wedgwood. If they are to prosper, they must produce what the tourist will like and with a better glaze than what they used to make. See the difference?" And she held up one of her new shining pieces to be compared with an old-time plate which had gold-brown glaze running crude and at ease over a bird done with a few slight, sure strokes. We nodded but said little. Lawrence was taciturn. After tea with rum in it and lively chat, mostly between Mrs. Holmes and Frieda, we left and Lawrence gave a sigh of relief immediately outside the doorway, wriggling his lean shoulders as if to shake off the spirit of the house and of its inmates.

"Did you see them sullen in rows," he commented, "not once looking up at us, the mechanical motions of their hands, just slaves, galley slaves, under the whip of that woman and her money! We have no business here in Mexico, we foreigners. We should get out."

"She meant to be kind," remarked Frieda. "I don't think she's so rich. And it was good tea."

"Always your stomach!" he retorted.

But he approved of her buying some good simple Tonalá pottery in the open market just beyond and approved also, when we stopped at a glass factory on the drive back, her selection of amber-colored pieces for their dining room. The glass blowers, with molten globes aglow at the ends of their rods, held us gazing for many minutes.

"That was different," said Lawrence, in the calandria again. "A Mexican owner, Mexican energy, Mexican products."

"But wasn't it taught them by foreigners, by Spaniards?" I challenged.

"Those red throbbing bits being thrust into the furnaces!" he ignored me. "I could only think of red throbbing hearts thrust on altars! It was natural to them. And yet it was frightening too. It was frightening, Frieda."

"No more frightening than in Venice, Lorenzo."

He withdrew into brooding, and then he uttered like an oracle: "The Aztecs knew that Death takes the heart out of life. They thought they could satisfy Death with the hearts of their victims, distract Death away from their own hearts. They did think that, Frieda. So they'd prance in the skins of the dead as if to fool Him—'You have my heart, you Dark Deity, so spare me!'—not realizing how right they were, that their own hearts were gone too. And so it has continued. You remember that fellow at Teotihuacan, the meat vendor, and what was in his filthy bag? That's all they have inside them, instead of hearts,— a death's head!" He was flushed.

I couldn't help suggesting, "It seems to me that that fellow with the sheepskull had a sense of humor inside him."

"*Ja!*" agreed Frieda gustily.

But Lawrence was back in his brooding.

We visited the orphanage, a noble building with a succession of finely proportioned patios graced by lofty cottonwood trees, trees gone now, cut and sold, I was informed by a later manager, to buy needles and thread for the orphans. The broad laurels are gone too from the Zócalo, their beauty banished because noisy starlings congregated in them and soiled the park benches. We drove out past the austerely beautiful Carmen Convent, that too now gone in the erasure of juts and variations welcome to the eye in those days but obstructive to the straightness of a modern boulevard.

"I did look for a smaller house in Chapala," resumed Lawrence, "but none was to be found. I had to take this one. It has a living room, a dining room, a kitchen, a patio full of trees and flowers, a pleasant woman servant who lives outside and three good bedrooms, plenty for all of us."

"I told you," I replied as evenly as I could, "that on no condition were we to share a house."

He made no answer.

We came to the Penitentiary, which, on the whole, though my thoughts were now obscuring my vision, I admired more than any building I had seen in Mexico, with its massive slabs of chocolate-colored stone and its wide, huge-pillared portico. That too was torn down later to make space for a straight highway, in lieu of the two streets which used to pass around it, giving variety and grace to the city landscaping. But destiny settles down in Mexico as elsewhere. Too much of the charm which Guadalajara had for the Lawrences and for us, when we drove round it that day, is now only memory.

"The hotels are noisy." Lawrence was looking sidelong at me. "I doubt if you could work in them. Somebody else was looking at the house. So I had to decide and take it. Besides, it's too big and expensive for just Frieda and me." He had the meek look of a child winning his way. "You will like it, Bynner."

"We'll see," I answered weakly.

Spud winked again. And Frieda digressed, "Idella said that we could buy trinkets here made by the prisoners, some of them quite pretty. Shall we go in, Lorenzo?"

We entered the penitentiary and passed into a large, round, flower-bedded court, from which the cell alleys spoked as from the hub of a wheel. Some of the male prisoners were lolling about, and we bought from them miniature plaited baskets and a woven belt or two. Lawrence chose and gave me with, I thought, too much gesture, a neatly carved monkey which one of the men had made of a peach stone.

He thinks, I brooded, that he can make a monkey of me. We'll see.

15. Chapala

IT was Lawrence's idea that, instead of going to Chapala by camion, we take a train to Ocotlan and then cover the two thirds of the lake to Chapala by launch, as he had done when arriving from Mexico City. But that meant another night in Guadalajara and possibly two days for the trip.

"No," he concluded, "we'll wait and do all that later in a *canoa.*"

"A canoe?" blurted Spud from his fragility.

"A canoe?" protested Frieda with her bulk.

"A canoa is not a canoe, Frieda. I've told you. I've shown you. But you never remember."

"*Ja,*" she assented, trying hard to remember.

So we decided to go by the spur train which traversed the forty-mile run to Chapala on narrow gauge. Except for typically reckless Mexican drivers of the camions, few motorists used to venture the cobble-stoned highway with its broken culverts and rough detours. Wet weather made the road a high-ridged marsh. Access to the resort was mostly in railway cars that several years later, when the line was discontinued, were lugged aside as ready-made houses for Mexican families, even the rails going into other houses as beams for ceilings.

With his usual avidity for information, Lawrence had already collected no end of local data. He told us on the train about an hacienda which the tracks skirted at the edge of Guadalajara, a stylish establishment with various buildings enclosed by high walls, how two rich brothers hurried its new main house nearly to completion through forced labor by peons whom they paid almost nothing, and how Pancho Villa, when he took over Guadalajara, had avenged the workers and invited them to the hanging of the two brothers from a beam in an unfinished room. The room had remained unfinished ever since and the house was standing in unoccupied elegance.

When we approached Chapala he told us that a foreigner—Scandinavian I think—had planned development of a bay colony a mile from the village, had bought the long tract bordering an inlet from the station to the town, had divided it into lots and erected several villas as a start for his colony, with sales of land not only to trusting Mexicans but to foreigners as well, "including a whole moony cult from California," he said. The Scandinavian had sold enough stock in his enterprise to finance the railroad, the station, the big stone pier, which now stands high and dry back from a sunken lake, and the two-deck steamer which, lashed into pieces since by a storm, still was moored there then and plied good reaches of the sixty-mile lake from village to village. But because of far too much financial outlay at the start, the Scandinavian's scheme had collapsed and with it his title and the titles of his victims. The little train was still running then, but travel was scanter than had been expected; and the elaborate two-story station, with its huge waiting room and offices, its arched portals and its twin towers, was already looming, as it does now, over the decay of a colony intended.

Lawrence went on unfolding his verbal map.

Mineral baths at the center of Chapala had long been popular. He had seen photographs of the place in the Diaz days showing flocks of fashionable visitors, even tallyhos and silk hats, had been told that gowns and jewels which would have graced France had floated and flashed at dances in the Hotels Palmera and Arzapalo. Doña Maria Pacheco viuda de Arzapalo, widow of the owner of the second best of the hotels, had once, on a trip to Europe with her family, taken along a complete outfit of mattresses for fear the continent would afford them inferior comfort. Don Porfirio himself, the risen, ruthless, Europeanized Indian dictator, approved of not only by favored foreign plutocrats, who afforded him power in return for concessions at the expense of humbler Indians, but by the Mexican aristocracy whose wealth he was protecting and increasing, had often relaxed at his brother's villa on the lake, bringing there his showy friends and attendants from the capital. The villa, El Manglar, restored and enlarged, has now become again a sleek, major estate; but in 1923 half the building had sunk into ruin and we used to tread perilous floors in the upstairs rooms which Lawrence was presently to describe in *The*

Plumed Serpent as being perilous for another reason—the scene of a lively battle.

I remember the balmy Chapalan air which entered our nostrils even at the station. We were driven in a ramshackle car the kilometer or so from the station to town, the running boards thick with noisy urchins. On the drive we passed three or four of the villas built in sanguine days but already crumbling down in 1923 and used, in parts that were still fairly sound, by local fishermen or farmers for their combined families, fowls, dogs, burros, cows, and pigs.

The house Lawrence had found was very different. On one of the side streets leading to the lake and not far back from the water, its brick front, then unplastered, stood flush with the edge of the broken brick sidewalk and adjoined a gateway of stout pillars and thick wooden doors. Our procession entered a garden bright with bloom, cool with shade. Each of the six rooms in the T-square house had its own entrance opening on this garden and the whole place withdrew from the bleak street into a pleasant privacy. It had been built when Mexican progress had not modified hereditary Spanish patios beyond the change to sheltered gardens. This garden was enclosed on two sides by house and gate and on the other sides by high walls. American influence had not yet begun setting houses back from the sidewalk and giving them, instead of their patios, strips of useless street-side garden with low railings, good only for what uninvited persons leave behind them.

Lawrence began directing where in the house our various bags, baskets, and bundles were to go; but I clung to my typewriter, shook my head and hardened my heels for the tug of war. A knock at the gate interrupted. In came a cordial-faced woman with effusions of welcome. Lawrence introduced her as Isabel, the *criada*. We spattered our Spanish. Isabel had the usual sentences for us all; but when she had made the round, she turned back to Frieda and, tiptoeing like a dark Lilliputian, embraced Olympian hips and cried, *"Mi niña!"* (My little girl!) That much Spanish we all understood and we burst out laughing. So did Isabel. We did not know then that *Mi niña* is a customary term of Mexican address from woman servant to mistress; and I am convinced that our ignorance saved two of us from an unhappy spat. The general good humor precluded altercation.

"Lorenzo," I said with no remnant of rancor, "the house is just right, you had to take it of course, you can't be anything but happy here, and you were generous when you thought of sharing it with us. But it's not going to be too big for you and Frieda—the living room, the big bedroom, and this other room for a study. You'll need it all. If you added Spud and me, we'd be constantly under your feet. And besides, when we settle down and are all at work, our hours wouldn't fit. You know that the two of you are early birds and we're not, so that breakfast would be stretching out all morning. You like to go to bed early and we jabber on into the night, which would be sure to disturb you in the next room. It would be silly for any of us to have to sleep in the living room, especially since you've found a town where we can stay for some time. Don't you think so yourself, Lorenzo?" I sped on, "Perhaps we could have suppers here together, with Spud and me taking other meals at the hotel. You'll see all you'll want to see of us, only a street or two away. It's really better. Don't you agree?"

Lawrence had not intercepted my argument nor once bristled. But he did not answer when I paused. So I made a move which I feared, during the second when I could not unmake it, might be unwise. "What does the *"Niña"* think?" I asked. "Don't you agree, Frieda?"

Spud meantime had maintained his natural silence.

She looked at the three of us in turn, replied questioningly, *"Ja?"* then nodded a thoughtful head and concluded definitely, *"Ja."* Without further ado, with only equanimity from that moment, Lawrence acquiesced. "I'll take you over to the Arzapalo," he said, "and we'll come back here for tea."

The Mexican boys, who had been standing by with graceful and impassive patience, picked up our luggage, helped hoist our trunk on the back of a porter waiting outside the gate, and part of the procession moved again.

16. Hotel Arzapalo

AS yet we had had only a view of the inlet by the station and of the sealike stretch beyond it toward the Ocotlan end of the lake. Now, coming through the Lawrences' street to the waterfront, we turned west and faced the massive roll of the mountains on the other side like arrested waves, their violet crevices covered with a faint spray of haze. We came by a pretentious Victorian brick villa, in the convulsive school of architecture—bay windows, turrets, cupolas, stained-glass windows. The church, with modern but pleasant white façade and steeples and a fine, solid, stone nave of much older period, is set just beyond it toward the town; and Lawrence told us that the grounds themselves, full of palm trees, oleanders, and flower beds, had once belonged to the church and should belong to it still but had been sold by a venal priest, so that the two buildings have had to stand alongside each other ever since, maintaining an incongruous likeness to a misshapen American businessman in a red-brown suit being married to a slim Mexican beauty in wedding veil.

An open-air pavilion with tables for drinkers offered shade at the end of the two streets leading to the stone pier. Pepe Sanchez, who conducted this *pabellón,* was an expert photographer, whose prints of Chapala are a selective and artistic record of its aspects in those years. Beyond the pavilion we saw the outline of Ajijic hills descending into the lake with the grace a Chinese painter gives the unseen line that follows wild geese alighting. And sunsets over those hills were often then, as they are now, volcanoes and lakes and pools of golden fire. Across from the Sanchez pavilion was our hotel, the Arzapalo, standing full on the lake, a tawny oblong structure, with high, corniced, iron-balconied windows at the sides and a second story deeply open at the front, roofed but facing the lake through three airy arches. On the

upper floor of the western wing we chose two rooms, just over a corn-
field and with railed windows toward the beach and the sunsets. On
the ground level, in front, was an earth-floored terrace with tables and
over them an arbor supporting a thick-stemmed wide-spreading bou-
gainvillea. It was very different, this free exposure to the beauties of
lake, mountain, and cloud, from the snug seclusion of the Lawrence
house; and, without saying so to them, we preferred it. I felt sure that
the voices of bathers, or children playing ball, or loiterers on the beach
below would be little or no disturbance. When Spud and I were left
to an hour of relaxation in our rooms, we were pleased for the Lawrences in their choice, pleased for ourselves in ours, pleased for all four
of us in a personal world at peace.

With teatime a shadow came over the peace. After our first exchanges of general felicitation, we heard quick dark tales from Lorenzo
which he had heard from Isabel. Already she had introduced her two
sons, Jesús, the elder, who ran the little gasoline motor for the town's
electric light system, and Daniel, who was both farmer and boatman;
and they had corroborated the dark tales. All was not well in Mexico,
in Jalisco, in Chapala. Peons were being mistreated everywhere, and
there were whispers of coming reprisal against the masters and against
foreigners, too, whom the masters were supposed to be imitating. "It
was not a stray bullet that killed Ewart," said Lawrence. "We must
be very careful. We must not walk beyond town. We must keep doors
and windows locked and we must be ready to leave quickly at any
moment."

Then he told us over the strong tea a specific story. In Jocotepec, at
the western end of the lake, lived four or five skillful weavers whose
serapes were deservedly popular in Jalisco. Under back-yard portales,
or in rooms darkened by blocked-out windows—all over Mexico one
sees this phenomenon of window openings filled solid with adobe or
brick, as if the inmates preferred to change from a nest to a warren—
the weavers' families would all be busily bent over rough wool of
various colors, assorting it, carding it, running it and clamping it into
the cross strings of looms. Then on market days in Chapala and other
villages, even in Guadalajara, the weaver would bring armfuls of
finished blanketry to be bargained for. At that time wool was cheap,
beans were cheap, life was cheap, and the average final price of a colorful, well-woven blanket was ten or fifteen pesos. Daniel had set his eye
and heart on a particular serape belonging to the manager of an

hacienda some twenty miles from Chapala. It was not new, it was worn thin in places and, if bid for off some back in a crowd, would have fetched perhaps twelve pesos; but it was of very special design, not only richly patterned around the neck opening but covered all over at intervals with varicolored stars. Daniel had wanted it. So he had walked to the hacienda and offered to give a month's work there in exchange for it.

"The *hacendado* agreed!" railed Lorenzo. "And he let the boy work there for thirty-one days! Then he went on a trip and Daniel had to walk from Chapala to the hacienda three times before he found the man. And when he did find him, the brute sneered at him, 'You not only don't get the blanket, you don't get a centavo. Then you'll learn not to covet things that belong to your betters.'"

"But what about the authorities?" demanded Frieda. "Why didn't he go to the law?"

"He did, Frieda. I told you he did. But they took the hacendado's word that the story was a lie. I told you that but you don't listen."

"If I were Daniel, I'd kill the man," said Frieda.

"And then get killed yourself?"

"No," persisted Frieda, "Isabel told me that they let people kill one another here, like killing rabbits, and then say it's God's will, and there's nothing done about it. I did listen to that, I did."

"It's never God's will to kill a master, Frieda, until men themselves make it God's will. And they'll do it. There'll be a leader, like Villa or Zapata, or somebody stronger." His face became intense. "And once they have a strong leader, these people will be strong too. They'll be as merciless to their masters as their masters have been to them. And they won't know the difference between their masters and foreigners like us who are their friends. It's no good trying to be their friends, Spoodle. They'll never understand. You can see it in their eyes. These people are volcanoes. The volcanoes all over the land are symbols of the people, who will erupt again as they have erupted before. What seems laughter in their eyes, Bynner, isn't laughter. It's heat turning back into lava."

"It's pretty in the meantime," suggested Spud.

"Listen to the Spoodle," replied Lorenzo, indulgent. "How happy he is in the little he knows!"

"But who knows as much as you know?" charged Frieda. "You're an idiot, a madman. I know what a fool you are. You're trying to frighten us, and I'll thank you to hold your silly tongue unless you have something sensible to say." Without looking at him she picked up her sewing. Without being torrential this time, she had dampened him. His feathers rose a little, but he shook them back into place.

"Some night," he prophesied, as though to himself, "we'll find out." And then his voice trailed off, with no spirit, "Go on with your silly sewing."

Our talk then eased away from black topics and stayed comfortable until the supper hour, when the Lawrences walked part way with us to the hotel, far enough to see that a sculptured sunset had left in the sky above the mountain slope three narrow lagoons of jade green, their edges seeming to be crisp, incandescent shores in China. And the mariachis were giving a last song, one of their simpler, older songs, not in the characteristic trip-hammer beat of mariachi music, and yet not saccharine-slow like many of the songs by Agustin Lara and other popular composers. The thrum of the homemade, man-tall harp and the throb of a single plaintiff voice were melting into the quiet of the sky, and only a few of the ending day's sounds were heard against the lap of the lake waves. Suddenly something went wrong at the electric light plant. All lights flickered out. Without a good night, Lawrence hurried away into the shadow, a little ahead of Frieda who half said good night. He was frightened. He would bolt the gate; he would lock the doors.

Spud and I looked at each other later across the hotel supper table.

"Housed with that?" I exclaimed.

We laughed. We relaxed.

This was the very time when Lawrence was writing Middleton Murry, "The end of the lost trail is here in Mexico. *Aqui esta. Yo lo digo."*

"Here it is. I say so."

In saying so to Murry, he was trying to convince himself.

17. The Village

IN spite of the dry season, which was parching to a close, in spite of what Lawrence called the "stale earth" all around us, we found plenty in the Chapala scene to hold our eyes and our attention. Even at their dryest, the strangely shapely mountains in their changes of light were vital enough. In certain lights cultivated, furrowed slopes, sometimes almost vertical, looked like wrinkled sides of mastodons in harness. The earth was at work. But the row of mountains to our west, on the north side of the lake toward Jocotepec, when one saw it from the water, or from Ajijic, was to me more like leathery elephants alongside in a circus. This analogy pleased Lawrence, who called my attention to a similar elephant-leather look in the thick legs of ancient Indian laurel trees in the plaza. He warmed to any reminder of animals. The fact fascinated him that mastodons had once roamed these hills. And the present fact that, in our own momentary era, animals were living in the houses with the people always drew his eye, though I doubt if he would have enjoyed in his own abode the constant entrance, which we saw among houses around us, of fowl and flea-bitten hounds, of pigs, even of cattle and horses. But birds could not come close enough to him. He was ever pointing out to us hummingbirds, wild doves, house finches, black-and-yellow birds like orioles or like big grosbeaks, who would squawk back and forth, mate to mate, from trees at some distance apart, and slender blackbirds whose tails had one slice longer than the other, and mouse-like wrens among the roof tiles. Terry for once was right.

The birds were as numerous as the tiles themselves and as natural to the village as though the tiles now and then took wing. The lake bobbed with ducks, mud hens, grebes, and the dark edge of shore accentuated ivory-carved shapes of egrets, cranes, and herons, with

now and then a heron of blue jade. Cormorants, wild geese sped over
the lake, and even sea gulls who had flown inland and remained there.
Lawrence was puzzled as to birds who came out every twilight from
the little hill above the town, taking a hoarse croak with them into
the darkness over the water. They looked and sounded like sea gulls;
but why this emerging at night? At the same hour bats would flitter
from the upper story of one of the rusty mansions on the lake edge—
"seven clouds of them," he said, "at seven-minute intervals"—and, like
the night birds, fade into the lake sky. It interested him to be told by
an old-timer that these bats flew ten or fifteen miles across the lake
for their fare in abundant orchards but returned before dawn to sleep
in Chapala. Fruit bats, I think they were called. We found the pits of
their fruit, sometimes, in Chapala patios. These night flights were the
more eerie when they happened against an amphitheater of sunset.
Often at Chapala the clouds will glow not only in the west but on all
sides, as though Vulcan's forges were making a heavenly round. There
were other silhouettes against the sunsets; idlers or mariachis poised or
moving slowly in the peace of the evening, boatmen beaching their
craft or poling it to anchor, and all the figures black against the sky,
as though cut sharp from black paper.

"No wonder Mexican children are born to be painters!" exclaimed
Lawrence. Several times he and Frieda led us to the village school to
see artistry on display there, pictures imaginative, bold, alive. Again
said Lawrence, as if feathering an arrow, "Better than Rivera!"

On occasion we used to eat at the restaurant of Inocencio Cervantes,
where dinner was seventy-five centavos and on holidays a peso. We
liked to sip the thick cinnamon-flavored chocolate at supper. Then we
would sit in the *jardin,* the public square, where the life of the people
flowed around us. The voices of some of the little boys were hoarse as
if they were old too soon; but the little girls shrilled like cicadas. It
was strange, Lawrence remarked, that such shrieks could subside into
the lullaby music of the middle-aged Indian women's speech. The
men's voices were often grating and insistent, yet with a melancholy
inflection which made them sound, he said once, "like an excited
dirge." And he never wearied of watching the withdrawn expressions
of the *musicos* who, when they sang, would not look at one another or
at a listener, or yet far away, but apart from everybody as if distance
were close. It was like our actors in films who not once give the
audience a straight look. His favorite mariachi song was "The Jail-

keeper's Daughter." He would not let them sing him "The Dying Bull." He laughed over small girls in white veiling led to their first communion, their faces little black moons and their toes alert for escape to the swishing caper of ballet infants.

Always on Saturday evenings we would stroll on the pier alongside the beach to watch the canoas arrive and unload for Sunday market: tomatoes, melons, cucumbers, sacks of charcoal, bricks, earthenware, serapes, huaraches, sombreros. Lawrence was making mental notes for *The Plumed Serpent*. He tells about it in that book, and about the evening market place, the tin torch lamps with floating oil wicks, the shadowed faces, and in the mornings men bringing water, each with two gasoline cans slung from a pole across his shoulders or the girls with the jars on their shoulders. And the Indians who stand resting or rest standing. All these he saw and records. But from the clay grave figures he stays clear. They bothered him, much as, among the birds, buzzards always bothered him. He was with us when we dug up some of the images. In every grave there would be pottery portraits of the dead, each with lips at the ear-opening in the skull of his prototype. These figurines estranged him. One could wash them, brighten them alive, only to see them quickly fade and whiten dead again. He drew away from them, uneasy. He would turn to other objects found in the graves: *tecomates, molcajetes,* and *naguales,* painted bowls, three-legged Chinese-looking plates, and animals with baskets on their backs. These last he liked the best. They would be found always with a dead man, never with a dead woman; and it appeared that the dog or whatever it was would, with goods on its back, accompany his master—swimming across the river of death to survival on the other side. There would have been no good in affording a woman one of these burden bearers, because no woman is allowed to cross the river into the future world. "You see, Frieda," said Lawrence softly.

One market day a canoa brought across the lake a huge hog which so violently resisted attempts to unload it that it fell screaming overboard alongside the pier and, because its legs were tied, drowned there before it could be rescued. Jumping into the water, its owners lugged it ashore, bloodied the small shore waves by slitting its throat and promptly held market on the beach. Crowding Chapalans made offers for this cut or that. Legs, ribs, haunches, head, and hoofs were severed with the deftest dispatch and handed to the highest bidders. The Lawrences fled; but I stayed, risking the beratement I received later for my bloodthirsty American curiosity. "You have to see every-thing," said Lawrence. "You can't resist."

He liked little better another Chapalan experience. Youngsters had brought from a slope of the pyramidal hill by the village two rattle-snakes which I promptly bought and ordered parboiled and fried for supper. Delicious though the meat was, better than the tenderest frog's legs, he would have none of it. You would have thought we were feasting on Quetzalcoatl. "Where did you learn to be a cannibal?" he asked; and when I answered, "Devil's Lake, Wisconsin," he growled, "You should have drowned in it."

Both Lawrences were delighted that one robust, grizzle-mustached fellow in Chapala was a spiritualist, defied the entrenched Catholic Church and conducted meetings at which the medium was Voltaire. "Better than the Pope," agreed Lawrence. "And better than those Aztec ideas," added Frieda. "Are you so sure of that?" asked her husband—one of the few hints he gave Spud and me of his then reverent absorption in Mexican mythology.

After our wanderings we would sit at an outdoor table in the plaza or on the hotel terrace for an absinthe, a vermouth and soda, a tequila lemonade, or else go back to Calle Zaragoza for tea, with biscuits baked by Lawrence and the native fruit pastes he liked, made of guava, quince, and pear.

And there we would usually find Isabel and a daughter on their knees swabbing the tiled floors. Then Lawrence would bridle. "You did that this morning!" he would fling his Spanish at them. And they would look up with sweet surprise and continue scrubbing the already spotless tiles. All over Mexico this happens. Perhaps because the bare-foot Indian in his thatched *jacal,* with droppings of fowl or beast ever left there, and with little furniture beyond the *petate,* the plaited sleeping mat, has long required that the earthen floor be repeatedly cleaned and cannot shake loose from hereditary practice. When he has a tiled floor of his own, he continues the endless swabbing. Furniture may become layered with dust, windows streaked with stain from bird or bat or insect, woodwork splashed with plaster, all are neglected in favor of the floor. And the furniture which has to be moved for the mopping is never returned to place but always left helter-skelter where it stands. This happens country-wide. But to Lawrence's mind the practice seemed personal and malevolent, even from gentle Isabel.

I doubt if he would have seen the fun in similar stubbornness when,

Frieda Lawrence

Spud Johnson

D. H. Lawrence

D. H. Lawrence

Caricatures by Witter Bynner

Portrait of D. H. Lawrence by Knud Merrild (Courtesy of the artist and custodians of the Louise and Walter C. Arensberg Collection at the Philadelphia Art Museum)

many years later, I had screened the two entrances of the kitchen in my Chapala house and my servant Ysidoro persistently propped the outer door open with a stone or a chair for easier access to the yard. Each time I would shut it he would wait till my back was turned and then stubbornly prop it open again. I had learned or thought I had learned that the best way to give orders in Mexico is by example rather than by dictate or debate; but finally I broke down and, with an almost Lawrencian flare, asked, "Why do you suppose I paid money for those screen doors? It was to shut out flies!" With the greatest calm and yet with that glint of Mexican opposition which always infuriated Lawrence, Ysidoro answered, "I shut one door to keep them out and I open the other to let them out." I doubt if Lawrence would have laughed and thereby won Ysidoro's good will and co-operation with the screens at least most of the time. Now and then, to this day, when Ysidoro asserts his independent dignity by propping the yard door open, I leave it open. Soon after he knows I have seen it, he will whisk the kitchen clear of flies, remove the chair or the stone, and leave both screen doors closed, with nothing said by either of us.

Once when Lawrence had stormed at the tile scrubbers and they had disappeared and we had calmed ourselves into a half-hour's conversation on the porch, I saw his quick head jerk toward the kitchen end of the garden and the bad look come into his eyes. The look that would presage trouble with Frieda was different. Whereas that would be a hardening of the iris into cold scales like a snakehead, this was the hot glare enlarging the eye of a night animal and it was directed at Isabel and Maria who sat together by the well, the mother combing the daughter's head for lice. Among the poor in Mexico such attention may be seen in doorways, in windows, in the market place, in the street. It is no shameful practice. On the contrary, it betokens open preference for cleanliness, like a cat washing a kitten. And to them it seems as acceptable a performance in public as sewing. But to Lawrence it was odious. "Always when we have guests!" he squealed and then, jumping at them, he ordered them off into the street. "Get out!" They splayed away like a frightened pair of fowl, with muted clucks. "Fear is the only force they know," he said, glowering. "They knew what they were doing disgusts us. They do it when we have people. They do it to annoy us. They were getting even with us about the mopping. In their hearts they hate us. Yet Frieda here believes in treating them kindly!"

"*Ja!*" boomed Frieda.

"But you see what it gets you!" his voice rocketed over her. "You are always giving them presents out of kindness; but they take it as a sign of weakness—they think that you're afraid of them, that you are buying them off with kindness, that you owe them whatever you give them and more. So then they tread on your patience, on your time, on your will. They set their wills against yours, their power!"

He continued to me, "It's not just Mexico. It's your western continent. Everywhere in America it's the same. Everywhere in America they do that. It's an everlasting battle of wills. Your servant, your neighbor, your tradesman, everyone you meet flaunts his will at you and is determined to master yours, not for any real result but just for some petty satisfaction in their silly, barren natures. Look at those women now!"

They had come back through the gate, the two other daughters with them this time, and were edging along the wall toward the kitchen. He strode at them, summoning weight to his thin stature, gravity to his piping voice, and all the authority of Moses to his beard. "Get out, you bitches!" he chanted like a priest. It subdued them. Not only two faces as earlier but four now were stricken into sudden quiet pain, their eyes looking nowhere, like those of dogs maltreated. But there was no slinking away. They walked out erect.

"They don't understand," interposed Frieda.

"Oh, but they do," he shouted back. "Let them go with their lice. They need a Diaz and they know it. What you think of Diaz is wrong, Bynner; that was the only kind of government they could ever understand or respect. They need a Diaz—or they need America. It might be best for them, after all, if you Americans should annex them! There must be command; there must be obedience," he continued, with a voice grown from petulance to that of a Hebrew prophet. "These people are devils and always will be. There is only evil on this continent and death."

"On all the continents, Lorenzo," said Frieda with gravity, "it is like that for you. But look there, Lorenzo, see Isabel."

Somehow, without our noticing, Isabel and Maria had by-passed the *portal* and the two were on their knees with mop rags wiping the tiles outside the dining room.

"They are smiling at you," nodded Frieda.

"No, no," he dissented with almost a wail, "that's not a smile, it's a sneer. They've beaten us again. I can't stay in the house with them. I won't watch them, Frieda. We'll go to the beach till they're done!"

But they were never done, especially if any of us were in the house; partly because they wanted to be observed working but mostly because they liked to be among us, watching us with eyes which seemed not to see.

The women and children annoyed Lawrence more than the men did. In the men he mostly preferred to perceive an ancient dark power, a magnetic menace. He would have been at odds with Graham Greene who remarked long afterward, in *Another Mexico,* "Grown men cannot meet in the street without sparring like schoolboys. One must be as a little child, we are told, to enter the kingdom of heaven, but they have passed childhood and remain forever in a cruel anarchic adolescence."

Usually, after Lawrence's petty frets over the women and enjoyable frights over the men, the sky would calm him. Before sunset an amber glow would settle on the town, suffusing houses and gilding the inner bones of people. While we relaxed in our beach chairs, the long hills across the lake would float in mist, the boats nearby would be dreaming downward. Day voices were stilled. In the church a soft anthem would give treble to the organ. Feet on the paved lake-walk would sound like goslings quacking to rest under a wing; and low-lying light would recline on the water with a night sigh. Or else, toward the rainy season, the mottled sky would look like a vast plum-stuffed cake, with the moon in the middle for a prize; and, unlike the usual stiff evening wind, a cool breath would come as from a glacier just far enough away.

For his tender lungs and sensibilities Mexico's air felt kinder to Lorenzo than its earth, its people.

18. Diary

THAT night, ruminating over Lawrence's apparently settled dislike of the Mexican Indian's character, I put down in my notebook my own reaction.

"He knows better than I, because much more of a reader, that centuries of fear have been exerted upon Mexico, almost nothing but fear. And the Indian has resisted, resisted and come through. These Indians, who have bent and bent under the long winds of fear, have never been broken, never been severed from their roots, their tough roots. Even to this day the descendants of the Spanish conquerors are outsiders, ill at ease in Mexico, for all the blandishments of material well-being. They pitch their voices high, to overcome misgivings, especially their women who toward sunset become as sharp as starlings, while the Indian women's voices stay low and sure. The Spanish blood is not at home here, or the French, or the English, or the American— nor Lawrence's.

"In the Museum of the City of Mexico you see again and again the feathered serpent, 'a low deity,' according to Lawrence, who is properly versed in his histories and mysteries. He fails to see how that feathered serpent has guarded Mexico against the higher gods, the devouring gods of Europe. Effigies of Christ bleed in the churches of every Mexican town, great clots of blood oozing from the brow, the side, the arms and hands, the knees and ankles. The people hitch forward to him on their knees, the penitents outstretch their arms, the priests bind Christian mourning about the eyes and mouths of their people like blindfolds and gags. But in the end this misnamed Christ is helpless to lead the greedy armies which try to use him. This fake Jesus has been slain not by mortal Jews but by the immortal winged serpent.

"At first the Mexican Christ and his blood had made me think of Aztec altars, of an ancient priesthood lifting to heaven unnumbered human hearts torn from live bodies. I had visioned all those hearts gathered into the one heart, the Sacred Heart of Jesus, torn again from the living body, lifted again on the pyramid—the same human sacrifice, the same religion of blood, the same murderous priesthood and the same people with their twisted minds, glorying in the pain and beseeching good from it. 'They are devils,' says Lawrence, 'and always will be. There is only darkness on this continent and violence.' Does he long for the sweet corruption of Europe to become an incense here, covering the smell of blood? The very fruits here taste to him of blood, the pitahayas, the ciruelas, the mangoes, the guavas. No wonder he shudders. It is his own blood he tastes, the blood of a decadent Europe, of a decadent religion, of a decadent Christ. But alongside images of Quetzalcoatl in the Hall of Ancient Stones are images of other gods: gods in the shape of men, squat gods with huddled knees, thick gods with snaky bowels and no wings, bent and brooding gods. And always in the middle of these gods, where there might be the navel, symbol of separation, of the cord broken between person and person, of the individualizing knot, always where the navel should be, there gapes instead an opening, a hole, a vacuum, a receptacle. It is the receptacle for what gods and men may or may not create within themselves, the womb of the imagination, the tabernacle of the soul, the nest of another god, the lung of the breathing presence of all life beyond and including the single self. And woe to him who carries in that cavity only incense or oil or gold. These Mexicans, with breath at their core, have continued against the majesties of the world a profound resistance. And so these little Lawrences with their little nerve patterns have grown frightened and querulous. 'They would kill you and not care,' he exclaims. 'Nobody would care. See how they kill one another and nobody cares. See how they skin a lamb!'

"There is after all no retreat for Lawrence. From country to country he flees the agglomerated particles of himself, of his own factions, of his own weakness, of his own strength."

There was to have been more of this, but I left off, because of tired eyes in candlelight. And I never resumed it, except through a poem which I showed Lawrence and which he said he liked:

The Winged Serpent

The eagle is of the air toward the sun,
And the rattlesnake is of the air toward the sun;
And the mewing of the eagle is the sound of many people under
 the sun,
And the rattle of the snake is the sound of many people under
 the sun.
But where are the people who can make the sound of the winged
 serpent,
Clapping the air into thunder
And shaking lightning from his scales?
This is the bird of the wonder that prevails,
The serpent of the wonder that prevails;
This is the dream that lives in the mountains above the yellow
 people of the middle kingdom,
This is the dream that lives in the lake among the red people of
 the outer kingdom;
This is the heaver of earthquakes,
This is the dreamer of rain:
This is the earth in the air
And the air in the earth;
This is the winged terror in the hearts of men
Because a snake can be so high in the air
And a bird can be so low on the ground,
With a hiss of fire from the scaly girth
And a stir of rainbows through the feathered mane.
  Pray to him well,
He will dart through your prayer,
Through the very heart and center of your prayer,
And out of the words of your mouth
He will scatter a mist that will reassemble in a great cloud,
And out of the cloud will come rain.
  Laugh for him well,
And he will dart through your laughter,
Dashing it into splinters and spars of light
To be reassembled in the sun.
  Die for him well,

And out of your death he will make darkness.
　And if you have lived for him,
He will add the breath, that you have sung with,
To the everlasting wind of his plumes.

I believed that in this poem I was successfully challenging Lawrence's fear of Mexico and of Quetzalcoatl; and Lawrence quite
meekly allowed me my belief.

19. The Beach

THE water of Lake Chapala is warm in May, almost too warm, and through the sunny hours there is little change for the skin between basking and bathing, except a change of element. Its temperature was the same then as now; but the long, high bowl of the lake was much fuller. I have wondered since, remembering rollers gathering tall over the shallow beach at Waikiki, why Chapala winds which usually begin blowing toward shore in late afternoon do not now pile up the sealike breakers they used to bring when there was depth, before this bowl was overdrained for irrigation, service, and industry. Constantly, in the dark of our rooms at the Arzapalo, we seemed to be in steamer berths hearing the heave and fall of ocean waves. All night there would be the ebb and flow and crash. Late afternoons in those days there was a chance now and then to ride a considerable incoming wave, with refreshing change of temperature from the breeze of the beach to the warmth of the water and then back to the cooling shore.

Most Mexicans of that period, especially the city Mexicans, were apprehensive of sun. Not till after their siestas, when the sun was low, would they come out to the beach and even then they would wear their bathrobes to the brink and slide quickly out of them and under the water's protective surface. Sometimes we would see bare-legged servants wading out to their calves, holding the robes over the shoulders not only of women but of men too, and then watchfully waiting to slip the robes back when the bathers returned. This dodging of sun, akin to the peons' custom of blocking windows in their houses or of wearing wide sombreros, was also dread of darkening the skin. Through later years foreigners with their zeal to be tanned have broken down the old prejudice. Mexicans of all classes now accept the sun's rays. But in those early days, till four or five o'clock, the beach would be given over mostly to villagers: fishermen casting their hand nets; boatmen wading round their craft or sleeping on the sand; women in figured cotton dresses sitting arm-pit high and vigorously soaping their long black locks and, under cover, their bodies; postcard and candy vendors, newsboys, bootblacks, and other youngsters pranking like dolphins in the water or drying their white, pajama-leg *calzones* in groups ashore.

Lawrence never joined us in the lake. I know now that he, the caveman in fiction, was acutely sensitive concerning his bony, pinched, pigeon-breasted, clay-white body, and I believe he was a touch jealous when Frieda would gaily join us on sand and in water. Spud and I, with a North American craving of sun, continually took our books, magazines, or manuscripts to the shore and lazed in the brazen day, to be joined toward evening by Frieda for a dip. We had quickly made friends with the newsboys and vendors, who would sit in a huddling circle round us, exchanging Spanish for English, trying to impose postcards or chewing gum on us, or peanuts or pop or beer or small lengths of water ices impaled on sticks. Gradually learning that we liked to read or write uninterrupted, they respected our peculiarity and would wait till we entered the lake before they joined us in their bevies, diving from our shoulders, swimming between our legs, tipping us over with unexpected underwater assaults, racing us to moored rowboats or launches, climbing aboard with us and plunging out again. The daytime beach belonged very much then to the villagers who, puzzled at first by our unusual beach timing, soon welcomed us and made us members of their community. For the most part, our young companions, aged from six to sixteen, would slip ashore when the fashionables emerged from shaded cover. The boys were not only hesitant to swim among these haughty elders but were mostly eager to sell papers and shine shoes. Week ends, when crowds came from Guadalajara, the vendors and bootblacks would leave off swimming and idling; but through the week, when business was sparse, they were with us constantly, even into the hour when Frieda would join us. They had soon learned to say "shine," "pos'card," "Hallo," and "meestair." "My particular friends here," I wrote my mother on May 19, "are the bootblacks, nine of them in this tiny village, plying very little trade except on Saturday and Sunday when enough Guadalajarans come to enliven the place without crowding it. When I appear at the tall window of my room in this bare barracks of a ramshackle hotel, my bootblacks hail me from the beach, urging that I go out for my Spanish lesson in the sun and to be their diving board."

Lawrence was to depict them in *The Plumed Serpent:* "Darting among the trees, bare-legged boys went skylarking in and out of the shadow, in and out of the quiet people. They were the irrepressible bootblacks, who swarm like tiresome flies." Though tiresome to Lawrence, they were not tiresome to us nor, I think, to Frieda.

They all had nicknames, such as Pepino and Zorrillo—Cucumber and Skunk. One of them who had a change of caps, was dubbed Gorras, the Spanish plural for such headgear. Because adult Mexican civilians did not wear caps and I usually did wear one on the beach, the youngsters thought at first that I must be either a priest or a soldier. For a while they called me Padre; but later, when my tan had deepened, they shifted to El Cristo Negro, the Black Christ, an alias still remembered by older Chapalans. Spud was El Flaco, translatable as Skinny; Frieda remained La Niña; but they did not have, at least in public, a by-name for her husband, who was glad and yet sad that he awed them.

Daily Lawrence would accompany Frieda from their house to the beach and would then stroll along the sand or sit on the terrace while the three of us bathed or chatted at the water's edge. They would arrive together, he in shirt and trousers, she in bathing clothes and bath wrap. It occurred to Spud that it would be easier if she used one of our rooms for changing. This would save her having to walk home sometimes with the bathrobe over chilly wetness. She liked the idea and Lorenzo nodded. So for several weeks it was daily custom that she shift clothes in Spud's room while he and I used mine. Lorenzo then discontinued coming with her. I judged that he had thought it more seemly to accompany her when she walked through the streets in her bathrobe but that now, since she came and went conventionally clothed, she did not need escort. We all felt, moreover, that he was glad of extra hours for his writing which had begun in earnest; and we knew well by this time that the beach was not his happy terrain.

During the third week, he followed along one day an hour behind Frieda, and it happened to be a time when most of our young friends were romping in the lake with us, the usual games, the shoulder divings forward or backward with newly learned somersaults, the races, the swimming between legs with occasional heaves from underwater and more somersaults. Frieda would give buoyant approbation, sometimes clapping her hands, but never participated in the games. Lawrence was now watching with visible disapproval. If she had been looking at him, she might have let loose one of her verbal bolts and scotched him. Spud called my attention to him. He stood staring like an angry schoolmaster, his red beard stuck out toward us accusingly. Nor did he stir for some ten or fifteen minutes but waited till our bathing was ended for the day and we came ashore.

Fortunately none of the Mexicans near us, young or old, knew English.

"Why do you act like this?" he rasped at Spud and me. "Making idiots of yourselves with all these little fools! It isn't dignified and what's more it's dangerous."

"D-dangerous?" we stammered.

"Yes, dangerous! Don't you realize how dirty these little chits are? They begin early down here doing everything. And you let them shin up on your shoulders and clutch you round the neck and rub their dirt into you. You don't know what diseases they have, what you might catch. It's outrageous, it's reckless, and it's a silly spectacle. People are talking."

Frieda failed us this time. She had been taken as unaware as we. She did boom, "Lorenzo!!" But that was all. The boys knew that something was wrong and waded offshore.

As for ourselves, we were surprised but not dumb. "Enough of that, Lawrence" was my hot retort. "You can yell at Frieda if she'll take it. But you can't yell at me. I won't take it and you'd better find that out. Good night."

Spud followed me into the hotel. When we reached the terrace, I remembered Frieda. We looked back. She had not moved but was standing like Lot's wife. Suddenly Lawrence seized her arm and she swayed off beside him, wet and unwilling. Each time she pulled back, he jerked her forward.

We sent her clothes along after them by Ysidoro, one of the boys he had lambasted.

Next afternoon when they came to the beach, Frieda was already in her bathing clothes. They joined us in some beach chairs.

"Lorenzo prefers that I dress at home," she remarked, with a slight edge of relish. "He's being considerate. He thinks I'm a nuisance to you."

"A nuisance?" wondered Spud.

"No, he doesn't," I twitted. "You're not being considerate, Lorenzo. That's not it."

"I'm not considerate at all," he flared. "But I don't like her dressing there and she's not going to dress there."

"If it's convenient for her," I retorted, still smarting from his lecture of the day before, "she's the one you might be thinking of."

He seemed to take no offense but turned his beard toward others around us and then toward us and hesitantly, as if afraid of his own remark but unable to restrain it, whispered the strangest sentence I ever heard from him, "It's not a question of being considerate of any of you. It's what people will think."

Frieda gave a deep sigh, then suddenly laughed and so did Spud. Too disgusted to laugh, I tried to down a new ground swell of dislike for the man by what I thought a friendly gesture. "Mr. Scott and his daughter want to see something of you and Frieda and I think you'd find him interesting. Why don't you join us all for supper tonight?"

I doubted, from his grimace toward Frieda, if he wished to accept. He apparently had not found the Scotts interesting; but when Frieda said, "Gladly we'll come, not tonight, tomorrow," he did not demur.

We sat at a table and lapsed into silence, while the sunset became radiance through which at any moment the hand of Michaelangelo's God might have reached to touch our fingers and set them busy again about small matters, touched our minds too and set them busy again about such small questions as "What will people think?"

20. The Willow Tree

B Y this time Lawrence had begun daily, sustained work on his novel. For his open-air study he had chosen a shady spot under a willow tree on the water front at the end of his street, Zaragoza. On his street and on the shore street at the end of it there were then but few houses and those mostly sealed until caretakers should open them to families thronging from Guadalajara and Mexico City for the gay blare of Holy Week.

Then as now Carnival Week, preceding Lent, was celebrated by the villagers with excited voting for a queen who, accompanied by her ladies in waiting, the runners-up, would preside daily in the bandstand over various outdoor functions, over brisk competitive sidewalk performances by young and old of the *Jarabe Tapatio* and other dances. Each night until Ash Wednesday, on a dais in a cavernous ballroom, either at the Arzapalo or one of the other hotels, she would queen it over a formal ball, all the older female worthies sitting along the walls, with children at their knees begging for pop, while the older male worthies steered constantly around the corner for beer or tequila and then swayed back again for stronger dancing. As Holy Week belonged to absentee landlords and other visitors, *Carnaval* belonged to the village.

And so did Thursday and Sunday nights when the town band would play for *serenatas,* the girls in pairs or clusters all circling in one direction round the bandstand and the men outer-circling them in the other. It would always play at some point "Ojos de Juventud," and the Diaz waltz and always end with "La Golondrina." Vendors sold boutonnieres which were slipped into ready hands, or eggshells full of confetti which were cracked on favored heads, while whole families of onlookers, largely countryfolk, sat on benches or squatted on curb-stones with stolid enjoyment. These celebrations were local, though occasional Mexican hotel guests or foreign visitors like ourselves would join the circling. Lawrence, when he joined, always followed the example of one or two other husbands and walked with his wife in the inner female file. Frieda would beam broadly when we broke the confetti-filled eggshells on her, and Lorenzo would smile a dim approval. Basically he was too shy for this sort of playful mingling; but Mexicans have an adroit way of letting a stranger feel unobserved. You come along a sidewalk blocked by a group of them who seem unaware of you. You think you will be stepping off the curb to pass them. Just before you reach them, one or two of them, without looking at you, will move aside and give you clearance or, rather, flow aside like a turn of water round a rock or, in Lawrence's words, "as a flame leans from a draught." Mexicans perceive without looking, much as Lawrence himself did. In this respect I think he felt a sympathetic catlike kinship with them.

Holy Week was another matter in Chapala. The villas of the rich, most of which had been barred and shuttered the rest of the year, were opened wide for as many as they could hold. Ghost houses came alive. Gay gowns bloomed throughout the week, as they burgeon in New York on Easter Sunday. Priests had long deplored revelry through Holy Thursday and Good Friday; but the Latin custom would not be downed and, though church was visited all day by suddenly solemn worshipers coming and going, the streets outside were strident with musicians, eddying merrymakers with games and gamblings, eatings and drinkings and bargainings.

When we reached Chapala, with Holy Week over, the town was limp after its whirl, the Lord had risen but the people had sunk back, the *elegancia* had departed with its finery and parrot chatter, the softer voices of Indian women were lullabying the air, houses behind Lawrence's tree on the beach had shut their openings for another long sleep: he could once more sit at peace with his back against his tree trunk and write. The willow tree is gone now, but I still see him sitting under it. Its leafy image stirs above his bearded own. A few fishermen and boatmen pass softly between him and the lake or shove from shore in their high-prowed dugouts, burros come within six feet of him and let their noses hang toward him as though they were contemplating him in a long trance. Meantime his hand moves rapidly down the right-hand pages of his schoolboy's copybook, leaving paragraphs of legible, flowing script, with seldom erasure or correction but now and then an asterisk indicating that an added phrase or passage is to be inserted from the left-hand page opposite.

Idella Purnell writes me: "I remember Lawrence used to go down to the beach, where the women washed their clothes, and sit under a large tree like a willow writing for hours in long hand in the dime copy books he used for composing. I remember one time he complained bitterly of being annoyed by a goat."

The manuscripts were miraculously precise. As O. Henry used to know whole stories by heart before he set them down, so Lawrence must have composed firmly in his mind before his hand moved, although he did tell Dorothy Brett once that he seldom knew ahead what he was going to write. For some time, long afterward, two complete versions of *Lady Chatterley's Lover* were stored in my safe at Santa Fe. Page after page after page in the two would be almost identical, and yet I doubt if he copied one from the other. Through considerable portions the changes would be so slight that he might easily have made them on the original and saved much toil; but no, the second version was as entire as the first, each direct from the man.

Toward the cool of the Chapala evening, when his solitary sessions were ended, he would return to the house and lead Frieda, she in her bathing dress, he in shorts, to a shallow neck of the inlet leading to the station. She seldom came to the public beach now but accompanied him instead to this secluded spot for an uncomfortable dip. The shallows were only waist-deep, the shore an almost solid jumble of sharp rocks and stones, with interstices of mud and slimy reeds; but here the two figures would arrive each afternoon, once in a while with Johnson and me in attendance but seldom with anyone else about. They would pick a painful way into the water, hand in hand, teetering and wobbling, till they were submerged to the hips, whereupon with the utmost gravity and with hands clasped as they faced each other, he would start them bobbing up and down, a bit deeper each time, till shoulders were covered and then he would bob gradually up again, freeing himself, shining white, and stumble back to shore. Sometimes Frieda would laugh aloud over the absurdity of the show, but Lorenzo would end it with the look a child might wear if he felt growing through his chin a wet red beard. It was comic and yet pathetic—the red beard bobbing over the pinched torso of sheetlike pallor. A narrow, iron-banded keg painted white might so have bobbed adrift at sea. I thought one afternoon that Spud and I ought to have gone and bobbed with them; but we never did. It may have been the sharp stones or we may have thought we should be intruding on a private ritual.

I had not then read *The Trespasser,* that young novel, not heard what Lawrence was wanting from earth and water and sky. I wish I had known the passages: "The sand was warm to his breast, and his belly, and his arms. It was like a great body he cleaved to. Almost, he fancied, he felt it heaving under him in its breathing. Then he turned his face to the sun and laughed. All the while, he hugged the warm body of the sea bay beneath him. He spread his hands upon the sand; he took it in handfuls, and let it run smooth, warm, delightful, through his fingers. . . . He was a poor swimmer. Sometimes a choppy wave swamped him, and he rose gasping, wringing the water from his eyes and nostrils, while he heaved and sank with the rocking of the waves that clasped his breast. Then he stooped again to resume his game with the sea. It is splendid to play, even at middle age, and the sea is a fine partner."

Not quite sensing what Lawrence was needing from the elements, Spud and I were only realizing afresh those afternoons, as we had realized before, that it was his physical shyness, his dislike of his own physique together with a jealousy of the physique of stronger men, which was often at the root of his seeming arrogances. William Gerhardi, in his *Memoirs of a Polyglot,* records that at mention of "the lucidity, the suppleness and pliability of Bertrand Russell's mind," Lawrence "sniffed, 'Have you ever seen him in a bathing dress? Poor Bertie Russell! He's all Disembodied Mind!'" Had Bertie Russell ever had a similar look at Bertie Lawrence? It would have been fun to watch the exchanged glances of the two of them. At least Russell openly valued his mind, while Lawrence was vaunting the blood stream. The sad point was that he seldom could have seen a body weaker than his own and that actually he was proud of the muscles of his mind. He had a stout mind and he would show us all!

21. John Dibrell

M R. Winfield Scott, an American who had married and out-
lived a Mexican wife, was manager of the Arzapalo Hotel,
and he and his daughter, Margaret, occupied front rooms in
the west wing of the ground floor, just under ours. The whole corre-
sponding east wing, with a door opening on the terrace, was reserved
by the owner, of whom Lawrence had told us on the train, the widowed Doña Maria Pacheco viuda de Arzapalo, a majestic lady of the
old school, crowned with an enormous crop of yellow curls natural
both in their color and their kink. Her evening strolls, in lavender
and white, with shawl and parasol of silk, were tours of triumph—
queenly bows here and there along the walk above the beach or an
occasional pause for rapid, eager, shrill twitterings with favored
friends. She had a rare gift of melodramatic narrative ending with a
cascade of irresistible laughter over some comic brink. I constantly
wondered that Lawrence did not recognize in her an extraordinary
figure for the Mexican novel on which he was intent, for I had not
realized as yet his prime attachment to multiple fictional figures of
himself. In a short story of her or a sketch, he might have kept alive
her lusty magnificence. But she had as little engaged his attention as
had the Scotts.

Besides Doña Maria at the Arzapalo, there were others who, I
thought, might have interested him for his Mexican scene.

The Pani family, whose head was then or later Minister of the
Treasury, was forever playing poker in the big lobby and exchanging
fine chatter; a young American named Taylor, manager of the
Y.M.C.A. in Mexico City, was on vacation with wife and brood and
maintaining remarkable Christianity toward the latter; there were
seven or eight other family groups, Mexican and American, whose

stories of the country were to Spud and me welcome corollaries to Mme Calderon de la Barca's *Life in Mexico* and Charles Flandrau's *Viva Mexico*. But none of the guests were distracting Lawrence from the inner absorption which was planning *The Plumed Serpent*. I should have guessed that he was looking for heroic Indians and finding them on the inner stage of his imaginings. I have stressed his voluble irritations, his tempers, and his flames, but he had frequent periods also of quiet withdrawal and reserve.

On one occasion, Spud's twenty-fifth birthday, he did bring Frieda to an Arzapalo noon meal at which there was a considerable company. Among the guests were two Americans: an alluring lady from Tampico with an immolated swain who constantly tripped over himself to please her. Lawrence's nostrils, when he was near them, grew the cruel dent he had observed in the *aficionados*. The lady complained, having been served chicken at the birthday feast, that she disliked dark meat. The swain at once gave her his plateful of white. "So you're offering her your breast," said Spud. Neither guest favored the sally, so Lawrence applauded, his laugh like a snarl.

On Sundays, Dr. Purnell and his daughter were often among the Guadalajarans who came to the resort; and the doctor's gentle spirit had much to do, on those occasions, with Lawrence's untroubled intervals. "He always treated Daddy," Idella recalls, "with a real consideration, even affection. I attributed his liking for hour-long strolls along the *playa* with Daddy to two factors: one, that he liked Daddy; two, that he liked all the wonderful material he could glean for books." Idella's own fresh youthful sallies with him, which might have seemed impertinences in someone else, engaged his amused liking. I remember that he was always happy and vivacious when the Purnells arrived. Nor did he demur when we told him that Leighton was coming for a short stay at the hotel. With Leighton, as with the Doctor, he took long conversational walks. It was as though there had been no friction, no dismissal, at the Monte Carlo. To Frieda's relief, as well as ours, all was ease. This was the more surprising since heat had aggravated Chapala's dryness and some of the days were oppressive. He would complain of them now and then, and of the brittle brown landscape in its dead haze; but as yet he remained equable with all of us.

Apart from the Purnells and Leighton, apart from Isabel's tribe and a few boatmen and fishermen with whom he was genial on the way to and from his beach retreat and through whom he was attentive to back-yard rehearsals of the everlasting dance pageant concerning Montezuma, Malinche, and Cortes, with its crude finery, stylized battles, and singsong couplets, his interest had been caught by only one person in Chapala, a young foreigner with a rich black beard who, proficient in Spanish, sometimes brought Mexican friends to the open-air cantinas and the hotel terrace. Lawrence, certain at first that the man was a Russian spy, would strain ears for proof when we would be sitting at a table near enough. Why a Russian spy I never quite knew, it was before their heyday; but Lorenzo continued for a period to relish a suspicion of sinister mystery and was disappointed, almost annoyed, when we presently met the young man as John Dibrell who, for all his having been a champion boxer at Johns Hopkins, was as gentle as the little finger of Jesus and more interested in secrets of courtship than of state. Contemptuous of conventional behavior in the northern country, his mother having been State President of the Federation of Women's Clubs, he was out to shock his kin by marrying a Mexican villager. Some years later, having been rejected in Chapala, he outraged his unwarned family and friends by marching, wound in an Indian blanket, across a Texan ballroom to a dais where his sister sat enthroned as queen of some festival and blandly introducing his wife. The wife, legitimate but frightened to tears, was a little Navajo squaw in native dress who would not once take her running nose out of the crook of his arm. I am certain that the gleam in his eye on that occasion, as on any occasion, was not Russian.

Johnson and I had already seen a good deal of Dibrell and liked him. We sympathized with his irritation against authorities all over Mexico who were discouraging the peons' native attire, white, pleated shirts with crescent pockets, wide-flowing, pajamalike calzones which were tied crisscross at the waist and bound with broad red cotton sashes. On a board hung against one of the big laurels near the bandstand an official order was chalked, forbidding the wearing of this apparel in Chapala streets. Indians arriving from the country, or on canoas from across the lake, would have to stop at the edge of town and shift into dark blue overalls, which at once blotted out their grace and made them look wooden. Lawrence knew about these regulations and the false pride which motivated them; but through Kate in *The Plumed Serpent,* which he was then writing, he could not resist giving the motive a sexual accent: "She understood why the cotton pantaloons were forbidden on the plaza. The living flesh seemed to emanate through them." I have laughed at the notion of Mexican officialdom saying, "Brother, brother, you look too alive in those clothes! You must change." What it did say was, "Brother, brother, you look too provincial in those clothes. You must change." Johnson and I had seen Cuernavaca police seizing sombreros from heads in the plaza there and slicing off rims which exceeded the stipulated width. Already in Chapala a few of the Indians were limping about in tight airless American-style shoes, instead of in huaraches, the open-work sandals of plaited leather which gave them a tread of ease and spring. When I left Mexico that year, border officials, finding huaraches in my trunk, tried to confiscate them. It seemed to be the first pair an American had tried to take out of the country. "You want to show these things round up there and make fun of us, of our poverty," they protested. "Not at all. I want to wear them and be comfortable," I replied and proved it by changing into them on the spot and crossing the border in them. It happens that I have worn Mexican huaraches most of the time ever since.

Dibrell had been fuming over this trend in Mexico and believed that by personally disproving supposed foreign contempt for native dress, by adopting it ourselves, we might not only relieve the Indians in both pocketbook and spirit but possibly start a move which could save the national costume from extinction. He already had a *charro* outfit, the approved cavalier rig of the country gentleman; but he had decided that that was snobbery. Every friendly foreigner in Chapala, he was convinced, should at once order pleated shirts, flowing calzones, huaraches, should buy red sashes and the widest sombreros and then in a body join the next serenata and invite arrest. Here was a humble version of the Indian resurrection which was stirring on grand scale in a novelist's fancy; and at first Lawrence warmed to the plan. While the rest of us put in our orders with the seamstress, he designed a serape which Antonio Gutierrez should weave for him at Jocotepec. I do not think he followed us any further than that, even though we interested Sr. Luis Murillo, a sympathetic local official, and through him his brother Sr. Farías, curator of the Museum in Guadalajara, and through Sr. Farías, finally, the Governor of Jalisco himself. By the time our attire was ready, Governor Zuno had given us a signed letter rescinding the order of our local Presidente. This letter we tacked on the board in the jardin alongside the chalked interdict; and on the night of the serenata, when we headed the male line in the concentric circle—some eight or ten foreigners with serapes and big hats, the black chin ribbons hanging behind like Chinese queues—we were followed by a solid, swollen file of delighted natives, all in calzones. The band played well that night. Lawrence walked beside Frieda in the women's line and nodded with a smile when we met, and she would stop and pin little nosegays on us or break a confetti-filled eggshell over our heads. As long as we stayed in Chapala, the Governor's order held good; but after we left, an American influence stronger than ours prevailed. The white calzones we had worn were like long drawers! The Presidente's ban was restored.

Dibrell's belief in the Indians, their liking for him and his handsome, easy leadership among them, had, I am certain, much to do with Lawrence's concept of Don Ramon in *The Plumed Serpent*. If only the novelist might have appreciated Dibrell's laughing side, as Spud and I did, Ramon would have been a more human figure.

I think that in 1923 Chapala already had its cinema, a large open-air court with rough wooden benches fore and aft and around the sides. The village did offer certain other amusements, in the patio of a sizable hotel on a back street. One wing of the hotel was reserved for women of occasional virtue, the others for families of modest and tolerant circumstance. Frieda liked especially the deftly run one-man puppet shows which would come there; and one night the four of us went with Dibrell to see a traveling vaudeville troupe perform in the courtyard. There were dancers, singers, comedians; but the star of the lot was a buxom, luscious, widowed contralto. Though in the show she was well spangled, on the street she wore mourning. The performance ran for a week; and Dibrell, who had soon made her acquaintance, introduced her to the Lawrences and ourselves. Her sparkle was contagious, her smile a delight, her elegances an opera. We saw her several times. Then toward the end of the week I received at the Arzapalo an envelope with deep black edge, containing her signed photograph and a flowery acceptance of my hand in marriage. Dibrell, charged with the prank, confessed it. In my reply to the lady, I enclosed a photograph, affectionately signed. The name was my name; but the photograph was of Dibrell. Proper extrication from the tangle I left to him; and the lady, before she departed, gave deep sighs, one in his direction, one in mine, then broke into gurgles of warm laughter. Such monkeyshines would not, of course, have done for Don Ramon in *The Plumed Serpent*. But if only that hero's earnestness might have been leavened with fun, as Dibrell's was, if only Kate, the heroine might have laughed, even once, as the contralto laughed—or as Frieda laughed!

22. Mr. Winfield Scott

T HE night of our supper with the Scotts, Dibrell with a Mexican
group was near us on the terrace; and Lorenzo's ears had been
leaning toward their Spanish until the little manager's English
began telling a gruesome local tale. Lawrence's chair was soon shifted
back close at our table and his beard pointed toward the speaker.

"Tell him about it, Mr. Scott," I said.

Only the previous year there had been bandits in the hills above
San Antonio, four miles away. The Presidente himself, Chapala's
Mayor, had been caught by them a mile from town but had promptly
summoned ransom money from his family. Though visitors in Chapala
were warned at the time not to stray beyond the village limits, an
American woman who was at the Arzapalo with her six-year-old son
scoffed and took the boy with her on a ride about the same distance
out. She was a Westerner, an experienced horsewoman, and had the
little fellow perched between her and the pommel. Then, alone and
frantic, she spurred back to the hotel. They had stolen the boy from
her very arms. Police and townsfolk shook their heads. The police were
not strong enough to attempt a rescue. She would be sent a demand
for money and she had better pay it. Next morning came the note in
crude Spanish, demanding ten thousand pesos within three days. She
took the train to Guadalajara, where the American consul advised
payment. But no, she would see the Governor. That meant another
day's delay and then, through postponement, another day.

"He was a Vasconcelos!" yapped Lawrence. The room looked toward
us. But Scott, undisturbed, resumed his narrative. The Governor had
promised soldiers. The mother returned to Chapala and waited. No
soldiers came from Guadalajara. On the fourth day came instead, from
the other direction, an envelope containing only her son's ear. A second

wild rush to the city resulted in successful borrowing. The money was placed under a bridge as directed, and a few hours later a sobbing child, with his other ear still intact, was found on the bridge and brought back to his mother.

Lawrence sat rigid. Mr. Scott, who was to figure slightly in *The Plumed Serpent* as Mr. Bell, now interested him. Frieda, who had children, was unhappy. Much though I disliked her being hurt, malice still pricked at me and I asked Scott for the story he had told me one night about the Hotel Ribera at El Fuerte. I enjoyed having Lawrence frightened, the man who enjoyed trying to frighten others.

"I was in it," complied Scott, "in what happened at the Ribera."

"What happened there?" breathed Lawrence.

But at that moment, late though it was, Ysidoro came up from the walk to the terrace and asked if I wished a shine. I often let him polish my huaraches while at table. It was as much a custom on the terrace as in a barbershop. Usually he came at breakfast but had missed us this morning, and I had just placed my foot on his shinebox when Lawrence turned and bade him go away. "They shouldn't be allowed up here," he complained to Scott. "The smell of the stuff turns my stomach. It's bad enough having them follow one all over the rest of town. This terrace should be private. Please tell him, Mr. Scott, that you forbid him or any of them pursuing your guests here. Please make it an order. Keep them off the terrace and I am sure that your other guests will be as grateful as I."

Mr. Scott, always obliging, mildly asked Ysidoro not to come soliciting shines at the tables. "And the others, all of them," insisted Lawrence. Scott gave the order. The boy, looking as surprised as though he had been told not to breathe, went away.

"The Ribera?" continued Lawrence, "isn't that the hotel where I stayed, at the far end of the lake, beyond Ocotlan, when I came from Mexico City?"

"Yes," Mr. Scott resumed, "near La Palma. It was built there by a German, and it was different from any of the other hotels around here. It was all made of logs, like buildings I have seen pictures of in Switzerland."

"A chalet," Lawrence urged, impatient.

"Yes, a chalet," assented Mr. Scott, unhurried. "And a few years ago it was popular. Duck hunters stayed there and other people, too. I had met the German when I was running a hotel in Ocotlan and, after he bought the point and a big stretch of land behind it and put up the hotel, he asked me, in 1919, to be his manager. It looked like a good thing and I accepted, though I didn't care much for the German. I soon found out that the natives didn't like him either."

"Whom do they like?" quacked Lawrence.

"You'll hear," said I.

Scott went on at his slow tempo, "For years and years, when the property belonged to Mexicans, the poor people around had been allowed to gather fallen wood on the hills. They had been allowed to as long as anyone could remember and they had never cut trees, they had just kept the land cleaned of dead wood. But this fellow was a regular overbearing Prussian. It wasn't the wood so much; it was just that he didn't want the peons on his place."

"I can understand that," defended Lawrence, sensitive for Frieda, because the man was of her race.

The story continued. "One day when he was riding in the woods with his son, he came across a Mexican with an armful of wood. Well, sir, he pulled out his pistol, ordered him down to the hotel, and when they arrived got out a whip and lashed the fellow within an inch of his life, and it was an old man."

"An old man!" I echoed.

"Why didn't you stop him?" challenged Frieda.

"Some of the guests and I tried to. But he had the whip and the pistol. Then the poor thing crawled away on all fours. I felt so bad about it that I made up my mind to quit the job. But I never had a chance. That very night somebody forced my door and next thing I knew there was steel on my neck and I was yanked out of bed, pushed over to the office and made to open the safe and fork out the money. There were five men in the gang. They didn't say anything much but they kept me moving in my bare feet and underwear on through the lobby and out the door. It was after dawn and I saw another bunch of 'em outside. There must have been fifteen or twenty all told, all with guns, and in the middle of 'em the German and his wife and son. And I can tell you he didn't look so German right then."

"Is cruelty always German?" challenged Frieda.

"Well, Prussian," granted Mr. Scott, going on. "As soon as we were up with 'em, I was shoved into the middle and we were all prodded along across the road, into the woods and then up to the top of the hill, where they stood the four of us side by side in a line. The German was saying something, offering them money, I think, but I couldn't listen, what with my own mind working fast and my heart making a racket. I don't know whether it was my mind working or what it was, but I do know that when I heard a shot and then another and another and saw three bodies tumble and my own turn next, I lit out like kingdom come down that slope, cactus or no cactus, with the shots flying after me. I slid round the hotel. I made a streak for the lake and got under the pier, with the water all bloody from my feet. They didn't follow me. I'll never know why. Perhaps someone told 'em I didn't have anything to do with the whipping. Anyway, after a spell of waiting and listening, I got back to the hotel. There were around ten guests. They'd all been robbed and then locked in their rooms. I let 'em out and in somebody's car we went to Ocotlan, where we told the police. I never heard that anything more happened about it. I guess the police knew what kind of a cuss the German was and didn't mind his getting his come-uppance."

"All Germans aren't like that," boomed Frieda, from a swelling bosom, her pride topping other emotions. "I'm German."

"But that was one German got what was coming to him, don't you think?"

"*Ja?*" she hesitated. "And now do the Indians here hate all Germans?"

"They hate all foreigners," I said for her relief and for general annoyance.

"How long ago did this happen?" asked Lorenzo.

"1919."

Lawrence, nibbling his lower lip, shifted in his chair, looked away from Mr. Scott and then back to him. "Where," he asked uneasily and clearing his throat, "where have the San Antonio bandits gone? The ones that were near here?"

"Oh, they're still around," said Scott with a nonchalant shrug, odd in one who had been as close as he had been to Mexican violence. "The richest man in Ajijic has been waylaid twice this year but he always takes guards with him who are good shots."

We walked home with the Lawrences.

"It made my flesh creep," said Frieda. "*Ach,* that ear!"

"He wasn't exaggerating," stressed Lawrence. "It wasn't just a

Yankee yarn. I thought at first it might be. But Scott wouldn't have wits enough to tell anything that didn't happen." And when we reached the house he remembered something in Terry and found it and read it to us, accenting its verbiage: " 'Albeit the days of brigandage are past, the timid traveller finds it easy to recall the times when *bandidos* haunted this same highway'—our highway, Frieda, the one from Atequisa"—and he found the place again in Terry, " 'stripped unfortunate travellers of every stitch of clothing and usually sent them into Chapala clad in rustling newspapers pinned together with mimosa thorns.' "

I wonder now, having read the "Nightmare" chapter in *Kangaroo,* if Lawrence was visioning himself ignominiously stripped again, as he had been by examiners for the British army and fearing physical exposure more than other violence.

"A pretty picture *I'd* be!" laughed plump Frieda.

"Don't laugh!" snapped her husband. "Terry's as wrong as he always is. It could happen any minute. That's the reason for these tight-shuttered windows and watchmen sleeping inside all the doors."

Watchmen did sleep on their *petates* inside hotel doors, yes, to let in late guests. We had had to rouse the doorman at the Arzapalo several times to admit us after night sessions with Dibrell over *canelas,* a strong native potion of tequila or straight alcohol, hot water, and cinnamon sticks, a glowing drink.

This night we went to our favorite cantina, played dice for canelas till ten and then banged for a full minute on the great side door of the Arzapalo, with the carved wooden lion in the half moon over it. We finally heard a growl and were admitted by a sleepy but most amiable Rumaldo.

"Did Scott know he was scaring Lawrence?" I asked of Spud upstairs.

"I don't think so," said Spud with a yawn. "After all, it all happened three years ago."

"But it scared him," I gloated, quietly.

From our beds, we heard some shots in the distance. A burro, under the moon, let out his down-scaling love bray. And I who should have been immune, having heard the El Fuerte story twice now, waked later from a dream of running barefoot over cactus and never coming anywhere.

In *The Plumed Serpent* we were to read: "Last year the peons had murdered the manager of one of the estates across the lake. They had stripped him and left him naked on his back, with his sexual organs cut off and put into his mouth, his nose slit and pinned back, the two halves, to his cheeks, with long cactus spines."

23. The Orphans

B Y this time we had discovered that half of our young friends on the beach were known as *"los huérfanos."* Some of the group were actual orphans; some were sons of widows too poor to provide for them; some were sons of drunken widowers; and some were just jolly sons of the world who enjoyed taking care of themselves. Together they had organized a loose alliance and pooled their resources to rent a disused and partially caved-in convent in the heart of the village, with enough roofing left so that each boy had his own cell. It was a sort of club and they were proud of it and of their ability to maintain it. They shared expenses in a gaily communistic way, took turns at repairing, water-carrying, and other co-operative duties and apparently could just about meet the day's needs from their meager earnings. Their clothes were few and ragged, in case of illness they were doctored by the Lord; but their spirits were abundant and sound, and the more Johnson and I saw of them the better we liked them. No wonder they tried to penetrate anywhere with their packets of postcards, their trays of sweets, their shoeshine boxes; and I was glad to see Mr. Scott ignore their gradual disregard of his order that they stay clear of the terrace. Lawrence, the only one who appeared to have strong objection to their presence, was seldom there. Spud and I did concede transfer of shoeshining to the plaza benches or the beach or our rooms.

Ysidoro, then sixteen, had come to regard himself as our special room attendant, being adept not only at shoeshining but at filling missions for us with tailor, seamstress, grocer, post office, or bar. In fact we had soon set up a small bar of our own in our front room at the hotel and taught him various skills for mixing drinks. Tequila [with lemon, orange, or grapefruit and mineral water] was the staple ingredient. And the sweet Martinis he made of poor gin and good vermouth we dubbed *"chatos,"* Snub Nose. Some of our concoctions became popular in the Sanchez pavilion. And we could always fall back, for quick stimulus, on tequila *con limon* and enjoy the ritual of a lick of salt from the back of the hand, a small toss of the tequila, and then a bite into the juice of a lime. One other and very special way of drinking tequila was to follow a straight swig of it with a cardinal-red liquid called *sangre,* blood, a secret preparation made by Sra. Sanchez. It appeared to be orange juice, tomato juice, grenadine, and chile; but only she could so blend whatever the portions were as to give exactly the right suavity and bite to the chaser. Ysidoro, trying his hand at it, failed and was vexed. However, when I told him that it was his first failure at anything, he gave the Mexican smile, which illumines eyes and teeth as though a flashlight were on them and then suddenly not on them.

The Lawrences came to our rooms one noon just before Spud and I were off for a two- or three-day stay in Guadalajara. Ysidoro dared in their honor a special new invention which he had not even tested on us. It was pineapple juice and gin and white of egg, most palatable. Frieda, licking her lips over several fills of it, became radiantly groggy; and I saw Lorenzo, trying to be surreptitious, slip our bootblack bar boy a *tostón,* half a peso—a high tip for those days.

Ysidoro and one of the others carried our bags to the station this day and a dozen of them saw us off. We were to stay at the Purnells and the doctor was to fill some teeth for me. On the third day we returned, as I had said we would; but there was no contingent at the station, none of our familiars, not even Ysidoro.

Reaching Mr. Scott, I mentioned their absence.

"No wonder," he said. "Mr. Lawrence had them all arrested."

"What do you mean?"

"He brought Mrs. Lawrence here for *comida,* and six or eight of the kids were on the terrace, some of them with their shoe kits. I ought to have noticed, but I'd forgotten, and the first thing I knew Gorras was shining a shoe at the next table and Mr. Lawrence had hopped up like a jumping jack and left. Mrs. Lawrence gave me a smile and shrugged her shoulders, as much as to say, 'Well, he's gone, you can't do anything about it now, you might as well let the boys stay, I don't mind them.' So I did nothing. But in two minutes Mr. Lawrence was back with a soldier and came up and said, 'You gave orders, Mr. Scott, that these boys were to stay off the terrace?' I had to agree and he went on, 'But they won't obey your orders and they need to be taught a lesson. The only way you can teach them is to punish them, so will you please make the proper complaint to this officer?' He browbeat me into it and then he browbeat even the cop and said, 'You'd better take the rest in, the whole lot of them that live together, one's as bad as another, they've all disobeyed you, Mr. Scott, and they all need the discipline. They're a public nuisance.' I didn't think the police would give them anything," Mr. Scott continued, "more than a talking to; but Mr. Lawrence went along, helped round up the rest of the kids, and he himself signed a complaint at the Presidencia. They can't pay their fines, so they've been there two nights. Mr. Lawrence has a way with him when his mind's made up. He was like a Mexican general. And then he came back and grabbed his wife away from the table, though she'd only had her fish, and began letting loose on her. I could still hear him squalling at her as far off as the church. . . ."

This time my irritation became contagious. Spud was irritated, roused out of his usual mute acceptance of whatever might happen. Those urchins stoutheartedly struggling for the day's sustenance and now facing fines because of a bad-tempered mean-spirited Britisher! "He wouldn't have done it if we'd been here," muttered Spud. "But he couldn't wait till we were out of sight," I barked, "to vent his spleen on a lot of children. And it wasn't really spleen against them, it was spleen against us or against me anyway for having a good time with them and for giving Frieda a good time. He doesn't want anyone to have a good time, that's what his damn theories amount to. He wants suspicion and spite, meanness and rage, he wants to indulge his contemptible ill nature and call it living according to the blood stream or any crazy folderol which will let him have his own way. And it's a way that isn't worth having. It's denial of all happiness, all comradeship, all decency, all positive living, all humanness. He'd better stay with the beasts he belongs with. But even they're too good for him. He's a death worm."

The explosion seemed to do me good, though I had a momentary intuition that his influence was becoming too strong for me, that, if I did not take care, I might become like him and enjoy on my own account animal outbursts. I could feel the thought of him lift my lip in a snarl against my teeth. I could not arrest swell after swell in me of physical dislike for him, and I did not want to. If Spud had tried to stem my tide, he would only have swollen it. Luckily he turned it, instead, by suggesting that we go to the Presidencia and see what could be done for the jailed orphans.

The front of the two-story Presidencia was all offices for town officials and judges and clerks, a courtyard behind it and behind that the jail, a large iron-grated enclosure with earthen floor, no sleeping mats, no conveniences. Inside it, together with village drunks and other offenders, huddled our friends.

They came cramming against the bars when they saw us, and a great chatter went up, only a bit of which we understood. However, we did manage enough Spanish to find that, by paying their fines, we could release them; and the transaction was effected.

In the midst of it there had entered from the street a town character, La Francesa, a short, sweet-faced, white-haired Frenchwoman in her middle fifties, who had a candy stand near the beach and who, with just enough private means for livelihood, devoted all profits of her trade to buying food for prisoners in the jail. She had tortillas for them now, with meat and beans and chile. Save for her, our friends would have gone unfed through their durance. She had witnessed the arrest, followed them to the jail, and vainly pleaded with Lawrence and the Presidente.

"Your friend is a very strange man," she said to me the day after.' "He must be very unhappy. I am sorry for him."

"So are we," I nodded, doing my troubled best to absorb some of her goodness. But that night, when I set down notes by candlelight, my goodness had evaporated. I found resentment returning in hot waves and, yes, a palatable though slightly sickening savor in the stir of goose flesh. "I am becoming like him," I said to myself. "I must stop it."

I did stop it, to the extent of self-repression in his presence. We had no open argument or conflict. Frieda privately deplored his jailing of the orphans; but with Lawrence we left the event untouched. Nor did I divulge it in writing others, as I wish now I had done when it was fresh. I have, however, in letters to myself, so to speak, a record of its drastic effect on me. Probably at the time, even in the heat of the happening, I felt it a story too ignoble to tell. Perhaps unconsciously, against my will, I was protecting Lawrence.

I did realize now a deep-seated jealousy in Lawrence's nature which he would have been the last to acknowledge but which he could not unseat. He cared nothing about the orphans but it was insupportable that they should be shying away from him and be liking Spud and me. And they liked Frieda.

Entering the plaza a few days later, I saw him on an iron bench letting Ysidoro shine his shoes, the Ysidoro who had offended his nostrils and been jailed for it. I turned back before they noticed me.

24. Notes and Letters

HERE are the "letters to myself," notes set in my diary soon after the episode of the orphans and written when a shocked distrust of Lawrence was tiding back into me and increasing my distaste for the book of his I was reading, *Women in Love*.

"D. H. Lawrence pushes everything away from nothing. He vituperates any religion but his own—which is himself in a vacuum. He values the British Empire because he is himself its peak. He thanks Heaven that he is an Englishman—but there are no others. Finally he turns upon even his own stupid master, Freud. He damns idealists but madly idealizes himself. He is a true Englishman in that his wife is his cattle. He sees free love come into vogue; so he grimly, somewhat primly, idealizes monogamy again. He makes the importance of life consist in attenuated flurries of the nerves. A fastidious cannibal, he blames the flesh of other men instead of his own ulcerated tooth.

"He is a man with nothing whatever at his core—except the worm that has consumed him. And from that fatal worm radiate odors that are sweet in the nostrils of jaded people. He is a writer keenly gifted in the vocabulary of hatred and rancor, which with a sinister ease he makes seem the language of psychology. His moments are little hymns of hate; and, in order to make his rancor the more incisive, he pretends to be radiating those moments from an enlarged and esoteric soul. His soul was long since eaten by the worm of envy and malice. In its place are spleen and black bile. And he is alert forever to find in people signs of decency and of happiness that he may twist those signs into malevolence and futility. With the tongue of a singing serpent, he searches for Edens. And in all the lost gardens he finds on the way, he adds to the damage already done. Essentially evil and essentially false, he is inordinately clever. Hence his appeal to this casual generation. He is a new, fantastic Satan, offering all the mystic kingdoms of Los Angeles to a tired Christ. It is time for a new Satan to destroy magnificently with a sweep of noble despair. But this is surely the smallest potato that ever wore horns. See him, garnished with parsley, on the tables of the *bourgeoisie!* The potato that thinks itself an egg. The egg that thinks itself an eagle. The eagle that thinks itself an Egyptian soul."

"This is literature in which moods become motives, indigestion becomes indignation, heartburn become hatred and constipation becomes tragedy! His people need not analysis but pills. If he might know some well people, really and openly know them, not just meeting and ticketing them according to ill images of himself, his novels would behave better, and the earth—though not perhaps the critics—would be kinder to him. It is a sad commentary on the generation that he has not been laughed out of countenance for so wryly sentimentalizing minor and momentary moods. He makes mountains out of six-year molars. He makes three torrid summers out of a louse under the wing of one swallow."

"Of course we all have many half-conscious irritations and vanities compounded with our clearer, better impulses. Of course there are reactions as well as actions. But the sentimental exaggeration of impatience into a hate motive, of self-importance into a power motive, belongs with the outworn literature in which every gesture or sigh or quickening step or loss of appetite meant love. A plague upon both their houses! Between them they can kill off sound emotion, not only honest love but honest hate.

"He is his own Peter and his own Judas. He has denied himself thrice. He has sold himself for thirty pieces of silver, and he kisses his own lips with treachery. Henceforth he acidly observes other people —ashamed of watching himself.

"Old Dr. Earth-Worm!"

My resentment of the death motive I felt in Lawrence, as though a living corpse shook his finger at me alongside, bidding me join or leave him, has been abetted since by what Knud Merrild has written, in *A Poet and Two Painters,* concerning the Lawrence of about the same period: "All this devastation, destruction, and death—death—he breathed death, spake, and saw death everywhere, and only darkness, the darkness of death. And when he spoke of new creations, his creations, his gods, his souls, his ideas, they were always shrouded in darkness not yet visible."

Perhaps Merrild had read, as I had, a passage in *Women in Love* and pointed it at Lawrence himself, the passage in which Ursula says to Birkin: " 'What you are is a foul, deathly thing, obscene, that's what you are, obscene and perverse. You and love! You may well say, you don't want love. No, you want *yourself,* and dirt, and death—that's what you want. You are so *perverse,* so death-eating.' " Out of his own mouth it had come—and he must have known he meant himself. I would charge him with it flat, on rare Chapala occasions, and he would give me a flat glare, like stone, and then wince, like water, and say, "But you don't understand me, Bynner."

From Jalisco at this time, I wrote letters to others besides myself; one to Alice Corbin Henderson, May 4, 1923: "Lawrence, for the most part, is a bad little boy who probably needs to sit for an hour a day in ice-cold water. I really believe that some sort of medical treatment might make him the artist he promised to be in *Sons and Lovers. Aaron's Rod* and *Women in Love,* as far as I've read the latter, seem to me not far removed from the work of Bertha M. Clay—the sort of thing the English lower middle class has always delighted in but which he has now made pretentious with a smear of pseudo science and made semioccasionally rewarding with a paragraph of masterly observation. He is utterly without imagination, humor, or warmth—the qualities of any first-rate creator. The man ought to have been a naturalist. He might then have done less for the titillation of nervous women, but more for the world and his own happiness. Personally he continues very amiable to Spud and me. My fatigue with him results from his unfailing and unfeeling contempt for all things mortal save himself. Secretly I am convinced that it is himself that he despises and makes mankind vicariously suffer for. In Mexico City when for the eleventh time he wavered in his hot resolve to sail to England and for the eleventh time discovered that he hated England also, he set out alone to reconnoiter along Lake Chapala before removing from the capital Frieda and his other luggage. As Frieda prophesied, 'When he finds a place by himself, he always likes it.' His psychology is simple. He telegraphed his pleasure. Spud and I brought Frieda along to Guadalajara, and then we suddenly swerved off from the Lawrences to be in touch again for a little while with humanity. Mind you, I like Frieda better than ever. A solid, hearty, wise, and delightful woman. The few days we had alone with her in Mexico City were a solace. Her love for Lawrence, probably her worst fault, is genuine and forgivable."

And there were several letters to others, written from Jalisco at this time, one to Haniel Long from Guadalajara, May 9, 1923, shortly after our arrival from Mexico City:

"I'm halfway through *Women in Love,* detesting it and yet granting something of what you say about it. Mrs. is a German brick with plenty of straw to stand the rough usage. The man is much more concerned with hate than with love; but I'm enjoying him at intervals. Really, though, his work seems to me unimportant—till it touches animals. He should have been a naturalist. Hatred can be a worse form of sentimentality than ever love can be. That's what this little generation doesn't see."

Another letter went to Long from Chapala, not dated but obviously somewhat later, when I was recovering from wrath: "My relationships here—with Lawrence and his wife—are much more comfortable than they were. I heartily like Frieda and always shall. Lawrence and I are in pretty thorough disaccord in our views of life, nor are we physically congenial enough to create the real ease which sometimes exists between people with opposite convictions. Without impudence, I am certain that I am more securely grounded in my beliefs than he is in his. Loss of temper, to which he is a chronic victim, is almost always a sign of interior uncertainty, is an attempt to attain equilibrium with wild gestures. Lawrence is a selfish egoist and he assembles all sorts of vehement theories to dispose of his own inner misgivings. On the other hand, he has a flexible mind, is a mass of inconsistencies and, in spite of a mature verbal skill, is probably at a very early stage of his development. He seems to me to have found in life almost nothing that is worth finding and almost everything that is of no value. This may of course be the best possible foundation for a later structure. He is only thirty-six. His profundities are marvelously young."

So were mine, I now realize, though I was four years his senior; and I am amused to find jotted alongside the Lawrence notes in my diary a quotation from Hugo Münsterberg: "The story of the subconscious mind can be told in three words. There is none." I must have smacked my lips when I entered that item. And when I answered a note from Richard Le Gallienne, I must have been not only still smart-ing but feeling smart. Alongside his sentence, "You say that solitude is what you needed and yet you went to Mexico with D. H. Lawrence!" I find penciled in the margin, doubtless to use in an answer: "Could there be a greater solitude?"

Though my resentments were unaired with Lawrence himself, or with Frieda, they were aired with Johnson and with Idella Purnell, as well as in verses about him, not then revealed to him. Idella acted openly. She writes me: "After much brooding over Lawrence and his malevolence (as seen through your eyes), I wrote a rather long poem about him, in which he was called 'the white white slayer with red red beard,' and so on. And then, motivated by who knows what impulse, I showed it to him. He liked it and spent hours of one sunny Chapala morning working over it, polishing it, revising it."

Here are two stanzas which Lawrence excised from the Purnell original:

> The fangs of glories he was denied
> Stung like serpents to torture his side.
> He lifted the great sword he was heir to,
> Piercing mountains, cleaving them through.
> He hurled lightning, proclaimed thunder,
> To smite the world and cast it asunder.
> He edged his thunder with obscene red
> And hurtled it forth that the quick might be dead.
>
> And the mountains that were beautiful
> Like slow slugs snake their way
> Over the unrelenting plains
> Into a savage day;
> And the cocks, the donkeys and one white mule,
> Under the black rain
> Of his sinister magic, shrink with pain
> At the mouthings of a fool.

And here is the second and best of several adaptations he made of other stanzas which were retained:

> In that light wood
> By the length of the beautiful lake,

Under the tavachin trees,
With red beard to his knees,
A prophet stood.

He lifted his voice to make mountains break,
He lifted his voice and spake
The word for the earth to quake.

And the red of the tavachin trees
Was no redder than his beard
Against the breeze.

He was one torn and speared
By demonish ecstasies
And given to naming them.

He broke the sacred bud from its stem
By the soft and holy lake
And spoke for the earth to quake.

There is marked likeness between these lines and his Quetzalcoatl chants in *The Plumed Serpent;* and his attention to Idella's theme confirms abundant evidence in the novel that he enjoyed identifying himself with Don Ramon's role of prophet.

It is amusing now to realize that, in writing her poems about Lawrence, Idella had been more or less under the influence of my opinion of him and then had let it be revised by his opinion of himself.

Her letter tells other reactions: "I remember that whenever you were splashing in the lake with fifteen or twenty bootblacks, having a marvelous time, Lawrence on shore would rail against your indiscriminate friendliness; he would say that since you loved everybody, your love had no meaning at all. This used to make me furious; although I was actually half way between his philosophy and yours, his attacks on yours always seemed to me attacks on your *The New World* and the whole principle of democracy, even of Christianity. I was fascinated by him; and he was no doubt exceedingly amused by me. I was also alarmed by him, for I had been surrounded largely by people who tried to be courteous, and he was quite lacking in most of what I regarded as necessary amenities. But after the outburst at the tea party, he was never again offensive: I always felt that he might be teetering on the brink of explosion. And you, with your poems about Lawrence and your hatred of much of what he stood for, influenced me to a point of considering him a wicked man, an anti-Christ. Now, in the perspective which the reading of a few of his books and the long years have given me, my feelings have reversed: I think of you—well, not as wicked, but as pagan, and Lawrence I think was a Puritan out of his time. He would have fitted beautifully into the New England of witches . . . and would have hustled them to ducking-stool and fire."

Here I disagree with her.

He would only have given them a piece of his mind for punishment, as he was constantly giving pieces of it to Frieda.

Convinced in Chapala that his emotion toward Frieda was less love than jealous possessiveness or the bossiness of a thwarted cave man, I was the more readily estranged by his impatience with some love poems of my own in particular and with the love doctrine of the Christian world in general. At times I suspected that he would talk just for the sake of talking or shocking; at other times I felt that he believed what he said when he said it, that by the very saying of it he would persuade himself. At least he was not like Montaigne who confessed, "I speak truth, not so much as I would, but as much as I dare; and I dare a little more as I grow older." Lawrence always dared to speak whatever he thought truth, but it seemed to me too often an imposed or transient truth—a truth felt irresponsibly under stress or impatience, rather than truth considered, orderly truth related from moment to month, from month to year, or to another individual however different from himself. His autocratic tenet, "I am the truth," could not lead to amiable connections; and I at the time was regarding the two words on the title page of E. M. Forster's *Howards End* as a supreme commandment: "Only connect." I admit now that I might myself have made better efforts to connect, instead of enjoying my self-righteous condemnation of Lawrence's frenzies and arrogances as those of a lost evil spirit and assuring myself that his chronic dissatisfaction with the world was due to his fatal resolve that he would not love people. No wonder I kept thinking that he distrusted and feared the Mexican natives! How could there be understanding between a Mexican too happy to be busy and an Englishman too busy to be happy! His abuse of the bootblacks stemmed partly, I continued to believe, from a jealous resentment of the fact that Johnson and I did like the natives and that they liked us. Or he might possibly have feared lest people misinterpret this friendliness. Again, as about Frieda's changing clothes in our rooms, "What will people say?"

Oh, yes, I was smug enough and must have been as hard for him to bear as he was for me. On the other hand I think we partly envied each other, he my attachments, I his detachment.

In his *Plumed Serpent* and in several of my poems records remain that each of us was more or less secretly accusing the other's mind of being not "a native feather" but "a nest of worms." Our awareness of the unvoiced challenge was probably a good spur for both; but at times it was uncomfortable.

One of my poems, "Loosen Your Marrow," written at this period, was, I can now see, an expression quite in sympathy with his own constant advice to dismiss the brain and the will in favor of the blood's native impulses, and yet I thought I was aiming it at him:

> That little tangled thing you call your brain,
> Which has not lived before nor will again
> In any such compartment of distress,
> Is an abominable restlessness.

> Loosen your marrow from corrupting thought
> And be as inattentive as you ought
> To all the little motions of the will
> Which feed upon the happiness they kill.

> Open your being to the flows of air
> Which form its destiny from everywhere
> And let your mind become a native feather
> And not a nest of worms, tangled together.

Because of what I thought Lawrence's literary stress on sexual fervors disconnected with aught else—revolting against themselves yet, apparently by his doctrine, remaining the ultimate and total values of life—I wrote at this time "A Wayside Tree":

> Lust is a lovely thing if taken
> As fruit from a wayside tree;
> But why should an apple-bough be shaken
> Too much? Let it be.

> Bring your quick blood to bear
> On greater ways, why not,

Than on this greedy care
To catch and be caught?

The time would soon enough come round
Through less than you have done,
With no more apples on the tree or ground
And even the leaves gone.

I did not show him any of these lines at the time. We might have connected better if I had. But I did show him some others, written about the kindly Frenchwoman in Chapala, because I thought he would like them, which he did. We never told him that she fed the orphans when he jailed them. Perhaps, in the last line of "La Francesa," I thought, he saw something of himself:

Selling her candies at a corner-booth
To spend the profit on prisoners in jail,
The little old Frenchwoman would watch the beach
From under the white halo of her hair.
She told me once, "I have three ages, different:
My hair, they are white, they are one hundred years;
My body, it is fifty-six; but my heart
Only fifteen because never have I loved."

"Sometimes I think he's crazy," said Frieda, "and so does he." And he would subscribe with a pleased grin, "Yes, so do I." Then I would try to take it all seriously and argue that if there were enough insane, the sane would be locked up, that the authority of the sane derives only from their numbers. I wanted to be a bit odd too. But I did wonder why we could not both content ourselves with unquestioning or unprobing or undemanding enjoyment in the felicity of the natural earth. Apparently that enjoyment was not enough. We conjectured, with heat. My conviction that the joy, the blending, of bodily love was partial experience of the final integration of all the fragments of life, seemed to him as crooked-minded as his contracting of it into something purely animal and sufficient seemed to me. So we prowled around each other, faced each other, reluctantly, suspiciously respectful, and went on thinking, each in his own way: I still thinking that physical and spiritual joy could and should be joint, he still thinking that such thinking as mine was an abomination.

Little realizing that the goad of Lawrence's presence was good medicine for my complacence, I continued fondly pitying Frieda and deploring the lack of love in her husband, deeming him full of fine, fussy, inconsistent theories: stubborn-minded, self-willed, and as bloodless as a worm.

But there was always anodyne in Chapala—still the sculptured sunsets, the mountainous Indian laurel trees and a golden air alive with the voices and dartings and circlings of birds, visible bits of the wind, the aloe eyes of the women, the graceful repose of the men, the high-prowed junks with their full-moon sails, the fishermen casting their nets, the ducks and wild geese arrowing overhead, the honied voices singing, and the great, firm, natural presence of Frieda.

I find, in my diary of those days: "The mind clears at Chapala. Questions answer themselves. Tasks become easy."

I wonder now if they were so easy. At least Spud seemed at ease, with his fixed silences, his brooding eyes, his faithful attentions to all of us, and his occasional, sudden, apparently irrelevant chucklings, which sometimes Frieda would abet with an outright laugh, while her husband would look at her, irresolute. Should anyone laugh?—except at his prompting.

25. Agreements and Disagreements

T HE Lawrences' house being more comfortable than the hotel, we usually gathered there after supper. I realize now that Lawrence seldom talked about what he was writing, or even about what he had published. He was an egocentric in other ways, but not as a writing man. Although I was older than he in years, I was younger in writers' egocentricity. He would show us poems now and then; but I did not care so much about his poems as I did about mine and Johnson's.

In these poetry readings, I remember his mention of the Imagist group in London. He was amused by the callow pranks of Ezra Pound and was gently snobbish toward him, as an Englishman toward an American, I thought, because I had a slight pride in having arranged initial book publication of Pound in the States, his young volumes, *Personae* and *Exultations*. Lawrence was diverted by my first encounter with Pound, who coming to call on me in New York and bringing a great sheaf of manuscripts, floored me with his costume. Although the weather was autumnal, he wore a wide-brimmed straw hat of coarse shiny weave, the band on it white with large pink polka dots. Jacket, vest, and trousers were, in my remembrance, of three colors—mauve, snuff-colored, and purplish—and his socks bright-hued in shoes one black, one blue. He told me that he yearned to go to Europe and that his father, for some reason, wanted advice according to my judgment of the son's manuscripts. I think there was a note to the effect, "I'll help him if you say so." And I said so. Lawrence did not that evening enlarge, as we shall see he did later in the year to

144

Idella Purnell, upon his own first meeting with Pound. He said little beyond a shrug and beyond what he has written somewhere: "In the old London days, Pound wasn't so literary as he is now. He was more of a mountebank then. He practiced more than he preached, for he had no audience. He was always amusing." He did enlarge, with comment I am sorry to have forgotten, upon another Imagist, H. D., referring to her longer poems: "She is like a person walking a tightrope; you wonder if she'll get across." I recalled to him the fact that Amy Lowell had been the first person wishing to connect us. I do not remember his saying anything favorable about her or anything unfavorable; but I do remember him, with one of those shrugs and with a cat smile, deprecating her "ambitious insistence" that she include him in her Imagist anthology. His attitude was apparently amused consent. "Why not?" he asked, shrugging again, "though it was all nonsense."

I believe I have read somewhere about Miss Lowell's contributing fifty dollars to the Lawrences when they were in special poverty. To Lawrence this would not have seemed an unnatural gratuity. He was himself always ready to hand over a sizable part of his own small balance, when he had one, to almost any friend in need, with no thought of gratitude or even repayment. Yet I remember his own punctiliousness in repayment, his assuring us, for instance, as Frieda has lately reminded me, that he refunded to Mrs. Lujan what she had advanced for the Lawrences' expenses from San Francisco to Santa Fe and that he met rent for the Taos house. It belonged to Tony Lujan and was on Indian land. So he gladly paid. He was always only too willing to use and share his wherewithal. I remember also his statement, in his introduction to *Memoirs of the Foreign Legion,* after the suicide of its author, Maurice Magnus: "I could, by giving half my money, have saved his life. I had chosen not to save his life. . . . I respect him for dying when he was cornered." Norman Douglas has castigated the choice; but I do not think it was made from lack of generosity, either financial or spiritual, in spite of a lesser instance cited by Douglas when Lawrence dodged a luncheon debt and left "with the phantom of a smile creeping over his wan face." Lawrence's face closed that evening in Chapala, at mention of Douglas, with a slight frown which seemed to prefer not remembering. The two men had already disagreed concerning their more or less shadily distinguished friend, Magnus, though Lawrence's introduction had not yet appeared to the latter's book nor had the quarrel between the novelists yet broken into print. Frieda, however, contributed, smiling, "Norman Douglas took to me but could not bear Lawrence. He's a wicked one, that Douglas, but you'd like him."

Twenty-seven years later Robert Hunt and I spent several afternoons with Douglas on his island, where he is an honorary citizen, and found that we did like him. At eighty-two he was still a doughty one, both physically and mentally, the old visage stout and the old speech lusty. Twice he walked half the length of Capri to see us at Anacapri. He plied us with snuff from a little box he carried. Though, because of some illness, he was coy toward drink, he always took it. He had an occasionally absent look, which made me wonder if he had grown inward as aging people often do, if his ears quickly forgot what they heard, but I guess not. I told him of Frieda's remark, no news to him, that he could not bear Lawrence and the rest of it. "Neither could she," he chortled. "They used to beat each other to a jelly. She *is* somebody. She would say something; and, unexpectedly, especially to herself, it would be sound, even profound. She was plump at first; but afterward, the last time I saw her, in Florence, she was noble, seasoned, patrician. She was better than he. But I have forgotten my row with him. Those things pass. Through one edition, people wanted my pamphlet about him; through a second they wanted it; and then when a third was printed, they had forgotten. I have eleven copies left and shall give each of you one." He took another pinch of snuff and looked far away. "So Frieda told you that I am wicked? Oh, that Frieda," he said, twinkling, "*she* is the wicked one!" When we invited him to visit us in New Mexico, he chuckled, "Look out now!" Then, with a great hoot, "Once I come, I stay. It's easier to invite me than to dislodge me." His handsome ruddy face grew pensive. "I'm afraid that you needn't be alarmed. I shall never come to you now, I am too old—never shall cross the Atlantic." And then he made a remark which sounded exactly like Lawrence, "But Europe is dead."

Among the books in the mysteriously lost lot of the Lawrences' personal volumes offered for sale at Edinburgh in 1950 was, oddly enough, an "Association Copy," 1922, of *Aaron's Rod* with an inscription written by Norman Douglas to Pino Orioli, Lawrence's publisher in Florence: "For darling Pino from Uncle Norman, who bought this first edition at a street stall for one franc fifty centimes— a bloody stiff price, considering what trash it is. St. John's Day, 1932."

I asked the Lawrences, that year long back in Chapala, about Osbert

Sitwell with whom I had had a pleasant, brief correspondence. It had begun about a San Francisco waiter who had recited a long poem to me, wondered if I might happen to know its authorship, and been greatly pleased when I discovered for him later that it was by Sitwell. Frieda as well as Lorenzo was this time reticent, and had little or nothing to say about the Sitwell trio, beyond the fact of having met them. I wonder if aloofness on both sides had already existed some years before the Sitwells took umbrage at *Lady Chatterley's Lover*. Perhaps there is explanation in a vividly descriptive letter written by Sir Osbert's mother in Italy, and appearing in the fourth volume of his autobiography, *Laughter in the Next Room*: "A Mr. D. H. Lawrence came over the other day . . . a funny little *petit-maître* of a man with flat features and a beard. He says he is a writer and seems to know all of you. His wife is a large German. She went round the house with your father, and when he showed her anything, would look at him, lean against one of the gilded beds, and breathe heavily." The mother's remark about "flat features" reminds me that now and then, when he was not looking at me, Lawrence's face would give me the uncanny effect of a bird, a beast and a flower which had all been pressed together.

Johnson was at work in Chapala on his volume of poetry, *Horizontal Yellow,* and I on verse for my book, *Caravan*. We showed Lawrence, during our evenings, many manuscripts and benefited by his criticism. He was always attentive to our writings, generous and helpful; and he seemed to enjoy letting us see shorter pieces of both prose and verse with which he was now and then interrupting *The Plumed Serpent*. Rightly he preferred not to give or read us chapters of the novel. With a long piece of work, a writer is usually balked or confused if, before at least a first draft is finished, he admits to it other presence than his own. Verse, if mistakenly altered, can be restored easily; and Lawrence, showing us his verse, seemed as cordial to our comments as we were to his.

Among my *Caravan* poems were two verse portraits of him. The longer and sharper of them he did not see till two years later; but I did at the time show him the milder one, "Lorenzo":

> I had not known that there could be
> Men like Lorenzo and like me,
> Both in the world and both so right

That the world is dark and the world is light.
I had not thought that anyone
Would choose the dark for dwelling on,
Would dig and delve for the bitterest roots
Of sweetest and suavest fruits.
I never had presumed to doubt
That now and then the light went out;
But I had not known that there could be
Men like Lorenzo and like me,
Both in the world and both so right
That the world is dark and the world is light.
I had not guessed that joy could be
Selected for an enemy.

Frieda, when I read this, humped her eager head forward, ejaculating *"Ja!"* and intimating that a little more joy might be allowed in their life, distinct from the comfortable domesticity and the fiery love battles. *"Ja!"* she chimed again, "he is like that."

"Part of me is," he nodded, looking away as though joy were in the doorway, to be apprehensively appraised. "But you have seen only one side of the medal. I am not an enemy of life. Do you think I am, Spud?"

I let Spud say no, unchallenged, beginning myself to be unsure.

"I do not think I fight joy," he continued gravely, "but there's danger in going after it too hard. Joy can be a mirage."

Just then a downward turn of breeze flooded us with sweetness from a tree in their garden, called *huele de noche,* an attar comparable to that from the night-blooming cereus but more pervasive and overpowering. The little white feelers of the flower give out their scent only at night, but several times a year, and one is almost too drenched with it.

He also might become too overpowering, I thought; but if only he were oftener sweet, as he is now, I should not be afraid of his influencing me. His influential tempers had always rasped me into temper too. His deliberate Merlinism used a magnetic wand against which I was on guard. But I was becoming aware of a subtler influence which had not been staved off. Occasionally, in my writing, even in my speech, I found reflections and echoes of Lawrence's way of seeing and saying things. In notes made at the time, I have found two instances. Before Holy Week, Chapala like other Mexican towns, expects its householders to give their dwellings fresh coats of paint. The usual colors, partly because of their freshness but mostly because of choice, are hot and raw. "From the way they paint their houses," I said on a walk one day, hoping that Lawrence would like the way I said it, "you would think their national colors were not red, white, and green but blood, pus, and gangrene." It was a labored imitation; and even when I thought I was speaking like Lawrence, I could not ban my constitutional predilection for punning, which bored him. The other instance was a line of verse, in a poem I showed him about Mexican landscape. It described trees as being "hairy on a hill, topped by a phallic steeple." This was definitely a case of imitation—and very poor imitation. I think he recognized in both cases my attempts at the Lawrence manner and found them wanting, though the lake might for him still be "sperm" and mangoes be "bulls' organs."

Apart from these literary susceptibilities, I was still alert against Lawrence as a man, against what I thought, in almost his own terms about other men, was his hollow manhood. He had received life, it seemed to me, but not given it. He had not appreciated friendship because he was too damned important for it. Very well, he should have but little of mine. I should be immune to his Merlinism.

On one of our Chapala evenings he may have been feeling tequila and cassis, or he may have been feeling naturally savage, I now don't know. Frieda had told me of his rupture with Middleton Murry but not the reason. On this occasion I was a lone caller on Calle Zaragoza. Johnson had gone to bed early. With abruptness Lawrence pushed a letter toward me under the lamp. "Read that," he said.

At the other end of the table Frieda held a book in her hands but her head was slumped forward. "Is Frieda reading or sleeping?" I asked. "With Frieda it's the same thing. Read Murry's letter."

I did. It was highly overwrought—several closely written pages of adulation and of contrition concerning something he had done to alienate Lawrence. He begged at eloquent length for reconciliation. From quick reading of it years ago, I should say the letter, addressing Lawrence as Master, declared that, if only signal were given, the disciple would on his knees follow his master to the ends of the earth.

In *Son of Woman*, after Lawrence's death, Murry published a milder version of this dedicated sentiment. Oddly enough, it is in reference to *Fantasia of the Unconscious*, the very book which had soured my early liking for the Lawrence of *Sons and Lovers*. Writes Murry: "Here was something which I did verily believe with all my heart, and all my mind, and all my soul. What I had glimpsed in *Aaron's Rod,* I had now a full sight of. If this was what Lawrence believed and stood for, then I was his man: he should lead and I would follow."

I judge now that Murry's earlier published review of his friend's novel, *The Lost Girl,* must have been influenced by his wife, Katherine Mansfield, who felt an extreme and to me incomprehensible dislike of it. Murry publicly called it "sub-human," "mysteriously degraded," "slime," and said that he found in it "loss of creative vigour," "paralysis," and "decline"; and I can understand how Lawrence, caring little about ordinary reviewers but knowing the book good and expecting better from this particular reviewer and friend, was not now in a mood for the friend's penitent genuflections. But without this knowledge, as perhaps even with it if I had known, I felt the letter moving and worth sympathetic answer. I said so, whereat Lawrence turned on me like a knife. "Don't be a fool," he said. "I know Murry. He's a shit-head." Without blowing his nose on Murry's page, an occasional gesture of his when letters displeased him, he tore it into shreds. I said that I regretted his not saving it for calmer reading.

"Don't you be a shit-head too," he fanged at me. "Katherine Mansfield," he jumped to his feet, "was worth a thousand Murrys! But he drove her sick, neglected her, wandered away from her till she died, and then he prowled back like a hyena to make a meal of her! He'll do the same to me!" A year or two afterward, I received a letter from England in which he spoke of Murry with all friendliness again.

But in Chapala his angry voice had waked Frieda. Too sleepy to talk but wanting to rouse herself, she crossed to a chest of drawers and pulled out from under it a cardboard box tied with string.

"They won't interest him," said Lawrence.

"Yes, they will, *ja,*" she retorted, cutting the string with her sewing scissors.

"She's always boring the life out of people with her silly pile of pictures, like a child with paper dolls."

"No, I'm not."

"You never have the sense to know when people are bored."

"Yes, I do."

"You're not going to show those to Bynner."

"Yes, I am."

The box fell out of her round lap and photographs slid on the floor.

"That's where they belong. Leave them there."

"Hal will pick them up," she said defiantly.

"Always someone picking up for you! If you must show the silly things, hold on to them."

Gathering them off the floor and out of the box, I piled them on the table and drew my chair forward, while Lawrence sat aside and glanced at a copy of *El Informador*. Frieda, after her monosyllabic daze, began to waken, pounced on pictures at random and breathed little gurgles of interest over likenesses of her mother, her sisters, her cousins, one or two of the Hohenzollerns. Out came a portrait of a severe, pedantic-looking Englishman. "Do you wonder?" she asked, pointing to it and shaking her head. And then that rich, full voice broke, "But oh, my children! Look!"

I remember only two child pictures, a boy and a girl.

"Oh, Hal, I love my children and they don't write to me. Their father won't let them. . . . He wouldn't give me a divorce all that time. He wouldn't let me have love. And now he won't let me have my children. And I love my children." She took the photographs from me, stared into them, and clasped them to her breast.

Lawrence was out of his chair like a rattler. "You sniffling bitch!" The coil and the poise had taken a second. Then the venom struck. He snatched the pictures from Frieda, tore each one across the face twice, flung first one, then the other on the floor, treading on each in turn.

"That's better," he yelped, "much better. Now you can't be a fool over them any more."

The violence had been so swift that I was dazed, but I did manage to say, "You're being a he-bitch! Can't a woman love her children? She's no fool for that!"

Frieda stood panting, her wide eyes staring at him. Her hand went to her breast again, where the photographs had been and she stumbled blindly out of the room, closing the door behind her.

I made a move to pick up the pieces.

"Let them alone," he ordered and followed Frieda into the other room, where I could see her mounded form on the bed. Again the door was closed.

I heard a sob. And I heard his voice saying calmly, "It was better."

26. Japanese Comedy

"IT'S their business," counseled Spud, after I had told him, the
next morning.

Whenever they quarreled, Johnson would appear not to see
or hear and, if we were not at a meal or cornered together in the evening, would walk away from them. I remember, when they bickered
once in a rowboat, how Spud's quiet eyes looked toward the water
and remained looking as at a fixed fish.

"I wouldn't refer to it at all," he continued, "unless she does, and
I don't think she will. He won't."

"All right," I agreed. "We can talk about the Japanese book I lent
them, get going about that."

So that night we were at their house again and behaved as though
nothing unpleasant had happened.

Lawrence forestalled the planned topic by asking about Arthur
Davison Ficke, whose Anne Knish poems had amused him in *Spec-
tra*. I thought perhaps the two funniest stories I knew concerning the
Fickes might divert us.

One Sunday, in Davenport, Iowa, Arthur and his wife, Evelyn,
agreed that the time had come for divulgement to their eight-year-old
son, Stanhope, of the "facts of life" and that in the case of a son it was
the office of the father to make the revelation. The boy had been itching to join roller-skating playmates but was held a full hour for instruction in his father's study. When they emerged, the father was pale
but the boy unflurried except as he was still on edge to be outdoors.
"One moment, Stan," said his father, solemnly restraining him. "Before you go, I want you to be sure, and to say so to your mother, that
you understand what I have been telling you." "Yes, I understood it,"
granted Stanhope, "But I don't believe a word of it."

"Probably," commented Lawrence, "Ficke had tried to make it pretty, instead of telling the truth."

"It *can* be pretty, Lorenzo. But the story has a point," laughed Frieda, "a good finish. Most of my stories have no point, no finish."

Lawrence gurgled. He had been several times witness to my insistence, at the Kodak Shop in Guadalajara, that I wanted my prints with a dull finish. It was one of the very few times I ever heard him approach a pun. "Your stories don't shine, Frieda; they lack luster because they have a dull finish." She laughed. Whatever he had said to her after I left them the night before, she was herself again, she was comforted. She might not have the photographs, but she had Lawrence.

Years later I had begun telling the Stanhope story to Mrs. Roosevelt at the White House, when three elderly, pleasant, but rather severe-looking women entered the room, and I would gladly have desisted from the the anecdote but was persuaded by our hostess to begin it again for the newcomers who, as I foresaw they would be, were cold to it from start to finish. But Mrs. Roosevelt leaned toward them from her tea-pouring and assured them, with un-Lawrencian heartiness, "Obviously, a very pure child."

The other Davenport anecdote concerned an occasion when, early on a Saturday evening at a neighbor's house, Mrs. Ficke had invited some twelve friends there for Sunday lunch. Because we had subsequently stayed till four in the morning, her husband was gruff on the way home and told her that the suggestion should have been withdrawn. His Lawrence-like irritation with his wife, because he himself was irritated with the universe, lasted even to the Sunday lunch table where Mrs. Ficke was doing her best to enliven her heavy-lidded guests. Quite unlike herself, she told a salty, unladylike story she had picked up somewhere. When the maid had left the room, Ficke, ordinarily good-natured, administered a rebuke, "I disapprove, Evelyn, of your telling that story before the servants. And, besides, I don't think it was in the least funny." "But, Arthur," she replied demurely, "I don't always think your poetry funny."

"That was quick," said Lawrence. His eyes twinkled, then sobered. "But cruel, too. I am sorry for both of them."

I remember making caricatures of the Lawrences and Spud that evening, another diversion from what was on our minds.

Presently he picked up a book from the table. "Have you written your review of it?" he asked me.

"Not yet."

I had been sent, to review, *The Toils of Yoshimoto, a Tragedy of Ancient Japan,* by Torahiko Kori. Spud and I had read it, and we had handed it along to the Lawrences. Reading matter in English was scarce at Chapala.

"Lorenzo never reads a review of any of his books," Frieda crowed. "I bring them to him and he tosses them out."

"Why not?" he agreed. "I know what I intend better than they do. I know where I fail or where I succeed. And they only bore me by fumbling about for what they think I think."

"But isn't there a warmth in having people like what you do?" ventured Johnson.

"No, Spoodle. I've warmth enough without that. I know when I'm good and I know when I'm bad and I don't need other people telling me. If they attack me, even when I know they're right, their repeating of what I know depresses me. And overpraise makes me sick. So why read any of it? Criticism is not written, after all, for me or for those who read me. It's written for the vanity of those who write it—or for a few shillings. It's a shabby business, though I do sometimes have to engage in it myself."

"And you like to read what you write about others, Lorenzo, you do," hummed Frieda, like a cello string, "even though you don't like to read what they write about you."

"It's all vanity, Frieda."

"Saith the preacher," nodded she, "the great preacher, Lorenzo."

"Yes, I *am* a preacher," he admitted, then, turning to me, "You review this thing for what journal?"

"The New Republic."

"Yes, you read that, don't you, Bynner, and *The Nation,* too. You read them religiously, don't you. And you try to foist them on me."

I cared about current events. He was mostly indifferent to them. He felt that current events were not often eventual, that current events and then eventual events are created and formed by special human beings, by individuals who are the source of them all, that the individual is the eventuality. And though he highly valued the idea of heroic leadership by individuals, he gave, I used to insist, little thought to the potency of the millions of obscure individuals who, in combination, create lasting judgment and progress. The leader may be the tall light-house, but the people below are the hidden wires of electricity. When this is not the case, I used to urge, when the leader is detached from the people, or coerces them, a government or system results which, how-ever dominant and spectacular for a while, most of the world finally judges to be evil and throws away. "We are all members one of an-other," I said to him once, "doesn't go with your very special 'blood stream.'"

"Neither does *The New Republic*," he quipped back.

In *The Plumed Serpent* an interesting illustration occurs of Frieda and Lawrence blended in the one character, Kate, when Cipriano calls at her house in Chapala. She tells him, "'I have nothing to *do!* The servants won't let me do anything. If I sweep my room, they stand and say *Que Niña! Que Niña!* As if I was standing on my head for their benefit. I sew, though I've no interest in sewing. What is it, for a life?' 'You read!' he said, glancing at the magazines and books. 'Ah, it is all such stupid stuff, lifeless stuff, in the books and papers,' she said." The first voice is the voice of Frieda, the second voice is the voice of Lawrence.

On this occasion, while I was bridling a little at his contempt for my journals, he was gathering steam: "'Journals of opinion' they call themselves. Why be opined for? Why not read the news and opine for yourself?"

"But ordinary news is distorted or colored," I protested. "These journals give you the news behind the news."

"All news is colored, Bynner. News behind the news is colored. Find your own news behind the news and color it yourself. You can see it as clearly as they can see it and you have just as good a color to color it with."

"I'm opining for them this time about the play," I declared. "They're not opining for me. Have you read it?"

"Glanced into it."

"I've read it," asserted Frieda, "all of it and digested it."

"My glance is as good as your glutting," he taunted.

"What a book!" she rolled on. "What heroes! Are they still like that in Japan, Hal? Is it a modern play or an old one? How can a Japanese write such good English?"

"A new play," I explained, "on the one old Japanese theme of loyalty."

"No, no," Frieda disagreed. "That's not the real theme. You did not understand, Hal. It's the deep, proud power of the father."

"Can Frieda tell us the story?" teased Lawrence.

"*Ja, ja,* but let Hal do it. Let's see how he thinks it goes."

"All right," said I. "A bad emperor has deposed a good emperor. The good emperor decides to put up a fight and summons an old retired general who had been loyal to him. The eldest of the general's seven sons has compromised and been put at the head of the bad emperor's army. The general and his six other sons all join the good emperor, knowing that the eldest son cannot shift allegiance, must now fight not only against the good emperor but against his own father and brothers, just because of a formal pledge to the bad emperor. That's the Japanese code of honor. And you think a tragedy can be based on such piffle?"

"No, Hal," objected Frieda, "you should read it again for the real point."

"The real point?" I summoned all my sarcasm. "The eldest son defeats his brothers, one by one, and then when he's about to capture his father, he weakens and wants to let the old boy go. But the father orders him to do his Japanese duty. So Sonny Boy has his dear brothers and his nice old papa tortured and killed. And then, oh, no, that isn't enough. The bad emperor gives Mikimoto hell because he weakened for even a moment when he thought of letting papa get away. That wasn't gentlemanly. So Mikimoto makes up for it by getting rid of his last touch of natural affection and squalling out in the final scene that torturing and killing the lot of them was not only the deed of an honorable Japanese gentleman but the finest compliment he could possibly pay his family. Fine business!"

"Not at all, not at all," steamed Frieda. "You have missed the whole point of the play! It's the father complex, it's . . ."

"Rubbish, Frieda!" Lawrence jumped in. "You have a fool's complex. You don't know what you're talking about with your smatter of Freud. You have to drag him into whatever you read. You're an idiot!"

"Who's the idiot? You haven't even read the book—just a smatter yourself!"

"The first three or four pages were all I needed, to know what it's about."

"No, Lorenzo, it's the end that explains."

"But I read the end."

"No, it's somewhere in the middle, where the father will not let the son weaken. It's that, it's his power over his son, because his son takes his word for it, because his son loves him."

"Love, love, love!" flashed Lawrence. "That's the woman of you. Anything's all right if it's love."

"How can you talk about the book," Frieda hurled at him, "when you haven't even read it? It's in the middle."

"I've read the middle," he hurled back.

"You had the book in your hands three minutes . . ."

"But I've read the middle," he barked. "Loyalty was the great motive of man through all the great periods of history, for seven thousand Egyptian years before our twenty little piffling Christian centuries."

"Loyalty to royalty!" I jeered back at him.

But he reared toward Frieda, "It was you women who invented this damnable doctrine of love!"

I reared too. "Inner loyalty is the only real loyalty, devotion to a conscience instead of to a command, to an ideal instead of to a word!"

"Damn ideals!" blazed Lawrence.

Frieda sprang back at him with as good a gust. "No, it was not women who invented love, Lorenzo, it was you men."

"Of course," he gathered himself together, not heeding her at all and bringing his argument suddenly to a measured conclusion, "of course there can be misdirected loyalty, loyalty that doesn't see clearly. It mustn't be blind loyalty. It must be unity of faith—loyalty to oneself as well as to the leader."

"Oh, well . . ." said I.

Johnson had for some minutes been detached from the discussion, leafing through passages in the book.

"You had read it before, hadn't you, Spud?" inquired Frieda.

He nodded.

"And what do you think of it?" she urged, hoping for an ally in the general confusion.

"It's romantic," he said, mildly.

Lawrence held through the years to the romantic side of his conviction. Mrs. Carswell writes in 1927: "When I was shocked by the old Japanese play *Bushido,* in which the adoring parents of a talented and beautiful only boy, tell him that they must cut off his head to save that of his Emperor, and the boy, like his parents, purifies himself and is willing for the sacrifice, Lawrence told me I was wrong to be offended. 'It is the only way to happiness,' he said, 'the only way for life to be rich, for people to have something apart from their own little individual souls that is worth the sacrifice of life itself.'"

And yet he had resented Frieda's loyal craving for her children and fought with all fours the chance that she might have sacrificed him for them.

One must not sacrifice the Emperor.

27. The Spectral Visitor

THE man is a tangle, I thought that night in bed, neither flesh, fowl, nor good red herring, only tangled red beard.

How can he put all this together? He wants the heroic savage, whose quality bubbles up from bowels like something at Yellowstone Park. Then he wants the leader, the hero, ever held up by the flame, like a bouncing phoenix. Then he wants adherence from the dedicated masses to the inspired hero, while the leader must be motivated from the bowels, never trust his head, any more than the followers do, but just his guts. Now comes the trouble. Lawrence, I realized again, wants to be both his own leader and his own follower. Nobody else is good enough for either role. Contained in himself must be all the panoplied pomp of the Roman Church with a Perfect Pope and the sweet earthy utter clutter of the purring Perfect Peon. But never in either the leader or the follower must an idea intrude or an ideal. Everything done all round by surges of the sacred blood! Leaders and followers all spouting fiery blood streams from a single magnificent intestinal crater!

What continued to shock him, time after time, as he quested through the world, was a growing suspicion that he himself might really be the only Rousseau, the only being, both natural and noble. He saw and saw and saw the supposedly noble savages. The trouble was that he did not, like Rousseau, sit at home and populate some vast wilderness with figments of his own image. He went about and found out that, save himself, nobles were not natural and naturals were not noble. Still he sought among the primitives. Still Mexico held him while it frightened him. And so he would continue seeking, until he should find surcease in the most primitive land of all, the land where no inhabitant, apparently, disappoints.

Daniel, Isabel's son—Lawrence has described his "domed Indian head with its thick black hair"—wakened us at nine one morning with a grave face and the written message: "Please come for breakfast as soon as you can." Nine-thirty was a generous compromise between their seven and our ten. So we felt bounden and went, weak-eyed after late writing and reading by candlelight.

Frieda was at the gate. "Wait, wait, wait till you hear!" she chanted, as though Medea sang the "Marseillaise." We could not tell whether it was triumph or disaster.

"I am afraid," said Lawrence grimly, hurrying in her wake, "that me must all leave Chapala."

"Why?"

"What I warned you of!"

"Tell it with coffee, Lorenzo, with coffee and eggs," burbled Frieda. "The boys are here, Isabel." And Isabel came from the tiny kitchen with coffee. "Now tell them, Lorenzo."

"I was wakened in the night," he confided, "by a sound of breaking glass. The moon was across my door. The small pane by the lock had been broken and a hand came through. I couldn't think at first."

"You didn't think," interrupted Frieda. "You jumped. I heard him jump in the other room, a great thump on the floor, a noise in his throat, and then he was in my bed, his head against my shoulder, saying 'They've come!' 'What? Where?' I asked. 'My door,' he answered. And I was out of bed and his door was not bolted, but there was no one in his room, in any room, no one in the house, no one in the garden, only the moonlight."

"It's not good, Bynner," he said gravely. "We must leave."

"Did he get anything?" came Johnson's practical query.

"He wanted Lorenzo," explained Frieda, with a grand gesture like something in opera.

"Are you sure you had had your door locked?" I wondered.

"I always lock it. I saw the hand unbolt it, the moonlight on the fingers, and there was a knife in the hand. We must leave this place, Bynner."

"Don't leave your coffee," advised Frieda. "And now some eggs."

When Isabel brought the eggs, Lawrence asked her if there was not danger when men scaled walls and broke panes in doors.

"*Mucho,*" said Isabel, like a pleased Cassandra. "You must have Daniel. We must have him bring his petate and serape and sleep there by the door outside. We must have him bring his *pistola*. Then no one will dare."

Before we had finished breakfast, Daniel had arrived, poising his slim, firm figure in the door and smiling an inquiry. To Lawrence's story, told again, and to Isabel's interpolated suggestions, Daniel nodded his low-growing forelock and agreed, "*Si, señor.*" He had his pistol with him, and Isabel expanded the plan, "By day he can garden, by night he can guard. It is better, *señor.*" Daniel, with a kindly light in his face, echoed, "*Si, señor, it is better.*"

So arrangements were made then and there for another servant in the Lawrences' household; and thenceforward Daniel lay on his mat in the portal every night, like a faithful dog at his master's door.

Discussing the episode with Spud, I wondered if our friend, Nacho, had not had something to do with it. Idella Purnell had sent Nacho to us early in our stay with a card of introduction and also posted me a letter concerning him: "He is a member of one of the most aristocratic families, so he knows all the who's whos; but he is blessed with a happy-go-lucky spirit, so he also knows everyone else, including cargadors, beggars, and tamale women. This makes his older brother very angry, but Nacho says, 'What do I care? I know how to enjoy myself.' He is an entertaining, erratic, irresponsible fellow. However, it is silly to try to describe people . . . when you can see for yourself."

So Nacho had come and been seen and had conquered. Besides being a fine figure, which most of the young dandies down there were not, he had all the ease of aristocracy with no arrogance and with a sort of heroic dash which had caught the Lawrences' imagination. Besides, he spoke flowing English, which was a blessing for Spud and me. I remember Lorenzo's special delight in Nacho's description of a little sewing girl he had discovered who had a good voice: "She is of humble people, you know, but she has a proud throat." Though Nacho lived in Guadalajara, he had rented a lake house near the Lawrences and each time he came to stay in it we saw something of him. Lawrence liked him, drawing upon him more and more trustfully for information about Mexicans of all conditions.

Within the week I had received a letter from Idella: "Nacho says he is leaving Chapala because he no longer considered it safe to live at Zaragoza 18. That is why he had moved to the Hotel Chapala. He says to tell the Lawrences immediately to move to the Hotel. He states that the hotels are perfectly safe. He alleges that there is in Chapala a band of Bolsheviks (*Bolcheviques*) with whom the Chief of Police sympathizes and works, that they have confiscated large sections of land; that they plan to seize more houses, *and* the people in them; and that they wish to make the people who own the houses suffer for being rich. Therefore it would perhaps be wise for the Lawrences to move to a hotel. Nacho knows people of every class; his information is probably authentic.

"Incidentally, Nacho is certainly a wonder. There were two little boys travelling home with him and his young bride. She told me to ask him in English who they were: she didn't know. They called him Papa. They were obviously his own kids. How is that? To take a fifteen-year-old girl on a honeymoon and return from it that way! Wonderful, wonderful Nacho!"

Wonderful Nacho indeed! Relishing credulity, he had undoubtedly been pouring alarm into Lawrence. He had probably known better than to try to scare Frieda. Her comfortable fatalism was like the Mexican "what God wills," except that when occasion demanded she had a will too. She was not scared easily—even by Lawrence. And she was healthily skeptical and immune to most mischief.

"The door pane was broken when we took the house," she smiled later in the day when we were alone with her, "but we have not told him. He is having too good a time."

"Hadn't he known it?" we asked.

"*Quién sabe,*" came her bit of Spanish.

"But didn't he see that there was no broken glass on the floor?"

"*Ach!*" replied Frieda, indulgently. "It was more exciting to see a knife in the moonlight."

In *The Plumed Serpent* this experience is used, in subdued form, and transferred, of course, to Kate: "Her doors on the verandah had shutters. The doors themselves were fastened, but the shutters were open for air, leaving the upper space, like the window of the door, open. And against the dark grey of the night she saw what looked like a black cat crouching on the bottom of the panel space. 'What is that?' she said automatically. Instantly the thing moved, slid away, and she knew it was the arm of a man that had been reaching inside to pull the bolt of the door. She lay for a second paralyzed, prepared to scream. There was no movement. So she leaned and lit a candle."

Elsewhere in the novel is a passage which sheds more light than the candle on Lawrence's nervous apprehensions and on his insistences that he had actually seen that hand. A little before the visitation he had heard vaguely that bandits were busy again near San Antonio; and he writes in *The Plumed Serpent:* "The fact that a gang of bandits was out always set the isolated thieves and scoundrels in action. Whatever happened, it would be attributed to the bandits. And so, many an unsuspected, seemingly honest man, with the old lust in his soul, would steal out by night with his machete and perhaps a pistol, to put his fingers in the pie of the darkness."

The knife had become "a machete and perhaps a pistol" and Lawrence a plum "in the pie of the darkness."

He wrote Knud Merrild on April 21: "We have a man to sleep on the verandah with a pistol: and we may not walk outside the village for fear of being robbed or carried off by bandits."

Years before, in his boyhood, his brother had told Jessie Chambers (E. T.): "He isn't at all well. . . . He calls out in his sleep, thinks somebody's trying to kill him."

And Anton Skrebensky had said in *The Rainbow:* "I am not afraid of the darkness in England. . . . It is soft and natural to me, it is my medium. . . . But in Africa it seems massive and fluid with terror—not fear of anything—just fear. One breathes it like a smell of blood. The blacks know it. They worship it, really, the darkness. One almost likes it—the fear—something sensual."

28. Reflections

SPUD and I agreed that, even if Lawrence's panic lasted and he insisted on leaving Chapala, we would let him go, taking Frieda away from us, that we would not accompany them. After Chapala we doubted if he would be content anywhere else in Mexico for more than a few days. Moving about, without steady work on the novel to absorb him and distract him from his petulant vagaries, he might become irascible to the point of an open break. We remembered his turn against Fred Leighton. We were both enjoying the lake town, where our laziness and our literary pursuits moved in fine balance. Dibrell was still genially at hand for likable companionship. The fly season had not begun. We had become accustomed to *bobos,* little fools, tiny transparent stingless insects, revolving swarms of which would hang here and there in the evening air, entering one's eyes and nose, or would take deadly dives into candle flame or, near any light, stipple the walls and tables with their spent wings. Having only candles or lamps to read or work by after ten, we had found that, except for our Lawrence evenings of talk, early to bed and early to rise was making us feel both healthy and wise. Chapalan prices, moreover, were sparing our funds. At that time a servant's monthly wage, even though a householder did need two or three of them, was ten American dollars and a person's daily bill at the hotel, for bed and board, not more than two dollars. The air was good vintage. The lake was exercise. To us, if not to Lawrence, the people seemed friendly. Why should we leave all this, to satisfy his neurotic whims? Might it not be better if the Lawrences did leave, letting us relax into a season of peace, without ruffle or apprehension?

"Yes," said Spud.

With that issue settled, I wrote a few letters to vent the bile which still blackened in me. To Alice Corbin I declaimed: "The longer I think about him, the cleverer and shallower he seems, a thoroughly specious person. He knows the characters in his books as a specialist knows patients who dislike him. He never knows them personally and never will, nor does he know them impersonally. He knows them as objects. Sometimes he slays them. And so he flees from land to land, as from book to book, a quick-witted but miserable Cain."

"Chapala," I wrote my mother on June 22, 1923, "besides being for the most part a serene place, acts as a tonic on the writer. Lawrence agrees. Despite this, he is afraid of it and is starting soon for New York. I shall give him your address. Be very careful, however, what you say to him and shake a lot of salt on what he says. He is a strange person, as you have seen, gifted as a writer; but as a human being, built on sand. He is curiously unreal: agreeable as a companion if one accepts only his flashes of wit and wisdom and discounts him as an entire being. Of course if he were cured of whatever ails him, he would probably stop writing. Even while he flees Chapala, he already plans coming back again. So do I."

To Eunice Tietjens I reported: "He's one of the uncanniest human beings imaginable. Did I say human? Slowly I am coming to the conclusion that he was misborn as a man, that he is a four-footer of some sort, chafing against human bondage. . . . I usually care very little for his writings; but when he begins on any animal or any bird, I am spellbound. He ought to have been a bird or an animal—or, at least, a naturalist. Think of him again, from that point of view. Think of him waking up in the dawn, without his beautiful claws or feathers and, because of his lack, hating humanity afresh each day. From my point of view, there has seldom been a writer less fitted to discuss human affairs. He struggles and struggles to think as a man, with all those acute animal perceptions, but he cannot. By paying no attention to him, I have won his tolerance for this considerable period, just as I might have won the tolerance of any other self-respecting beast. But he has the contempt for me that he has for all humans. And how can such a man, who could never really care for any human being, treat of human life? He can see it and feel it, but he can never know it."

Years later, in a book by Sakya Muni, I ran across the observation: "Whoso discovers that grief comes from affection will retire into the jungles and there remain," and in Lawrence's own *Studies in Classical American Literature:* "I only know that my body doesn't by any means gravitate to all I meet or know. I find I can shake hands with a few people. But most I wouldn't touch with a long prop." Diana Trilling wrote of him recently in *The Saturday Review of Literature:* "The quick warm touch of instinctive sympathy for his fellowman is indeed what we have always most missed in Lawrence's work—this and its counterpart, humor. Their absence is bound to be regretted. One of the things we all of us unconsciously seek in art, particularly in fiction, is the knowledge of ready love and forgiveness, the promise of the kind of understanding that is shared in laughter."

Turning from letters that night and with humorless Lawrence still in mind, I set down the first draught of my poem, "O For a Witless Age," which finally reads:

> Humor is warm, wit cold,
> Wit can be a common scold,
> But humor can laugh and do no harm:
> For wit is cold and humor warm.
>
> O for a witless age again
> Of clear upstanding laughing men,
> After a humorless age like this
> Of dapper coils and lisping hiss!
>
> Nothing hearty, not even hate,
> Never a rollicking reprobate,
> But only fangs that peer and piddle—
> O for some laughter from the middle!

I was wishing that there might be some laughter in that "dark center" of Lawrence, laughter not only at others but at himself.

In my diary I entered: "He will not let well enough alone until it is ill enough."

And finally, ruminating over the likelihood that his "dynamic consciousness" had forced the moonlit knife into his "mental consciousness" because his dynamo was determined upon his own undoing, was determined to flog him ever away from contentment and peace, I wrote Harriet Monroe: "D. H. Lawrence is the most brilliantly lost man I can imagine, fleeing always, with a violent grace, from his own shadow."

29. The Canoa

NEXT day neither of the Lawrences made any reference to departure, nor the next, nor the next. Life continued its previous tenor. By the week's end, with Daniel now happily and usefully attendant night and day, Lawrence himself brushed aside the prowler as only a would-be thief and came as near to laughing at himself as I had known him to do. We dared to rib him over his having rushed from danger to Frieda's bosom, like a child to its mother, and he relished and joined our mirth. Slightly shamefaced for having relinquished to her the courageous role, he quipped, "She could face it because she has no imagination," but the picture of his flight amused him and he himself drew it out for us with comic detail.

The following week he proposed our renting a canoa for a leisurely sail around the lake and inviting the Purnells to join us. Routine trips on the little steamer had given us brief stops ashore at various villages. With this excursion, lasting as long as we liked, we could touch everywhere and roam and linger. Daniel had broached the idea already to a boatman from Tuxcueca, whom he found not only willing but eager to pilot these foreign passengers and at slight cost. So a date was set and a few provisions purchased from the market to supplement what we might buy in the sleepy lake hamlets.

On July 4 I wrote home: "Tomorrow we are starting on a three or four day sail in what they call a canoa, a fairly large primitive half-enclosed vessel, like a Chinese junk, with one enormous rounded sail. Until our return, you shall have no word—unless in the meantime you receive a peremptory summons from Mexican bandits!"

The idea of bandits, however, did not disturb me as it did Lawrence. My only misgiving, which I thought too trifling to mention, was concern over an eruption at the base of my spine, dismissed by the village doctor as of no importance.

The Purnells had arrived from Guadalajara and all was set for departure, when an unexpected storm broke over the town. The normal rainy season was several weeks off; but this *tormenta* gave us an exciting foretaste of what we were to experience later. Tempests in Chapala are wild. They occur usually at night, have spent their fury by morning, and given way to bright sun again; but while they last they are Walpurgisnacht. Thunder crashes like a tumbling of mountains, lightning crackles blue and lashes its bolts while the lake is a stampede rearing thousands of white manes. This time the attack came not from across the lake as usual but from inland and not by night but by day. We could see it approaching, bearing down on us, before it struck. We postponed embarkation, glad not to have been caught by the storm dragon in mid-lake. But next morning a freshness in air and foliage and puddles underfoot were all that was left of the deluge, the sun was serene, the lake calm. So aboard our canoa we went, ten of us, the six passengers, the captain and his crew of three, including Daniel.

The captain was an erect fifty-year-old Indian with a square black beard and the dignity of Michelangelo's "Moses." The canoa was all cabin, so to speak—a spacious, roofed hold, open at bow and stern and edged outside the roof with runways. On these, to push the craft through shallow water or to make progress when there was no wind, the barefooted boatmen, planting their poles and leaning on them, would first face toward the stern and then patter catlike prow-ward to place the poles again. Three years previously I had traveled on houseboats in China; and, though to the ornately fitted houseboat this bark was as a shed to a parlor, I was reminded of those Oriental river trips. There, with no sail, our whole progress had been dependent on poling; here the method of our occasional poling was the same; and the dress, motion, and faces of the boatmen might have come in one generation from China.

Idella Purnell writes about the expedition: "Lawrence and you and Daddy and Spud had spent hours conferring with one another and going to the water front in a sort of 'leave this all to us' attitude which was very masterful indeed. The great day came when Frieda and I were invited to see our new home. It was a rather stripped, rather decrepit canoa—and we wondered why all the men beamed with such pride until they took us to see the toilet they had made of a reed mat swung down across the niche formed by the bow, [a petate which ended knee high]; and behind it a big wooden box with a hole at the top to fit over a bucket. You men all stood there waiting for our approval. Frieda and I exchanged one look and then burst into the praise which was so clearly expected of us."

I had forgotten this episode and also the detail, which she remembers, that "we took off amid the applause of the population of Chapala, a large part of which was at the beach."

As we poled out from the pier, with Idella waving at the population, silken, violet-shadowed mountains opposite might have been a mile away, instead of ten miles off, so clear was the day, so clean washed with yesterday's rain; and we could see San Luis Soyotlán, Tuxcueca, San Nicolas, and even more distant Tizapan catch the sun like toy villages. Our taking off is well pictured in *The Plumed Serpent*: "The two peons on the ship's rims were poling her out, pressing their poles and walking heavily till they reached the stern, then lifting their poles and running to the high prow. She slid slowly out on to the lake. Then quickly they hoisted the wide white sail. The sail thrust up her horn and curved in a whorl to the wind."

We planned mooring near Tuxcueca that night and loafing through town on the morrow; but we had reckoned without the storm dragon. Before the rest of us were aware of threat in the air, the captain, like Moses toward the burning bush, kept giving the sky anxious looks. Yes, it was clouding ominously. The wind was against us. The sail was ordered down in mid-lake, its bellying flaps furled and secured on the hatch. We became nervous. If there was to be another downpour like yesterday's, we were in for a great blowing and wetting. But it was still warm and we played up our spirits all we could.

Idella remembers that "everyone went swimming over the side. Blankets," she writes, "were swung down from the beams under the hatch. These made a dressing room for Frieda and me. I was reluctant to go in, since I could not swim, but finally succumbed to urging. By then the rest had come out, dripping, very gay and very happy. I was not happy, for I felt queasy; but everyone said a dip would make me feel better. So down I went, and the moment I accidentally lost hold of the rope ladder I began to drown. On deck all of you laughed; you thought I was having fun. I thrashed about desperately and finally found the ladder and clung to it, very miserable indeed, while my friends above roared with laughter. The dip did not help my seasickness. That evening passed rather pleasantly, though. Frieda and Isabel cooked a good, simple supper, and after supper one of the boatmen played my guitar, while we sang. Then three mattresses were spread on the floor by the stern. Frieda and Lawrence occupied the outside mattress, then came Spud and you, then I, with Daddy on the inside. The first four slept with their feet pointing north, and we slept with ours pointing south. No sooner had we all settled down than Lawrence, very quiet and catlike, crept over us all to visit the seat in the bow. Somehow in the dark he kicked over the bucket, and a loud clatter resounded through the boat. You of course could not resist; you never can; you sang out, 'We all know what you're up to, Lorenzo.' And the dark seemed suddenly to surge with waves of pure hate coming from the affronted dignity of D. H. L. Finally everyone seemed to quiet down, except you, who kept tossing and turning and sighing, and me, who was still seasick and miserable. About two in the morning rain began to splatter on the roof and to leak in. I asked in a small voice, 'Hadn't we better fix the camera so it won't get rained on?' and you agreed, as if pleased to have the night broken by some activity. We fixed the camera, under other packages. Then again we were fairly quiet for a while, until my seasickness became too much for me and I began to fumble for the flashlight. This time Frieda aroused, to know what was wanted. 'The flash,' I said, and promptly she passed me the flask, full of tequila. 'No, I said the flash. The flashlight!' and this time she gave me the right thing. Fortunately I had fewer people to climb over than Lorenzo had had; I managed to reach the toilet without waking everybody and there I was very miserable, retching without relief. Back I went, with a cold sweat on me. And fell asleep, at last!"

Idella was the first to be seasick; but Spud and I felt squeamish, as I think the Lawrences did also. My memory of the night is that the canoa tossed hard. I dozed for a while, then waked as though on a sweating broncho. I found that the sweat was water in the hold. Our blankets were wet, and it was pouring outside. Somebody was vomiting in the dark. And what had happened to my back? I turned stiffly and slid my hand down my rump to realize that the rash had become aggravated, swollen, and painful. Then I was suddenly seasick and had to crawl to the bow with the flashlight. Sheets of water fell over me till I slunk back like a drenched dog. It was only three in the morning and the rain gave no sign of abating.

Again and again, sick, anxious, shivering, I turned the flash on my wrist watch while the night moved like slow, black lava. At last wind and rain lessened, the canoa's rocking quieted, and a film of light entered the hold, enough so that I could see Idella, beyond Spud, sitting upright on her pallet and swaying from side to side like a mourner. We gazed at each other with a dumb stare of misery, I too sitting upright. Lorenzo waked, Spud, Frieda, each of them as in a slow-motion movie. Daniel was already making coffee, which did not smell good.

"I am very sick," said Idella humbly.

"So am I," came from me. And the two remarks seemed slightly to cheer the others, the more so as there was now a pale sun which might later warm us and perhaps dry our clothing. We exchanged a few words. No one left his mattress, though, and we must all have fallen uncomfortably asleep again.

Idella's letter recounts our rising: "The next thing I knew my father was excitedly summoning us all to come and see a water snake. I couldn't see why a water snake was of any interest, nor why we had to be awakened so early to see one; there was only a faint gray light under our shelter. But obediently we all went up on top of the hatch. The water snake was a waterspout, a black funnel reaching from the lake to the sky, or rather a chimney, with an elbow in it about half way up. The lake was now gray and angry, a thin rain spattered down, and it was cold. My seasickness was upon me again."

Daniel tried to enliven us by telling us that the people in Chapala were probably on their knees praying, because last year a waterspout had reached the town and taken a whole tree up by the roots, carrying it two blocks, and another one the year before had taken up a whole house. He seemed to have hopes that the canoa and all of us aboard might be caught up in a sky dance; but the spout slowly split at the elbow and then all of it misted and drifted away. Lawrence was entering notes in a little book from his pocket, something he seldom did.

Idella continues: "The sail was put up while breakfast was made. The wind blew up rapidly across the lake, and soon we were in danger of shipwreck on the rocky shores just west of Tuxcueca. Now all the men began to pole to keep us off the rocks. Then they saw an Indian who had come down to the desolate shore to watch. By much shouting they made him understand that he was to run for help. Somehow, finally, we reached the wharf and went ashore. You and I sat on the breakwater, while the others set off to buy chickens. And as I revived, you wilted. When the rest came back, they told us that the steamer was soon due. The steamer came, and with relief the others got rid of us. I was thankful that the Y.M.C.A. Taylors were at the hotel and that I could turn you over to him, for by the time we reached there you were very ill indeed. When the rest came back to Chapala, three or four days later, you were in a Guadalajara hospital; and only I welcomed them back. How unkempt and unshaven and happy they looked! And how filled they were with the delight of their adventure!"

My own remembrance is that, after coffee and beans and tortillas, I took Dr. Purnell beyond the hatch and asked him to look at my hindside. He called Spud and Lorenzo. They were both alarmed. My whole middle was puffed and inflamed.

"I shall go back with you," said Lawrence.

"*I* will," said Spud.

"I *must*," said Idella so miserably that we all laughed.

The two of us were landed at Tuxcueca. At the last moment Frieda almost stayed with us; but we would not let her, telling her that she looked the most stalwart of the lot and they might need her. Beyond the breakwater, where the roadway took off for town, we found a slope with sparse grass on it already dry; and there we lay down side by side, both of us so sick that we wished they would stop prolonging their farewells. We waved feebly. They poled out again, found a wind, hoisted a sail, and slowly glided off.

30. The Hospital

SINCE the only practicing American physician in Guadalajara had gone to Mexico City, our Consul took me to the hospital of Dr. Barrierre, a big, businesslike Mexican, who told me that my trouble was an infected fistula and that he would operate in the morning. The Consul, lingering behind in my room, shook his head and said that he would summon the American doctor back from the Capital by telephone and that I must wait. I must on no condition let the Mexican doctor operate. My only feeling was an ache for the Consul to leave. Why couldn't Frieda be there to manage for me?

In the morning there was no sign of the American doctor or the Consul. I was told later that the doctor had been taken very ill the same morning in Guadalajara, with the Consul at his bedside, and had died shortly after. My operation proceeded. And the following morning the nurse found me on the floor by the door to the adjoining room in which a ranch owner with a broken leg, a guitar, and two attendant ranch hands had been softly singing Mexican songs into the night.

By the time the Lawrences and Spud reached the hospital, I was being wheel-chaired for an hour or two daily in the garden with bougainvillaea, oleander, hibiscus all about, and was rereading *Sons and Lovers,* liking it still better than I had liked it the first time. Though sure that Frieda and Spud would be concerned and attentive, as they were, I had not expected constant, thoughtful tenderness from Lawrence. When I began to walk again, he would ease me out of the chair, help adjust the crutches and reassure me, with a soothing sort of authority, that inability to manage my legs was natural and did not mean a derangement of the spine. At first, mindful of the warnings and head shakings from the Consul, I feared that it had been a mistake to let the Mexican doctor operate, that I was permanently injured and that they were not letting me know. The Lawrences, bringing flowers, magazines, and mail to the room, brought also personal cheer and quietly did away with my perturbations.

On that first day Lorenzo had with him a note acknowledging payment of an account at a Guadalajara provision store and pointed out for my amusement the floral formality of salutation and signature: "Appreciable cavalier and friend," "your account in this your house," and the concluding "your most affectionate and attentive friend and servant." Such trifles were proper fare for an invalid.

I wondered a little if his attitude meant that, sick, I was in his power. But soon I thought better than that.

He came several times during my two weeks of hospitalization. One day, at the outset, noticing that I did not progress much with books or magazines, he advised, "Do something with your hands. When you are too weak to read, you can do something with your hands." He took out of his pocket a slim silver chain and a handful of silver votive offerings, which the faithful bring to saints' altars in token of cures: a heart, an eye, a leg, a liver, a dog, a burro. "String these," he said. "Make a necklace."

A day or two later he fetched from Chapala a serape which I had bought off the back of a bearded farmer at one of the serenatas a month before. Though beautiful in its seasoned color and its Michoacan design, it was badly frayed. I was in bed and he spread it over me.

"Because it's gayer than the hospital blanket?" I asked.

"No," he smiled, "I want you to mend it. I'll show you how." He produced bodkin and skeins of red, black, gray, and yellow wool wound around twisted lengths of paper. Sitting close by the bed, he deftly slipped his needle horizontally into the serape an inch or two back from a ragged hole and then over and under the sound strands, across the opening and into firmness again on the other side. Under his fingers, which moved like hummingbirds, each new strand followed its proper line of color until a dozen of them lay across the gap, neat and regular as the strings of a harp. He then repeated the process vertically. One patch was done. He was proud eyed. And, though the new colors were brighter than the old, they blended as naturally into the rejuvenated edge of the serape as though a touch of sun were gleaming on it. He showed me next the more intricate process of making new edges where the old had fringed away. He bade me try. I fumbled and poked and made a messy crisscross which he promptly unraveled, saying, "Do it again." Before he left, I had learned the method and, after repeated unravelings, I made a fair showing. Visitors in my Santa Fe house where the repaired serape hangs as a curtain have to look close now to distinguish one old wool from the other, though it is still easy to distinguish Lawrence's handiwork from that of his pupil.

His hospital attentions touched me, the more so since patience in visiting sickrooms is not one of my own virtues.

It was during the weaving lesson that we discussed a pet theory of mine as to education. Having taught poetry at the University of California in 1918, with relish on the part of Idella and other students and with even more relish on my own part, and having realized that I could not evoke or experience anything like that relish if I were to continue giving the course, I had nursed an idea that repetition by one person of courses on any one subject made them stale for both instructor and pupil.

"We have conscription for destructive purposes. Why not for constructive, for creative purposes?" I suggested. Why should not school boards, under combined federal and state authority, select men and women who had become or promised to become in their profession expert and eminent and draft them for a single year's service as teachers? Never more than a year, lest they go stale. Persons so chosen, though shy or awkward at first, would soon make up for their ignorance of pedagogy by their special knowledge, their fresh approach and enthusiasm, and would themselves receive as much stimulus as they gave their students. "Wouldn't you like to teach that way? Just one year?"

"Perhaps," considered Lawrence, "but you like people better than I do, Bynner, especially young people."

"You'd like them too, Lorenzo, if you ever let yourself."

"Perhaps." He pursed his brow.

"Haven't you any such pet ideas?" I asked.

He veered back with sudden finality, "I'd force all women to spin and weave."

On another of our hospital days I said to him, "Spud tells me that you are leaving Chapala. Why?"

"I think we've had enough," he answered, "but I don't yet know what we'll do. We have the Del Monte ranch of course. But no! Not Kiowa!" He was suddenly antagonistic. "No! I don't want to go back to America. It's both uncivilized and sterile. There is nothing really good, Bynner, on the whole continent. I ought to go back to England. And yet I don't know. I may keep the house in Chapala or another somewhere else in Mexico and be near enough to run up to New York now and again, because New York, after all, is my business center. My books have no sale in England, only in America. That is the one thing," he smiled, "which makes me think there may be some good in America, something of civilization. I can at least say for Americans that you read my books. But when an Englishman does read a novel of mine, I can be certain that he understands it. Americans buy it and read it but they haven't the least idea what it's about."

This was the old Lawrence again, and yet there had been a smile. I wondered if the old Lawrence would ever anger me again, now that I knew the kindness which underlay him. He would have recoiled if I had mentioned that kindness. The hard blue gleam would have returned, the mineral eye. Kind he would never be if he could help it. Or so he thought. So he theorized. There is more in your dark center, I meditated, than is dreamed of in your philosophy. Instead of thanking him for kindness, I took the opposite tack.

"I scribbled something about you last night, Lorenzo." It was in the commode drawer. I read it to him: " 'On the sixth day he had eliminated everyone from his possible world, leaving only Himself to whom to be superior, but on the seventh day he refused to rest.' "

He laughed a little and at the same time frowned.

"Why doesn't that mind of yours ever rest? Why don't you ever give it a rest, Lorenzo, from this incessant theorizing? Americans aren't irrevocably this and Englishmen irrevocably that and Mexicans irrevocably something else. We're just people, the whole lot of us."

"But you like democracy and I don't," he persisted. Then he gave a slight shrug and smiled, with the look of an innocent but puzzled child, like Stanhope Ficke reacting to his father's exposition of the facts of life: "I understand what you say, but I don't believe a word of it."

I never knew what he was going to be, this odd man-child: winning, flashing, sulking, malicious, angry, or merely innocent: He was himself aware of the contradictory changes and of the child element. In *The Plumed Serpent* he describes himself in Kate's watching Mexico "like a child looking through a railing, rather wistful and rather frightened." In my Chapala diary was entered: "He's a child, a good child, a naughty child, a spoiled child, a frightened child. He's afraid of the dark and he tries to talk the darkness down."

I wondered if he was still frightened of Mexico, if that was why they were leaving. Or was he wistful for some other place, the right place yet unfound? He had seemed, on the whole, happy in Chapala. Did even happiness frighten him?

31. Reflections Again

THE period around the Lawrences' leaving and my return to Chapala is vague to me. I suffered for some time the effects of illness and operation. It was weeks before I could direct my limbs with precision. And so I suppose the brain too was wobbly.

Our good-byes were said at the hospital in a vein of jollity. Through a haze, I remember a flat sense of void when Frieda, laughing, "I have the umbrellas this time," waved from the doorway and faded into the corridor. Lorenzo lingered to say, "Get well." It was no solemn leave-taking. There was no reason for melancholy. Even if they went to England for a bit, as he said they might do after their business visit in New York, we should soon be seeing one another in New Mexico and then perhaps the four of us return together to Old Mexico for the winter.

Lawrence had too often been on the nervous point of sailing from Vera Cruz, and then changed his mind, for me to believe that they would go abroad at this juncture. *The Plumed Serpent* was not finished, nor was he out from under the spell of New Mexican Indians. He would look around for a while longer in the New World and listen to its tom-toms.

As to myself, Johnson writes me: "When you were able to be up, you came back to Chapala; but soon we moved into Guadalajara, staying at the Purnells', where we lingered for some weeks, most of August, I think. That was when I saw the Mexican issue of *The Laughing Horse* through the press at Idella's printer's, the printer speaking no English, I no Spanish. We returned to Santa Fe within two months after the Lawrences had left. I think it was just that all of us had had enough of Mexico for the moment, all of us were homesick."

Johnson remembers, as I do, that during our first days at Chapala, they had considered buying a small house on the lake. It is interesting to find that, despite apprehensions as to banditry, the idea had lingered in their minds to the very end of their stay. "We were away travelling on the lake," Lawrence writes to Knud Merrild, June 27, 1923, "and looking at haciendas. One could easily get a little place. But now they are expecting more revolution, and it is risky. . . . We shall leave next Monday for Mexico City—and shall probably be in New York by July 15th. I don't expect to care for the east; don't intend to stay more than a month. Then to England. It's no good, I know I am European, so I may as well go back and try it once more."

Idella Purnell tells of the actual leave-taking: "When they left Chapala, Mr. Scott's daughter and I accompanied them to the station in a boat, round trip paid for by Lawrence. When we got to the station, Frieda unabashedly blew her nose several times with deep emotion into a big, man's handkerchief, saying, 'I *like* Chapala, I *like* Chapala!' But Lawrence was glad to go."

Something, as forgotten by me as apparently by Spud and Idella, must have occurred toward the end to revive my intransigency, since it figures in letters of my own written shortly after their departure. I remember also pouncing with mean relish on what seemed to me a pertinent passage in Charles Lamb: "To think the very idea of right and fit fled from the earth, or your breast the solitary receptacle of it . . . to grow bigger every moment in your own conceit, and the world to lessen; to deify yourself at the expense of your species; to judge the world, this is the acme and supreme point of your mystery." Something in me still resisted Lawrence; and I fell back on doctrinal statements in his books to support that resistance. Something deeper in me, though, was being drawn to him. It was not only his solicitude at the hospital. Though still disliking his self-indulgences, I was haunted by the lost-child look underlying the occasional adult look of determined innocence. It must have reached me that, whatever he did, he was genuine. He often advocated, or defended, sincerity, his doing or saying at any moment whatever he felt like doing or saying, without considering the effect on others or on himself. By such definition any vagary, any willfulness, any selfishness might justify itself as being sincere. What a fine justification for naughty children! "Why are you doing that, dear?" "Because I want to."

I once saw an eight-year-old great-nephew of Henry James, suddenly and with no provocation whatever, give his younger sister a good blow in the face. When gravely asked, "Why did you do that?" he replied as gravely, "An irresistible impulse, Father." Said Lawrence, "That which I, being myself, am in myself may make the hair bristle on a man who is also himself, but very different from me. Then let it bristle. And if mine bristle back again, then let us, if we must, fly at one another like two savage men. It is how it should be. We've got to learn to live from the center of our own responsibility only, and let other people do the same." My instinct about some of his antics and much of his writing was that he was dodging the conscience of a man's blood stream and wantonly substituting the irresponsibility of a child's blood stream. On the other hand, the mistakes he made in his childish moods he seldom followed with defensive rationalizations; and my instinct was that the core of his manhood clung to the qualities which make childhood happy and lovable: wonder and faith.

For all that, I wrote Haniel Long: "The Lawrences are gone. I still like her but find him pretty odious—intelligent, witty, perceptive in ways, but on the whole a poor beast." I may have continued this strain through stubborn pride of opinion, remembering what I had written Long earlier. I did say in another letter to him, perhaps priggishly, perhaps in simple truth: "I watched Lawrence learn." I should have added: "He watched me learn, too."

After my return to Chapala on July 14, there followed three letters to my mother. It is odd to me now that I did not report to her Lawrence's happy days, of which there were many, or his long working hours on the beach, or our hearty good times with Frieda. Probably such reports had been made in briefer letters, not preserved; and these final, summary readings of him were set down at a time when, because of physical debility, my own spirits were drained. One of them says, with literary effort: "His body was visibly ribbed as the underside of a horse-chestnut leaf in the sun. His mind was colored and spired like the pyramidal orchidlike bloom on the same tree. But when the nut was born in its spiked shell, it was of no nutrition to men." In the second letter I confessed: "I envy Lawrence his complete indifference to praise or blame." In the third I used my convalescence to set down a lengthy review of our Chapala months: "We had dared, in early May, to doubt Chapala. There were insects almost every evening, midges, beetles, flying ants; and on Saturdays and Sundays there would come, amid Guadalajara fashionables, an occasional American more obnoxious to Lawrence than the insects. The waters of the lake were warm, not invigorating, and of a gray or brown that seldom sparkled and never exhilarated. Although the rest of us relished the almost transparent whitefish, a famous gastronomic delicacy of the region, Lawrence lodged complaint against them. 'How could fish be good for either palate or stomach out of so dull a liquid?' Looking at the lake on another occasion, 'It's just a great basin,' he fretted, 'of dark, warm fish milk.'"

Then comes a paragraph about the bootblacks, concerning whom, as time went on, I seemed to have found Lawrence's judgment more reasonable than at first, for I wrote of them: "They are learning too readily to ask for cigarettes; and when they vie with one another, scrambling up to dive from my shoulders, they tear my bathing suit and dig me with their fingernails. I learn also, as I accumulate more Spanish, that their large-eyed, sparkling gaiety depends to a great degree upon obscenities. 'Cabron,' meaning not only billy goat, but cuckold, is their favorite epithet. One day they were gibing at little Carlos, whom they call Popo, making fun of his stammer. He retorted that he had two words for every one of theirs and that when the time came for their wives to have babies his action would be double theirs. I have found, as Lawrence warned me I should, that their light fearlessness becomes almost impertinence, an easygoing ingratitude. Good as one might be to them, they often act like suspicious animals, holding away on the instant, remote. 'They would betray you in a moment,' declared Lawrence. 'I let my servants know yesterday that I had brought back considerable money from Guadalajara. It was very foolish of me.'

"Apart from his general suspicion, he was haunted by the banditry which had been rampant shortly before our arrival and by tales of violence. A local butcher had recently suspected his wife of too much interest in a customer. When she entered the shop one morning she had found her husband absent but his rival's bloody severed head on the counter. Six months later the husband was back, suffering no harsher sentence than an order that he change his occupation. D. H. did not find this order amusing. On a market day the Lawrences and we, passing the jail, saw prisoners lowering baskets on ropes from the roof and women below filling the baskets with provisions. Little Pancho Real was watching with us. 'Each one up there has killed a man,' he said admiringly. 'And how long are their sentences?' demanded Lawrence. 'Six months,' answered Pancho, 'and it's worth serving.'

"Lawrence was shocked to see Mexicans give murderers the same sort of admiration an Anglo-Saxon gives soldiers; and yet he had to admit that the difference between the two kinds of killers consists only in the difference between personal and national motives. To a Mexican a personal motive seems clearer cut and better justified than a motive of state; and you would have thought that Lawrence, with his faith in the rightness of action rising direct from the individual blood stream, might have sympathized with their preference. The Mexican here has learned individualism the hard way. He has chosen ragged clothes for the street; and if he happened to forget and wear good huaraches, he has yielded them with the same gay salute to whichever partisan might spy them—Carranzista or Villista. Each man for himself is the law of this Mexican life. It is a gay grim game of individualism. This directness of individualism should, I repeat, have appealed to Lawrence; but their blood streams were too different from his. The natural man could, after all, be too natural."

While I was writing these letters, before Spud and I left Mexico, I wrote also a short poem about Lawrence called "A Foreigner," to which he never referred, though he saw it later in *Indian Earth,* a volume dedicated to him:

> Chapala still remembers the foreigner
> Who came with a pale red beard and pale blue eyes
> And a pale white skin that covered a dark soul;
> They remember the night when he thought he saw a hand
> Reach through a broken window and fumble at a lock;
> They remember a tree on the beach where he used to sit
> And ask the burros questions about peace;
> They remember him walking, walking away from something.

32. Leighton's Letter

IT will be interesting, I think, to insert here a letter from Fred Leighton about the Lawrences. When I wrote him, asking if he would tell me what he remembered of them, he responded with several pages in which I note his light skimming of Lawrence's rudeness to himself and no mention of his own generous and manly reaction recounted earlier.

On an accompanying sheet he said: "I hope you will not forget the picture of Spud owlishly secretarying simultaneously for you and Lawrence, grimly enjoying your guarded duel." I was amused to be reminded of that situation and to realize afresh that, except for Spud, Lawrence and I might have reached open battle early in the game. Spud, of course, was receptacle of spleen provoked in me by Lawrence. At the same time he was receptacle of spleen provoked in Lawrence by me. Far more temperate than either of us, he quietly enjoyed being septic tank for vents from both houses. He may have been aware of the ignominious figure Lawrence was planning for me as Owen in *The Plumed Serpent* and was certainly aware of the uncomplimentary Lawrence portraits I was sketching in verse. Less definitely but to good purpose, I believe that both Lawrence and I were content with the fact that Spud deflected our shafts from direct aim and saved our companionship. Beyond personal irritations, which we kept mainly concealed from each other, hidden between the paws of our friend the sphinx, we enjoyed open ideological combat, Lawrence repeatedly despising my faith in spiritual democracy and I challenging his in the divine right of heroes to judge for the masses. In *The Plumed Serpent* he made a good case against political aspects of socialism as he saw it developing in Mexico; but some years later he wrote me acknowledging a common sense of heroism in the mass of men as a

183

necessary element complementary to the heroism of individual leader-ship. And I could admit to him now not only that a good man has far more than the strength of ten but that great sections of mankind apparently enjoy being fooled all the time.

In 1923, though he was more mature for his thirty-seven years than I was for my forty-one, neither of us was inclined to open-minded concessions. I am sure, however, that we enjoyed our spoken or un-spoken duels, glad at the same time that a friend was there between us with his wise and healing silences. Frieda also, though seldom si-lent, would whack any of us with wholesome sense and knew that she was sparing the whole foursome by attracting great shots of her husband's venom and shooting back at him. Leighton reports, after the years, how these encounters appeared to one less used to them than we were and not then informed, I believe, of my having counseled Mrs. Lawrence to strike first and to strike hard. However much the result may have appalled outsiders, Frieda and I continued to believe the counsel sound.

"Twenty-six years have passed," wrote Leighton in April, 1949, "yet some impressions of D. H. Lawrence cling, powerful and vivid. The most vivid memories spring from his temper and his bad manners: the most powerful from the feeling he evoked in me of the tragic destiny of deep insight shackled to violent emotions in a frail body.

"His bad manners shocked me, made me wish to apologize for him to somebody, to anybody. Never before or since have I heard a human being, in educated society, repeatedly release such flow of obscene vile abuse on his wife (or on anyone) in the presence of comparative strangers as Lawrence did on Frieda; nor, I must admit, have I· heard such apparently uninhibited response. Lawrence was far more elo-quent, more varied in his vituperation, but Frieda hardly less emphatic.

"Those evenings at the Hotel Monte Carlo, those afternoons on the pretty terrace in Chapala in the spring of 1923 were memorable ones with much conversation, both trivial and important; the words have all fled my memory long ago, a few only of the ideas remain, but there persists sharply today that feeling of wishing to be somewhere else when Lawrence started railing at Frieda.

"Anger in the grand manner I recall also. It was that day Lawrence was to lunch with the Minister of Education, José Vasconcelos. As a minor functionary of the Department of Education, and specifically through my immediate superior, Bob Haberman, I had arranged the affair. We gathered in the antechamber of the Minister; Lawrence, Frieda, you, Spud Johnson, Carleton Beals, and I. We announced our arrival; we waited and we waited. A *mozo* emerged from within, putting his thumb and first finger together in that inimitable, inevitable Mexican bureaucratic gesture, and said '*Un momentito,*' one little minute. How I recall those 'little minutes' in Mexico that so often stretched into hours! So we waited again. Lawrence was getting decidedly fidgety. Another *mozo* appeared—this one more important— probably a private secretary, and said, 'The Minister regrets, but urgent matters of State prevent his receiving you today and will you do him the honor to lunch with him tomorrow?' Lawrence sprang to his feet, blue eyes flashing hot blue fire, 'No! I shan't!' he shouted and strode from the room. Though visibly flustered, the rest of us including Frieda replied we'd be happy to accept for the morrow, and the private secretary who didn't know English retreated to inform Mr. Vasconcelos that we'd all accepted for the following day; a luncheon which was duly held at Sylvain's with the Minister at his charming best—but no Lawrence. Lawrence had stuck to his first utterance, 'I'll not go! I'll not think of it!' and he had strode back and forth on the third floor inner balcony of the Education building for fully ten minutes before he could be quieted sufficiently to leave. He felt he had been insulted; in him Art, Literature, History, the British Empire, Civilization itself, had been insulted! How anyone's body, to say nothing of a sick, fragile one, could withstand such berserk bursts of passion I did not know.

"Thereafter, while Lawrence remained at the Monte Carlo, I was in disgrace; for I had arranged this insulting affair. Of course I was about with you and Spud and Frieda, and Frieda was cordial as usual; but Lawrence, though civil, was distinctly frigid. Then off he went to Chapala. What a strange adventure that was! Nobody we knew had heard much of Chapala in those days, though I had been there the previous autumn and had mentioned it to Lawrence as a good quiet place in which to live and write."

Then, corroborating my memory of our wild rush from the Monte Carlo, Leighton remembers "finally unearthing a pushcart and a man to push it and piling mountains of luggage into it and myself escorting it all clear across the city to the old Colonia Station. How Frieda and the rest of you got there I don't seem to recall.

"Some weeks later," he continues, "when I visited Chapala, Lawrence was quite friendly again. It appeared I had been forgiven, because of my efforts in getting Frieda on to that train. He had then begun *The Plumed Serpent* and was daily entering neat meticulous lines into his copybook.

"It was in Chapala I felt that other deeper fire in Lawrence, that hot blue passion turned inward until it touched molten levels below. It was the Lawrence of *Mornings in Mexico,* the Lawrence who at times felt both Huitzilopochtli and Quetzalcoatl in himself, as he lived there on that quiet mountain-circled shore.

"I recall walking with him one bright morning along the beach. This was when he propounded his theory—it was no theory to him, it was direct inner apprehension of evident truth—of the races of men who live in mankind, not races with different colors of skin, but races of different capabilities; especially that aristocratic ruling race the members of which appeared from time to time in cottages and palaces, in slums and on farms, in every clime, and of course especially in England, that mystic superhuman near-divine race of aristocrats who were meant to lead and guide the world, who would do so now were its members fully conscious of themselves, who would do so certainly and inevitably in the future. So I recall his talk.

"It is hard to disentangle the threads of that conversation, twisted as they are by the rotation of the intervening years. Looking back, however, I remember Lawrence's struggles to emerge from the dull anonymity of a collier's family; looking back, I see in the frailty of his body, the torrential blast of his feelings, the intuitive perception of his mind and spirit, raw material for the forging of this theory. However he came by it, it was what made him the Imperial Englishman in Australia, the confused master-interpreter of sex and woman to America, the petulant mystic who at times rose volcanically to great perceptions.

"And who shall say and who can truly evaluate? Does not history reveal, and do we not constantly see, the continual emergence of the great individual from the seething mouldering mass of mediocrity around him? Lawrence, in mystic language and with confused consciousness, was struggling toward an explanation of some very rugged facts in the world of human personality."

33. *Wanderer*

WHILE we were still in Chapala, Lawrence wrote me a postcard from somewhere in Texas: "It rained all the way in
Mexico, but Texas is fierce—hot—queer show—don't feel
much elation being here in U. S. Do hope you're better," and then on
August 14 he wrote me from New Jersey that he was visiting the
Seltzers there. A 1949 letter from Mrs. Bernardine Fritz says of this
period: "I remember the first time I met him. The Seltzers published
him in this country. Adela Seltzer was my cousin and, like so many
women, she was utterly enslaved. We were at the Algonquin—about
eight of us—and Adela, usually so voluble, was barely able to stammer
introductions. She sat, entranced, doubtlessly torn between ecstasy
at breathing the same air and a sense of unworthiness to do so. I was
too young at that time to feel the awe and wonder—if anything I was
perhaps just a little smug over being at the same table and seen by so
many friends who envied me. He, Lawrence, said practically nothing.
Another evening, however, at the Seltzers' home, he was talkative and
morose by turns, but compelling and fascinating. It's odd about the
aura that certain people achieve. I am sure that if I had known nothing of him, I would, despite his silences, have been deeply impressed."
Mrs. Fritz fails on either occasion to mention Frieda, who was perhaps already on the sea, bound for England, the more resolute this
time of the two wanderers.

Lawrence's New Jersey letter said: "You may be home by now and
you may not. We are still here. Frieda sails on Saturday by the *Orbita*
to Southampton. I'm not going. Where am I going? Ask me. Perhaps
to Los Angeles, and then to the Islands, if I could find a sailing ship.
Quién sabe? It's pleasant here—the trees and hills and stillness. But it
is dim to me. Doesn't materialize. The same with New York: like a

house of cards set up. I like it best down at the Battery, where the ragtag lie on the grass. Have met practically nobody; and the same thing, nothing comes through to me from them. Tell Spoodle the Horse came. . . . The picture of the horse looks like a sobbing ass. The inside quite amused me. . . . A little more guts, a little less indigestion. Your plays came too. I had read them long ago—it seems long—and forgotten the titles, also *Beloved Stranger*. Many of these poems I really like. It hasn't been hot here—quite pleasant. I wish things were real to me. I see the lake at Chapala, not the hills of Jersey (New). And these people are just as you said of New England —quenched. I mean the natives. As for the trains full of businessmen! . . . I shall probably leave for somewhere next week. I've booked F's passage and she's setting off alone, quite perky."

I was sorry that he was without Frieda, wondered what he would do without her and where he would go. I was sorry now that they had not stayed in Chapala, that we had not all stayed. My first sense of relief from him had worn off. I missed them. I guessed that Frieda had wanted to see her children, that he had not, and that they had quarreled over it.

My surmise was borne out later by what I read in various accounts. The Lawrences had had on the pier in New York the most fiery and serious battle of their lives. His only mention of it to me was "she's setting off alone, quite perky." Knud Merrild's book relates the situation, since Lawrence, after the battle—when Frieda had insisted on sailing and he had refused to accompany her—had fled across continent to join him and Götzsche in Los Angeles, hopeful of inducing them to go with him back to Mexico and found that colony of the chosen which had been his perpetual chimera. He may have deceived himself that such an accomplishment would be the right and heroic solace for loss of Frieda. As Mrs. Carswell repeats, from Frieda's account to her in London, "When they parted, it was in such anger that both of them felt it might be for always." Mrs. Carswell records also that, seven years before, in 1916, two years after the marriage, Frieda's only way of seeing her children "in London when their autumn term began . . . was to wait outside of their schools as they came out, so to walk along, have a word with them, give them some small gifts, and keep herself fresh in their memories. . . . Lawrence hated and disapproved of this. But Frieda stayed firm." I remembered the husband's resentment in Chapala of even the children's photographs. I remem-

bered her quick forgiveness of him, even as she had forgiven him
earlier when her beloved father had died and the comfort she received
from her curiously jealous husband was the curt comment, "You
didn't expect to keep him forever, did you?" Though she loyally for-
gave Lawrence, in neither case would Frieda swerve from her other
loyalty, and was not loyalty the very quality he had told us he liked
best? May not Frieda have known that innerly he loved her loyalty
and because of it would the more surely come back to her? Or was
she for a while too hurt and angry to care? Whatever it was, in 1923
as in 1916, Frieda held her ground.

It was not her loyalty, after all, for which Lawrence felt dislike. It
was her maternal loyalty. Perhaps because he had no children of his
own, possibly because he could not have children—had he not written
Frieda even before their elopement that he hoped for children by her?
—he gave frequent evidence of repugnance toward maternal instincts
in women, in animals too. Because of his real or imagined semi-
amorous feeling toward his own mother, he probably avoided the
thought of her having physically borne him and so resented the
thought of other women, or of any creatures, as brooders and breeders.
Fond though he was of his little she-dog in Taos, the Pipsy he had
hoped to take along with us to Mexico, Merrild has related at vivid
length Lawrence's fury toward the animal when she was in heat. Lawrence has told of it too in a poem. And Dorothy Brett recounts his
flare-up toward another Taos pet, Smoky, the hen; how he came in
carrying the bird "headless and with wings still flapping" and how
he explained, " 'I chopped off her head . . . to relieve my feelings. She
was getting broody and then I hate them.' " Brett says that Frieda
"for some unknown reason," flew into a temper and ranted at Lawrence. The reason may have been unknown to Brett, but one may
guess that Frieda was remembering times when she herself had been
"broody" and had somehow managed to keep her head. She kept not
only her head but her heart. She kept both Lawrence and her children.
In one of his poems Lawrence expresses himself:

> The mother in you, fierce as a murdress, glaring to England,
> Yearning towards England, towards your young children.

This time she had glared and yearned toward England effectively
and had left her husband in the United Sates; but according to Mrs.
Carswell, "immediately upon her arrival in England she sent Lawrence
a wifely cable. He must come to her because she needed him . . ."

A steamer letter I received from Frieda, posted in London, contained no open mention of the rift: "Here I am on the boat 'all by mineself' on such a dull boat—Chapala seems a dream, an impossible dream—I was not happy in New York or New Jersey. The Seltzers are very nice, but I don't know what it was, I felt such a poor little nightlight, hateful. I met a few, very few people, the *nice* ones all knew you, but everybody seems so tired—I am sure all those layers of people put away in their apartments on top of each other like boxes of gloves or hankies make the air dead. It makes me feel drugged—Lawrence you *knew* wouldn't like it. I loved some of your poems, but the plays were *too* black, I hope you don't feel like that any more. I don't think Europe will be gay. It may not be possible to go to Germany at all—I do hope my journey won't be useless—especially as far as my children go. Lawrence wouldn't come, he is going to wander. Where we meet again I don't know. If Europe is possible he will come—I will also let you know how it is—that you don't come, just to be miserable. There was one interesting evening with a few people—rather nice but again 'from the head.' I wish you were with me in Europe. . . . I was very sad to part with you and especially you not well—I was very happy with you and Spoodle—I hope we shall have good times together again, we will have that monastery when we find the place. . . . How is Santa Fe? It's a thousand million times better than the East. It's just about the time when you mixed us a cocktail. . . . Lord, I am not at all gay on this beastly boat."

Within six weeks, accompanied by Kai Götzsche but not Merrild, Lawrence was headed again for Mexico, along the Pacific coast this time. Spud and I had left for the north only a brief while before Lorenzo was returning south again. I have wished often that we had stayed this long at Chapala and been with him for further Mexican experiences. On October 5, 1923, he wrote me from Navajoa, Sonora: "Here I am wandering slowly and hotly with Götzsche down this west coast. Where F is I don't know. This West is much wilder, emptier, more hopeless than Chapala. It makes one feel the door is shut on one. There is a blazing sun, a vast hot sky, big lonely green hills and mountains, a flat blazing littoral with a few palms, sometimes a dark blue sea which is not quite of this earth—then little towns that seem to be slipping down an abyss—and the door of life shut on it all, only the sun burning, the clouds of birds passing, the zopilotes like flies, the lost lonely palm trees, the deep dust of the roads, the donkeys moving in a gold dust cloud. In the mountains, lost, motionless silver mines. Alamos, a once lovely little town, lost, and slipping down the gulf in the mountains, forty miles up the awfullest road I've ever been bruised along. But somehow or other you get there. And more wonderful you get *out* again. There seems a sentence of extinction written over it all. In the middle of the little covered market at Alamos, between the meat and the vegetables, a dead dog lay stretched as if asleep. The meat vendor said to the vegetable man: 'You'd better throw it out.' The veg-man looked at the dead dog and saw no reason for throwing it out. So no doubt it still lies there. We went also to haciendas—a cattle hacienda: wild, weird, brutal with a devastating brutality. Many of the haciendas are in the hands of Chinese, who run about like vermin down this coast. So there we are. I think, when we get to Mazatlan, we shall take a boat down to Manzanillo, and so to Guadalajara. It is better there. At least there is not a dead dog in mid-market. . . ."

In *The Woman Who Rode Away,* Lawrence makes record of this dead dog in the market place.

The travelers went on south to Guadalajara, traveling by car, by horse, by burro, and seeing the bullfight near Tepic.

The Purnells gave them the use of a primitive house in Ajijic, beyond Chapala. Götzsche writes Merrild, October 22, 1923, with acute observation: "I cannot help being amused about L. You know he always scorns sentimentality, and likes to appear rational, which he isn't at all. Why, even before we got out here, he said he didn't like to go to Japala [*sic*] without Frieda (he is longing for her) and when we were out there, he was deeply moved, he thought it had changed so much. 'Somehow it becomes unreal to me now. I don't know why,' he said. He is always so concerned about the 'spirit' of the place that he isn't aware, I believe, that it is he, himself, his own mood or frame of mind, that determines his impressions of the moment, or the landscape. It is, of course, possible that the place has changed, it is fall now and he was there with Frieda in the spring. But of course that isn't it. It is the 'spirit.' 'The life has changed somehow, has gone dead, you know, I feel I shan't live my life here.' And so on. His eyes were glossy, to the point of tears. . . . He had willed himself into belief that this was the place he loved, and the place to live. And then he is offended and cross because Frieda is happy to be in England. She writes it is the best country in the world, and wants him to come, etc. Deepest inside himself he is proud of England and if it wasn't for his author ideas, he would go back at once. But he wants to start that 'new life' away from money, lust, and greediness, back to nature and serious-ness. . . . He maintains that people like Johnson only play life away. I am afraid that that applies to himself; everything becomes play to him; he has means enough not to take anything really seriously. . . . It is evident to me that, inside, he is fighting himself, what to do, because as an author, he likes best to stay here and build a new colony in this country, a new simple, ideal life, but as a man he likes to go back to England and culture. . . . I rather realize that if I leave him now and go back to America, he will continue to ramble about in the world, without peace. . . . He needs, in a high degree, something else to think about, and something else to do besides his writings. I am absolutely sure that he would feel happier and live more happily if he could go out for a few hours a day, and have some work to do, milk a cow or plow a field. As he lives now, he only writes a little in the morning and the rest of the day he just hangs around on a bench or drifts over to the market place, hands in pocket, perhaps buying some candy, fruit, or something. If he could only have access to a kitchen, so he could make our food, that would occupy him for a couple of hours."

And a few days later: "We are still in Guadalajara, it seems like Lawrence is too slothful to move away. I would like to go to Japala as it is easier to paint on the streets there, and get people to pose, than here where it is so overcrowded with people and too much traffic."

But Götzsche knew that Chapala was haunted with Frieda. And so he continues: "I can feel that Lawrence is working himself up to *will* to go to England. I believe Frieda has influenced his friends in Eng-land, because they all write that he must come back and that England is beginning to be the leading country in culture again. 'If I go, I shan't stay long, I know,' he says. Well! That means he is thinking strongly about departure." Götzsche goes on: "Poor Miss Purnell, who is poetry-mad and talks verse with L. when we are there, gets some very hard thumps from him. I am avoiding L. as much as possible at present, because, considering all things, he is really insane when he is as now. . . . You know his way, and how he bends his head far down, till his beard is resting on his chest and he says (not laughing), 'Hee, hee, hee' every time one talks to him. A cold stream always runs down my spine when he does that. I feel it is something insane about him. I am, considering everything, really glad that we have not been able to find a ranch here, because I realize it would be too difficult to live with a man like L. in the long run. Frieda is at least an absolute necessity as a quencher. I have sometimes the feeling that he is afraid she will run away from him now, and that he cannot bear to be alone." A few days later the report is that "Lawrence is more human again. At present, he excuses himself on the ground that the air is so changeable that it makes him 'crazy' once in a while. A poor excuse!"

Then Lawrence writes Merrild: "Götzsche will have told you that Frieda won't come back: not West any more. I had a cable yesterday asking me to go to England. So there's nothing for it but to go." And Götzsche adds: "The last couple of weeks, Lawrence has been himself again. . . . Lawrence is a queer snail and impossible to understand. He seems to be absolutely nuts at times, and to have a hard time with himself. He overestimates himself. . . . At other times he is so reasonable and so overwhelmingly good that there is no end to it. . . . He makes everything much more artificial and complicated than it is in reality. He is afraid Frieda will avoid him; he says that she can have a house in London and have her children with her, then he can travel alone. 'She will hate it before long,' he says, biting his lower lip and nodding small, quick nods. Do you know him? The fact is that he is afraid she will like the arrangement only too well. Nevertheless, he has a large heart and means well, but his ideas are so impractical that it is doubtful he will get anyone to accept them. . . ."

After another week Götzsche tells Merrild: "Lawrence was impossible the last days in Guadalajara, although rather nice. But one day he came and said he could not go to England. 'I am sure I will *die* if I have to see England again.' All right, we decided then to stay and look for a farm, so we went out to see people and ask for information as to where we could find a farm to live on for the winter. He looked really sick and so pale, and his head hung way down on his chest. Next morning he came in to me and said: 'It is just as well to go to Europe, don't you think? One might just as well, I feel I don't care any more. I just go.' All right, then we'll go, and Friday we drove off from Guadalajara."

So they sailed together: Lawrence to England and Götzsche to Copenhagen. The former wrote Merrild from Havana, "G. at last happy." And "G" reported from Denmark on February 4, 1924: "I have had several cards and notes from Lawrence, last from Paris, where he writes that he and Frieda are going to Baden-Baden and from there to the U.S.A., where he thinks we can meet in March. He has lauded Taos several times, but likes best to go to Mexico again. I think he ought to feel ashamed of the way he changes from hate to love about the different places where he has been. He surely has very little control over his ideas, extraordinarily little—he doesn't even in the least know what he wants. . . . Yes, it was remarkable with his friendship to us. I don't understand it either. He is sincere in it, I believe; he needs it, needs us, but I am also sure that he doesn't praise us to the skies when he talks about us to others, in periods when he doesn't need us. He doesn't even refrain from exposing Frieda. But I don't believe it is out of meanness; he doesn't mean it, as he says, and at bottom he is goodness itself, and I do like him even if I could never feel about him in the way one feels about comradeship."

Idella Purnell writes me recalling Lawrence and Götzsche in Guadalajara: "They stopped at the Hotel García. Lawrence made a habit of coming to our house every night for dinner. What Götzsche did I don't know; he came a few times. They seemed entirely casual in their relationship to each other, like people who are friends, without being all-out friends. They did not have the community of interests or of hates which would be necesary for any kind of deep affection. At that time Daddy was on a strict vegetarian diet, and Lawrence seemed to enjoy it very much: frijoles, *queso blanco,* tortillas, honey, vegetables, fruits, sometimes a fruit pie, or *bizcochos.* After dinner we would go upstairs to the verandah where we would sit under the jasmine and talk, or into my study, if the night was cool, where sometimes he and Daddy talked while I worked or we all three talked. One night Lawrence got very 'high,' almost as though he had had too much to drink: he was gay and more charming than I had ever seen him—and he could charm when he wished. He stood by the fireplace in my study and told us all about Ezra Pound's advent in London. Lawrence with the red beard vanished, and there stood a young, callow, swashbuckling Ezra, with an earring in one ear, very affected and silly. Then came his parents to London to see him, after Ezra had the London drawing rooms bewitched by his mannerisms and affectations; and they were good plain middle-western folks—and Ezra died away, and there were pa and ma, good and plain and middle-western, and poor Ezra not knowing what to do about them. Lawrence made us see the parents and feel sorry for them as they sensed their son's attitude; and see the son, and even feel a little sorry for him! Then he went on and told us autobiographical details which later I recognized in *Sons and Lovers*. I never liked Lawrence better, except maybe one time on the train coming from Chapala, where we spent the whole trip discussing the Witter Bynner issue of *Palms,* for which I think he drew the cover design. He drew me a number of very fine cover designs for *Palms,* several of which I used. He also made various excellent suggestions for editing, raising funds, etc., quite as if he had forgotten I was an impertinent, egotistical little wretch! After he left, we had some notes from him, always kind and friendly. He always wanted to return to Jalisco."

Though while he was with the Purnells, I had had no word from Lawrence, he had written me on November 17, 1923, from the Monte Carlo, our old stamping ground in Mexico City, shortly before he sailed: "We got here this morning—hotel just the same, save fewer guests. All inquiring for you and the thin one and for F. But Mexico seems cold and dark after Jalisco. I like Jalisco very much—the plain around Guadalajara. It is Pacific Ocean influence, without too much softness. I want to get on a boat, as soon as I can now, to England. God knows how long I shall stay there. This cold, glowing morning in this city makes me think of it with repugnance. It was just nicely warm in Guadalajara. But we must bring penalties on ourselves. Perhaps later we'll all meet and make a place in Jalisco, even Mabel Lujan. It's terrible here, I can't speak Italian any more, only bad Spanish. We had a flask of the *very* good Chianti for lunch. Tonight we're going to dinner with the Brit. Consul General at Tlalpam—all in evening dress. How's that for committing suicide on the spot? My dinner jacket is so green with overripeness. I'm going to look for Covarrubias. . . . I miss you at the corner table—miss everybody and everything here. Don't like it—want to get out quick. This city doesn't feel *right,* feels like a criminal plotting his next rather mean crime. . . . '*Una arancia, una banana, o dolce di prugne?*' Mine's a banana. *Hasta luego.*"

Then within the month, December 7, 1923, came a note from London: "Here I am—London—gloom—yellow air—bad cold—bed—old house—Morris wallpaper—visitors—English voices—tea in old cups—poor D.H.L. perfectly miserable, as if he was in his tomb. You don't need his advice, so take it: Never come to Europe any more. In a fortnight I intend to go to Paris then to Spain—and in the early spring I hope to be back on the western continent. I wish I was in Santa Fe at this moment. As it is, for my sins, and Frieda's, I am in London. I only hope Mexico will stop revoluting. De Profundis."

A fortnight later he wrote concerning an English friend: "He has a son with lung trouble and thinks he might get him to New Mexico. Money scarce. Said son has wife and three baby girls—don't know ages. Do you think he could find a house for $50 or $60 a month in Santa Fe? . . . Don't curse me for bothering you—you are nice about these things. Ask Alice Corbin to help you think of a place. Tell her I consider we never quarrelled in the least, therefore are friends. Also Frieda and I think of coming to New Mex. in early spring, on way to Old Mex. And Middleton Murry says he wants to come too and probably another friend. How's that? I wrote you, *don't* come to Europe, it's awful. I hate being here—plainly—New Mexico is far far far better. Dead this side. Stay in N.M. Greet Spoodle and the Alices and be greeted by me and F. As I said to Spoodle, I get so cross with you for still being a democrat, but hombre, there is the underlying affection."

He seemed to be friends with Murry again, friends with Alice Corbin, friends with me, and no longer to feel that the Americas were the "death continent." I wrote him and Frieda that we happily looked forward to their return, and on March 3, 1924 he reported: "We sail on Wednesday on the *Aquitania* for New York, arrive about March 12th. We shall stay a week or so—then on to New Mexico. Seltzer has been behaving queerly. I must see to him. Dorothy Brett is coming with us—she is deaf—and a painter—and daughter of Viscount Esher. I think we shall stay a while in Taos. I want to go back to Mexico—particularly I want to go to Oaxaca. What do you think of that? We look forward to seeing you, and to making plans. Thankful to be leaving Europe—were in Paris and Germany. Au revoir."

He was still wandering. In *The Rainbow*, years before, he had reflected himself when he said of Fred Brangwen: "There seemed to him to be no root to his life, no place for him to get satisfied in. He dreamed of going abroad. But his instinct knew that change of place would not solve his problem. He wanted change, deep, vital change of living. And he did not know how to get it." Then of Alvina, *The Lost Girl,* he had written: "She took the timetable that hung in the hall: the timetable, that magic carpet of today. When in doubt, *move.* That was the maxim. Move. Where to?" Other passages declare: "I feel a stranger everywhere and nowhere" or "I feel sometimes I shall go mad, because there is nowhere to go, no 'new world.'" In *Sea and Sardinia* he answers: "What does one care? What does one care for precept and mental dictation? Is there not the massive, brilliant, out-flinging recklessness in the male soul, summed up in the sudden word: *Andiamo! Andiamo!* Let us go on! *Andiamo!*—Let us go hell knows where, but let us go on." In *Aaron's Rod* he has said through Lilly, "'I am a vagrant really, or a migrant. I must migrate. . . . It's just my nature.'" Professor Joseph Spencer's description of Lady Mary Wortley Montagu is apposite: "She is one of the most shining characters in the world but shines like a comet; she is all irregularity and always wandering."

I wonder if Lawrence had read St. Augustine's passage: "For he does not say, go to the East, and seek justice, travel far to the West to find peace; where you are, there He is, for to Him Who is everywhere present, one comes by love and not by sail."

Lawrence did, in his essay on Herman Melville make an almost final admission: ". . . you can't fight it out by running away. When you have run a long way from Home and Mother, then you realize that the earth is round, and if you keep on running you'll be back on the same old doorstep—like a fatality." He declares elsewhere: "Men are free when they are in a living homeland, not when they are straying and breaking away. . . . Men are free when they belong to a living, organic, believing community, active in fulfilling some unfulfilled, perhaps unrealized purpose."

Might not the Indians be this "believing community?" Might he not somehow join them? As he said in one of his verses, "I am so weary of pale-face importance," and in another passage, "There are unknown, unworked lands where the salt has not lost its savor."

The Indians were still calling him. He was still wandering, even though he could write Merrild: "I feel as if I should wander over the brink of existence."

34. Colonist

ALTHOUGH Lawrence had never definitely broached the colony idea to me, the little Eden in which there was to be no governing serpent but himself, I had realized that he kept dreaming toward something of the sort to be found in Mexico. Except for his persistent, fundamental fear, localized and quickened in Mexico by outward conditions, he would have liked nothing better than to seat the hoped-for ranch in one of the lake's small communities, to which a group of friends might come, the Danes from Taos, a few from Europe and, possibly, Johnson and I. But he wanted the group's members to be his dedicated followers and he knew that from Johnson and me he would receive no such discipleship. Though he could be amazingly magnetic and persuasive on occasion, he felt certain that neither of us would yield to commandments. Knud Merrild had inclined to yield and follow but had rebelled in time—a gentle but firm defection. "Something in me revolted," he writes, "many voices in me spoke: 'You are talking Lawrence, thinking Lawrence, living and acting Lawrence, your being is through Lawrence, you are saturated with Lawrence. Shed the burden of Lawrence. . . . Go your own way. . . . and know by yourself.' Yet I liked Lawrence," he continues, "I believed in him and I had the greatest admiration and respect for him." Merrild, however, like Götzsche, was not at all built for what is described in *Aaron's Rod* as "the deep, fathomless submission to the heroic soul in a greater man."

Götzsche, who went along on the second trip to Mexico, proved there to be a self-guided, stable fellow, liking his own keel, so that he lost Lawrence's attention. In some way I had been able to hold that attention, perhaps through Frieda, or perhaps because I was not fanatically turned inward to my own ideas but liked listening, even, or especially, to this man who seemed to me now and then, as he did to Götzsche, more than a touch mad. But it was a kind of madness which is sometimes sounder than sanity.

Mad or sane, the colony dream continued to plague Lawrence and had, I am more and more convinced, bolstered his angry willingness to let Frieda sail alone for England. While she was gone, he could be showing Mexico to the Danes. They were strong boys. They might kindle to the colony idea. They might be sentinels and guardians in this dangerous country, as well as disciples. And then from Europe might follow rare spirits. He never opened the scheme to me in its Utopian terms. He knew that I could only have dodged it, as first Merrild had and then Götzsche. But apparently he had maintained hope that, in "decadent Europe," there might yet live spirits innocent enough to believe with him, followers faithful enough to be drawn by his spell into the dreamed-of heaven.

The idea had always obsessed him. In 1915 he had tried to persuade Philip Heseltine (Peter Warlock) and Dikron Koujoumdjian (Michael Arlen) to join a colony. The location was then, or perhaps on another occasion, to be Florida. He had written Mrs. Carswell in 1916: "It is always my idea, that a few people by being together should bring to pass a new earth and a new heaven." True enough, he wrote her differently in 1917: "It is wrong to seek adherents. One must be single." But the doubt passed, the idea revived. From Chapala he again wrote Mrs. Carswell, in 1923: "I wish it could be that I *could* start a little centre—a ranch—where we could have our little adobe house and make a life . . . here in Mexico, in Jalisco. . . . It may be my destiny is in Europe. . . . If it is, I'll come back." He went back, not once but twice, the second time to die. But meanwhile, still from Chapala, he was writing Knud Merrild, first doubtfully on June 17, 1923, as to a possible farm in Ocotlan at the end of the lake: "Why should one work to build a place and make it nice, only to have it destroyed? So, for the present at least, I give it up. Mankind is too unkind," and then, ten days later: "We will go on looking and preparing, you and Götzsche and us, till we can really make a life that is not killed off as it was in Del Monte. . . . We have to be a few men with honour and fearlessness, and make a life together. There is nothing else, believe me." After he had left Chapala, July 2, on his way to New York, he was writing Merrild, July 15, from New Orleans: "What I would like best would be to go back to Mexico. If we were a few people, we could make a life in Mexico."

About an earlier appeal to Middleton Murry and Katherine Mansfield: "Let us all live together and create a new world," Murry asks in *Son of Woman,* "What was in his mind?" and answers, "I think nothing less than to be the founder of culture in one of these 'unknown,' not yet humanised lands: to be the Moses, the law-giver who should bring its soul to consciousness."

William York Tindall in *D. H. Lawrence and Susan His Cow* extends the comment: "Lawrence wanted tyranny on his own terms and only on condition that he be tyrant. It is in this way that he managed to reconcile his individualism, which had found itself so uneasy under democracy, with dictatorship. Throughout his life he dreamed of starting a community over which he could rule, and throughout his life this desire was frustrated by an individualism in others nearly as great as his own."

The dream is flatly stated by Count Dionys in Lawrence's *The Ladybird:* "Not as a hereditary aristocrat, but as a *man* who is by nature an aristocrat . . . it is my sacred duty to hold the lives of other men in my hands, and to shape the issue. But I can never fulfil my destiny till men will willingly put their lives in my hands."

On his first Mexican quest he had had only Johnson and me, who did not believe in him at all except as an artist. On the second Mexican quest Götzsche had had trials with Lawrence and reported to Merrild in rotating irritation, patience, and despair.

Wistfully Lawrence wrote Merrild on October 5, 1923, that somebody "said he'd *give* me six or eight acres of land near Guaymas, near the sea, in a very wild, very strange and beautiful country, if I'd only build a house on the place"; but a postscript is added to the letter: "When I look at the ranches, I doubt very much whether I shall ever try to live on one for ever and a day."

In England, however, the colonizing urge seized Lawrence again, despite the setback it had received from both Danes. Looking around his circle and seeing Lady Ottoline Morrell, Lady Cynthia Asquith, and the Honorable Dorothy Brett, as well as Bohemians like the Murrys and Koteliansky and comfortable middle-class friends like the Carswells, he wrote Lady Ottoline, "I do believe that there are enough decent people to make a start with. . . . We will be aristocrats. . . . We will found an order, and we will all be Princes. . . ."

Tindall finds in Coleridge a similar dream and quotes from the poet's essay, *The Friend:* "What I dared not expect from constitutions of governments and whole nations I hoped from religion and a small company of chosen individuals, and formed a plan, as harmless as it was extravagant, of trying the experiment of human perfectibility on the banks of the Susquehannah; where our little society . . . was to have combined the innocence of the Patriarchal Age with the knowledge of and general refinements of European culture."

Tindall may remember that long before Coleridge, St. Augustine had projected a colonizing venture of ten congenial men: "But when we began to reflect whether the wives some of us had already and others hoped to have would permit this, all that plan which was being so well framed broke to pieces in our hands and was utterly wrecked and cast aside."

Coleridge should have come to Taos or Chapala and explained to Lawrence the natural harmlessness of the later poet's vacillations between the old world and the new. St. Augustine should have come and cautioned him concerning wives. But Lawrence never woke up to the "extravagance" of his quest. And that is why he persuaded Frieda to plan the fabulous Café Royal dinner and, after it, when he had drunk too much of the port which was bad for him, issued his pathetic invitation, calculated to challenge and test the group closest to him in England. He had decided to make dramatic proposal of a joint exodus for them all to New Mexico. His dream colony was to be rooted at Del Monte—with perhaps a ranch later in Old Mexico.

Mrs. Carswell tells of it, as do others. She was present with her husband, and with Mary Cannan, Dorothy Brett, Mark Gertler, Koteliansky, and Middleton Murry. When I asked Frieda twenty-nine years later about Koteliansky, she beamed back at me: "He did not like me, but he loved Lawrence and he used to cheer Lawrence by roaring Russian songs at him. He was a mystery because he was supposed to be in a law office but he would take us there and bounce his boss out of the place and mix up sour herring and mashed potatoes for us on the spot with any old plates and then sing for us. Yes, he loved Lawrence. *Ja!*" She nodded, gurgling with the memories and with no resentment left, if ever there had been any. At the Café Royal dinner, according to Mrs. Carswell, when Koteliansky had made his tipsy speech in Lawrence's praise, punctuated with smashed wine glasses, he culminated: " 'Nobody here realizes how great he is. . . . Especially no woman here or anywhere can possibly realize the greatness of Lawrence. . . . Frieda does not count. Frieda is different. I understand and don't include her.' " Apparently this was too much for one of the other guests. Mrs. Carswell remembers Murry going up to Lawrence and kissing him "with a kind of effusiveness which afflicted me. 'Women can't understand this,' he said. 'This is an affair between men.'. . . 'Maybe,' said I. 'But anyhow it wasn't a woman who betrayed Jesus with a kiss.' At this Murry again embraced Lawrence, who sat perfectly still and unresponsive, with a dead-white face in which the eyes alone were alive. . . . 'I *have* betrayed you, old chap, I confess it,' continued Murry. 'In the past I *have* betrayed you. But never again. I call you all to witness, never again.' " From Murry's own writings as well as Mrs. Carswell's, I gather that the betrayals had consisted not only in harsh reviews of Lawrence's work as against protestation of deep personal affection but in Murry's not having been always on hand with his wife, Katherine Mansfield, at Lawrence's beck and call. "Throughout all this," the Carswell narrative continues as to the dinner, "Frieda remained aloof and scornful—excluded. Her innings would be later. She reminded me of King David looking down in derision from an upper window. One could not but admire her."

I summarize from several accounts the scenes that followed. First Lawrence, answering the toasts, sprang his proposal that the whole group should cast aside practical and mundane considerations and follow him and Frieda to New Mexico for the founding of his New Jerusalem. Murry is said to have assented with fervor, the others one by one to have declined or demurred for this or that valid reason— all except the Honorable Dorothy Brett who, to the prophet's call, gave acceptance and meant it. At least one disciple was ready to follow. But Lawrence, having shot his bolt and taken too much port, fell forward on the table and lost consciousness.

Ernest Boyd has commented: "Perhaps the choicest example of the insensitive humorlessness of the would-be guardians of Lawrence's integrity is the story of the dinner party at the Café Royal in London, when Lawrence became very drunk, vomited over the table, and fell into a stupor. The Honorable Dorothy Brett and Mrs. Carswell discuss this disgusting incident with almost religious reverence. . . . Mrs. Carswell even goes so far as to recall the Last Supper . . . and when Lawrence was frog-marched up the stairs to his flat, she adds that her brother 'saw clearly before him St. John and St. Peter (or was it St. Thomas) bearing between them the limp figure of their master.'"

Lawrence himself wrote Murry early in 1925: "You remember that charming dinner at the Café Royal that night? You remember saying: I love you, Lorenzo, but I won't promise not to betray you? Let's wipe off all that Judas-Jesus slime. Remember, you have betrayed everything and everybody up to now. . . . Best drop that Christ stuff; it's putrescence." And Murry declared later: "Lawrence is a revolutionary experience for anyone who takes him seriously. It is safer to leave him alone."

But Brett took him seriously, was ready to follow anywhere. She stood by her word. Hers had been an open-eyed resolve. She accompanied the Lawrences to the New World, to the New Jerusalem, to Taos, and staunchly stayed alongside—too staunchly sometimes for Frieda's comfort. In the fall of 1924 she left Taos with them for Oaxaca, where she records: "I try to urge you to start a little group, however small, to put your authority over it and build some new way of living among the few of us. 'I wish I could,' you say sadly, 'but what is the use—it's no good.'"

The Brett who still believed was presently banished from Oaxaca by the prime colonist, Frieda, who had tired of the disciple's perpetual attendance. The kingdom of heaven on earth was not to be announced through an ear trumpet by a female Gabriel. Apparently a colony of even three would have been too many. St. Augustine knew. "There can be too much of a good thing," as Frieda has said to me since.

35. *"The Plumed Serpent"*

I
N 1926 *The Plumed Serpent* was published.

"Surely here," writes Catherine Carswell of *The Plumed Serpent,* "is the most ambitious and most impressive novel of our generation." Tindall also acclaims it "by far his best novel." Murry reacts differently and oddly, saying, "At bottom he was not interested in art. . . . His aim was to discover authority, not to create art." Yet Murry thinks that the novelist "who discarded art for prophecy . . . reached a point where he must discard prophecy for 'art.' And this is acknowledged," he says, "consciously or unconsciously, in *The Plumed Serpent,*" which he calls Lawrence's greatest work of art. An amazing statement, when the book is almost devoid of the art which distinguishes *Sons and Lovers, The Lost Girl,* much of *The Rainbow,* and many of his short stories and essays. Even Frieda is reported to have had special weakness for the Mexican novel. John C. Neff has described in *The New Mexico Quarterly* a fairly recent encounter with Mrs. Lawrence and her daughter and son-in-law during "A Visit to Kiowa Ranch," in which he quotes Frieda as saying: " 'You must never read Lawrence while you are young. Too many young people read him, and they do not know what he is saying. It is so difficult, then, to explain to them what he is saying. You must have had experiences and bitter tastes of life before you can read him with intelligence.' The son-in-law interrupted," says Neff, "to ask if I'd read *Sons and Lovers.* He thought, along with the rest of England, that it was the best book. But Mrs. Lawrence broke in, saying, 'No, no, you must read *The Plumed Serpent.* All of Lawrence is in that book. Two years he spent writing it, one winter in Chapala and the next winter in Oaxaca.' " Although Frieda had apparently joined those who placed *The Plumed Serpent* at the top, she has said to me still more recently and, I think, rightly, "Lawrence was not so good in that book." She had in fact told me several times that she considered it "not so good," and a 1928 letter from her contains a caustic comment: "the religious part isn't religious, but dessicated swelled head." During Mr. Neff's call, she may have been thinking that her son-in-law considered *Sons and Lovers* Lawrence's only good novel, so that she was exaggerating the defense. Or on this occasion her remarks may have been absent-minded, since Lawrence never spent a "winter in Chapala."

When the book appeared, I was naturally eager to see what had been made of the material which Johnson and I had watched Lawrence gathering; and I have recently read it all again with better informed attention but with the same mixed reactions it brought me earlier. This time, aware of the strong pull Mexico continued to exert on him until his grave illness in Oaxaca, I have pondered over his original fear of the country and its people and over the elaborate fictional measures he took, as the book progressed, to dignify and offset, exalt and justify his fear.

Again and again he observes "that heavy, black Mexican fatality," the "glassy darkness" of their "centerless eyes"; "their sudden, charming smile, when you smile first, but the eyes unchanged"; "in the eyes of each, the uncreated center, where the evil and the insolence lurked." "The black eyes of the people," he says, "really make my heart contract, and my flesh shrink," "They oppress me like a weight on my heart," "the mysterious faculty of the Indians, as they sit there, so quiet and dense, for killing off any ebullient life, for quenching any light and colorful effervescence." Again, "Those big handsome men, under their big hats, they aren't really there. They have no center, no real *I*. Their middle is a raging black hole, like the middle of a maelstrom." He was seeing from the canoa the waterspout on the lake, had probably conceived his image on the spot. I remember the notebook.

Then, beyond imagery, he connects this black heaviness of the Indians with their country: "Down on it all like a weight of obsidian, comes the passive negation of the Indian." To his imagination the country itself was determined to "pull one down. It was what the country wanted to do all the time, with a slow, reptilian insistence, to pull one down." "Perhaps something came out of the earth," another passage suggests, "the dragon of the earth, some effluence, some vibration which militated against the very composition of the blood and nerves of human beings. Perhaps it came from the volcanoes. Or perhaps," he blames the people again, "from the silent, serpent-like dark resistance of those masses of ponderous natives. . . . Kate lay on her bed and brooded her own organic rage. There was nothing to be done?"

It was Lawrence himself saying, "What shall I do? What shall I think? What shall I write?" His vexation with himself was for a while making a whole race the scapegoat.

Sometimes he gives a homely and mistaken illustration of what he felt to be the Indian's attitude toward the Caucasian: he notes of Isabel and her daughters that the women "squatted on the gravel with their splendid black hair down their backs, displaying themselves as they hunted in each other's hair for lice. They wanted to be in full view. . . . They wanted the basic fact of lice to be thrust under the noses of those white people." He was quite wrong as I have said earlier: one sees this louse hunt in many doorways of every village, with the passing foreigner unconsidered.

Sometimes Lawrence attributes or transfers to the servants his own nervous apprehensions. He tells of fitful electricity in Chapala: "The electric light . . . would come on at half-past six in the evening, and it *might* bravely burn till ten at night, when the village went dark with a click. But usually it did no such thing. Often it refused to sputter into being till seven, or half-past, or even eight o'clock. But its worst trick was that of popping out just in the middle of supper or just when you were writing a letter. All of a sudden the black Mexican night came down on us with a thud. And then everybody running blindly for matches and candles, with a calling of frightened voices. Why were they always frightened? Then the electric light, like a wounded thing, would try to revive, and a red glow would burn in the bulbs, sinister." The servants were not frightened. They were fluttering and running in pleasant excitement. The glow was sinister only to Lawrence. He himself was the "wounded thing," trying "to revive."

Finally *The Plumed Serpent* touches on its author's true perplexity concerning the natives. Though his faith was that life breeds a cross section of recognizably superior men, and that he was surely one of them, he was baffled by the level serenity and natural aristocracy of the Mexican. He was forever irritated that his own sharp personality could not impress the native, could not awe him, alienate him or apparently move him in any way. This was what kept Lawrence in a state of unrest toward Mexicans. Their occasional violence, outwardly hot but inwardly cold, was in some respects akin to his own violence but was based on a more solid dignity. He was at odds with their poise, their fearlessness, their fatalism. In one passage the essential dislike emerges clear, through Kate's revulsion against their pretending to share the same human blood stream as his own. "A strange, almost torn nausea would come over Kate, she felt she must go away, to spare herself. The strange, reptilian insistence of her very servants. *Blood is one blood. We are all of one blood stream.* Something aboriginal and tribal, and almost worse than death to the white individual. Out of the dark eyes and the powerful spines of these people, all the time the unknown assertion: *The blood is one blood.* It was a strange, overbearing insistence, a claim of blood-unison." Here the miner's son borrows Frieda's degree of caste as the reason for his own individualistic pride: "Kate was of a proud old family. She had been brought up with the English-Germanic idea of the *intrinsic* superiority of the hereditary aristocrat. Her blood was different from the common blood, another, finer fluid. But in Mexico none of this. Her criada Juana, the *aguador* who carried the water, the boatman who rowed her on the lake, all looked at her with one look in their eyes. *The blood is one blood. In the blood, you and I are undifferentiated.* She saw it in their eyes, she heard it in their words. It tinged their deference and their mockery. And sometimes it made her feel physically sick: this overbearing blood-familiarity."

It was more than this "blood-familiarity" which offended Lawrence. It was the Mexicans' calm assumption of equality with Englishmen, even of superiority to them, and was especially obnoxious, even frightening, when exhibited by curt officials.

On the third Mexican trip, Dorothy Brett was with the Lawrences when a guard asked him take off his hat in the Mexico City Museum. She recalls his outbreak: "'They want to show their power over strangers, that's all it is. They want to show they have authority to make a white man take off his hat.'"

Even toward the end of his life, in his *Apocalypse* he wrote: "As a citizen, as a collective being, man has his fulfillment in the gratification of his power-sense. If he belongs to one of the so-called 'ruling nations,' his soul is fulfilled in the sense of his country's power or strength." Here in Mexico Lawrence was far removed from Britannia's muscular arm, an admirable limb when protective of a citizen rather than demanding of him; and, without its comparative nearness, beyond its mighty reach, he flinched from the menace he felt in this dark, haughty race.

Through Kate in the novel, he finally puts his finger full on his own pulse: "'I am afraid of fear,' she said." Earlier we remember Kate had asked herself if there was nothing to be done. Of course there was for the author. He would return to the motive which had brought him to Mexico, the expectation of finding not just the high nose of presumption but the fine brow of intrinsic primitive nobility. He would make himself admire these people. He would force himself to discover within them, beyond their puzzling darkness, a meaningful light, "The mystery of the natives," as Kate begins to perceive it, "the strange and mysterious gentleness between a Scylla and a Charybdis of violence." She now feels both "tenderness and revulsion," "but stronger than her fear was a certain sympathy with these dark-faced silent men in their big straw hats and naïve little cotton blouses." Anyhow they had blood in their veins: they were "columns of dark blood," "they touched the bowels with a strange compassion." "There was a beauty in these men, a wistful beauty and great physical strength. Why had she felt so bitterly about the country?"

The next step is inevitable in his imagination. They must become the heroic men, the deliverers, in whose ranks Lawrence, their author-creator would like to be. They must become Lawrences. They must bring people deliverance with a new religion. So he manufactures his wish-fulfilling marionettes. As middlemen between himself and his fantasy of himself he fashions the flimsy Cipriano and the still more unlifelike Titan, Ramon, the latter as a living Quetzalcoatl. The living Buddha would not have been a role for Lawrence. Thereupon these two puppet leaders and their numerous puppet followers prepare to send Jesus and his Mother gently back to sleep. The Holy Family is too tired to exert its godhood any more, at least for a while. Perhaps it will be regenerated in space and in the hearts of men and return later to resume its good works; but for the present its mission is over. It must recharge its mystic batteries. Meanwhile Quetzalcoatl, having enjoyed a good rest and been properly recharged, is primed to return and give guidance to his people. He will fulfill the center of their eyes and the hollow at their core. He will make the maelstrom strike from steady guts. As he wrote elsewhere, with naïve master-minded arrogance, ". . . if I want Mexicans to learn the name of Quetzalcoatl, it is because I want them to speak with the tongues of their own blood.

I wish the Teutonic world would once more think in terms of Thor and Wotan . . . and a new Hermes should come back to the Mediterranean, and a new Ashtaroth to Tunis; and Mithras again to Persia." Frank Waters, in *The Southwest Review,* has called the Mexican book "a ghastly prophecy. . . . As a pattern for one of the holocausts in history," he continues, "*The Plumed Serpent* has no parallel. Indeed, on close reading, it might well seem more Hitler's original blueprint than *Mein Kampf.*" Unlike Waters and others of us, Lawrence did not live to see what could happen when some of the old gods come back.

Tindall, in his scholarly searching, says: "From Mrs. Lawrence I learned that her husband read Mrs. Nuttall's *Fundamental Principles of Old and New World Civilizations,* 1901. To this formidable work Lawrence owed most of his wide but inaccurate knowledge of primitive Mexico." "It is probable," proceeds Tindall, "that he read Lewis Spence's *Gods of Mexico,* . . . This likelihood is increased by the presence in Spence's book of Aztec hymns so close in character to those in *The Plumed Serpent* as to appear to have suggested their use to Lawrence."

At the very outset of his literary plan, in revising his concept of the Mexican Indian, Lawrence reverts to what he has seen of Indians above the border. Instead of describing the Hispanicized dance steps and vocalisms of Mexico, he turns back to the Tewas, the Kiowas, the Apaches: "They were all afoot, with bare torsos and bare feet, dancing the savage bird tread." He dodges the fact that these northern ceremonies are hardly the Spanish fandango step—with the crude courtly costumes, reflecting more of Cortes than of Montezuma—which one sees all over Mexico and sometimes even as far as New Mexico in one imported dance, the Matachina. Kate joins a dance of the cultists: "The outer wheel was all men. . . . Men, dark, collective men, non-individual. And herself woman wheeling upon the great wheel of womanhood. . . . What a beautiful slow wheel of dance, two great streams streaming in opposite directions." But Lawrence knew well enough this was not Mexico. Though in the Mexican social serenatas around the bandstands, knots of men and of women stream "in contact, in opposite directions," what Lawrence is describing is the wheeling dance he had seen and joined in Taos. Rereading *The Plumed Serpent* and *Mornings in Mexico,* I regret again that he had not gone with us to the Shalako ceremony at Zuñi. According to Edmund Wilson, in *The New Yorker:* "The white visitor . . . becomes rapt . . . feels the thrill and awe of the elemental power summoned. It seems as if the dancer, by his pounding, were really generating energy for the Zuñis: by his discipline, reinforcing their fortitude; by his endurance, guaranteeing their permanence . . . it is startling . . . to see all the life of the animal world and the power of the natural elements made continuous with human vitality and endowed with semi-human form." This is good. For Lawrence, the Shalako, the ten-foot bird man, might well have become infused into the deity he conceived, compounded of man and winged serpent.

The American Southwestern Indian is explicitly reflected by Lawrence when Ramon, with one of his Quetzalcoatl chants, "sang in the fashion of the old Red Indians, with intensity and restraint, singing inwardly, singing to his own soul, not outward to the world, not yet even upward to God, as the Christians sing. But with a sort of suppressed, tranced intensity, singing not into space, but into the other dimension of man's existence, where he finds himself in the infinite room that lies inside the axis of our wheeling space." This again is not Mexico, this is the singing of the Tewa or the Hopi.

Sometimes, however, when our Southwestern Indian is "singing inwardly," he is but running softly through the song to himself, making sure of the words before giving them full voice. One evening in New York, Carl Van Vechten and I took Tony Lujan along with a group to a Negro dance hall in Harlem which had a good orchestra. He was the Taos Indian who had originally driven the Lawrences to my house in Santa Fe with Mrs. Mabel Sterne, whom he shortly afterward married. Tony was immediately caught by the rhythms, both of music and step. "Best time I've had in New York," said he. First he danced with Mrs. Van Vechten, then he wanted to sing. It was quickly arranged by Carl, who knew the place well. Tony went to the orchestra platform, tested the drum with low beats, and, to assure an especially good performance among people he liked, rehearsed his song for some three minutes in a beelike hum, with his broad rear to the roomful. His audience, all Negro but ourselves, not guessing that he was "inside the axis of our wheeling space," was politely perplexed until he turned and pleased them with the collected song—and then finally there were too many stanzas for them. I do not mean, by this reminiscence, to imply that Lawrence had not every right to be moved by Indian singing; but I do mean that his overwrought development of ritualistic song and symbol, in the Mexican cult he creates fictionally, takes him astray. The chants, or psalms, bulk large in the book. Heard just as music without words, they might have been effective: but they become long pages of invented liturgy which, however devout his intent, seem to me, for the most part, familiar mummery. We hear Ramon, in one of his chants as the living Quetzalcoatl: "There is no Before and After, there is only Now. . . . There is always and only Now, Now and I Am." Platform runes like this, but far less terse, remind one who lives in Santa Fe of a lingo introduced there by a sect from Los Angeles, locally called the "I Ammers," and of what Lawrence himself would have thought of it all, observed outside himself. Its extant priestess is said to wear diamonds set in her palms, an extreme to which Frieda might conceivably have been brought, in the person of Kate become priestess of Quetzalcoatl. The North American cult, I acknowledge, accents the collective power of "I Amness" in relation to life, whereas Don Ramon and his followers, speaking for Lawrence himself, accent often the sheer and withdrawn loneness of it: "I am weary of the things men call life. Living, I want to depart to where *I am*." Perhaps the current cult was born blindly of the book. It might have been.

Sometimes the voice of Lawrence, as it comes through Ramon's liturgy or rumination, is memorably moving, as when we hear him say: "The hearts of living men are the very middle of the sky. And there God is; and Paradise; inside the hearts of living men and women. And there the souls of the dead come to rest, there, at the very centre where the blood turns and returns; that is where the dead sleep best." But, often while the puppet Ramon gesticulates, the puppeteer Lawrence comes into full view repeating: "Only the Natural Aristocrats can rise above their nation; and even then they do not rise beyond their race. Only the Natural Aristocrats of the World can be international, or cosmopolitan, or cosmic." He did not add comic. Again from the visible puppet master one hears, and wonders that the counsel is not followed: "Man is a column of blood, with a voice in it. And when the voice is still, and he is only a column of blood, he is better."

The persistent chants and rituals with the drum symbolization of divine heartbeats become more and more embarrassing, because Lawrence is forcing himself to believe in something in which he did not believe, any more than he could have believed in the tenets and rituals of an established theology. The fact that he himself was establishing tenets and rituals made them still hollower. He was not one of those who, when they find they have frail support inside themselves, fall flatly and helplessly back upon an orthodoxy. He needed no dogma, no theology, no revelation save sacredly from inside. And I believe he was himself ashamed to be apparently recommending that such inner revelation should be organized, standardized, made uniform for man, even among Indians in Mexico.

The simplest explanation is that he always felt a carry-over from some childish uplift experienced through congregational or domestic singing of hymns in his boyhood. Though he had his full say later against Christianity as an organized religion, or even as a sound teaching, his sensory nerves loved the joint vocal offering of faith, and some sense of drama in him craved pageantry as an expression of faith. It is odd that the Roman Catholic drama never drew him. On the contrary, though his sympathy was drawn often by the lone Christ, by a wayside figure drooping in the dark, he felt in Mexico and elsewhere that the Roman show, as well as the Christian mythology, was at least temporarily dead and no longer useful. Like his feeling for the crucifixes of *Twilight in Italy,* his feeling toward Christian symbols in Mexico was tender. But it was the tenderness of an earnest gravedigger.

In the novel, the reverent burning of the Christian images on the Island of the Scorpions and the attack on Ramon at Jamiltipec—which is an elaborated picture of El Manglar, Don Porfirio's brother's villa— are almost straight narrative and, due to that fact and to Lawrence's simple relief after having had to maintain spiritual posture and declamation, are by far the best chapters in *The Plumed Serpent.* One of them immediately follows the other and they bring the reader also a sense of relief. I have wondered if they were written at a single period when the impulse and pitch of story-telling rose high enough to rescue Lawrence from himself, to banish his eternal self-quizzing and the almost hysterical fantasy of cult which overpowers and smothers his otherwise keen observation of people and doings in Chapala as they actually were. He might have written a rich book if he had not yielded to his ambitious attempt at mystic dealings. The performance which emerges from the attempt is sometimes like an ambitious high school presentation of *Aïda,* sometimes like the eager antics of the "I Am" cult, sometimes like a rally of the Ku Klux Klan, sometimes like Wagner without music. In many of Don Ramon's moments of exultation, one definitely feels a forecast of the fanatical Hitler. The elements of darkness which oppressed Lawrence in Mexico were none of them so sinister as the element which he himself brought there, his imagination training the natives in articles like Fascist philosophy and gestures like the Nazi salute. I quote Edmund Wilson again: "The Christian mythology is obsolete. . . . On the other hand, modern attempts to create a non-Christian mythology produce cults like that of Hitler and his hero-race of Germans."

I also, at Chapala, as I realize now from my poem, "The Winged Serpent," quoted herein earlier, inclined toward a mystical sense of a living Quetzalcoatl. This was too bad for us. And yet it seemed then a large cause, a whole cause.

In *The Plumed Serpent* most of the characters join the author in his attempt at a mystic cult. Certainly all the native characters do except Carlota and Teresa—who come nearest to flesh and blood— Ramon's successive wives whom Kate would have liked to replace with herself as a being superior to them. The other characters not only join the author but are the author, ever pricking himself into importance and leadership. He interrupts all his characters with his own rhapsodic or vehement chatter. When Ramon talks, it is Lawrence, except now and then when Frieda buoyantly forces her way through. Even when little Teresa talks, it becomes Lawrence. Teresa enters the story as a separate and real person; but her creator cannot help making her over into his own image, so that she finally uses his very own words to present his very own doctrine: "He is a man and a column of blood." She says, "I am a woman and a valley of blood." And then to conclude his portrait of her, he has her confess, in complete contradiction of the character he had first created: "I have a very great fear of love. It is so personal."

The main figures in the book, one and all, end by seeming to have no relation to anything personal. What they had at the outset they have lost in a mesh of doctrine. Elizabeth Shepley Sergeant says truly: "The persons of the tale are indifferent to us, their destinies are without meaning except as they bear on the haunting subjective consciousness that underlies the flow and the imagery, the consciousness of a great lost Englishman, engaged in a tragic war with his own sources of life, and a febrile search for an elusive mystery . . . this book is less a picture of Mexico than an almost demented state of homesickness."

Rereading *The Plumed Serpent* lately, I have been saddened again by Lawrence's not having confined himself to truth about Chapala and its Mexicans instead of burdening the book with a hundred and seventy-two pages of fabricated, melodramatic myth.

What he does tell in straight description could not have been told better. Chapala and Chapalans breathe alive on page after page, from which follow a few fragments. "The peons, sitting immobile on their seats in the background, looked on with basilisk eyes from under the great hats." Lawrence sees the plaza again, at night—one end of which was then a market: "On the north side, the booths were still flaring, people were buying and selling. But this quarter too looked lonely, and outside the actual reality, almost like memory." He notes the girls from Guadalajara as they appeared in those days, "their dark faces curiously macabre in the heavy make-up; approximating to white, but the white of a clown or a corpse." As to the city boys of that period, "The supply of fifis, the young male elegants . . . was small . . . in white flannel trousers and white shoes, dark jackets, correct straw hats and canes . . . more ladylike than the reckless flappers; and far more nervous, wincing . . . looking as if they were going to be sacrificed to some Mexican god within a twelvemonth; when they were properly plumped and perfumed."

He was always noticing the motionless postures of the Indian male, which is suspended animation without being suspended vigor. He may have noticed that when a Negro leaves work and lies asleep in any posture into which he has happened to fall, he is a picture of complete relaxation, somewhat like a wet cloth tossed down. The Mexican Indian, standing or lying, may stay still as death; but, whether awake or asleep in his immobility, he is an undead ember. Lawrence carves him in a few words: "Often a single man would stand alone at a street corner in his serape, motionless for hours, like some powerful spectre." In another instance he sees immobility even in a moving rider: "There was a curious motionlessness about him as he rode horseback, an old, male pride, and at the same time the half-ghostly, dark invisibility of the Indian, sitting close upon the horse as if he and it belonged to one birth." This particular passage connects with a 1923 letter he wrote Johnson, acknowledging a copy of *The Laughing Horse,* and flickering with his ever-romantic sense of Indians: "Two-legged man is no good. If he's going to stand steady, he must stand on four feet. Like the Centaur. . . . This two-legged forked radish is going flabby. . . . Sense! Sound Horse Sense! Sound, powerful, four-footed *sense,* that's the Centaur. . . . Horse-sense. Horse-laughter . . . ask the

Indians if it is not so." Lawrence may often have felt a twinge of jealousy when from his meager frame he looked upon these men of ample, easy strength and sense.

Besides the Chapalan Indians, the Chapalan landscape comes alive in his book. When he arrives in dry early May, "big hills rose up to high, blunt points, baked incredibly dry, like biscuit." But on dustless days he saw the beauty of the "grooved" or "fluted" mountains across the lake, with shadows "almost corn-flower blue." Or again Kate's feeling that "the green furrows of the mountain-sides were as if in her own hand." Though he scolded the color of the landscape and lake, yet it fascinated him. "The land so dry as to have a quality of invisibility, the water earth-filmy, hardly water at all." . . . "the great lymphatic expanse of water, like a sea, trembling, trembling to a far distance, to the mountains of substantial nothingness." He repeatedly calls the water "sperm-like" but presently finds other gentle colors in it: "the color of turtle-doves," "the dove-pale lake," "the full, pale dove-brown water of the lake." And then at sunset, when the rains have begun: "The hills stood up bluish, all the air was a salmon-red flush, the fawn water had pinkish ripples. Boys and men, bathing along the shore, were the color of deep flame." And the rains themselves: "There was a distant noise of thunders, several storms prowling round like hungry jaguars, above the lake." Or "down came the rain with a smash, as if some great vessel had broken," or "she could hear the drum again like a pulse inside a stone beating."

Beasts and birds, his familiars, figure in his imagery: doves, fawns, jaguars; and he is at his descriptive best whenever their actual presence enters the book. "On the nets a small bird sat facing the sun; he was red as a drop of new blood, from the arteries of the air." Other birds are "like new-opened buds sparking in the air" and cardinal birds are "poppies on wings."

Such passages come as easements to the reader, and one guesses that they came as easement to Lawrence, from fretful cerebration. Alas, alas, that the miner's son thought he must be more than a sensitive, articulate celebrant of the wonder of life, thought for a while he must devise an oracular ritual and be its pope.

Brought up by his mother as a Congregationalist, not only at Sunday School but in the Christian Endeavor Society and the Band of Hope, Lawrence had been a fervent singer of hymns, concerning which he eventually wrote *Hymns in a Man's Life*. Mrs. Carswell, who met him much later, comments: "When I heard him lift up his voice in 'Sun of my soul, thou Savior dear,' I thought he would not be content to die without having written hymns of his own. We have his hymns," she concludes, "in *The Plumed Serpent.*"

I never met Mrs. Carswell; but in 1950, I went to see at Hampstead Heath, on the edge of London, a woman with the rare signature, Poppoea Vanda, who had apparently always lived there. She told me that for a while, during her girlhood, Lawrence and Frieda had lived there too, in one of a row of houses named Byron Villas, in a section called The Vale of Health. This must have been shortly before Australia and New Mexico. His house had been next door to that of the English poet, Anna Wickham, under whose wing Poppoea used to sit on the back porch alongside the Lawrences on theirs. "And he used to lead us singing hymns, what time he wasn't trimming hats for Frieda." I had a quick sense of his innerly making, even then, Quetzalcoatl chants out of the English hymns and Malinche's heroic spreading plumes for Frieda's head.

The Plumed Serpent at one point, in relation to the Quetzalcoatl mysticism and mummery, lets Kate come to her senses or, rather, lets the straightforward, real Frieda come clean and speak her sound mind through the composite character of Kate. I suspect that Lawrence longed to come through to his own senses; but I can hear Frieda's wholesome, throaty voice, her enormous, beautiful vigor, booming the words Kate uses: "For heaven's sake let me get out of this and back to simple human people. I loathe the very sound of Quetzalcoatl and Huizilpochotli. I would rather die than be mixed up in it any more. . . . They want to put it over me with their high-flown bunk. . . . I've had it put over me." I am sure that this is what Frieda sprang at Lawrence when he read her the latter half of *The Plumed Serpent.*

On the other hand, her voice comes through again, firm, positive and good, when Kate speaks of her second husband, who had died: "With Joachim I came to realize that a woman like me *can* only love a man who is fighting to *change* the world, to make it freer, more alive. Men like my first husband who are good and trustworthy and who work to keep the world going on well in the same state they found it in, they let you down horribly, somewhere. You feel so terribly sold. Everything is just a sell; it becomes so small. A woman who isn't quite ordinary herself can only love a man who is fighting for something beyond the ordinary life."

I am confident that these were Frieda's own words. Only recently she sent me a letter to Chapala, in which she says: "When I meet ordinary people, I am thankful not to be so ordinary and to have unordinary friends." Such words might be misconstrued by a stranger but not by anyone, even anyone "ordinary," who has been warmed with the rays of her full, sunny spirit or blown by her stiff breeze. Aristocrat she may be but could not grow, if she would, the heart of a snob.

She has never returned to Chapala; and her letter goes on to ask, after clearing a few points for my own memory, "Isn't it strange that things past can often be more vivid than the present! Are the heavy boats still on the lake? And the birds? Those little figures on stands? And the crystallized fruit on trays?"

Yes, they are, and the sunsets and the Indians and the street singers, and Isabel who used to call Frieda, "Niña," and who, like Daniel her son and like Ysidoro, caretaker of my house near the lake these twenty-five years, still ask about the Lawrences. Quetzalcoatl's drums throb yet with thunderclaps over Chapala, and once in a while rises a water-spout. But Lawrence is gone, and the chieftains of *The Plumed Serpent*, with their imagined chanting, are as silent as he.

36. Would-Be Aristocrat

WITH Lawrence personally beyond my reach in Europe, I began trying more and more to reach what I could of him in his books. After these many years I have been reading him yet again, not only in his own books but in books about him, have been reconsidering what I find in printed record concerning the various persons he was: the wanderer, the would-be colonizer, the would-be aristocrat, the would-be leader of men and their thought, the mate, the would-be comrade, the born artist, and the resolving man.

I have in earlier chapters watched his loose wandering, his vain colonizing and regretted the errors and excesses in his literary dream of Mexican leadership. More slowly I arrive at conclusions concerning the qualities of his nature which lay behind his restless drive to lead.

Lawrence had given me in Chapala no hint of the grand opera he was planning to stage there with his novel; but he had spoken much of his belief in natural aristocracy, of his hope to find it in some Indian, and I am again interested to find in *The Plumed Serpent* extravagant records of the conviction which then possessed him and which used to sharpen his resistance to my naïve faith in the beneficence of democracy. He was, after all, a stimulating and not too aristocratic companion. As I look back on it now and had begun to feel at the hospital, despite the opposition between his dark center and my light head, between his advocacy of divinely anointed leadership and mine of humanly appointed fellowship, and underneath whatever heated debate happened between us, we had been quietly drawn together. I had begun to know it at the hospital. It is ironic in the present world, to see our ideals, and they were ideals on both our parts, betrayed into pretended fellowship under deified dictatorship, Lawrence's ideal of hero and my ideal of fellow man teamed into an inhuman blend which would have been as abhorrent to him as it is to me. His nature was dual in this respect, as perhaps mine was. He wanted to be a leader but would have liked also to be a follower. Since he could find no one else completely worth leading, he was following himself. Richard Aldington said of him in his lifetime: "He is a true Anarchist (this Lawrence denies but it is true) living outside human society, rejecting all its values, fiercely concentrating on his own values." Aldington's comment reminds me that, while a hero-worshiper like Vachel Lindsay named his heroes, Lincoln, Jackson, Altgeld, General Booth, this other hero-worshiper refrained from specification, except to name such an ancient as Osiris with whom, in two instances at least, he identified himself. His *Movements in European History* does cite for praise Attila, Augustus, and Bismarck.

But he could not keep away from Jesus, who, I sometimes think, for all his critical protests, was the only imaginable rival he respected, another humbly born aristocrat. "There was in Lawrence," says Norman Douglas, "a masochistic strain, a strain of Christ, prophet and sufferer. Both of them were in disharmony with their environment; both took every opportunity of saying so, although in Jesus . . . we find less hysteria than in Lawrence, whose Messianic utterances are delivered in shrill tones." In his second novel, *The Trespasser,* Lawrence considered Jesus and said, through Siegmund: " 'Thirty years of earnest love; three years' life like a passionate ecstasy—and it was finished. He was very great and very wonderful. I am very insignificant, and shall go out ignobly.' . . . Siegmund felt his heart very heavy, sad, and at fault, in presence of the Christ. Yet he derived comfort from the knowledge that life was treating him in the same manner as it had treated the Master." From the beginning Lawrence thought of himself as a fellow of Jesus; and at the beginning his thought was humble. When he was ordered to leave Cornwall during the war because of suspicion that he was a spy, when like Jesus he was taken by soldiers, he tells it in *Kangaroo:* "He sat with his immobile face of a crucified Christ who makes no complaint, only broods silently and alone, remote." When, as a dying man in France, he was reviewing his life and wondering what he had made of it and writing *The Man Who Died,* his story of Christ, he found himself a ghost not of himself but of Jesus. One of the bravest and most pathetic self-revelations in all literary history is his account of this Jesus who has been taken down from the cross too soon and must still live and must now learn that physical release of body to body is the only use of life which can make spirit. Jesus has pushed aside his cerements and has felt again "the animal onrush of light." He returns into the world. He changes his cerements for worldly clothes. Atop them all is Lawrence's cowboy hat: He comes within range of the Priestess of Isis and "as she watched, she saw . . . a stranger in a low, broad hat." Dorothy Brett has several times painted him in this hat. Later the priestess "looked at the sleeping face. It was worn, hollow, and rather ugly. But, a true priestess, she saw the other kind of beauty in it, the sheer stillness of the deeper life." And then the would-be aristocrat: "There was even a sort of majesty in the dark brows, over the still, hollow cheeks." And then the would-be young spirit with dark skin: "His dusky skin had the silvery glisten of youth still. There was a beauty of much suffering, and the strange calm candour of finer life in the whole delicate ugliness of the face." This is Lawrence in the shape of the hero, Lawrence and Jesus in their joint aloneness, above aristocrats. Of the returned Christ he sighs: ". . . with the peasants he could be alone but his own friends would never let him be alone."

"Only when he is alone," he says in *Apocalypse,* another of his last few books, "can man be a Christian, a Buddhist or a Platonist . . . . When he is with other men, instantly distinctions occur, and levels are formed. As soon as he is with other men, Jesus is an aristocrat, a master. Buddha is always the lord Buddha. Francis of Assisi, trying to be so humble, as a matter of fact finds a subtle means to absolute power over his followers. Shelley could not *bear* not to be the aristocrat of his company. Lenin was a Tyrannus in shabby clothes. . . . A man like Lenin is a great evil saint . . . Abraham Lincoln is a half-evil saint. . . . President Wilson is a quite evil saint. . . . Every saint becomes evil— and Lenin, Lincoln, Wilson are true saints so long as they remain purely individual—every saint becomes evil the moment he touches the collective self of men. Then he is a perverter—Plato the same."

Here we find his partial heroes named—the saints who would not remain saints because they strayed away from themselves toward mankind, because they would not remain with their aloneness. And so he himself, fighting to the very last for man to be open and free and clean in the essential element of life and in expression of it, was sad because Jesus and he had not had sense enough to stay within themselves, within their own saintliness, had tried disastrously to share it, to preach it among other men. Christ, returning in *The Man Who Died,* says.

"Now I will wander among the stirring of the phenomenal world, for it is the stirring of all things among themselves which leaves me purely alone." "I tried to compel them to live, so they compelled me to die. It is always so, with compulsion. The recoil kills the advance. Now it is my time to be alone."

Lawrence's essay, *The Risen Lord,* in *Assorted Articles,* whatever the date of its writing, is a sort of program note for *The Man Who Died* and considering the fragile second half of the latter, should be taken perhaps as his clearer statement of his theme. The essay modifies the stress on the desired loneness of Jesus returned, transfers the stress more definitely to Lawrence's sense of the values of life, as a sick man realizing that in imagination he has died and come back again to earth. As ever he interweaves his own character with that of Jesus. What should I have felt and done if I had been He and come back? So he resumes his own experience, and the experience of a modern man in the Christian era. He remembers the stages: "the man sees himself as a child, the innocent saviour-child enthroned on the lap of the all-pitying virgin mother. He lives according to this image of himself . . . until the image breaks in his heart" and he finds "left in its place the image of Christ crucified." This, he believes, is the image for those who go through the first World War. Then follow the young. "Neither of the great images is *their* image," says he. "And the churches, instead of preaching the Risen Lord, go on preaching the Christ-child and Christ Crucified."

Then Lawrence emphasizes: "Christ risen in the flesh! We must accept the image complete, if we accept it at all. . . . He rises from the dead, in the flesh, not merely as spirit. He rises with hands and feet, as Thomas knew for certain; and if with hands and feet, then with lips and stomach and genitals of a man. Christ risen, and risen in the whole of His flesh, and not with some left out. Christ risen in the full flesh! What for? It is here the gospels are all vague and faltering, and the Churches leave us in the lurch. Christ rises in the flesh in order to lurk obscurely for six weeks on earth, then be taken vaguely up into heaven in a cloud? Flesh, solid flesh, feet and bowels and teeth and eyes of a man, taken up into heaven in a cloud, and never put down again? . . . Flesh and blood belong to the earth, and only to the earth. We know it. And Jesus was risen flesh-and-blood. . . . The greatest test was still before Him: His life as man on earth. Hitherto He had been a sacred child, a teacher, a messiah, but never

a full man. Now, risen from the dead, he rises to be a man on earth
. . . to live the great life of the flesh and the soul together; as peonies
and foxes do, in their lesser way. If Jesus rose as a full man, in full
flesh and soul, then He rose to take a woman to Himself, to live with
her, and to know the tenderness and blossoming of the twoness with
her; He who had been hitherto so limited to His oneness, or His uni-
versality, which is the same thing." Here Lawrence, as always, suddenly intrudes his own person. In the fiction of *The Man Who Died*
he does not use the "I." Here he does. "The earth is the Lord's, and
the fulness thereof, and I, the Risen Lord, am here to take possession.
For now I am fully a man, and free above all from my own self-importance. I want life, and the pure contact with life."

Going back to 1923: in Lawrence's own eyes—and already to great
degree in mine, opened by his absence and by closer reading of him—
he had made himself worth deep respect for his honest, eager experi-
ments or adventures of heart and spirit. And I warmly began to sense
from him, now that we were not together, feelers of friendship. He
wanted friendship, I surmised, in the way Proust said he wanted
friendship, not because it "involved a man's essential self" but because
it "diminished loneliness." Much as Lawrence, like Jesus, craved aloneness, loneliness was something else. Frieda could be with him somehow in his aloneness; but even with her beside him he could be
lonely.

Yes, he had been lonely in Chapala, as he would have been lonely
anywhere, because of his disappointment in mankind and in his inability to make a satisfactory mankind out of himself. But while he
continued seeking surcease of loneliness, he remained stubbornly English with his insistence upon caste among men, not, let me repeat,
conventional caste according to pedigree or inherited wealth and
power but dependent upon the naturally ordained superiority of individuals: the cross section, through mankind, of native aristocracy,
the aristocracy to which he himself could belong, lonely and defiant.

This son of a miner was, however, a combination of pithead and
godhead; and try as he might to ideologize his cross-section nobility,
he could never quite shake off his island's hereditary sense of abiding
social levels. Despite all his protestations, the conventional sense of
caste dominant in novels by Jane Austen, George Meredith, Thacke-
ray, Henry James underlies much of Lawrence's writing. The deference of these earlier writers toward assumptions and fripperies and

the dog-show ribbons of pedigree is not fundamentally unlike their successor's deference toward a natural class of leaders as distinguished from a natural class of followers. And then when his spirit rebelled against those who might pretend to lead and he felt himself a lone wolf, he was troubled by his own incongruity, the natural aristocrat, ill-born. As he noted in *Sea and Sardinia:* "I like the lone wolf souls best—better than the sheep. If only they didn't feel mongrel inside themselves." One of his biographers, Hugh Kingsmill, comments, "To despise the class immediately above him seemed to him, as it has seemed to many poor men of ability, proof that he was by nature an aristocrat"; but Tindall, another biographer, observes astutely, "He was at home with members of no class." Tindall might have quoted him as saying to all of them, even the aristocrats, as he did say once to somebody: "Not so close, please. I am a little particular." He made to Dr. Burrow, the psychologist, the rather Wildean complaint: "I am weary of my own individuality and simply nauseated by other people's." Sometimes, like Lovatt in *Kangaroo,* he was, even more fastidiously, "thrilled with spite against everyone." This was the aristocrat with a vengeance.

To the very end, in *Apocalypse,* Lawrence was appraising and commending his "natural aristocrat": "There's no getting away from it, mankind falls forever into the two divisions of aristocrats and democrats. The purest aristocrats during the Christian era have taught democracy, and the purest democrats try to turn themselves into the most absolute aristocracy. . . . We are speaking now not of political parties, but of the two sorts of human nature: those that feel themselves strong in their souls, and those that feel themselves weak."

I believe that he had reached in Chapala a point of bewildered inner tangle over almost everything. He says of Kate in *The Plumed Serpent:* "Her soul and spirit were gone, departed into the middle of some desert, and the efforts of reaching across to people to effect an apparent meeting, or contact, was almost more than she could bear. . . . Never had she passed her days so blindly, so unknowingly, in stretches of nothingness." This was Lawrence. I have thought he might even have turned to a belief in democracy if he had not felt so strong a physical dislike for most of his species. As with Kate, so it was with him: "Brief contacts were all right, thrilling even. But close contacts, or long contacts, were short and long revulsions of violent disgust." " 'I like the world, the sky and the earth and the greater mystery beyond. But people—yes, they are all monkeys to me!'" "Between herself and humanity there was the bond of subtle, helpless antagonism."

It is known that Lawrence, after his marriage to Frieda, wrote letters—even twice to the same person, Ivy Low, later Mme Litvinov—on his wife's family's stationery, striking out the coronet and noting alongside, "My wife's father is a baron." Here, although trying to deny itself, was his insular, incurable crisscross of pride and humility. Well-born establishment impressed him. If only he himself had been born to so-called "nobility," he might have thought less about it. Under his earthy violence and wisdom, and undisguised by them, was a childish wistfulness toward higher rank and better breeding than his own. He still tried to content himself by believing that there could happen in any class quality quite as good as quality established by a few privileged generations. He would have liked to think it a finer nobility than the merely titular; yet how he would have loathed being called in America, "one of nature's noblemen," as much as he would have disliked being told that he belonged to the "century of the common man." When Ursula of *The Rainbow* says to Skrebensky, "'I hate democracy,' 'What do you want then—an aristocracy?' he asked, secretly moved. He always felt," the passage continues, "that by rights he belonged to the ruling aristocracy." In *Kangaroo* his combined humility and pride acknowledge "the mystic recognition of difference and innate priority, the joy of obedience and the sacred responsibility of authority." Vicariously, in the same book, "He felt himself to be one of the *responsible* members of society, as contrasted with the innumerable *irresponsible* members . . . the ideal of democratic liberty is an exploded ideal. . . . The men with soul and with passionate truth in them must control the world's material riches and supplies: absolutely put possession out of the reach of the mass of mankind, and let them begin to live again, in place of this struggle for existence, or struggle for wealth." Somewhere else he had said: "Let us submit to the knowledge that there are aristocrats and plebeians born, not made." And again: "The sight of a true lord, a noble, a nature-hero, puts the sun into the heart of the ordinary man."

But he never named a living hero, named only a vagueness of lords Egyptian or Etruscan or Aztec whose noble deeds were prehistoric or apocryphal. As late as *Apocalypse* he said: "Give homage and allegiance to a hero and you become yourself heroic." He did add: "Perhaps the law of woman is different." Lovatt, in *Kangaroo,* had proclaimed: "All this theoretical socialism started by Jews like Marx and appealing only to the will-power in the masses, making money the whole crux, this has cruelly injured the working people of Europe. . . . It has been a great treacherous conspiracy against the generous heart of the people. And that heart is betrayed: and knows it. . . . You've got to have an awakening of the old recognition of the aristocratic principle, the *innate* difference between people."

To the end—whatever he might write me or others—he could not forsake his concept of the illumined and life-dispensing hero. He visioned in Tarquinina, and tells it in *Etruscan Places,* a Lucumo "sitting very noble in his chariot, driven by an erect charioteer . . . he was divine, sitting on his chair in the stillness of power. The people drew strength even from looking at him." Lawrence, against his own occasionally dissenting judgment, could not relinquish his instinct toward some sort of personal pomp; and to the end the chariot was his, in which he could sit secure, awing and ennobling men with the bearded dignity of his superior loneness.

For dicta such as these, Lawrence, the perfectionist of individualism, has been accused of fascism. But the actuality of Mussolini failed to attract him. In 1942 I wrote Frieda: "Of one thing we may be sure, viz: that Lorenzo would not have cared for such heroes as Hitler and Mussolini—unless, say I, with slight malice, he might have happened to be one of them himself." In 1951 I can feel certain that he would not have liked his own political ideals, any more than anyone else's, in practice. And he might as well have been accused of bolshevism, because of what he had to say occasionally on the other side, for instance, in *Assorted Articles:* "The whole industrial system will undergo a change. Work will be different. Class will be different. . . . I know a change is coming—and I know we must have a more generous, more human system based on the life values and not on the money values." In 1921 he had written: "If I knew how to, I'd really join myself to the revolutionary socialists now. I think the time has come for a real struggle. That's the only thing I care for. . . . I don't care for politics. But I know there *must* and *should* be a deadly revolution very soon and I would take part in it if I knew how." He printed a *New Year's Greeting to the Willington Men for 1929:*

> O! start a revolution, somebody! . . .
> Not to install the working classes,
> But to abolish the working classes forever
> And have a world of men.

My Republican mother one morning, having cut coupons the day before and looking up from a newspaper account of a sit-down strike in some factory, cried out with equal vim, "If labor doesn't take care, we'll abolish it altogether!" In lines called *Politics,* among his *Last Poems,* Lawrence had finally to say:

> O you hard-boiled conservatives and you soft-boiled liberals
> Don't you *see* how you make bolshevism inevitable?

He had considered bolshevism in practice and despaired of "the dead materialism of Marx." "Bolshevism is one sort of bullying, capitalism another; and liberty is a change of chains." From Oaxaca he had written Murry as to socialism: "It is a dud. It makes a mush of the people." His conclusion is the sadder inasmuch as the nearest he had ever come to describing a practical political system of which he might approve had been in letters written to Lady Cynthia Asquith as far back as 1915. It was a system close to that which the Chinese had practiced locally for centuries and which Bolshevists pretend to have devised. The Soviet system is from China to Russia, not from Russia to China. "I don't believe in the democratic (republican) form of election," Lawrence wrote. "I think the artisan is fit to elect for his immediate surroundings, but not for ultimate government. The electors for the highest places should be governors of the bigger districts—the whole thing should work upwards, every man voting for that which he more or less understands through contact—no canvassing of mass votes. And women should not vote equally with the men, but for different things. Women *must* govern such things as the feeding and housing of the race. And if the system works up to a Dictator who controls the greater industrial side of the national life, it must work up to a Dictatrix who controls the things relating to private life."

That same year he wrote to Bertrand Russell: "There must be revolution in the state. It shall begin by the nationalising of all industries and means of communication, and of the land—in one fell blow. Then a man shall have his wages whether he is sick or well or old—if anything prevents his working, he shall have his wages just the same. So we shall not live in fear of the wolf—no man amongst us, and no woman, shall have any fear of the wolf at the door, for all wolves are dead. . . . The working man must elect the immediate government, of his work, of his district, not the ultimate government of the nation. There must be a body of chosen patricians. . . . It will be a ghastly chaos of destruction, if it is left to Labour to be constructive. . . . Above all there must be no democratic control—that is the worst of all. There must be an elected aristocracy."

I wonder what he would have made of Henry Ford's reply to me during the First World War, when I asked him how soon he thought it would be over and was answered, "When the idlers have killed off enough of the workers to feel safe." For whom, after all, did Lawrence intend the real fruits of the fight, for the idlers or for the workers, for the "elected aristocracy" or for the supporting plebeians, when he advised Russell that "there must be revolution in the state"?

In Lawrence's private life, as concerns his revolutionary tendencies, his wife kept watch on him, as he confesses in *Kangaroo*, when Frieda, under the guise of Harriet, protests: " 'There have been revolutions enough, in my opinion, and each one more foolish than the last. . . . And what have *you* got to do with revolutions, you petty and conceited creature? You're not big enough, not grateful enough to do anything real. I give you my energy and my life, and you want to put me aside as if I was a charwoman. Acknowledge *me* first, before you can be any good.' With which she swallowed her coffee and rose from the table. . . ." Yes, he had better acknowledge the Dictatrix, as well as the Dictator.

Considering what has been called Lawrence's fascism, Eric Russell Bentley has written, in the *New Mexico Quarterly Review*: "Thomas Carlyle, Friedrich Nietzsche, D. H. Lawrence, in their study of perfection rejected democracy. All were extreme nonconformists and could have been miserable under any despotism but their own." Bentley devised the term Heroic Vitalism to express the general impulses of these men and says: "The Heroic Vitalist thinks in terms not of good and bad but of high and low, courageous and cowardly. . . . Attacking democracy for its vulgarity, and hoping for aristocracy in a post-industrial world, he formulates a new religion of which the pivotal concepts are Heroism and Life." Mrs. Lawrence, reading the article and not liking it, missed the main phrase in it and wrote me: "I hated the spirit of that article, . . . that man doesn't know the simplest thing about living—with his 'historic vitalism,' what a phrase, it wouldn't fetch a cat from the fire!" If her cigarette eye had read "heroic," I think that her reaction would have been an equally instinctive antagonism against the intellectualized, categoric approach toward her husband's spasmodic thinkings and recordings. She knew that toward people in general, as toward a person in particular, he was deeply but resistantly drawn. For all his condemnations, it was a fond hatred toward this mass of mankind, an inner allegiance, a bond, like the sex bond. He was at depth a philosophical anarchist, as all good egoists have to be; but his rejection of political, ecclesiastical or intellectual harness was based not only on his knowledge of himself as a superior creature, with no need of blinders for guidance, but also on his faith in the inherent goodness of the individual man. For all his flinching from the touch of Tom, Dick, and Harry, this faith continued in him. Why else his everlasting search, and among the simplest people, as well as among the most complicated, for the proper stature of human decency? "I can never see how my fellow man should make me kill another man. . . . I do esteem the individual above everything else." "I am glad," he had written in *Sea and Sardinia,* "that Russia flies back into savage Russianism, Scythism, savagely self-pivoting. I am glad that America is doing the same. I shall be glad when men hate their common, world-alike clothes, when they tear them up and clothe themselves fiercely for distinction, savage distinction against the rest of the creeping world." Be distinguished, yes, Mr. Lawrence, and dress as you like, but why so savage unless you are willing to shoot some fellow man who, with an aristocratic individualism as intense and stubborn as your own, gets in your way?

"Democracy is not a good government, but it is the best we can get while we have only this poor, rotten human nature to work with." Wendell Phillips, who said this, an aristocrat by both nature and birth, had more faith in democracy and less in aristocracy than had Lawrence, the aristocrat by choice.

When an old loafer once exclaimed to Abraham Lincoln, "I feel patriotic," and Lincoln asked, "What do you mean by feeling patriotic?" the answer was, "I feel like I want to kill somebody or steal something." Melvin Lasky has connected this encounter with a quotation from Walt Whitman: "As one sees the shallowness and miserable selfism of these crowds of men, with all their minds so blank of high humanity and aspiration—then comes the terrible query, and will not be denied: Is not Democracy of human rights humbug after all? Are these flippant people with hearts of rags and souls of chalk, are these worth preaching for and dying for upon the cross? May be not—may be it is indeed a dream—yet one thing sure remains—that the exercise of Democracy, equality, to him who, believing, preached, and to the people who work it out—this is not a dream—to work for Democracy is good, the exercise is good—strength it makes and lessons it teaches—gods it makes, though it crucifies them often."

Lawrence's own attitude was: if you respect yourself and do your best by yourself, you will do your best by others. But they don't deserve it. And they like to crucify.

In his *Autobiographical Sketch*, written late, he still says flatly: "I don't feel there is any very cordial or fundamental contact between me and society, or me and other people. There is a breach. And my contact is with something that is non-human, non-vocal." He grants, however: "I find, here in Italy . . . that I live in a certain silent contact with the peasants who work the land of this villa. I am not intimate with them, hardly speak to them except to say good day. . . . Yet it is they who form my *ambiente,* and it is from them that the human flow comes to me. . . . I want to live near them, because their life still flows." His enjoyment in seeing the peasants and the fields at one was a little more than this. There was in it a touch of feudal luxury: in his small way, economically as well as imaginatively, he could be a lord affording to watch.

Even at the end, while he was wavering away from his theory of innately anointed leadership, he was wavering back to the sense that many men are born to remain as no more than the soil which grows sustenance for their betters.

He puts this conviction into the thoughts of Christ in *The Man Who Died*: " 'Let the earth remain earthy and hold its own against the sky. I was wrong to seek to lift it up. I was wrong to try to interfere. . . . It is tillage, not salvation.' " "The peasant had no rebirth in him."

The woman with whom Christ finally mates, goes even further: "She found slaves invariably repellent, a little repulsive." But she finds that "the man who died" and returned to life was a man whom an aristocrat might worthily choose.

Once again, as at first with Frieda, Lawrence felt that the passion of mating, as the supremely important expression of life, is not necessarily impaired by progeny. His jealousy of Frieda's children was over now. His feeling toward human maternity—except as his own mother's "son and lover" fiercely reverent toward her possessive tenderness—had mainly been uninterested or averse. Now—at least on a written page and as concerns the priestess—it has changed to bland tolerance. The tired, disillusioned Christ achieves with the woman a thornless crown of physical intercourse, exchanges with her what human creatures should exchange. Presently she says to him, "I am with young by thee." And then he becomes indifferent again. The fact that they have been together and that she has conceived seems to be enough and his feeling becomes much what it had been toward Mary Magdalene, with whom he had had no bodily bond: "Now I belong to no one and have no connection, and mission or gospel is gone from me. Lo! I cannot make even my own life and what have I to save?" He asks himself then the ultimate question: "I can learn to be alone?"

Frieda need not have worried when Lawrence told her that he might become a revolutionist. He was no revolutionist for his fellows. He could only fight for the individual. And the individual he fought for was himself, through whose liberation others might benefit. He was the "I Am" to which everything else flowed, as the life of the Italian peasant outside his window flowed to him and he had hoped that the life of the Mexican peon would flow to him.

Caste? Where, after all, was room for caste, when there was only one person, one lonely aristocrat, swimming in the chill of life as finely as Byron in the Hellespont? His own words tell it, in *Kangaroo:* "He wanted to be cold, cold, and alone like a single fish, with no feeling in his heart at all except a certain icy exultance and wild fish-like rapacity. '*Homo sum.*' All right. Who sets a limit to what a man is? Man is also a fierce and cold-fish devil, in his hour, filled with cold fury of desire to get away from the cloy of human life altogether, not into death, but into that icily self-sufficient vigor of a fish."

This is forceful writing and sleek thinking; but, as I ponder it, Guadalajara comes back to me and I remember anew aristocratic Frieda's delight in the American slang she hurled at him long ago, for no perceptible reason: "You poor fish!"

Jesus, that other aristocrat, had been called a fish too. From the fish, the phoenix.

37. Watcher

DESPITE his fishy vigor, Lawrence remained disturbed by the state and the fate of the ego in its necessary relationships to the world. There is a difference between being on the earth and being in the world.

We have considered his sympathy toward Jesus as a brave, distinguished man, with whom he felt that he himself, though a better thinker, had much in common. Conventional religion in the West no longer meant anything to him except through what he thought the mistakenly gallant humanness of its founder. As to the jealous, pretentious, emptily contradictory sects into which later men have divided the simple intent of Jesus, we know that when Lawrence left Westwood for the Teachers' College at Nottingham University—perhaps even earlier at Croyden—Darwin, Huxley, Haeckel, Spencer, and others had helped to free him from orthodox allegiance. "By the time I was sixteen," he says, "I had criticized and got over the Christian dogma." He wrote Bertrand Russell in 1915: "I have been wrong, much too Christian in my philosophy. . . . I am rid of all my Christian religiosity. It was only a muddiness . . . the Christian Metaphysic, which each man severally rejects, but to which we all subscribe as a State or Society." And the Christian Church was no Goliath worthy of David Lawrence's sling and pebbles. Walt Whitman had already said: "It does seem as if Ingersoll and Huxley without any others could unhorse the whole Christian giant. They are master-pilgrims with a fighting gift that would appall me if I was in the opposition."

But that was not the fighting pilgrimage on which Lawrence was bent. Let others than he see that the Christian Church had vitiated Western civilization. He had to see that it was the very nature of the founder himself which would have done the damage, if the thieves of his dignity and the betrayers of his spirit had not done it in the founder's name. Lawrence was now definitely at odds with the very intention of Jesus, whom he came more and more to distrust as a mistaken prophet. Rebelling against democratic precepts and Christian meekness, he was longing, as Tindall says, "for a return to the 'old religious faculty' of intuition and wonder." Although he could still feel tenderness for the Galilean, Lawrence was declaring, by the time he wrote *Kangaroo:* "If Jesus had been a kind master, he would have hit Judas across the mouth and said: 'Get back, you swine.' It was a very subtle cruelty on Jesus' part, to take that kiss. . . . It is a master's duty to *prevent* his man from treachery."

Lawrence's alienation from the teachings and example of Jesus grew with time. After he had left the Judases and soldiers of England behind him and arrived in Mexico, he wrote Mrs. Lujan: "Jesus, and the Good as you see it, are poison for the Indians. One feels it intensely here." And to Brett he said: "Christ was a rotter, though a fine rotter. He never *experienced* life as the old Pagan Gods did. His merit was that he went through with his job; but that was soft, squashy and also political—a labor leader. He never knew animals, or women, from a child—never. He held forth in the temple and never *lived*. Oh, basta! He was out to die, that's what makes his preaching disastrous." I wish Lawrence might have heard an elderly Quaker spinster, a good thorny saint, say to me years ago: "Jesus was a good man; but he dodged the real ordeal of life—he never married."

This was not the kind of blood, thought Lawrence, in which men should take communion. Among primitive races it has been common for a victor, in order to absorb the valor of heroic enemies killed in battle, to eat and drink their flesh and blood. Lawrence's essay on Melville in *Studies in Classical American Literature* contains a passage: ". . . if the savages liked to partake of their sacrament without raising the transubstantiation quibble, and if they liked to say, directly: 'This is thy body, which I take from thee, and eat, this is thy blood, which I sip in annihilation of thee,' why surely their sacred ceremony was as awe-inspiring as the one Jesus substituted. . . . The savage sacrament seems to me more valid than the Christian: less sidetracking about it." Here Lawrence should have made his point clearer: that Christian communicants are borrowing poorly from the custom of noble savages, that there had been better founded meals of transubstantiation before the Last Supper, better founded because the savages were absorbing valor instead of meekness.

Mrs. Carswell gives her judgment of what was going through Lawrence's sense of religion at this period and later: "By the Jewish-Christian ideal . . . we suffer either as a punishment for sin or in furtherance of our spiritual purification, this being undertaken by a loving God for his own inscrutable ends. In either case we are victims. As it works out in practice, we can become godlike only by welcoming suffering, not by resisting it. The more a victim, the nearer to the divine. . . . But the whole of the ascetic practice is an exact antithesis to the hardships undergone in the non-Christian initiation to adult life. The first seeks to weaken the flesh which already it has ideally degraded; the second seeks to strengthen an ideally potent flesh in the conflict between man and the unseen. Both would have man partake of the divine, but submission is the secret communion of the one, while the other communicates by way of a challenge which is none the less worship."

In the autumn of 1925 Lawrence challenged Murry as to a book upon which the latter was engaged: "Must you really write about Jesus? Jesus becomes more unsympathetic to me, the longer I live: crosses and nails and all that stuff!" And the short story, *Glad Ghosts,* contains a passage: "Think how ghastly for Jesus, when he was risen and wasn't touchable! . . . Ah, touch me, touch me *alive!*"

No, Jesus was not the prophet. Who was?

The great lumbering god of the Jewish Old Testament had been forgotten by Lawrence, before he set aside Jesus. One might think that on occasion Jehovah had been "dark" enough even for this latter-day rebel.

Although Jessie Chambers' careful memory of the books which nourished Lawrence's boyhood and youth gives us mainly literary titles, I am sure that he must have delved then or soon afterward into the records of mankind's religious inquiries and its conclusions which, however impressive, can only be reverently assumptive. He would not have been like the man who, remarking in a lecture that the Christian Gospels presented the last word, was quietly answered by Emerson from the audience: "The gentleman's remark proves only how narrowly he has read."

The mysticism of India might have drawn him, if he had not had a romantic preconception of the mysticism of Egypt—and the Americas. By his own account, Buddhism scarcely interested him. Nor did any other ready-made religion. He had touched at Ceylon on his eastward circling to the Americas and had stayed with Western friends, the Earl Brewsters, who were converts to Buddhism. His spokesman Lilly says in *Aaron's Rod:* "I can't do with folk who teem by the billion. Higher types breed slower." And yet India had haunted the Lawrence imagination. Mme Blavatsky, the theosophist, had liked India and he had liked Mme Blavatsky. India's dark millions grew a flamboyance of mysticism—architecture, sculpture, strong deities—not unakin to Egypt's. Different, though. Buddha denied too calmly his own or any godship. Lilly does go on to say: "I think a man may come into possession of his own soul at last—as the Buddhists teach—but without teaching to love, or even to hate. One loves, one hates—but somewhere beyond it all, one understands, one possesses one's soul in patience and in peace." Lawrence now and then under his tree on that beach in Chapala had looked like a lean, bearded Buddha—but a Buddha with a pencil pushing away peace.

Mrs. Carswell assumes, concerning the Ceylon visit, that Lawrence had to be fortified by a country with religion for one that had none. "So he withdrew for a breathing-space," she says, "would see if the 'old, old East' would sweeten the gall in his blood." By his own brief accounts it did not, at least through his pause on the edge of India. He did not like what he called "the boneless suavity of the Oriental."

I am constantly puzzled by the fact that Lawrence did not go farther east than a footstep on an island at only the edge of the far Orient, that he did not look for other ancients besides the Egyptian, Etruscan, and Aztec.

Why, if not drawn by his blood to China, was he not drawn, through his reading, by the classic Chinese tradition of a remote past in which a perfect society of men had lived with natural goodness, with natural leaders and natural followers bound in balanced and happy relationship, much as in his own dreams of heroic antiquity.

One of Laotzu's sayings begins:

> Sound old rulers, it is said
> Left people to themselves, instead
> Of wanting to teach everything
> And start the people arguing . . .
> With mere instruction in command,

So that people understand
Less than they know, woe is the land;
But happy the land that is ordered so
That they understand more than they know.

What could be closer than this to Lawrence's social faith? He said himself: "To pump education into the mind is fatal. That which sublimates from the dynamic consciousness into the mental consciousness has alone any value. This, in most individuals, is very little indeed. So that most individuals, under a wise government, would be most carefully protected from all vicious attempts to inject extraneous ideas into them."

He had written Bertrand Russell in 1916, and I wish Russell had quoted him to me when we were together in Peking the following year, five years before I was to meet Lawrence: "Do for heaven's sake be a baby and not a savant any more. Don't *do* anything any more—but for heaven's sake begin to *be*—start at the very beginning and be a perfect baby: in the name of courage. . . . Nothing is born by taking thought." This again might have been Laotzu speaking.

Laotzu had called himself only a glorious infant still nursing at the breast.

Laotzu had noted that:

. . . men of culture came, with their grades and their
    distinctions;
And as soon as such differences had been devised,
No one knew where to end them.

Laotzu had advised:

Leave off fine learning! End the nuisance
Of saying yes to this and perhaps to that.

Laotzu had said, long before Lawrence:

There is no need to run outside
For better seeing,
Nor to peer from a window. Rather abide
At the center of your being;
For the more you leave it, the less you learn.
Search your heart and see
If he is wise who takes each turn:
The way to do is to be.

It is likely that innate democracy in Chinese character alienated Lawrence: their belief that any man might prove to be as good as any other and their disbelief in divinely ordained rights. Throughout Chinese history a hero is a hero because of democratic understanding and compassion, because of his kinship to other men rather than because of superiority over them. The superior man in China is not the Genghis Khan but the Sun Yat-sen, the Lincoln, not a massive stone-visaged mystic, not a fine muscular monster, not a Wagnerian swashbuckler, not a dark power, but a man enlightened by and toward his fellow man. Lordly and poetic though this superior man is in the instinct of China, he may have seemed to Lawrence humble and prosaic. Pearl Buck, introducing a late edition of *The Good Earth,* explains that in China "basic and popular democracy has for centuries been successful, and this in spite of governments, old and new, which have often been far from democratic. . . . Chinese," she notes, "have lived longer upon their earth than any other human group. . . . What have they," she asks, "which has set them apart from others who have disappeared from the face of the earth? Nothing indeed except the belief that life is good and because it is good, it is to be preserved and continued. The present is all that we can grasp beyond doubt, and since this is true, life must not be wasted in folly. It must be savored in every mouthful of food, in every moment's sleep, in a bowl of hot wine, in an hour of sunshine, in rain drifting across the mountains, in a flower, in a bird, in a mountain stream, in the companionship of a friend, in the satisfaction of a lover. . . . The Chinese alone have come to the high point of understanding that life in and of itself is the most valuable possession of the human being, and life therefore is to be held in higher estimation than any religion, than any ideology, even than any dream."

Here, where he never cared to look for it, is the simple core of Lawrence. When all his other doctrines failed, the sense remained in him, firm, fine, and final, that bodily life is sacred. This is what we have, was his text. Let us use it well.

"Bodiless God," in Lawrence's *Last Poems,* declares:

> Everything that has beauty has a body, and is a body;
> everything that has being has being in the flesh;
> and dreams are only drawn from the bodies that are.

And in *Apocalypse,* toward the end of his life, he maintains: "Man wants his physical fulfillment first and foremost, since now, once and once only, he is in the flesh and potent. For man, the vast marvel is to be alive. For man, as for flower and beast and bird, the supreme triumph is to be most vividly, most perfectly alive. . . . We ought to dance with rapture that we should be alive and in the flesh, and part of the living, incarnate cosmos."

Around this conception Lawrence hovered all his life like a desperate moth. He should have realized, I must repeat, that it was a conception prevalent in China's civilization, in a large part of the world's population; and yet he dodged looking in that direction, perhaps because the conception there was not as excited as he would have it be, had grown too sober for him, or perhaps, incurable romantic and egoist that he was, because he did not wish to acknowledge that the best living of which he could conceive could exist anywhere except in a lost Atlantis, or in "those Middle Ages when men were lordly and violent and shadowed with death," or in his own imagination, or in some primitive race among whom he and his followers might kindle the embers alive.

Lawrence might have found the quietism of Tao more dynamic than all his own fevers, because by "dynamic" he meant the urge of growth, which is as quiet as it is dynamic. Growth was his central idea. As he breathed aloud, he would have liked to know the language of a tree, which grows better than man does, takes on its leaves, throws them off, and takes them on again. Once man's leaves are gone, they are gone except in shadow. Many of idealism's diagrams seemed to Lawrence a fixity of imagination and purpose. He would have agreed with Santayana's saying that "there is nothing cheaper than idealism. It can be had by . . . declaring that the first rhymes that have struck our ears are the eternal and necessary harmonies of the world." I think that he might have gone further with Santayana and agreed that metaphysics are "love affairs of the understanding." Certainly he would have agreed that "fanaticism consists in redoubling your effort when you have forgotten your aim," and that "activity does not consist in velocity of change, but in constancy of purpose." Every time Lawrence found an aim, he tripled his effort. But his aim was never a fixed idea. Lawrence's aim was a part of the growth of life; it was as natural as the uncurling of a fern. And that is why the man, because also he was an artist and was able to express what he was, stays vital into new generations.

He was a free and honest man. He had repudiated ecclesiastical dogma that you may be excused for misconduct merely by recognizing yourself responsible for it and working it off with penance and repetition. He had not accepted the psychiatric dogma that you are relieved of misconduct when you recognize your irresponsibility for it and brush it off with mental understanding and repetition. He had decided that any conduct which came from a pure blood impulse could not be misconduct, that, deeper than all reason, there is in the blood a conscience, an intuitive knowledge, through which we test instantly whether we do well or ill. By our conduct according to that knowingness of the blood, we may confidently and securely abide. Each man's church should be inside himself, his own daily life the liturgy, his pulsing blood the sacrament.

Lawrence was determined to find, inside human life, some meaning for it. Meanings, manufactured into creeds and philosophies, were but crutches of air. The meaning must be in the blood stream itself, the source and stay of life. He was often on the edge of that doctrine of cosmic instinct which Laotzu did not wish to put into words lest words obscure it—the solving of existence by solution in it, by the dissolving of one's own being in the being of the universe; but Lawrence felt his sort of Tao to be different: not a quiescent acceptance but an activity of his dynamic self participating in the generally dynamic lifeflow, recognizable by instinct and conscience. As I have remarked before, I do not think the Laotzu quietism and Lawrence dynamism are so different as they sound. Either one of them might have said with Don Ramon of *The Plumed Serpent:* "There is no liberty for a man, apart from the God of his manhood. . . . I can't find God, in the old sense. I know it's a sentimentalism if I pretend to. . . . I have realized that *my will* no matter how intelligent I am, is only another nuisance on the face of the earth. . . . Then! I ask what else is there in the world, besides human will, human appetite? because ideas and ideals are only instruments of human will and appetite. . . . And then when you find your own manhood . . . then you know it is not your own, to do as you like with. . . . It comes from—from the middle. . . . Beyond me, at the middle, is the God. And the God gives me my manhood, then leaves me to it . . . gives it me, and leaves me to do further." The figure Kate then takes over, both figures being Lawrence himself:

"She felt the fullness descend into her once more, the peace, and the power. The fulfillment filling her soul like the fullness of ripe grapes. And she thought to herself: 'Ah, how wrong I have been, not to turn sooner to the other presence, not to take the life-breath sooner!' "

The watcher had watched well. Life-breath was all the spiritual support his own nature needed. The rest was mostly something which other men had wrought out of nothing. And their hopeful business should have been none of his business. But that busy mind of his felt that he ought to be able to help direct other men in their hopeful business. His own direction would be too adult for them. They must have a perceptible god to follow. It was not he who needed the myth, it was his fellows, about whom for some reason he cared. He could never quite escape his responsibility for them. They were the children whom he had never had and almost forgotten to want from the body. He began trying to find for these other men who, without his knowing it, had become children of his breath, a faith he did not need for himself —pictures, faith-pictures on the nursery-wall. However, now and then the magic-lantern slide projected there a nursery tale in which he himself almost believed.

38. Seer

AT times this modern man, Lawrence, who knew himself a part
of growth, tried to combine some sort of formal orthodoxy with
his instinctive faith, with what Laotzu, despite the supposed
record of his *Sayings,* had felt to be incommunicable revelation inside
one's self, in one's universal identity. Lawrence stubbornly sought
now and then to subject the flexible tender moods of the self to some
more or less rigid outside control and to keep both the change and
the fixity valid. Never would he have adopted for his own self the
"willing suspension of disbelief." Never could he have accepted an
orthodoxy framed by other men. Yet at times he would swerve from
the truth of the inner revelation to some myth of the outer, would
even dream of himself being power and imposing a myth upon other
men.

His sense that the physical body is the holy temple of life remained
with him consistently, but just what god to seat there perplexed him all
his days. He felt at first, and I think finally, that his own identity was
enough, was all that had been really given him to know of the divine;
but betweenwhiles he flirted hard with various deities, most of them
created in his own image.

Professor William York Tindall, in his serious volume with the
superficially misleading title, *D. H. Lawrence and Susan His Cow,*
is the first as far as I know, to have traced his subject's early and
apparently continued interest in the high priestess of theosophy, Mme
Blavatsky, and in her books, *Isis Unveiled* and *The Secret Doctrine.*
Lawrence disparaged them, as at one time or another he disparaged
almost everything; but Mr. Tindall was informed by Mrs. Lawrence
"that her husband read and delighted in all of Mme Blavatsky's
works."

According to Tindall, Mme Blavatsky "gave Lawrence two important ideas: the idea of the primitive religious Utopia and the idea of ancient myths and symbols as the way of understanding and return." He suggests also that the Englishman may have picked up his heraldic personal symbol, his crest, from Mme Blavatsky who, in *The Secret Doctrine,* describes "the lonely, self-begetting Phoenix" as "an esoteric symbol of initiation and rebirth." But when Lawrence refers directly to theosophy, there is something of humor in the reference, if he meant it as humor. Brewster quotes him as saying: "Even theosophists don't realize that the universal lotus really blossoms in the abdomen." I wonder if there was any relation here to his confessed love of decking the navel with petals? Tindall says further: "The theosophical pursuit of the antedeluvian explains not only much of Lawrence's interest in the redskin but also much of his concern with the Egyptians, Chaldeans, Etruscans, and other ancient people, in whom Mme Blavatsky had detected traces of better days." He quotes Brewster's quotation from Lawrence, akin to the Blavatsky theory: "I believe that there was a great age, a great epoch . . . previous to 2000 B.C., apparently under a present ocean where the bright, lost world of Atlantis is buried." And Tindall points out agreement between the seeress and the seer that the ceremonies of the American Indians preserve, as Lawrence declares, "a living tradition going back far beyond the birth of Christ, beyond the pyramids, beyond Moses. A vast old religion," Lawrence continues, "which once swayed the earth . . . away back . . . before the Flood . . . lingers in unbroken practice there in New Mexico." Tindall finds in *The Plumed Serpent* mystic exercises and initiations previously described by Mme Blavatsky and comments that this work, "Lawrence's most animistic novel . . . is also his most theosophical. Its theme is that of Mme Blavatsky's *Secret Doctrine:* The recovery of lost Atlantis by means of myths and symbols." " 'I would like,' " says Don Ramon in the novel, " 'to be one of the Initiates of the Earth.' " I agree with Tindall: Lawrence would frequently try to find that the tremors of grave compassion in man's breast derive from the past are memories of Atlantis. Again he would feel them as creative pulsations of the future. Still again he would unite past and future into a symbolic rainbow, prehistoric Atlantis joining, merging, arching with posthistoric Paradise. It was a rainbow made of a hopeful mist from the unshed tears of his own eyes.

If such esoteric considerations were absorbing Lawrence toward the end of his Chapala stay, I have already indicated that they were not cheering his spirit. With recurrence of his Mexico City melancholy, he apparently felt depressed by life in general. Throughout his writing, when he is baffled, perhaps throughout his life, he imports something heroic or mystic to ease his physical or emotional shifts, vagaries or shortcomings. If he cannot invent a human being important enough to occasion or warrant his shift, he pulls in a ghost—as in short stories like *The Border Line*—or a god—as in *The Plumed Serpent*. I see now that there at the lake, temporarily weak in himself, he craved again a mysticism, a help from beyond or behind, and that he was still under the spell cast on him by Indians of New Mexico, by what Mrs. Lujan and others had told him of the North American Indians' spiritual power, and by ever-recurrent need of outer assistance for his boastful but dependent ego.

Tony Romero of the Taos pueblo has often explained to me that his fellow Indians would recover their land and rightful sovereignty when at last the moon had finished its office of hardening to arthritic stone the bones of all white men. Such prophecy coming out of handsome Indian presences continued to catch Lawrence's imagination and unsettle his security. Out of his bewilderment he turned to a God, partly to the God within him, but partly also to a new Saviour. So he declares, through Don Ramon: "Man loses his connection with God. And then he can never recover it again, unless some new Saviour comes to give him his new connection. And every new connection is different from the last, though God is always God." It was this swerving to outer revelation which introduced into *The Plumed Serpent* the pretentious pageantry of Quetzalcoatl, through which he chose to exteriorize and melodramatize his own inner combats and cravings. Oliver La Farge describes authors like Lawrence who come to Mexico and New Mexico as "setting out in a complex search for simplicity, peering through refractions of a mysticism they have brought with them and superimposed upon the country, a sort of prismatic vulva in which they see only their own problems surrounded by rainbows."

Lawrence often felt that no one is eventually great as a mere thinker, because mortal thought decays and is gone in the cleansing course of time. In theory he agreed with Dostoyevsky, his precursor and blood brother, concerning the "heart-emptiness" and homelessness of the intellectual as compared to the peasant's heart bonds with the earth and its divine source, and yet he ever remained the bewildered intellectual himself, wandering the earth in search of a natural home. He used to nod occasional assent to my belief that finally only common sense persists with purity and force. And common sense is anybody's possession against all proud pretensions of the intellect. In this respect, I used to insist to him, he was a democrat, because common sense in its essential meaning, is the rock-bottom base of democracy. And yet, though Lawrence exclaimed, declaimed, proclaimed against merely cerebral processes, he constantly seemed—more in his books than in conversation—to depend upon a prop of theory to hold up common sense. For all his distrust of intellect, for all his trust in common sense or "horse sense," his mind craved and his tongue drummed incessant theory. For Frieda the strong earth was support enough; and all places, wide or narrow, were the earth. If he had had more of her fundament, he would have been a happier native of the universe. He was wise in his concept of what he wished to be; but he could not resist darkening it with theory, giving it sharp angles, instead of radiating simplicity from its round center as she did. Her amber was clear. His had flowed over insects.

The new god, for whom Lawrence was looking, was greening in the smallest pea. And yet he wanted another new god beyond the pea—a god with power beyond the vegetating beauty of the world. At times he even wanted, as we have seen, some such fine pomp as the Tibetans or the Papists expensively afford, an artistic hierarchy in control. He wanted this easing of personal effort, some outside authority; and yet his dignity would never yield to it, to a substitute for man's own dignity—the only god that any man really knows being his own receptive and creative wonder that he shall be worthy of having the god within him.

In 1913, he had written Ernest Collings: "Isn't it hard, hard work to come to real grips with one's imagination—throw everything overboard? I always feel as if I stood naked for the fire of Almighty God to go through me—and it's rather an awful feeling. One has to be so terribly religious to be an artist. I often think of my dear St. Lawrence on his gridiron, when he said, 'Turn me over, brothers, I am done enough on this side.'" In 1915 he wrote to Lady Ottoline Morrell: "Let us have no personal influence, if possible—nor personal magnetism, as they used to call it, nor persuasion—no 'Follow me'—but only 'Behold.' And a man shall not come to save his own soul. Let his soul go to hell. He shall come because he knows that his own soul is not the be-all and the end-all, but that all souls of all things do but compose the body of God and that God indeed shall *Be."* He also said: "There is, in our sense of the word, no God. But all is Godly."

This was much like the faith I had tried to enjoin upon him in Chapala; but by then he had violently cast off his own heresy of Oneness. Tindall comments that in Lawrence's late work, *Apocalypse,* "he rejects individuality in favor of oneness with all. At times," continues Tindall, "he wavered between preserving the identity and merging with the whole, preferring, in the same essay, now one now the other. At other times, however, he tried to reconcile relationship with individuality by making the former a necessary condition for the attainment of the latter."

Let Mrs. Carswell summarize the conception which she thought underlay Lawrence's apparent vacillations: "Nothing was needed but for us to perceive religiously that the cosmos itself was alive and to enter into the richness of that perception. In wrestling with a live cosmos men would immediately become themselves gods of a kind— fallible still, but potent with cosmic energy. On Monte Cassino . . . he saw his temptation and his destiny, and he put the first from him and accepted the second open-eyed. To the lovely past, as worshipped by the monks behind him, he would not bow down, though it might bring peace. He must live in the hard and often loathsome present, and individual man's life, with all its needs, contradictions and errors proclaimed as it goes along; and at the same time he must be an unswerving conduit from the very origins of life—so far back that they were lost—to the undiscovered future, in some way that transcended while it never eliminated or absolved the individual."

In one of his letters he said: "Primarily I am a passionately religous man, and my novels must be written from the depths of my religious experience," in another, "There is a *principle* in the universe towards which man turns religiously—a *life* of the universe itself, and the hero is he who touches and transmits the life of the universe," in another, "I take on a very important attitude of profundity . . . and so feel happy."

In later days his attitude of profundity continued but became simplified. Let me put together, from *Assorted Articles,* passages in several of his essays—*On Human Destiny, Autobiographical Sketch, Hymns in a Man's Life, Men Must Work and Women as Well*—together with two passages from *Etruscan Places,* to condense his conclusions toward the end of his life. First his perceptions of the beginning and finish of Christianity under Empire and under Democracy: "Rome was pot-bound, the pot was smashed to atoms, and the highly developed Roman tree of life lay on its side and died. But not before a new young seed had germinated. There in the split soil, small, humble, almost undiscernible, was the little tree of Christianity." "To-day, the long light of Christianity is guttering to go out and we have to get at new resources in ourselves." "Now the great and fatal fruit of our civilisation, which is a civilisation based on knowledge, and hostile to experience, is boredom. All our wonderful education and learning is producing a grand sum-total of boredom. Modern people are inwardly thoroughly bored. Do as they may, they are bored. They are bored because they experience nothing. And they experience nothing because the wonder has gone out of them. And when the wonder has gone out of a man he is dead. He is henceforth only an insect. When all comes to all, the most precious element in life is wonder. Love is a great emotion, and power is power. But both love and power are based on wonder." "The mind by itself is just a sterile thing, makes everything sterile." "Man, poor, conscious, forever-animal man, has a very stern destiny. . . . The moment he builds himself a house and begins to think he can sit still in his knowledge, his soul becomes deranged, and he begins to pull down the house over his own head." "All western civilisation is now mechanised, materialised and ready for an outburst of insanity which shall throw us all into some purely machine-driven unity of lunatics." "One can save one's pennies. But how can one save one's soul? One can only *live* one's soul." "The old idea of the vitality of the universe was evolved long before history begins. . . . The active idea was that man, by vivid attention and subtlety and exerting all his strength, could draw more life into himself . . . more and more glistening vitality, till he became shining like the morning, blazing like a god. . . . This was the idea at the back of all the great old civilisations. . . . But it is truly a question of *divination.* As soon as there is any pretence of infallibility, and pure scientific calculation, the whole thing becomes a fraud and a jugglery . . . the same is true not only of augury and astrology, but also of prayer and pure reason, and even of the discoveries of the great laws and principles of science."

William Butler Yeats, in his *Essays,* 1924, asked: "How can the arts overcome the slow dying of men's hearts that we call the progress of the world, and lay their hands upon men's heartstrings again, without becoming the garment of religion as in old times? . . . We are about to substitute once more the distillations of alchemy for the analysis of chemistry."

Tindall notices, in Lawrence's essay on Melville, two passages within a few pages of each other: one, "No men are so evil today as the idealists," and the other, "Melville was, at the core, a mystic and an idealist. Perhaps, so am I." Lawrence's characters, observes Tindall concisely, "wandering through intense landscapes . . . utter improbable sermons."

"Gray," said Goethe, "is the color of all theory." In the long sections of Lawrence's novels, where he leaves narrative, leaves landscape, leaves animals and birds and real people, leaves the concrete, the objective, turns instead to subjective dialogues of idealism, of theory, or monologues of it, or disquisitions or sermons, turns to the abstract, the pages go gray.

But Lawrence in these moods did not think himself a theorist: he thought himself a seer.

William Marion Reedy, an American not yet held in enough esteem, has said that "happiness and goodness may be attained by making the most, in a high way, of this, the only world we surely know; by cultivating in the senses the soul until the senses, as soul, seem to reach out and apprehend in almost tangible fashion the realities of the unseen." Here would appear to me to be the resting place of Lawrence's pendulum; but if the Englishman had let it rest so simply, he might not, to himself or to others, have seemed a soothsayer, a Merlin, a mystic, a seer. As it was, the pendulum swung him back again to New Mexico and ancient magic.

39. The Mexicos Again

RETURNING from England, the Lawrences had touched only briefly in New York; for on March 21, 1924, I wrote my mother from Santa Fe that they "came at six this evening, with an English viscountess or something, deaf but likable, and left at tenthirty. They go along to Taos tomorrow, to see whether this time he can refrain from quarreling with Mabel. He's a man with a mind, anyway. I was glad to see him and really joyous in seeing the greathearted Frieda." I might have written more. I might have told her that I had read him and found him a man with more than a mind. I might have told her, to her satisfaction, that Frieda was not so meek now toward the spouse. If Lawrence condemned Christian meekness, why should he wish it in his wife? Because women were not capable of valor? Because meekness was their sphere? She would show him. He was always showing people this or that. It was high time that he were shown something. And by her. She loved him, yes, more securely than ever; but she had enjoyed her taste of their separation more than he had enjoyed his. She had seen her children and been sustained by them; and she had found that his friends in England liked her on her own account. His theories as to male and female were all very well, except as they gave more importance to the one than to the other. She was an individual too. She had found herself and where she belonged in life quite as well as he had found where he belonged. She would no longer let him encourage a court of eager women at her expense, and he knew it. She had had her taste of independence and found that it was quite as important to her as his was to him, although none of this interfered with her love of their interdependence. Brett quotes her as saying to him: " 'you want to make a God of yourself! You are no more important than I am. . . . Always at home I played first fiddle.

When I again saw my children after all these years, they said how surprised they were to see me playing second fiddle. I am as important as Lawrence, he says so himself.' "

I wondered if fearsome foresight of this wholesome change in her was why he had not wanted her to see her children.

It was during the following summer, I think, that the lodge on the mountain beyond Taos was transferred to the Lawrences; and there is a fine legend concerning the deal. Frieda, with her nostalgic and prudent craving for a home, coveted the cabin and the mountain grounds but had no funds. Mrs. Lujan is said to have suggested a Lawrence manuscript and Frieda to have remembered that *Sons and Lovers,* in Lawrence's fine hand, was at the bottom of one of his trunks. He had saved it, probably hoping that it would have a value; but he was away at an Apache dance with Tony Lujan. The ranch belonged to young John Evans, Mabel Lujan's son, who, it appears, was no more consulted than Lawrence was as to the transaction; but that fact seems to have been no deterrent to the two women in an exchange of possessions they did not own: the son's ranch for the husband's manuscript. Perhaps Lawrence, when he returned, shrugged acquiescence, and John Evans, if he had regrets, dutifully swallowed them. Dorothy Brett's account of the transaction is that Lawrence himself had decided "to give Mabel the MS of *Sons and Lovers* for the Ranch" but that the manuscript could not be found and he thought "Frieda's mother had it in Germany." That, however, does not build so good a tale.

The ranch house, with stout improvements, and with now another, more comfortable and ample dwelling built beside it by Captain Angelino Ravagli—the Lawrence's friend when they returned to Europe the second time, in later years Frieda's ranch manager, and in 1950 her husband—stands monumental as the nearest to a home of his own that the wanderer ever enjoyed; and it is said that the manuscript of *Sons and Lovers,* given to Dr. Brill by Mrs. Lujan in exchange for psychoanalyzing, was eventually sold, either before the doctor's death or afterward among his effects, for a substantial sum. Lawrence himself should have written the story! In a 1928 letter he asked me, "Do you know, by the way, how much Mabel got for the manuscript of *Sons and Lovers?* Has she really sold it? News!" I lacked the news for him. But it has now come to this: the ranch was Lawrence's for a while, is still Frieda's, and has been in both their lives a rich return.

Through the spring of 1924 we exchanged visits back and forth between Taos and Santa Fe, half a day's trip then each way.

On one occasion in Taos, the Lujans drove us all to the Manby Springs, at the foot of a side canyon—an extraordinary pothole of hot water directly adjoining the cold water of the Rio Grande. Arthur Rockfort Manby, a remittance Englishman, had come to Taos fairly early, had built a solid, gloomy house there, and had bought various properties round about, including gold mines and this hot spring. He would obtain money at the bank from nuggets which he carried to the wicket in a cigar box. He was said to be involved with shady characters in such deals as tapping through tunnel mines neighboring his own, or as organizing a racket of supposed watchmen who would hold up residents for fees under the pretext of protecting them and punish by theft or fire those who withheld dues. Eventually, when Manby had not appeared for a few days, his next-door neighbor, Dr. T. P. Martin —the self-styled "American Consul in Taos"—noted too many flies at a window. When the sheriff and he had broken the locked entrance and shot a savage dog, they found a headless body in one of the Manby rooms and in another room with a shut door, beyond which they shot another dog, a skull, eaten bare of flesh. The mystery has never been solved; and I understand that the hot spring is now as lifeless as its owner. In those days, remote though it was, Spanish-Americans took needed baths in it, and a few members of the foreign colony had discovered it and would lie in it, wondering if Manby might have been right that it contained beneficial radium. The Englishman had built a one-room wooden shack over it, from which by a ladder you descended into what felt at first like a pitch-black dungeon, large enough to contain six or eight persons. On this occasion, as I remember it, Mrs. Lujan, Mrs. Lawrence, and Ida Rauh, who was then Mrs. Andrew Dasburg, enjoyed the first soak, after which Tony, Lawrence, Johnson, and I took our turn. The water was hot, somewhat debilitating, the hole dark and for me a clamp of claustrophobia. When our eyes began to see, Lawrence asked Tony what the flaky, silicate-looking scale was on the water's surface. "Mexican skin," explained Tony easily. I wanted no more such ease and was glad that Lorenzo gave a quick jump, an example which Spud and I followed, out of the scum into daylight again. "Not so close," Lawrence might have quoted himself to the Mexican skin. "I am a little particular."

The ranch house on the mountainside was meanwhile being made permanently habitable—or at least ready for as much permanence as a chronic wanderer could manage. Mattresses in which chipmunks had nested were being mended. And a cabin alongside the main lodge was being restored. Brett was with them. In her book she describes Del Monte: "One house has been a cowshed for years, by the look of it: it is full of cow dung. The second house is better, and with cleaning could be made fit to live in. The third house is tiny, so tiny we wonder if it is possible to get a bed in it." She tells of the additional construction, partly logs, partly adobe, and reports the hard work in which she shares while Frieda cooks and watches and smokes—the cutting of trees for logs in new walls around a new chimney, the making of porches, cupboards, bedsteads, chairs, and a meat safe to hang in a tree.

Lawrence wrote me at the time: "We've finished all our hard work —and the little guesthouse is ready. If you and Spoodle would like to come up for a week, let us know, and come. I think we can manage to be good-tempered and amiable for a while. And we can talk Mexico plans. I still feel very much drawn down there. . . . It is fresh up here, and not dusty. And as a rule, the wicked cease from troubling, and the weary are, thank goodness, more or less at rest again, after five weeks slaving. . . . If you wish we'll arrange for you to come straight out here, without staying in Taos at all. We are very rarely down there, either. . . . I myself am sick to death of personalities and personalisms and tittle-tattle and threads back and forth, like a lot of ravelled knitting, and oneself the kitten trying to pick one's way out of it. Basta! to it all, and ten times basta. We keep fairly cool up here—but you'll have more or less to *camp*, help with the chores and all that. You won't be particularly comfortable, and of course society is strictly limited. But you can always depart when you've had enough, and in the meantime it's not bad. I will keep my irritatingness in bounds, I hope. Frieda sends a bright Hello!"

It was during these months that Mrs. Lujan was asking Johnson to be her secretary. After initial hesitation, concerning which Lawrence wrote, "I'm rather glad he's being wise and wary," Spud finally decided on Taos. I should have gone along with him for the Del Monte visit but was prevented by having visitors of my own.

Lawrence wrote soon again: "But come up before you—or we—go far away. I've not seen any of your poems or things about me. I never care, so long as it isn't mean, what people say about me. I've really reached the point of realizing that most people naturally dislike me—especially on second thoughts, they do. It's just part of the chemistry of life. Spoodle may come tomorrow—quién sabe? It's a world of maybes."

The world of maybes so arranged our lives that I saw Lawrence only once again and then but briefly, the following spring.

In the autumn of 1924 they returned to Mexico, with Dorothy Brett. My reasons for not accompanying them that year seemed sufficient to me then: spectacular trips into far reaches of Hopi and Navajo country, presidency of the Spanish-Indian Trading Post in which I worked enjoyably and profitably with Andrew Dasburg, B. J. O. Nordfeldt, and John Evans (Mabel Lujan's son), and, above all, ardent organization of New Mexicans who hoped to seat La Follette in the White House. I did plan to attend in Mexico City the inauguration of Calles as President; but exhaustion after the La Follette campaign and increased activity in the Trading Post kept me at home. I am sorry now that I did not give up these lesser pursuits and pursue the Lawrences instead. I might have helped them through their harassed winter months. Until he became ill, Lawrence's mellower attitude toward the western continent, and toward life in general, would have given us a comfortable time together. He had by no means entirely forgiven Mexico; but it had obviously become a magnet to his spirit. At least it now attracted him more than it repelled.

Idella Purnell had urged his return to Jalisco; but he wrote me from the Monte Carlo again: "We got in after midnight on Wed., train so late—journey otherwise uneventful and not unpleasant. . . . But the food in the Pullman the same swindle. There has been a good deal of rain here—country looks nice, and it's almost chilly. The capital is shabby and depressed—not a very nice feeling in the town. I think we shall go in a fortnight to Oaxaca. The English Vice Consul has a brother, a priest in the Cathedral Chapter there, and he would sponsor us! Ye gods! . . . The Monte Carlo is almost unchanged, but not many guests. We chose to go upstairs—Brett in your old room, we in the one inside where the monkey, the parrot and the Chihuahua dog abode. With a bowl of candied fruit, a flask of Chianti, those coloured majolica cups and tea, we only need you two to push back the clock. They're *very* nice to us in the hotel." In a second letter from the Monte Carlo, October 29, 1924, Lawrence wrote: "We've both had terrible colds like the one I had in Puebla. And if it's merely Mexico City, it's not worth coming for. Chilly, reeking with influenza, and in bad spirits, the town. I think we go down to Oaxaca on Monday. Somerset Maugham left for Cuernavaca the day we got in, but apparently he too is no loss. Disagreeable, with no fun left in him, and terrified for fear he won't be able to do his next great book, with a vivid Mexican background, before Christmas. A narrow-gutted 'artist' with a stutter.

"We lunched with the venerable Mrs. Nuttall: who has been nine months in California without, apparently, bringing forth. But she was nice, and gave us lots of flowers. Dinner at Coyoacán, and drank absinthe, gin, poilly, chablis, beaune, port, and whiskey from beginning to end of an evening, and was not comforted.

"Genaro Estrada of the PEN club called on me—fat and bourgeois but nice and I'm in for a supper at the Oriental Café on Friday evening, to meet the PENS. Don't like the thought of it one bit.

"Want to get away into the country and be by myself. . . ."

Shortly after this they went to Oaxaca. Meanwhile I had sent him in manuscript a copy of a poem of mine on an Indian dance. He wrote me, December 10: "Thank you for your letter and the poem: makes me wish I had seen that Buffalo dance. Dasburg said you were probably going to the Calles inauguration, so half expected to hear of you or from you in La Capital. . . .

"We are here in a house—perfect town. Brett is in the hotel. Heaven knows what we shall do in the spring. Frieda is sniffing Europe-ward once more: her mother and children. If we go, it will be from Vera Cruz. But will let you know. Brett has taken to photography."

He wrote Idella on March 3, 1925, from the Imperial Hotel in Mexico City: "We both got malaria so badly in Oaxaca, we can hardly crawl. I never knew the town was reeking with malaria, till I had it myself and was in bed a month. We struggled up here last week—and are sailing for England on the 17th—just two weeks from today. This time I *really* want to get back to Europe, for this sickness has taken all the energy out of me. We had much better have come to Chapala, but Frieda didn't want to. She now hates Mexico: and I no longer like it. . . . Believe me, Guadalajara is about the best place in this damned republic. . . ." Then from the Imperial again, eight days later: "The doctor has kept me in bed since Friday—blood tests, etc. and *insists* we must not go to England, but that we return to New Mexico. So we give in. If possible we'll leave next week for Santa Fe.

I'm sorry not to have seen you and your father—am still in bed here—and a perfect rag. . . . We'll meet on a happier day than this." Again he wrote her, a little later: "The doctor put me in bed again, and kept me there: threat of pneumonia. Now I'm up and about. The ship has gone—but doctor says I *must not* go to England now: so we're going to the ranch—Del Monte Ranch, Valdez, New Mexico.

"This time nothing has gone right. Let's hope for the next time. If you come to the U.S., come and see us at the ranch—really."

By April 12, 1925, he was in Valdez; but he and Frieda had already relented again toward Mexico, or at least toward Chapala. In a letter of that date he wrote Idella: "We have got back to our own ranch. . . . You know, we had booked berths to England from Vera Cruz, and the doctor wouldn't let us go. Said we must come here and stay in the quiet and cool and sun. I should really have liked to see your place in the barranca: but the Lord disposes! Wish we'd never gone to Oaxaca.

"We saw Bynner in Santa Fe. We talked of Mexico-Chapala in May or June. . . . We shall stay on here, I expect till late autumn. . . . I think for the winter itself we shall go to Europe. I've got a bit of a *Heim-weh*—a nostalgia—for Europe—though that may be only because I have been ill.

"The ranch is very beautiful, now in the April sunshine: and very clean, having emerged from under three feet of snow. But the winds come sometimes very cold, with a flurry of snow: so of course I got a chill and was in bed again. It is unlike me to keep on being sick, and I hate it. But I hope this is the last set-back.

"I'll send you my little novel *St. Mawr* when it comes out—next month. Remember me to Dr. Purnell. How I regret we didn't come to Guadalajara to drink anise with him, instead of going to that beastly Oaxaca."

The Lawrences had stopped but briefly in Santa Fe and I had been so dismayed by the physical change in him that little remains with me of what we discussed, except his strange pitiable longing for our return together to the country in which he had been stricken. I remembered Amy Lowell's speaking to me of tuberculosis; but Frieda avoided the word in Santa Fe.

I wonder if Idella had guessed the doctor's knowledge in forbidding England and sending Lawrence back to the high, dry mountains; and I wonder if the Mexico City doctor knew how cold and windy and snowy early spring can be in northern New Mexico, when he said to Frieda: "Take him to the ranch. He has tuberculosis in the third degree. A year or two at the most." I wonder if Lawrence himself realized, or had been told, what the orders meant. If so, it is sadly strange that, instead of Valdez, he did not choose Chapala, where he had been well, and again later that he did not choose Chapala, instead of Europe. In subsequent letters from both Valdez and Europe, his regret over the moves he made becomes evident and the fact that his heart and health, however much at home through the summers on his ranch, belonged through the winters in Jalisco. He discovered too late that Oaxaca and Mexico City and Valdez had drawn him away from the temperateness and relaxation he could have found in Chapala.

On June 5 he wrote Idella, who had carried herself and *Palms* to California: "We sit tight here on the ranch. I find in myself very little inclination to move. . . . Haven't seen anybody from Santa Fe—or even Taos—since we are here. Bynner may run up. Ask your father to ask Robles Gil how many pesos I have left in their bank—and I can give you a cheque for a subscription or two—or should it be dollars now?" And then, on the twenty-ninth, he gave evidence that at least one review had caught his attention: "I'm glad you like *St. Mawr.* Did you see Stuart P. Sherman in the *N. Y. Tribune,* on me and my beard? As if my beard didn't cultivate itself! It is merely that I refuse to extinguish it."

Dr. Purnell had had at this time a chance to buy an extensive tract of beautiful wild acreage with waterfalls and marble quarries not too far from Guadalajara, and Idella had toyed with the idea of founding a colony on it for artists and "live people," an idea to which Lawrence responded: "The 10,000 acres of yours really sounds fascinating. But heaven knows about the 'colony.' Artists and 'live people' are usually most lively hating one another. But try it and see. Anything's worth a try.

"We are due to go to Europe for the winter. I feel a little relief from the American Continent will be good for me. But I have been inoculated with Mexico: who knows when it will fetch me back. When it does, I shall write post haste to you and your Daddy to know if I can come to the ranch. No more Oaxacas for me. I loved Chapala, Guadalajara, Jalisco, much the best: and I do wish we had come there again. But never mind. We shall see what we shall see.

"Frieda was asking me if, by chance, you have that little book of poems *Bay*—from which you printed some bits in *Palms*. The one copy we had in Chapala was the only one—and F's. But I am almost certain you brought it me back. It has disappeared.

"Your letters are getting a California note to them: a certain cheery look-into-the-future-with-bright-eyes touch. I suppose that's why you want to go back to Guad. where the future doesn't really exist. When we came down to Guad., Götzsche and I, we came from California—Los Angeles. I wonder how I'll come next time."

The copy of *Bay* must have reappeared at Kiowa Ranch, since later it disappeared again. The second time was from Florence, with nearly all of Frieda's copies of Lawrence's books, inscribed to her, and with a number of his own, like *Love Poems,* inscribed in his hand: "D. H. Lawrence—His own copy not given to anybody." *Bay* had been given to Frieda by E. D. McDonald, Lawrence's first bibliographer, with the inscription: "For Mrs. Lawrence and not to be carted away by any of her friends. E. D. McD." to which was added, "This is my copy not given to anyone—Frieda Lawrence." Yet these two books and forty-four others, mostly rare editions belonging to the Lawrences' personal library, jumped somehow from Florence to Edinburgh, where in 1949 they were offered to the public at high prices. I have already mentioned Orioli's copy of *Aaron's Rod* being included, with the Norman Douglas inscription. Mrs. Lawrence's London agent has, she tells me, managed to recover for her a considerable part of her lost property, which had warranted a finely printed catalogue all to itself of *Valuable Books by D. H. Lawrence.*

From April to September of 1925 the Lawrences were at their ranch; but I was in Santa Fe only a month of that time. It happened too that just then, sitting in the sun, I had finished the manuscript of my verse play *Cake,* placed a stone over it, left it on the ground, and was stretching muscles by making a bonfire nearby of strayed newspapers and waste. A neighbor's little boy had, perhaps justly, thought my pile of scribbled sheets rubbish too, so that by the time I came back with my own next armful the whole manuscript was consumed. This mishap, catastrophic to me, meant that the only weeks which were left me near the Lawrences were spent in piecemeal remembering and painful reconstruction of my months of work. When that was done, Chapala seemed the natural refuge from fatigue, and I urged Lorenzo and

Frieda to come along. Their reason for not making the move was more compelling than mine had been the year before: it was Lawrence's ill-health and also his nagging need to have at least one more look at Europe. But I thought that he would improve in health and would finally prefer Chapala, just as they had thought that I would join them via the Calles inauguration the previous winter. And so we failed to join in either year. If I had not felt sure of their choice and of seeing them in Mexico, I should have made a trip to the ranch before departure. Instead I sent Frieda a necklace I had brought from China and Lawrence a poem, though not yet one of the poems about himself. Acknowledgment came from Frieda: "Quite out of the blue your little parcel was handed me and when I saw the new cigarette box, I thought you had sent me some specially good ones, but no—inside was the lovely jade—I am making myself a green linen dress for it. So many thanks. . . . Do come up sometime the middle of June or after. We have got 9 chickens, an irrigation ditch that looks like a brook, tomorrow comes a black cow. Lawrence is much better. It's *raining*. We have also 4 grown up Indians and 2 little ones. Embarras de richesses!!" At the foot of the page was a postscript from Lawrence: "Thanks for sending the poem: thought it good. Run up and see us before you go south." And then a final note from Frieda: "Lovely days, come before you go to Mexico anyhow. Lawrence is better slowly. Do come and see us."

But it was not to be. I was the one this time who went to Mexico, still hoping that they would follow.

Lorenzo's yearning toward Jalisco stayed real. Mrs. Carswell records that "Mexico—horror and all—held something for Lawrence as a man and a writer that he needed." Again she says: "Of Mexico he spoke much, with loathing of many things about it, but saying that it had spoiled him, he feared, for Europe."

Perversely or by unhappy accident, he went that winter to Europe, from which he was not to return. Both Mexico and New Mexico were behind him. His body was not to dwell in them again; but to the end, his spirit never left them. His writings about them remind me of a comment in Washington Irving's notebooks concerning Thomas Campbell's *Gertrude of Wyoming,* which had appeared in 1809: "This is almost the only instance in which a British poet has thought proper to lay the scene of a poem in this country. He has convinced many that our native scenes are capable of poetic inspiration and that our country may be as capable of poetic fiction as the worn out scenes of classic Italy—the gay vallies of France—the gothic scene of England. A writer of this kind certainly benefits the country he honours with his notice—every work written concerning a country tends to increase local and national feeling—we cannot but notice it as a proof of his liberality." In Lawrence's case the proof was not so much of his liberality as of his liberation, and by New Mexico finally more than by Old Mexico.

He wrote Knud Merrild: "I think New Mexico was the greatest experience from the outside world that I have ever had. It certainly changed me forever . . . the moment I saw the brilliant proud morning shine high up over the deserts of Santa Fe, something stood still in my soul and I started to attend. . . . For a *greatness* of beauty I have never experienced anything like New Mexico."

He transferred bits of the Merrild letter to an essay. Perhaps he was writing the letter and the essay at the same time. "Spellbound in New Mexico," which first appeared in *Survey Graphic* (New York), May, 1931, and *John O'London's Weekly* (London), June 25, 1932, many months after his death, contains these passages: "The moment I saw the brilliant, proud morning shine high up over the deserts of Santa Fe something stood still in my soul. It was so different from the equally pristine and lovely morning of Australia, so soft, so utterly pure. In the lovely morning of Australia one went into a dream; in the magnificent, fierce morning of New Mexico one sprang awake, a new part of the soul woke up suddenly. There are all kinds of beauty in the world, thank God, but for a greatness of beauty I have never experienced anything like New Mexico . . . the greatest experience from the outside world I ever had. It changed me forever; it liberated me from the present era of civilization, of material and mechanical development. . . . It is curious that the land which has produced modern political democracy at its highest pitch should give one the greatest sense of overweening, terrible proudness and mercilessness; but God! how beautiful!" The country which he finally never denied was New Mexico.

He said in *St. Mawr*: "It was always beauty, *always!* It was always great, and splendid, and, for some reason, natural."

Lawrence had found men to be physically inwrought with their landscape, wrestling with it, and usually defeated by it. *Twilight in Italy* shows Bavarians and Italians subdued to their mountains, vainly pitting their warm valleys against deathy peaks. He himself in place after place wrestled and fell. Only in New Mexico did he feel himself not beaten by an alien element but liberated into his own, not a fight but an embrace.

40. Dark Gods

IN this new country Lawrence, the seer, felt that among Indians as well as in the landscape he had at last found an end of his wandering, a ready-made colony, the plumed serpent alive, the natural aristocrat, the dark god existent in the living blood stream. With Lawrence, as with Columbus, this old continent had long existed but needed new finding.

Says Lovatt in *Kangaroo,* where Lovatt is Lawrence: "Celts, Cornish, Irish, they always interest me. . . . They don't believe in our gods, in our ideals. They remember older gods, older ideals, different gods: before the Jews invented a mental Jehovah, and a spiritual Christ. They are nearer the magic of the dark world." Lovatt "would go into the blackness of night and listen to the blackness, and call, call softly, for the spirits, the presences he felt coming downhill from the moors in the night. 'Tuatha De Danaan!' he would call softly . . . 'Be with me!' . . . And it was as if he felt them come." In the same book he says, "The human heart must have an absolute. . . . The only thing is the God who is the source of all passion. Once go down before the God-passion, and human passions take their right rhythm . . . the God from whom the dark, sensual passion of love emanates, deeper than the spiritual love of Christ. . . . In his supreme being, man is alone, isolate, nakedly himself, in contact only with the unknown God. . . . The mystery of apartness. And the greater mystery of the dark God beyond a man, the God that gives a man passion, and the dark, unexplained blood-tenderness that is deeper than love, but so much more obscure, impersonal, and the brave, silent blood-pride, knowing his own separateness and the sword-strength of his derivation from the 'dark God.'" This does not sound to me, though there are other passages which come nearer to sounding so, like Hugh Kingsmill's conclusion that "the Dark Unconscious, the Dark God, the dark otherness which he preached, was the prenatal state from which he had never fully emerged, and into which he longed to be absorbed again." Kingsmill, it seems to me, missed the point that Lawrence's "dark god" was no foetus in a cave but a full-grown body in the universal shadow, even like a dreaded drunken father coming up out of a mine.

Lawrence was convinced that, however propriety, pretense, and self-evasion may deny it, the doings of mind and spirit are mankind's rather dubious avocations, not so trustworthy as the vocation of the body. So he was dissatisfied with both of the Jewish inventions, Jehovah and Jesus, gods of the mind and the spirit. They could never be the basic gods of man. There must be a god of the body, justifying and glorifying whatever the body does naturally and without direction by either mind or spirit. Why he persistently referred to this deity as "dark" is less easy to understand than the contention that the god enters man's consciousness "from below," through the noble nether regions of anatomy. It was "the great God, who enters us from below, not from above," he says, ". . . from the lower self, the dark self, the phallic self, if you like." Lawrence was more and more convinced that the god really controlling mankind is this god of the body, a god—or a galaxy of gods—known to the ancients but now ignored and lost, a god who, as body, was father in the trinity with mind and spirit, a god whose "dark" rightness should permeate all bodies, govern, and ennoble them. It is odd of him, I repeat, not to have more explicitly resented implications by the modern Christian Church that the body and its doings are unclean, that it would have been a shame for Jesus to be born carnally. He might aptly have linked Jehovah swooping in the form of a dove upon Mary with Zeus or Jove swooping upon human flesh in the form of eagle or bull or golden rain.

He did delight once in a story of a happening in San Francisco. My old friend, Bruce Porter of that town, who had been dubbed by Henry James "the only gentleman in America," and who later married the daughter of William James, had taken a group of us for dinner to a Bohemian resort there, The Manger. Its floor was laid with straw, its ceiling crossed with rafters, and its booths cut off like stalls. At one end of the room was a tethered cow. Fowl pecked among the feet of the guests and pigeons strutted on the partitions. The National Federation of Women's Clubs was convening in San Francisco and a contingent of its members was dining that night at the Manger, eight or ten of them, all lofty of manner and sequoian of build. Suddenly, for no apparent reason, into the bosom of the hostess, dove a dove. Yelping and heaving her haunches, she went over backward, her strong knees tipping the table forward and spilling all its spread upon her guests. Amid the uproar we heard the quiet voice of Mr. Porter, a devoted Swedenborgian, saying: "Now we know how Mary felt." "Yes," added Lawrence, when I told him the tale, "She might better have accepted Joseph. Who wants a Holy Ghost or any silly Christian myth!" Yet to other eyes than his the revised pagan mythology, with which he proposed to supplant Christian myths, looked silly too.

One wonders that, making as he did a fetish of the body, he was not more interested in a similar preoccupation on the part of the Christian Church with its doctrine of the body's resurrection. Most Christian sects agree with Rome concerning the ascension into heaven of the mortal body of Christ, after his condescension into it from his heavenly body, but do not go so far as to permit the Virgin Mother's bodily assumption. Lawrence inclines toward general physical assumption, without differentiating between the physical and the metaphysical, the chemical and the spiritual.

Do we come up as plants or as angels, do we revive as fish or as phoenixes? He prefers to keep us in the dark where, as sole wedding guest at the nuptials of earth and heaven, he only intimates for his followers, instead of defining like other popes, the supernatural truth. For bodily angels of light with wings he substitutes half-revealed angels of darkness with fangs, but without the definite motive of Greek Furies. He revels in a lovely horror of vague black magic.

He often bears witness to such envenomed revelry—in *The Lost Girl* for instance: "The puerile world went on crying for a new Jesus . . . when what was wanted was a Dark Master from the underworld. . . . Black and cruel presences were in the under-air. They were furtive and slinking. They bewitched you with loveliness and lurked with fangs to hurt you afterwards. There it was: the fangs sheathed in beauty: the beauty first, and then, horribly, inevitably, the fangs." In *The Rainbow* Lydia Lensky's desire had been "to seek satisfaction in dread . . . to satisfy the instincts of dread in her, through service of a dark religion." In the same book Ursula Brangwen "seemed to run in the shadow of some dark-potent secret . . . of whose existence even she dared not become conscious, it cast such a spell over her and so darkened her mind." It was "the vast darkness that wheeled round about, . . . the System of Righteousness . . . with half-revealed shapes lurking on the edge." For her, as for her grandmother, Lydia Lensky, "the angels in the darkness were lordly and terrible and not to be denied, like the flash of fangs."

In *Kangaroo* Lawrence cries out: "Commandments should fade as flowers do. . . . No everlasting decalogues. No sermons on mounts, either. The dark God, the forever unrevealed. . . . The source of passions and strange motives. . . . The ritual of supreme responsibility, and offering. Sacrifice to the dark God, and to the men in whom the dark God is manifest. Sacrifice to the strong, not to the weak. In awe, not in dribbling love. The communion in power, the assumption into glory."

Still he remains the theorist, setting up an assumption that gods somewhere in the prehistoric world were vital creatures connected in superb and unassailable dominion over earth and man: "The dead and everlasting Egyptians." Yet somehow, he feels, the dominion has been assaulted and the superbness swept aside. How this has been accomplished he never hints. Puny man could not have undone such vast power. How could man have beaten the gods? One's only conclusion must be that the early gods committed mystic suicide. But the suicide being mystic, the gods survived somewhere and are ready to return among men: not so augustly benign as before but with a dark, grim need of helpfully hurting men. It could not have been mystic suicide. Mortal man must have got the better of them once. Or why their pestering need of vengeance, when their great shadows gather back again even more jealous than Jehovah?

Lawrence had never been in Egypt. Yet however much he loved the Etruscans, the Aztecs, the Red Indians of his fancy, it was the Egyptians whom his heart held closest—until he found New Mexico. He had till then been faithful to Egypt. "His heart of hearts," he says himself in *Kangaroo,* "was stubbornly puritanical. There was a down slope into Orcus, and a vast, phallic, sacred darkness, where one was enveloped into the greater good as in an Egyptian darkness."

He had pictured himself, as Birkin of *Women in Love:* "He sat still like an Egyptian Pharaoh. . . . He felt as if he were in immemorial potency, like the great carven statues . . . fulfilled with subtle strength . . . with a vague inscrutable smile on the lips." In *Sea and Sardinia* he had said: "Italy has given me back I know not what of myself, but a very, very great deal. She has found for me so much that was lost: like a restored Osiris."

He says in *Kangaroo:* "You open the gate and sometimes in rushes Thor and gives you a bang on the head, with a hammer; or Bacchus comes mysteriously through, and your mind goes dark and your knees and thighs begin to glow; or it is Venus, and you close your eyes and open your nostrils to a perfume, like a bull. All the gods. When they come through the gate, they are personified. But outside the gate it is one dark God, the Unknown. . . . A fearfully vengeful god: Moloch, Astarte, Ashtaroth, and Baal. That is why we dare not open now. It would be a hell-god, and we know it."

Thus, in books earlier than *The Plumed Serpent,* he had admitted a pantheistic group of divinities to romp in his vitals, while he still barred his gate to the Dark Unknown, whom he visualized as a strong and fascinating Devil. His Dark Unknown would seem to me to be a reflection of the Satan about whom he had been taught in his orthodox days and toward whom he must always have had an admiring, as well as timorous, awe. Mixed in with his consciously, happily naughty heresy had been a wistfulness toward the possibility that he might somehow, somewhere, find, in the god who preferred earth to heaven, a comprehensible and finally beneficent deity. He later wrote a poem on "Lucifer":

> Angels are bright still, though the brightest fell.
> But tell me, tell me, how do you know he lost any of his bright-
> ness in the falling?
> In the dark-blue depths, under leaves and layers of darkness,
> I see him move like the ruby, a gleam from within of his own
> magnificence
> Coming like the ruby in the invisible dark, glowing with his
> own annunciation, towards us.

Like other Europeans, who have hoped to replace a dead with a live theology, Lawrence had followed his hungry spirit toward America's Red Indians, who might be finding heaven on earth. Here would be people, by-passed and unhurt by civilization, among whom the true gods of the ancients might have survived to mingle with their followers in pure and heoric living—here and now.

Several years before he came to America, as I have already noted elsewhere, he had expressed—badly—an early concept of Red Indians.

He had drawn some of it from James Fenimore Cooper's romantic presentation of these lordly savages but more of it from his own hopeful imagination. It remains very difficult to understand why the novelist permitted, in so fine a book as *The Lost Girl,* intrusion of such banality, except that with *The Plumed Serpent* he did almost the same thing again. In the younger novel appear those vaudevillians whose "great turn, of course, was the Natcha-Kee-Tawara Red Indian scene." One might guess from this beginning that a satirical account might follow; but no, like a small boy the narrator tells of the Red Indians bringing in a male white prisoner and a bear! The bear kills one of the Indians. The white prisoner, released from bonds by the Indian woman, kills the bear. This white male prisoner is the crude precursor of the Mexican Indians' white female prisoner in *The Woman Who Rode Away,* published seven years later (1927) and written after Lawrence had been among real Indians in both New and Old Mexico and should have been done with his play-acting. In this famous short story which, despite its pretensions, seems to me to be almost as good nursery stuff as the Natcha-Kee-Tawara Red Indian scene, he calls his Indians Chilchuis but describes them as idealized Huicholes, animally raw Indians from Sonora, whom one sees sometimes lagging and gawking in the streets of Guadalajara. Kai Götzsche had written about them to Merrild from that city, where Lawrence must have seen them too but with eagerer eyes: "They struck me as prehistoric, or like wild animals in the street." The mystic qualities Lawrence but not Götzsche attributes to them, and the ritualistic hocus-pocus which, in the story, induces psychic yielding by their captive, had been anticipated when Alvina joined the tribe of Natcha-Kee-Tawara. Her initiation rites are remindful of sophomore sororities, spiritualistic séances, Mme Blavatsky and grandiose passages in *The Plumed Serpent.* Red Indian rites, which had joined the Lawrence heroine to an Italian in *The Lost Girl* and to a Mexican in *The Plumed Serpent,* finally join her to death in *The Woman Who Rode Away,* the offices performed growing each time more and more pretentiously mystical, until Brunhilde becomes Mother Goose.

It is interesting to note again that in both these later writings, Lawrence elaborates and transfers to Mexican Indians—as the base of their rituals and incantations—rhythm and content from ceremonies he had witnessed in the States. Mexican Indian dances, besides being Hispanicized in rhythm and content, are dispirited performances in com-

parison with those of our northern Indians. I have remarked before
that he uses the Circle Dance, often sociably enjoyed in New Mexico,
like serenatas in villages below the border, as though it were an inherited ceremony in Old Mexico. Though I have never seen it performed in Mexico, Lawrence may be historically right. He may have
chanced upon information that it had once belonged there or have
discovered in the Mexico City Museum some small clay representa-
tions, which I have only lately chanced on, of such concentric dancing with a drummer seated at the core of it.

Not until he comes to *Mornings in Mexico* does Lawrence allocate
the ceremonies, their rhythm, their content and the spirit behind them
to the right region and people. And he does so with great seriousness:
he had not only found the land he loved, he had found the faith he
needed. His essay on *The Hopi Snake Dance* tells of it: "Strictly, in
the religion of aboriginal America, there is no Father, and no Maker.
There is the great living source of life: say the Sun of existence: to
which you can no more pray than you can pray to electricity. And
emerging from this Sun are the great potencies, the invisible influ-
ences which make shine and warmth and rain. From these great inter-
related potencies of rain and heat and thunder emerge the seeds of
life itself, corn, and creatures like snakes. And beyond these, men,
persons. But all emerge separately. There is no oneness, no sympathetic
identifying oneself with the rest. The law of isolation is heavy on
every creature. . . . The Potencies are not Gods. They are Dragons.
The Sun of Creation itself is a dragon most terrible, vast, and most
powerful, yet even so, less in being than we. The only gods on earth
are men. For gods, like man, do not exist beforehand. They are created
and evolved gradually, with aeons of effort, out of the fire and smelt-
ing of life. . . . So that gods are the outcome, not the origin. And the
best gods that have resulted, so far, are men."

Spellbound in New Mexico, which should have been part of *Mornings in Mexico,* continues his quieted observation of Indian dances:
"Never shall I forget the utter absorption of the dance, so quiet, so
timelessly rhythmic, and silent, with the ceaseless down-trend, always
to the earth's center, the very reverse of the upflow of Dyonysic or
Christian ecstasy. . . . It was more darkly and nakedly religious than
anything we know. There is no conception of a god, but all is God.
But it is not the pantheism we are accustomed to. In the oldest religion
everything is alive, not supernaturally, but naturally alive: the rock

and the mountain, which is a deeper, vaster life than a rock. To come into contact with the life of a mountain, man had to put forth a greater religious effort. This effort into sheer, naked contact, without an intermediary or mediator, is the real meaning of religion. . . . The newest democracy," he states his fear and his hope, "is ousting the oldest religion! And once the oldest religion is ousted, one feels that democracy and all its paraphernalia will collapse, and the oldest religion will start again." Still later, in *Phoenix,* he says: "It is curious that one should get a sense of living religion from the Red Indians, having failed to get it from Hindus or Sicilian Catholics or Cingalese. . . ." The Red Indians "connected with an ancient time when the whole life-effort of man was to get his life into direct contact with the elemental life of the cosmos, mountain-life, cloud-life, thunder-life, air-life, earth-life, sun-life. To come into immediate *felt* contact, and so derive energy, power, and a dark sort of joy." To Murry he wrote: "This animistic religion is the only live one."

Some of his dark gods, those of them whom he had feared, had become dragons, subject to the lance of living man. They were no longer to be feared. He had parted the waters and uncovered Atlantis, where other dark gods had become his comrades, dancing.

41. Passionate Puritan

HOWEVER much Lawrence knew that the earth itself was his final love, he incessantly concerned himself with the high worth of human living as animal, sexual activity. He was right that the body is usually far less hypocritical than the mind.

"Be a good animal, true to your animal instinct." This was from the gamekeeper, Annable, in Lawrence's first novel, *The White Peacock*, forebear of Mellors, gamekeeper in the culminating novel, *Lady Chatterley's Lover*. Somewhere else their author says, "We are just human beings with living sex. We are all right, if we had not unaccountable and disastrous fear of sex," and again in his essay, *Pornography and Obscenity*, "Sex is a creative flow, the excrementary flow is towards dissolution, de-creation. . . . Our profoundest instincts are perhaps our instincts of opposition between the two flows. But in the degraded human being . . . the two flows become identical. *This* is the secret of really vulgar and pornographic people: the sex flow and the excrement flow is the same thing to them." The Venerable Donald B. Harris, archdeacon of Bedford, has said, more blandly: "We all know that sex is supposed to be one of God's greatest gifts to the human race, but it has become misused by men."

Lawrence calls one of the characters in his short story, *A Modern Lover,* "an old-fashioned inarticulate lover." When a man I wish Lawrence might have known and written about quit his wife who was a public lecturer, his complaint was that she knew no difference between platform and bed. Lawrence often seems in a similar fix, but his wife never left him. Over and over, in all the books, he expatiates on sex sensations, like the French spinster who, when rebuked by her priest for repeatedly confessing a single sin, replied, "Yes, Father, but I love to talk about it." A new-fashioned lover in this same story, speaking of love, says: "If you pull your flowers to pieces, and find how they pollinate, and where are the ovaries, you don't go into blind ecstasies over them. But they mean more to you; they are intimate, like friends of your heart, not like wonderful, dazing fairies." Aldington remarks of Lawrence: "A puritan somewhere at heart—he treats lust as a serious passion—he is scandalised by the assertion that we ought to love everybody." Aldington is right that, at least in proclamation, Lawrence thoroughly disbelieved in the theory of Christian general tenderness toward all fellow humans and thoroughly believed that purely physical specific impulses are the right guide. It is too often forgotten, however, to my mind, that by purely physical he meant physically pure. Sexual impulse and procedure, as directed by "blood-consciousness," were for him mankind's divine guidance and the base of all other happiness, to be constantly respected as such.

To Ernest Collings he had written as early as 1913: "My great religion is a belief in the blood, the flesh, as being wiser than the intellect. We can go wrong in our minds. But what our blood feels and believes and says, is always true. . . . What do I care about knowledge. All I want is to answer to my blood, direct, without fribbling intervention of mind, or moral, or what-not. I conceive a man's body as a kind of flame, like a candle flame, forever upright and yet flowing: and the intellect is just the light that is shed on to the things around. . . . We have got so ridiculously mindful, that we never know that we ourselves are anything—we think there are only the objects we shine upon. . . . And instead of chasing the mystery in the fugitive, half-lighted things outside us, we ought to look at ourselves and say, 'My God, I am myself!' "

In a cross section among all classes, his fellow Englishmen have of late been interviewed as to sex, and the report discloses that, in a percentage tally on each question, 31 per cent of Britons were "perfectly happy without sex," 54 per cent found sexual relationships "unpleasant," 26 per cent believed sex is "wrong" and 56 per cent thought "it could prove harmful." Only 33 per cent believed sex "important to happiness." Such confusion as to what keeps life going relates, of course, the Christian world over, to such attacks as that by the New York State Catholic Welfare Committee, denouncing the sex education film, *Human Growth,* on the ground that it is "fundamentally at variance with traditional Christian teaching." The film shows a classroom of boys and girls being taught about sex. The committee says it "vehemently opposes" the showing of the film "even to parents and adult groups," because of the schoolroom background "with boys and girls in the same class discussing the most intimate matters of sex without a semblance of Christian modesty." Such objectors would forbid open-air butterfly hoverings without loud-speaker insistence that it might result in worms. For centuries the Church has exhibited the shamefulness of sex. The fact that it does not wish its main idols to have been touched by sex is exhibited daily not only to "parents and adult groups" but to children. And what more openly deleterious instruction could be given? Lawrence went to the very end of the opposite direction. He made sex an idol, would have liked, as primitive men have done, including his Red Indians, to set the phallus in a shrine.

Earth was to be the shrine—and the very shrine could be a symbol, as, in *The Rainbow,* "a high smooth land under heaven, acknowledging only the heavens in their great, sun-glowing strength, and suffering only a few bushes to trespass on the intercourse between their great unabateable body and the changeful body of the sky." His character, Ursula, opens herself to the earth-enshrined symbol, "She wished she could become a strong mound smooth under the sky, bosom and limbs bared to all winds and clouds and bursts of sunshine."

When I found, in *The Lost Girl,* one of his earthy sex symbols, "the burning gold maize cob . . . the long ruddy gold of fruition," I wished that he might have seen, as I have seen in a Pueblo village, a Koshare, a sacred clown, a mirthful spirit of the dead, with a corncob held between his thighs, dart suddenly like a rooster toward a woman among the watchers and chase her, while she waddled away clucking, capture her, fall upon her with the cob, the pair then to be covered with a blanket and jounced upon by other sacred clowns. Or at dawn in the dusty plaza, with men, women, and children watching from the sidelines, he should have seen two Koshare slice each an end off a melon on the ground, and then, lying prone, insert their penises to fertilize the fruit. Indian onlookers laughed their approval of the human episode; but toward the symbolized fertilization of acceptant melons they were solemn and still. To our Indians, as much as to us, human beings are apparently more comic than other growths.

Lawrence's insistence all his life that human attachment must be a hopeless combination of "yearning love and burning hate," is to me comic. When I come upon his repetitions of the theory, all I can see is the farce played in a pueblo village of the squawking hen and the fierce rooster. His major relish in sex was apparently not so much the sensual entanglement as the intervals when hostility of the flesh might be enjoyed, sullenly or blatantly, in preparation for the next orgasmic wrestle. Why did he never write about actual wrestling or boxing as the great human, sadistic ritual, round after round? He does celebrate male tussles or fisticuffs, as flesh release and attachment, in the famous *Women in Love* passage, in his short story, *The Old Adam,* and elsewhere. But he does not give his men, as he does his man and woman sex combatants, the glowering, lustful hatred between rounds. I wonder if he had ever chanced upon a passage in George Eliot's *Middlemarch:* "Although Sir James was a sportsman, he had some other feelings towards women than towards grouse and foxes, and did not regard his future wife in the light of prey, valuable chiefly for the excitement of the chase. Neither was he so well acquainted with the habits of primitive races as to feel that an ideal combat for her, tomahawk in hand, so to speak, was necessary to the continuity of the marriage-tie."

In *The Rainbow* Lawrence carries his doctrine of antagonistic physical love through three generations; and these three successive sex encounters are oddly like three poor matches in an arena, repetitiously lifeless. It is a play in three identical acts. Thomas Hardy's imagination had already bettered him with a novel, *The Well-Beloved,* in which the protagonist embraces successively, grandmother, daughter, and granddaughter. But in Hardy's theme, it is not three bodies which are desired but a single spirit continuing alive in three shapes, somewhat like Charpentier's theme in his opera *Julien,* the sequel to *Louise.* Seldom do people, leaving one mate for another, require in the successor an essential difference, a difference of spirit. It is less the body than the spirit which determines. Lawrence was wrong. Without spiritual inclination, all the sex in the world does nobody much good.

But, in fiction, he enjoys his mistake, or his stubborn pretense. In all of his novels and most of his short stories, out of a group of real people, minor for his interest, he brings sexual prima donnas of both sexes to the front of the stage in a great focus of theatric light. The other figures dim away, leaving Male and Female, who start with this name or that but are soon depersonalized into bright-painted puppets of sex, and enjoy first an alternation of sarcastic verbal interchange or sullen mutual loathing and then hysterical sex clutches. Often, at some breaking point between love and hate, the love cracks away and becomes dust, to the great convenience of one or the other doll and to the sadistic delight of the puppeteer.

In his essay, *The Crown,* he sought to symbolize and exalt sex conflict in the supposedly oppositional flow of a rainbow, like the oppositional flow of the Indian wheel dance. "It is thus, seeking consummation in the utter darkness, that I come to the woman in desire. She is in the doorway, she is the gate to the dark eternity of power. . . . Gradually my veins relax their gates, gradually the rocking blood goes forward, quivers on the edge of oblivion, then yields itself up, passes into the borderland of oblivion. Oh, and then I would die, I would quickly die, to have all power, all life at once, to come instantly to pure eternal oblivion, consummation, the source of life. . . . My source and issue is in the two eternities, I am founded in the two infinities. But absolute is the rainbow that goes between; the iris of my very being . . . God is not the one infinite, nor the other, our immortality is not in the original eternity, neither in the ultimate eternity. God is the utter relation between the two eternities. He is the flowing together (*i.e.,* unanimity and love in the spirit) and the flowing apart (*i.e.,* separateness and hatred in the flesh)."

With such dogmatism, Lawrence appears to me to have been forsaking the simplicity of his belief in anarchistic intuition, because it seemed to him on occasion that a man, to be important or profound, must formulate philosophical theories. And he was as earnest in his importance as he was in his simplicity. He strove to believe dogmatically in the sex battle as an excitation to the sex surrender and as a valid, necessary part of the whole relationship. Yet when Kate, in *The Plumed Serpent,* "realized how all her old love had been frictional, charged with fires of irritation and the spasms of frictional voluptuousness," Lawrence seems to have suspected that his heroine had overdone it and must experience something a little better, and so he tried, though rather helplessly, to give it to her in Cipriano.

Sometimes I have a feeling that Lawrence, despite all his protestations, retained his youthful shyness as to sex and thought that he ought to overcome it by manful strides. I do not, however, subscribe to the suspicion of those, including doctors and psychiatrists, who have suggested, since he overstressed sex, that he must have been impotent. I remember a question asked me in a puzzled way by a man who confessed himself never to have had any sex urge whatever. "Have I missed anything?" he asked. "They talk so much about it that I wonder." Though this fellow went to doctors and psychiatrists for help or advice, because he thought he ought to be like the rest of mankind, he was given no means, physical or mental, which could charge his sex batteries; whereupon he relaxed into great enjoyment of the natural world's beauty, the steadfast quality of persons and the joke on all mankind, himself excluded, in the vast dilemma of God's having apparently posed man a conundrum and never given him the answer: equipped and stimulated him to populate graves.

I wonder if Lawrence ever knew that, by reports of white doctors, Red Indians—for all their abdominal inheritance from the dark gods— will often come begging for medicine to quicken their prowess below the navel. Sex seems to have been lodged in their minds as much as it was in his, the very place from which he ever urged that it be driven out. The mind was no place for it, or the nerve system, or the spirit. It must live only in the blood stream. "There is another seat of consciousness than the brain and the nerve system," he wrote Bertrand Russell in 1915, "there is a blood-consciousness which exists in us independently of the ordinary mental consciousness, which depends on the eye as its source or connector. There is the blood-consciousness, with the sexual connection holding the same relation as the eye, in seeing, holds to the mental consciousness . . . when I take a woman, then the blood-percept is supreme, my blood-knowing is overwhelming." To William Gerhardi, Russell said of Lawrence, "He has no mind," and Lawrence of Russell, "He is all Disembodied Mind." Of himself Lorenzo might have said, "I am all Embodied Mind."

My surmise persists that at times Lawrence had doubts as to the complete dignity of sex and therefore he longed to set it apart from his spiritual or mental responsibility and to remain always a young blood, happily accountable only to animal nature. On the other hand, though with his countless dissertations on sex he might be thought to have had wide and varied experience, there is little or no evidence in his life story that he was inclined to varietism. I do not think he would have quite liked, although it came close to declarations of his own, Bernard Shaw's statement: "The sex relation is not a personal relation. It can be . . . rapturously consummated between persons who could not endure one another for a day in any other relation."

Certainly Lawrence gives testimony enough concerning his own separateness from the object of passion and concerning his use of sex for self-revelation, self-importance, self-love. His was a case of psychic narcissism: he was ever looking to find himself mirrored in mate or friend. Sometimes, frail though he was, it would seem even a case of physical narcissism. In *The Rainbow* he is Tom Brangwen thinking of Lydia: "How could a man be strong enough to take her, put his arms round her and have her, and be sure he could conquer this awful unknown next to his heart? . . . He let himself go from past and future, was reduced to the moment with her, in which he took her and was with her and there was nothing beyond, they were together in an elemental embrace beyond their superficial foreignness. But in the morning he was uneasy again. She was still foreign and unknown to him. Only, within the fear, was pride, belief in himself as mate for her. . . . Her hands on him seemed to reveal to him the mould of his own nakedness, he was passionately lovely to himself. He could not bear to look at her." Norman Douglas says, in his volume, *Looking Back,* that Lawrence "had a shuddering horror of Casanova's *Memoirs;* he was furious with a friend for keeping two mistresses instead of one, and even with Florentine boys for showing an inch or so of bare flesh above the knee—'I don't like it! I don't like it! Why can't they wear trousers?'" Chapala and the beach boys there came back to my mind. "Lawrence was no Bohemian," concludes Douglas, "he was a provincial, an inspired provincial with marked puritan leanings."

The obvious excuse for conjectural intrusion into Lawrence's sex life is that he has invited it by his own trumpetings. Whatever he thought about sex itself, its practices and purposes, he did believe firmly in plain-speaking about it. Only silliness, he felt, could come from romanticizing about it as a spiritual expression and only peril from making it a hidden business, a secretive phase of life. Surely it should be as openly surveyed as mental processes, bodily connection being a more primary and essential function of life than mental connection. That much at least was clear. He was not deterred by the fact that a normal man shrinks from exposing at random his most intimate spiritual experiences and quite as naturally, however cocky his occasional crowing, keeps to himself his tenderest bodily experiences. In life, Lawrence did shrink from such bleatings, but in literature it was different. Sex boastings in a roomful are not the same thing as confessions or exultations on a printed page, which the reader may take to himself in comparative privacy. The truth has been sometimes overlooked that these self-revelations, these body-searchings were to Law-

rence much the same reverent release that soul-searchings have meant
to conventionally religious persons. He deeply wanted to be a dedicated
saint of the flesh, and his revelations of the flesh were as prayerfully
offered as ever any spiritual communication has been offered by a
dedicated celibate.

Douglas, though, disapproved of such humorless publicists: "They
indulge in airing their own private sensations—a mild form of exhi-
bitionism—with a shamelessness that reminds one of nothing so much
as of a female dog." This dig was well calculated to wound the man
who, inconsistently, felt strong distaste for animals in heat, who seemed
at times to think that sex was all very fine for human beings but somehow impaired the dignity of his beloved beasts. Lawrence's own opinion of *Lady Chatterley's Lover* in a letter to Mrs. Carswell, was that
it is "very verbally improper . . . but very truly moral," whereas Dorothy
Brett reports his exclaiming to his wife over Joyce's *Ulysses:* "The last
part of it is the dirtiest, most indecent, obscene thing ever written.
Yes, it is, Frieda . . . it is filthy." A. E. Housman, according to Grant
Richards, said that *Lady Chatterley's Lover* "is much more wholesome than Frank Harris or James Joyce"; and, according to Sarah
Gertrude Millin, Bernard Shaw told General Smuts, "Every girl of
sixteen should read it."

"Opening a little window for the bourgeosie" was, according to
Norman Douglas, Lawrence's lifework; but for Lawrence himself it
was part of a noble and needed crusade. In his late essay, *Pornography
and Obscenity,* a too repetitious but wholly honest and fine challenge, he maintains that "secrecy and modesty are two utterly different things. . . . Away with the secret! No more secrecy! The
only way to stop the terrible mental itch about sex is to come out
quite simply and naturally into the open with it. . . . If the use of
a few so-called obscene words will startle man or woman out of
a mob-habit into an individual state, well and good. And word
prudery is so universal a mob-habit that it is time we were startled
out of it." Though believing that the nineteenth century was peculiarly
false and hypocritical and dirty minded as to sex, he felt that "the
length of a complete lie is never more than three generations, and the
young are the fourth generation of the nineteenth century lie." But
he finds the young, among Bohemians, too "sex free." "They have apparently killed the dirty little secret, but somehow, they have killed
everything else too. Some of the dirt still sticks, perhaps, sex still

remains dirty. . . . Hence the terrible dreariness and depression of modern Bohemia, and the inward dreariness and emptiness of so many young people of today." But even this state seems to him better than what had preceded it, the sentimental secrecy. "When obscenity becomes mawkish," he says, "which is its palatable form for the public, and when the Vox populi, vox Dei is hoarse with sentimental indecency, then I have to steer away, like a Pharisee, afraid of being contaminated. There is a certain kind of sticky universal pitch that I refuse to touch. . . . It was one of my fond illusions, when I was young, that the ordinary healthy seeming sort of men . . . had a wholesome rough devil-may-care attitude toward sex. All wrong! All wrong! . . . If such fellows have intercourse with a woman, they triumphantly feel that they have done her dirt, and now she is lower, cheaper, more contemptible than she was before."

Neither Dostoyevsky nor Lawrence enjoyed for long remaining calm. Though the Englishman grew gentler toward the end of his life, the spark of fight would not die out. Contrariness, opposition for its own sake or for the grim fun of it, was no longer in him—the earlier heatedly offensive or defensive overstatements on all sides of inconsistency; but his fist still tightened to defend or advance what he considered a vital cause. Since the very spring of life is sex, sex remained to him an element at least as sacred as spirit. Evasions of it as a natural, proper, clean and noble function, as godly as any function of man's heart or brain, repelled him and stirred him to combat. He had taken this stand since youth and would now, toward the end of his life, face the fight firmer than ever. I believe also that, if he had felt doubts as to the dignity of sex and had to down them, the doubts were now done with and the fervors of his crusade entirely sound. The office of religion, in making man ashamed of sex, through such dodges as celibacy, such charges as original sin, such doctrines as the immaculate conception, seemed to him more than ever to be prudery or pruriency toward the basic fact of life, a profoundly irreligious and perilous perversion of life. In a late letter to me he announced the fighting spirit of his final crusade: "One has to fight . . . one still has to fight for the phallic reality, as against the non-phallic cerebration unrealities."

He did say himself, "Though a woman be dearer to a man than his own life, yet he is he and she is she, and the gulf can never close up. Any attempt to close it is a violation, and the crime against the Holy Ghost." But the fact that neither sex partner must yield his individual integrity to the other did not mean to him that sex was not a right and rich relation. His own partnership with Frieda would appear to have been so right and rich that sexual vagrancies did not attract him. Though I never heard him flail promiscuity in others except when he thought it mere cheapening of the loins, he seems to have felt no need of it for himself. His sexual Puritanism, however, was his own affair, not a code to be imposed upon others and not a basic part of his theory. Idella Purnell erred, I think, when she visioned him as a potential witch burner. On the other hand he faced the fact that even those whom heaven had joined together might at times, and quite naturally, put themselves asunder and for a while not tolerate each other. Such rejection was a part of the rough love of animals; and for him, it cannot too often be repeated, the animal nature of man, when not warped by the spirit or whipped by the mind, was the safe element. Even the cells of frogs' eggs, pulled apart, draw together again.

F. Scott Fitzgerald has noted Lawrence's "great attempt to synthesize animal and emotional." Yes, the attempt was great; but let me still again emphasize the fact that it was not an attempt to synthesize animal and spiritual. I quote from *Twilight in Italy:* "Man knows the great consummation in the flesh, the sexual ecstasy of unanimity, that is eternal. But the two are separate and never to be confused. To neutralize the one with the other is unthinkable, an abomination." Because he wished, for some reason, to think that he himself could not combine the animal with the spiritual, he tried to believe that no one could combine them without neutralizing them and to resent anyone in whom such combination seemed possible, also and at the same time resenting himself, in whom it seemed impossible. So he continued to glorify sex as a power almost single in its sacredness.

V. S. Pritchett, in one of his essays, believing the "phallic cult a disaster to descriptive writing," observes further, "No one could possibly believe what Lawrence believed, and Lawrence hated people if they tried."

It must be clear, however, to Pritchett or to anyone, that Lawrence's fight to use the terms of sex openly and freely was an earnest crusade. He was by no means a sensationalist desiring excitement and publicity. It is certainly clear that the old-fashioned shabby artifice of employing blanks in place of forbidden words only dirties the words omitted. *The Laughing Horse* letter, as first printed, became naughty, whereas his own version was merely outspoken. Hemingway's wholesale substituting of the word "obscenity" for blanks was a similar injurious accent. Norman Mailer, defending the use of blunt words in *The Naked and the Dead,* believes it "very poor policy just to indicate obscenity. If you do, every time it comes up it has a kind of phony force—shock. My feeling was that after the first twenty or thirty pages the reader wouldn't notice it any more." That was what Lawrence had felt and hoped to prove in writing *Lady Chatterley's Lover.* The first edition of the book was on blue paper, one copy for Frieda and one for himself, both of them in the collection lost at Florence. In Frieda's copy was written: "This edition is limited to only two copies one for the Master one for the Dame none for the little boy that lives down the lane." In my own copy of the book I found jotted a passage from a letter I had written him about the little boys and girls who were shocked by it: "It wasn't the story, the essence, the facts, that so delightfully hurt them. They hate to have their private flippant vulgarities taken away from them and made serious and beautiful." But once more, in his high seriousness of purpose, Lawrence suffered from lack of humor. I am afraid that more people have merely laughed at *Lady Chatterley,* or been bored by it, than have been shocked.

His pioneering feat, however, has obviously had strong influence in killing tabu and in freeing speech for writers who have succeeded him. It has had influence even in general conversation. The effect has for the most part been wholesome, though freedom of speech, like other freedoms, is often taken less as release than as license. Whereas Lawrence wanted to write openly about sex because he felt it clean, he opened the way for others who want to write about it because they feel it unclean. It was his feeling of that difference which provoked Lawrence's attack on *Fantazius Mallare,* though he failed, I think, to take sufficiently into account Ben Hecht's intent light-handedly to satirize licentious writing. For Lawrence nobody's writing should be light-handed. I have wondered what he would have thought of a book like Erskine Caldwell's *God's Little Acre* which, backed by Judge Bok's tolerant and considered opinion, and taking public advantage of liberation for theme and word, has echoes in it of Lawrence's own accent, though in another dialect. Caldwell's character, Ty, says, in one of the book's superior passages: "The trouble with people is that they try to fool themselves into believing that they're different from the way God made them. . . . Some people talk about your head being the thing to go by, but it ain't so. . . . God put us in the bodies of animals and tried to make us act like people. . . . If He had made us like we are, and not called us people, the last one of us would know how to live. A man can't live, feeling himself from the inside, and listening to what the preachers say. . . . He can live like we were made to live, and feel himself on the inside, or he can live like the preachers say, and be dead on the inside. A man has got God in him from the start, and when he is made to live like a preacher says to live, there's going to be trouble. . . . God made pretty girls and He made men, and there was enough to go round. When you try to take a woman or a man and hold him off all for yourself, there ain't going to be nothing but trouble and sorrow the rest of your days."

My guess is that Lawrence would have sanctioned all of this except the denial that monogamy may be a possible and wholesome happiness. In 1915 Bertrand Russell, considerably Lawrence's senior, showed the younger man a typescript of a lecture to be given in a joint course between them. On the sentence, "Successful monogamy depends upon the successful substitution of habit for emotion in the course of years," Lawrence marked an emphatic "No!" And against Russell's, "A character which does not readily form habits, or does not find habits an adequate safeguard against emotion, is not suited to monogamy," Lawrence interlined, "The desire for monogamy is profound in us. But the most difficult thing in the world is to find a mate. It is still true, that a man and wife are one flesh. A man alone is only fragmentary—also a woman. Completeness is in marriage." Then against Russell's statement, "No need of hate or conflict: only the failure of inward joy brings them about," Lawrence sets down, "There will always be hate and conflict. It is a principle of growth: every bud must burst its cover, and the cover doesn't want to be burst. But let our hate and conflict be *really* part of our vital growth, the outcome of our growing, not of our desire for sensation."

It is a noteworthy fact, incidentally, that Lawrence seldom used in speech the sensation of words he demanded the right to use in print. Now and then a phrase would ring out, sexually or faecally laden, in anger or contempt, such as his outburst to me in Chapala about Middleton Murry, but not nearly so often as in the ordinary male's staple conversation. His pen was not so reticent; and Pritchett may be right that "the world is not saved by novelists." This novelist said himself in his last novel, *The Man Who Died:* "A sermon is so much more likely to cake into mud, and to close the fountains, than is a psalm or a song." He may have preached too much; but he practiced what he preached.

"Great becomes the fruit," said Buddha, "great the advantage of earnest contemplation, when it is set round with upright conduct"; and Lawrence strove ever, in his life as in his works, to assure and maintain healthy passage through the phallus of either urine or a god. He was a good man fighting for decency. Aware of the compelling power with which sex determines men's thoughts and deeds, he believed more and more that its acts and preoccupations should be brought into the light with candor, that men should not hide sex or smirk at it but, facing it openly, find it a clean, strong motive and a deeply proper function in the dignity of their lives.

When Lawrence wrote his article, *The State of Funk,* he was not far from physical death, but was ever a man more alive? He gives his own summation: "The whole trouble with sex is that we daren't speak of it and think of it naturally. We are not secretly sexual villains. We are not secretly sexually depraved. We are just human beings with living sex. . . . My sex is me as my mind is me, and nobody will make me feel shame about it. . . . I remember when I was a very young man I was enraged when, with a woman, I was reminded of her sexual actuality. I only wanted to be aware of her personality, her mind and spirit. The other had to be fiercely shut out. . . . Now I know that a woman is her sexual self too, and I can feel the normal sex sympathy with her. . . . Our civilisation, with its horrible fear and funk and repression and bullying, has almost destroyed the natural flow of common sympathy between men and men, and men and women. And it is this that I want to restore into life. . . . Many people hate it, of course. Many men hate it that one should tacitly take them for sexual, physical men instead of mere social and mental personalities. Many women hate it the same. . . . If there is one thing I don't like it is cheap and promiscuous sex. If there is one thing I insist on it is that sex is a delicate, vulnerable, vital thing that you mustn't fool with. If there is one thing I deplore it is heartless sex. Sex must be a real flow, a real flow of sympathy, generous and warm, and not a trick thing, or a moment's excitation, or a mere bit of bullying. . . . Be tacitly and simply aware of the sexual being in every man and woman, child and animal; and unless the man or woman is a bully, be sympathetically aware. It is the most important thing just now, this gentle physical awareness. It keeps us tender and alive at a moment when the great danger is to go brittle, hard, and in some way dead."

Gusts blew Lawrence's life; but the gusts were not, as he thought, out of the great dark edges of the universe so much as they were out of the crotchety corners of his desire. He wished to fuse his particles, like the earth itself, to be what he might have called the sure blue halo of the flame. He maintained to the very end that the germinal contact of man and woman was the lark-high be-all and end-all and found in sheer animal-human life, to quote his own words, "naked shapely animated fragments of earth active in heaven."

In late writings he called the celibate Jesus back to coitional heaven on earth. . . . The earth itself, he felt, is in the veins of man a better salvation than all the Christs. He wrestled with the angel of the Lord, because he liked the fleshly wrestling. It was a magnificent tussle. It was he and the angel and the earth. And after each bout, the earth supported his fainting fall. His weakness was that he liked to talk about it. And he told about the combat mostly in terms of defeat. If he had been true to his faith in the animal, if he had not allowed the beliefs and doubts of other men to twist him—masters or disciples, what matter?—he might have answered in plainer terms the everlasting need of a man to be at one not only with himself, but with his wrestling mate and with the earth to which he falls.

The elements of strange intimate trinity which he could never combine into one, and yet which he forever felt himself to be, as snakily entwined as the Laocoön, were self, sex, and the natural world. He liked every one of these elements by itself; but he hated the binding of any one of them to the others. Each was struggling away. Not only were they never made one; they were never equal, the three elements. Let anyone who thinks that the members of the trinity were self and man and woman look closer. They were himself and the wrestling angel and the earth—but the greatest of these was the earth, of which he was an incomparable seer. By one crocus bud and the early-morning wind his phallus was replaced and his doctrines blown away.

42. Comrade

AS far as I know, Lawrence never as a writer touched seriously on
the physical attraction of woman for woman; but the close tie
of male to male has been an heroic theme throughout history,
outbalancing the Sapphic theme, and he could not bear to leave alone
any experience which might make him feel heroic and historic, especially when he dreamed that his lonely blood stream, steering blindly
for haven, might discover a new continent. He imagined that for a
man to achieve another man's total devotion might be the noblest, most
heroic experience of all; but it was an adventure for which he was apparently not competent either in spirit or body.

With his lack of interest in Chinese character, he had probably not
heard of the Oriental oath of blood brotherhood, nor would he have
felt sympathy toward the Christ-like forgive-your-enemy conduct
which founded it. Kuan Ti, a great general, canonized in 1492 as the
God of War, had originated the blood brotherhood pledge with Chou
Ch'uan, a rebel general whom he had conquered and released several
times and whom he finally conquered again but pardoned with such
patient generosity that his enemy became his lifelong devoted friend.
Twenty-five years ago, as I can bear witness from formal participation,
their pledge had still lasted in Chinese custom—a slight cutting of
wrists, a blending of blood, and a recital: "We could not choose to be
born of the same parents on the same day at the same hour, but we can
choose to die at the same hour of the same day into the same earth."
Lawrence would not have liked this, unless he had been the one to go
first, with the comrade hurrying after! There could be only one leader.
But the Whitman creed of "adhesive" comradeship teased his interest.
At least it was no suicide pact; and perhaps the absence in it of actual
sex enslavement appealed to his ever-recurrent need of escape from

the physical bond. "All women," says he, as late as *Apocalypse,* "have a large streak of the policewoman in them." Scientists, psychologists, and other observers have indicated, more and more freely since Lawrence's time, that a considerable portion of the race feels inclination or response toward either sex or its own sex, which is perhaps why society has been so sensitive on the subject and has sternly driven aberrationists in upon themselves to an unwholesome, often grotesque, and sometimes tragic degree. Lawrence was very seldom afraid of any such attitude, would have been as contemptuous toward conventional society in this respect as he was in all other respects except trifles, such as Frieda's dressing in our rooms at Chapala. But his tendencies toward Whitmanic comradeship were mainly wistful, tentative, theoretical. Such natural instincts of physical liking as he felt toward the male were more hopeful than real, more historical than actual and, apparently, were abortive. Nevertheless, the possibility of such relationship had a mental attraction for him from the beginning: his novels and other writings touch on it frequently and idealize it.

George Saxton's inclination is an instance in *The White Peacock.* In *The Rainbow* Tom Brangwen "had loved one warm, clever boy who was frail in body, a consumptive type." The two, writes Lawrence, "had had an almost classic friendship, David and Jonathan." There were Cicio and Geoffrey in *The Lost Girl,* or Edgar Lievers in *Sons and Lovers.* In *Sea and Sardinia* Lawrence was moved by the simple, natural relation between the busman and the male "mate" who sat on the seat with him. In *The Prussian Officer* comes the violent flesh call between captain and orderly. *Women in Love* brings the naked wrestling match between Rupert Birkin and Gerald Critch and Birkin's statement to Critch: "You've got to take down the love-and-marriage ideal from its pedestal. We want something broader. I believe in the *additional* perfect relationship between man and man—additional to marriage." Says Hugh Kingsmill of the episode: "Gerald is represented as strangely elated by this proposal, yet still more elated when he rejects it." Mutual attraction between males is the point of the short story, *Jimmy and the Desperate Woman.* In *Kangaroo,* Lovatt, using the term "mate" in its masculine connotation, says . . . "you can't hold together the friable mixture of modern mankind without a new cohesive principle, a new unifying passion. And this will be the new passion of a man's absolute trust in his mate, his love for his mate. . . ." But Lovatt "had learned something else as well. He had learned the great danger of the new passion, which as yet lay only half-realized and half-recognized, half-effective." Again in *Kangaroo:* "He had all his life had this craving for an absolute friend, a David to his Jonathan, Pylades to his Orestes, a blood-brother. And now at last . . . he didn't want it. . . . Yet he wanted *some* living fellowship with other men . . . but not affection, not love, not comradeship. Not mates and equality and mingling. . . . What else? He didn't know. . . . Perhaps the thing that the dark races know: that one can still feel in India: the mystery of lordship." The essay on Whitman among his *Studies in Classic American Literature* says: "Woman is inadequate for the last merging. So the next step is the merging of man-for-man love. And this is on the brink of death. It slides over into death." In *Fantasia of the Unconscious* he had already written: ". . . wait, quietly, in possession of your own soul, till you meet another man who has made the choice, and kept it. Then you will know him by the look on his face: half a dangerous look, a look of Cain, and half a look of gathered beauty. Then you two will make the nucleus of a new society." How he liked his own dangerous look, the look of a dangerous Cain, who might kill off a silly brother!

Kingsmill concludes, from careful study: "Of sexual desire for a man, as opposed to a groping desire for an experience to which he might prove more adequate than to normal intercourse, there is no evidence in his writings." Tindall, on the other hand, concludes: "It is likely from the conduct of Lawrence's heroes in *The White Peacock, Aaron's Rod, Kangaroo,* and *Women in Love,* as it is from the affair of the farmer in Cornwall . . . that Lawrence had more than the proper regard for his fellow man. For this reason his experience with women was a disappointment to him." Murry, in *Son of Woman,* tells of the only time, apparently, when Lawrence tried to make his ideal of male attachment a reality—with the young Cornishman who, misunderstanding the spirit of the approach, would have none of it. For Lawrence, to apply Murry's words about the *Women in Love* episode, this was "another phallic failure." Commenting on the approacher in *Aaron's Rod,* Murry more than intimates Lawrence's excessive expectations: "Lilly tried to convince Aaron, but really to convince himself, that whereas it is right that he should depend upon a woman, it is right that Aaron should depend on a man. . . . Lilly is glad that he has no children, because it is 'against his instinct. . . . If childhood is more important than manhood, why live to be a man at all?'. . . Lilly," comments Murry, "would have had a better chance of convincing the unyielding Tanny that manhood was more than childhood if he had given her the children she wanted so badly. It is not easy for a man incapable of begetting children to convince a woman of his perfect manhood: . . . In other words, Lilly wants a homosexual relation with Aaron to complete his incomplete heterosexual relation with Tanny. This he calls 'extending' marriage. Other people might find another name for it." One easily sees how this passage of Murry's can have instigated or stimulated various questioning rumors as to the author of *Aaron's Rod,* although Murry concludes: "Lawrence's hunger for a man could never have been satisfied. He came to know, and in part to confess it later, in *Kangaroo."* In Chapala Lawrence spoke to me with scorn, of "a pederast who took photographs of naked boys at Taormina," and I do not think that he was pretending his distaste.

Mrs. Carswell, in *The Savage Pilgrimage,* makes sympathetic observations as to the farmer episode: "It is doubtful if the subtle, uncultured Cornishman understood much better than the subtle, cultured Londoner, or indeed than the simple German wife, who regarded any relegation of her man's emotion as a species of 'unfaithfulness.' It is even fairly certain that the Cornishman's mystification—as he was also given to talking—added to the cloud of suspicion. . . . It surely added greatly to the loneliness of Lawrence."

She continues: "Mrs. Lujan in her book has said that women meant more than men to Lawrence. This is not so. Apart from his mother and Frieda, it was men that really counted. . . . To a woman her children: to a man his comrade. . . . I have heard Lawrence say." He had told Mrs. Carswell "that sexual perversion was for him 'the sin against the Holy Ghost,' the hopeless sin. But he cherished," she concludes, "the deep longing to see revived a communion between man and man which should not lack its physical symbols. He even held that our modern denial of the communion in all but idea was largely the cause of our modern perversions. To recover true potency, and before there could be health and happiness between man and woman, he believed that there must be a renewal of the sacredness between man and man. But what he was to find later, to his deep delight, existing among the Mexican Indians,"—she should have said New Mexican— ". . . religious segregation of the male for the communal worship of something greater than himself, and so for the increase of his male power—he was excluded from by the barrier of race."

At Los Angeles, in 1923, the Danes, Merrild, and Götzsche were invited to speak on Lawrence. Introducing them, the chairman said: "I will ask each of the young artists to tell you about the private life of D. H. Lawrence." Whatever Merrild said at the time, and he was indignant enough to have said nothing, he wrote of Lawrence afterward in *A Poet and Two Painters:* "Of course he cared for manliness, and he was himself as manly as any other real man. . . . But he was more than just a man. He was an artist. . . . He was a complex of all mankind. . . . When he spoke of his beloved idea of starting a new life and forming a colony, he never included women. . . . Only at times he added, 'I suppose eventually the men shall want to take women unto themselves.'" Merrild might have noted the ironic fact that the only persons who finally accompanied Lawrence on a colonizing venture were women—Frieda and the Honorable Dorothy Brett. Quoting Horace Gregory's impression of Murry's trying in *Son of Woman* "to prove Lawrence's hatred of women and to hint broadly that he was spiritually undermined by homosexual tendencies," Merrild declares: "From the very beginning, we didn't believe what was said, and we soon learned to know it was untrue and false."

Merrild literally was right. Lawrence's peacock tail flaunted the plumage of male, while his female bill gathered kernels. To the end he imagined and craved and feared and dodged the male mate. It was usually the male mate about whom he wrote in his fiction; it was the male mate seen through the eyes of the female mate; but the focus was upon himself—he himself was the male mate. It is true that the idea of male attachment fascinated him as much as it finally disappointed him; but I doubt very much if homosexual mastery, or yielding, would have profited his existence or saved him from the abysmally antagonistic clasp.

Hugh Kingsmill mentions a 1925 conversation in which Murry maintained to Lawrence that the betrayal of Jesus by Judas was a story told by other followers, that Judas was the only one who had been wholly true and that he had "hanged himself in horror at the uselessness of the Crucifixion." According to Murry, "Judas was the broken-hearted lover." Lawrence, apparently, if Kingsmill's implications are correct, was cold to the personal pertinence of Murry's theory. In his last message to the latter, he wrote: "If I am the only man in your life, it is not because I am I, but merely because I provided the speck of dust on which you formed your crystal of an imaginary man.

. . . It is no good our meeting—even when we are immortal spirits, we shall dwell in different Hades. Why not accept it?"

He had rejected the comrade.

In 1915 he had written Bertrand Russell of E. M. Forster, in whom he had hoped for a literary comrade: "There is more in him than ever comes out. But he is not dead yet. I hope to see him pregnant with his own soul. We were on the edge of a fierce quarrel all the time." And again he wrote to Russell, in whom he had wanted a comrade on the lecture platform: "Let us become strangers again. I think it is better."

And yet the craving for ideal comradeship stayed with him to the end. His essay, "The Risen Lord," in *Assorted Articles,* contains the passage: "If Jesus rose in the full flesh, He rose to know the tenderness of a woman, and the great pleasure of her, and to have children by her. . . . He rose to have friends, to have a man-friend whom He would hold sometimes to His breast, in strong affection, and who would be dearer to Him than a brother, just out of the sheer mystery of sympathy. And how much more wonderful, this, than having disciples!"

In his play *David,* Jonathan says: "I would not see thy new day, David. For thy wisdom is the wisdom of the subtle, and behind thy passion lies prudence. And naked thou wilt not go into the fire. Yea, go thou forth, and let me die. . . . Yet my heart yearns hot over thee, as over a tender quick child."

Less heroic comrades than Jonathan would not have done.

43. The Man Himself

WHAT effect did these theories, these superstitions and intuitions, these fighting convictions, these disappointments, have on the character of the man in whom they dwelt? Or what had so molded him that he contained them? I am trying to find the differences between what Lawrence thought he wanted to be and what he had to be.

Much has been recorded of his early days, by himself and others. His novels go back to his boyhood, and so do his biographies. We have the picture of the lower- than middle-class household into which he was born: the loutish, drunken father, who was made to feel inferior; the supposedly superior, long-suffering, self-righteous mother, who instructed the son in a caste sense of condescension toward his sire and his neighbors; a group of brothers and sisters who existed for him more or less in amiable shadow; and Jessie Chambers, the Miriam of his *Sons and Lovers,* who afforded him, through her family, a cheery domestic warmth he could not find at home and, through herself, an eager, winsome, intelligent companion. When later he and she became aware of the fact that such companionship might lead to marriage, he balked, at times because she seemed to be too intellectual a woman to suit him, and at other times because she was too feminine. Doctors and critics have judged that he was "mother-sapped," that as a boy he could not have mated. His attempt presently with another girl, openly passionate, seems not to have been rewarding. He himself exclaims in his essay, *On Being a Man,* "Oh, women, beware the mother's boy!" Here he was, to begin with, torn at home between love for his mother and hate for his father, and at the house of the favorite neighbors divided between eager love for their whole family with whom he was connected by Jessie and apprehension lest she might appropriate that love all to herself, might try even to intrude where his mother should be.

He might have known, perhaps did know, that one parent may be superior while the other is better; but he was persuaded by the mother, as his father had been instructed before him, that she was both the superior and the better parent. Alive, she had made existence as wretched for her husband as, alive and dead, she had made it for her son. Jessie Chambers, though she may have felt a rightful grudge, spares the mother all she can; but the picture of Mrs. Lawrence, Sr., is not pretty, wherever it emerges, unless perhaps in the book by her daughter, which I have not read. In the son's fiction, his mother, for all his worship, still emerges a poor figure. In life, when she was down with her last illness, but not past ability to read, and when her son brought her the pages of a book he had just finished—his first— she let them dangle, did not look at them. It was he whom she wanted, not his book. The book would have been her son's importance, not hers. She had apparently never believed in his importance except as being her household pet. With all his conventional adoration of her, he the Holy Infant, she the Virgin of his bones, she does not, in his writings where she returns often, wear a nimbus for his readers. However hard a time she had in her household, she seems, from all accounts, to have brought the hardship on herself by her own character—conceited, possessive, captious, querulous. One wonders that Lawrence could have been grateful for his maternal inheritance. In his character, according to a remark Richard Aldington made some years ago, a difficulty existed yet to be divulged, even after all the divulging. The main difficulty would seem to me to have been an inherited likeness to the mother—an impatient, domineering, self-important snobbishness.

Though Lawrence rarely admitted the fact, there was also in his nature a through-shine from his father who was, almost unknown to him, his better genius. The father had wanted to relish life, even though he had been driven to do so through drink. Drink is not the worst false value. If only the mother had even once got drunk with liquor! Like her, Lawrence chose intoxication, but self-intoxication, instead of realizing that if there must be intoxication, it should come from the outside. Like a tipsy man the son made a noise in the world, and when they looked at him, he would lurch again. If only the son had given the father some of the tenderness his mother absorbed and given his mother some of the blame his father tried not to deserve! He knew that this was what he should have done. Instead, he chose to make of the parental conflict a fruitful darkness inside himself, expressing it through Lettie in *The White Peacock*: "You have to suffer before you blossom in this life. When death is just touching a plant, it forces it into a passion of flowering. You wonder how I have touched death. You don't know. There's always a sense of death in this home. I believe my mother hated my father before I was born. That was death in her veins for me before I was born. It makes a difference."

In the perceptive introduction to *Apocalypse,* Richard Aldington guesses that the father might have bequeathed to Lawrence the sharp outbreaks useful for venting irritation and purging the spirit. "In working-class homes," explains Aldington, "people let off steam much more freely than in bourgeois homes, where a sort of rancour often lurks under the superficial good manners. Very likely Lawrence was only doing what he had seen his father do a thousand times—work off his annoyance by shouting and apparently unnecessary violence. But with these people, once the scene is over, there is no ill-will at all." Aldington, like Brett and myself, may have heard Frieda saying to her husband on strained occasions, "If you'd been born to manners, you might have some," and suspecting, even while she spoke, that Lawrence's birthright from the rough paternal side was in the long run a valuable safeguard and a sounder trait than the nice gentility his mother tried to give him. He records, in his *Autobiographical Sketch*: "My father . . . was usually rather rude to his little immediate bosses at the pit. . . . He offended them all, almost on purpose, so how could he expect them to favour him? Yet he grumbled when they didn't." Like father, like son.

What he says of a character in *The Rainbow* obviously mirrors himself: "Sometimes," it reads, "he talked of his father, whom he hated with a hatred that was burningly close to love, of his mother, whom he loved, with a love that was keenly close to hatred, or to revolt." Jessie Chambers who tells simply of the constant, powerful interposition of the mother between the boy and herself, says, "I wondered often what was the secret of her power, and came to the conclusion that it lay in her unassailable belief in her own rightness."

But it was not the mother's belief in her own rightness and her use of that belief as power, it was not her personal intent and devices, which held the son away finally from their neighbors' daughter. It was the mother's blood inside the son himself which fought off trespass by another woman. The girl records it in her book through conversations with him. Lawrence says to her: " 'if only you'd been a man, things might have been perfect . . . but it wouldn't have been any good, because then you wouldn't have cared about me.' " Again: " 'I am *not* a complete whole. I tell you, I am two men. One man in me loves you, but the other can never love you. . . . I can't *make* myself love you, can I?' . . . 'Of course not!' I replied. 'But then why do you trouble about me? Why don't you leave me alone?' . . . 'Because you are necessary to me.' . . . I could not help feeling," she continues, "that the whole question of sex had for him the fascination of horror. . . . The theme of a 'physical' marriage . . . would crop up again. Lawrence looked at me with intensity. 'You know—I've always loved mother,' he said in a strangled voice. 'I know you have,' I replied. 'I don't mean that,' he returned quickly. 'I've *loved* her, like a lover. That's why I could never love you.' " On another occasion, " 'Fatherhood's a myth,' Lawrence declared. 'There's no such thing as fatherhood,' he concluded slowly, as though the words tasted sweet on his tongue."

In *Sons and Lovers* which his young friend had watched over, through two manuscript versions, he writes: "You will not easily get a man to believe that his carnal love for the woman he has made his wife is as high a love as that he felt for his mother." And at the end of the book, " 'Mother,' he whimpered, 'Mother!' " In an early poem, "The Virgin Mother," he protests:

> And so, my love, my mother,
> I shall be true to you.
> Twice I am born, my dearest:
> To life, and to death, in you;
> And this is the life hereafter
> Wherein I am true,

ending it,

> I must go but my soul lies helpless
> Beside your bed.

In another poem, "Spirits Summoned West," he writes: ". . . motherhood is jealous, But in virginity jealousy does not enter."

Did the girl guess that Lawrence might have enjoyed finding in his

side of their dilemma something "dark," something Greek and in-
cestuous, and also that such a solution might have been a dramatic
refuge for a man not yet sure of himself? His parents had damaged
for him the idea of fatherhood but they had not killed it. Through
Sons and Lovers he says of the mother's influence on the father. "In
seeking to make him nobler than he could be, she destroyed him."
There are indications of Lawrence's fearing that Jessie Chambers
sought to make the son nobler than he could be. From the beginning
he fought against such idealization of man by woman and, through it,
her subtle control over him. His mother obsessed his imagination; but
he felt in his body the image of his father and was bound not to be
subdued, destroyed, by any woman. Yet, in *Son of Woman,* Murry says
of him at a later period: "As Lawrence in childhood depended on his
mother, so now in manhood he depends upon his wife . . . after a long
and fearful struggle to be free, he is lapsing now back into the condition of child in relation to his own wife."

This is partially true. Lawrence had a childish craving to be important to women and at the same time to hide behind them like a tot
clinging behind skirts. His first published story hid behind the signature of Jessie Chambers. He hid behind his mother, behind Jessie,
then behind Frieda. A great deal of the time when he thought he was
talking about himself, he was talking about what mother or virgin or
wife felt him to be. He was not so much looking at them through his
eyes as at himself through theirs. In his later years he did not much
enjoy seeing people objectively and so saw human life less and less
except in some image of himself and, as often as not, through the eyes
of others as he imagined their seeing him. Perhaps he was right that all
life exists in one man. New Mexican Indians almost persuaded him
that all life exists in any one man. But he was not any egoist. He was
the one egoist.

Through Lovatt in *Kangaroo,* he says of his mother and wife: "They
neither of them believed in me." Wanting adherence to his ideas, to his
theories, to his preaching, to his important manhood, he had found, in
both of them, possessive fondness of his person, tenderness toward his
frailty, indulgence of his vagaries, appreciation of his talents, but not
what he craved most, faith subjugated to a master spirit, to a prophet.
Nor, as he realized early, could he have exacted that sort of belief from
Jessie Chambers. She had a mind of her own. So apparently had Jessie's
sister who told her that "in those days Lawrence impressed her with a

sense of his divine belief in himself. She said he seemed to feel he was important to the world, and he resented any claim that would curtail his experience and therefore his usefulness. He felt himself a medium charged with some power for the good of mankind. Yet he wished he could escape it and grow stout, and attractive to women. He longed to be loved as man instead of as a poet. He told her also that he was a common man with an intellect. . . . He would say one day that he must accept every experience that came to him, for the sake of his 'mission,' and the next that he was nothing but a simple, ordinary man, with a little more than the ordinary man's mental equipment. Her final verdict was: 'He sees the light and chooses the dark.' " Murry calls it "a fearful fate: to be believed in as prophet only by those whose belief is not worth having, and by those whose belief is worth having only to be loved." Lawrence's "message is a compound of truth and falsehood," thinks Murry, "and the truth and the falsehood are so subtly intertwined that it needs more understanding and love than most men possess to separate them out."

Murry would probably agree that, for Lawrence's good, women believed in him too much and men too little.

The fact that women fluttered like moths round his light did not mean that he beckoned them there, that he consciously exerted an appeal of sex. Augustus Saint-Gaudens used to tell me that with a species of African ape the male would seat himself at times at the center of a moonlit jungle clearing, then thump his great chest like drums and roar for appreciation, which would forthwith be given by a rapidly assembling circle of fascinated females. This is more Hemingway than Lawrence. The latter was tolerant and patient with women, perhaps flattered by their following him; but I doubt if either he or the titillated women who circled him were particularly loindrawn. They did not want to smother him so much as to mother him: to dominate him like Virgin Mary mothers. That "dark center" of his noisy chest was a magnet more powerful than the phallus. Or else what drew many of them to him was his purity, as many men are attracted to virginity. His female temple attendants would clutch at his innocence or his fastidiousness and then he would fall into a fit of resentment or into a trance of thinking.

One always finds foreign women sitting rapt at the feet of a Hindu yogi. And so I believe that, beyond the sure intimacy of Frieda, most of these other women remained foreign to Lawrence. Deeply he was alone. In the middle depths, where one can swim, he swam, or bobbed as at Chapala, with Frieda.

Occasionally the followers would be too much for him. His patience or his endurance would break. Idella Purnell remembers that "one evening when we were sitting in the lobby of the Hotel Arzapalo, Lawrence came in suddenly, looking pale and pursued, and sat by Frieda, saying to her, 'Oh, Frieda, protect me from these wretched women!' He almost put his head down in her lap, like a little boy. My feeling about him," Idella continues, "after all these years and in the light of the things I know now, is that he was sexually immature, upset over all the Freudian stuff and nonsense and preoccupied by a desire to understand, with his head, something he could never really understand with his body. Psychologists say that we progress from mother to father worship, then to a puerile form of homosexuality or lesbianism, then to heterosexuality, at last to switch into the 'normal' channels. My own feeling about Lawrence is that he never got beyond the first step, and I think he knew it, that that was his deep trouble. I think *Lady Chatterley's Lover* was an attempt to understand a lot which he never would understand."

Good, serious Idella would not have laughed at Lawrence; but I doubt if any of these women, or the women later, who did not believe in him but who loved him, would have done him any good by laughing at him, as I am sure that Frieda did laugh on occasion. No one who cannot laugh at himself must be laughed at by others. He had told Jessie Chambers that she had no sense of humor, "You have absolutely none. Everything has a fixed value for you." There appears to have been a little something in his charge; but he was far more vulnerable to the same charge, though on other counts. His young friend's heart held his person and personality as fixed values in her desire, and that annoyed him. Her head held his literary ability as a fixed value in her esteem, and that did not annoy him. Though I care little for *The White Peacock*, which passed under her critical eye, I have noted with respect that she lent not only criticism but possibly help here and there to the writing of *Sons and Lovers*. In fact she persuaded him to discard a whole first version, which did not seem to her worthy of him, and to produce a second. I suspect that she preferred his objective narrative to his philosophical, metaphysical, or theosophical dissertations and kept him as straightforward as she could. Though he did say to her, "The best man in me belongs to you," he never wanted her as his physical mate, and the likelihood is that he finally resented her as his literary mate. She doubtless had urged that he write intelligibly, which he would not always do. If I am right in this, I may be right too in thinking that I detect her influence lasting into the earlier half of *The Lost Girl,* before the author goes spinning off with his fantastic Red Indian troupe and then to the Continent. Frieda's influence on this book definitely takes over from her predecessor's, in the magnificently written move from England into Italy. Although Lawrence could never catch his wife's great sense of humor, her "heart-searching laughter," he recognizably absorbed into his writing some of her open-air gusto.

By E. T.'s account, which rings sincere, Jessie Chambers had offered Lawrence no theater to strut in with a Victor Hugo stride. Neither did Frieda. Despite a general impression, he was on the whole a lucky man in the women he knew. And despite Murry's judgment, these two women especially seem to me to have helped build the manhood he could not have built without women, although often he thought he would have liked to be clear of them, to be a high-standing male on some pedestal in Egypt. He had intended that beard of his to be of stone.

The rough sort of humor Lawrence himself possessed, perhaps inherited from his father—and I speak of humor quite apart from sarcasm or wit, which he possessed in cold abundance—was not the sort which could save him from being unconsciously comic in some of his postures. More in the quality of his humor than in any other aspect, he was the peasant, certainly as shown by his writings. When he observes and describes peasant humor, I should say that he relishes it. Not only his countryfolk but his cityfolk are often laughing over what, to most people, would seem nothing to laugh about, as in the following dull interchange, from his short story, *The Fox:* two experimenting amateur girl farmers, March and Banford, explain to Henry Grenfell, an intrusive overwhelming young male, their repentance over an agricultural venture. " 'Oh,' said March, 'we had a better opinion of the nature of fowls than we have now.' 'Of Nature altogether, I'm afraid,' said Banford. 'Don't talk to me about Nature.' 'You haven't a very high opinion of fowls and cattle . . . ?' he said. 'Neither fowls nor heifers,' said Banford, 'nor goats nor the weather.' The youth broke into a sharp yap of laughter, delighted." Then there is the bodily expression of humor, apart from laughter, the pokes and

shoves as in *The Rainbow* over some trifling impropriety in church:
"Fred was nudge-nudging at her. She nudged him back fiercely. Then
another vicious spasm of laughter seized her. She tried to ward
it off in a little cough. The cough ended in a suppressed whoop." In
its context this passage has a contagion, but not on second reading.
Connection with the warmth of laughter was not in Lawrence. I have
noticed that many very human Englishmen can laugh at or against
mere humanness, a shrill empty laughter which they need, apparently,
to save themselves from a momentary, shy weakness of sympathy.
Among Lawrence's characters laughter has little or no reason for being, except embarrassment or derision. It would not occur to any one
of them to share with others a laugh at his own expense. It would not
occur to them or to him that the best humor is not quick but slow,
not sharp but smooth, is the sun coming out and shining a puddle
back to good earth, putting the moisture underneath again where it
belongs.

I said to him once, sententiously enough, "I am above trouble," and
he answered, with happy quickness, "It is beneath an American to be
above trouble." Funny enough, I admit. But I remember wondering
at the time if Wilde's unfriendliest wit had conveyed more cutting
chill.

It is too bad that Lawrence could not have had the redeeming release in the solar plexus which has been recorded concerning a Swiss
minister, Johann Heinrich Pestalozzi, whose first sermon was so bad
that he laughed out loud in the middle of it. Pestalozzi knew that he
was just as funny as somebody else might have seemed to him, de-
livering the sermon. But that was not Lawrence's kind of humor.

Just once a Lawrence character almost laughs at himself. In *The
Captain's Doll,* the Captain's sweetheart has made a manikin in his
image which she hopes he will not see; but a painter acquires it and
uses it in a canvas. The *Muenchener Neue Zeitung*'s chitchat column
contains the announcement: "Theodor Worpswede's latest picture is
a still-life, containing an entertaining group of a doll, two sun-flowers
in a glass jar, and a poached egg on toast." The Captain, recognizing
his ridiculed self, buys the painting and should find a good laugh in it,
or a good ordinary lesson, instead of which it transforms him from a
credible ordinary human figure, into something else, with such suddenly soaring masculinity that the poor German Countess, who had
made a doll of him and loved him as a doll, has to take him as a

Titan. What had seemed the Captain was Lawrence. What had seemed the Countess was Frieda. What had seemed humor was not. Even the comedy with which he touches the portrayal of his father in *Sons and Lovers* is keen memory rather than creative humor.

Through his fictive characters he himself laughs but with no warmth, heartiness, no gay acknowledgment of the thwarting of human will or pretense. Seldom for Lawrence did laughter make the cheek wince with mirth or purge the heart of malice; it only made the jaw work into a snarl or a bark. He could objectively record humor in his characters; but usually his own rough humor would be what came through them, again illustrating the theory that laughter began with an animal showing its teeth. Passages in which I thought I had seen a laughing eye gleam would, when reread, lose the gleam. Each time the snarl would become both meaner and weaker. In his short story, *The Border Line:* "Alan just asserted himself like a pillar of rock, and expected the tides of the modern world to recede around him. They didn't"; in *Sun,* another short story: "The ship ebbed on, the Hudson seemed interminable. But at last they were round the bend, and there was the poor harvest of lights at the Battery. Liberty flung up her torch in a tantrum. There was the wash of the sea"; and in still another short story, *Glad Ghosts:* " 'I'm awfully sorry I can't drink wine. It has the wrong effect on me,' " answered by " 'I should say it has the wrong effect on everybody. But some people like the effect, and some don't.' " I had thought that one funny at first. Perhaps it is.

Apart from humor among his characters Lawrence's sense of it or lack of it breaks harshly or clumsily into his letters—which, for the most part, are moving and fine. What he thought was humorous speaking could sound like something else, as when he said after Rupert Brooke had left him a bequest of twenty pounds: "I have a great belief in the dead—in Rupert dead." Here was peasant humor again, embarrassment, or a stab at stylish wit.

When the project of joint lectures to be given by Bertrand Russell and himself went on the rocks in 1915, and when he directed his own private lectures against Russell in a series of caustic letters, condemning Russell's ideas and concluding, "Let us become strangers again, I think it is better," he had the audacity to say, ". . . when you make your will, do leave me enough to live on. I want you to live for ever. But I want you to make me in some part your heir." I doubt if to Russell this sounded like humor, but I am convinced that it was partly so intended. And, after all, the preceding passage in the letter had said: "Do for your very pride's sake become a mere nothing, a mole, a creature that feels its way and doesn't think."

Just once I have encountered an instance when Lawrence's humor seemed to me warm and funny and inclusive of a laughing look at himself. Brett tells it. It was one day when Lawrence and Frieda were out riding with her in Mexico and Frieda, exclaiming her delight in her horse, cried, "Oh, it's wonderful, wonderful, to feel his great thighs moving, to feel his powerful legs!" "Rubbish, Frieda," Lawrence shouted back. "Don't talk like that. You have been reading my books. You don't feel anything of the sort." Even then—though playfully—he was putting Frieda in her place.

"The young man who has not wept is a savage," says Santayana, "and the old man who will not laugh is a fool." Santayana might have regretted that Lawrence, who had been young enough to weep, did not live long enough to laugh.

Even in his last novel, *The Man Who Died,* he is not old enough to see that more than once what he presents soberly, tenderly, cannot but have a comic aspect for his reader. When Christ has come out of the sepulcher, he finds rest in a peasant's yard where a doughty gamecock is tethered. The passage as to their encounter is very Lawrencian at the outset, a bit Biblical at the center, and at the end downright funny. It is of course possible that Lawrence knew it would seem funny to a Philistine and, with his love of birds and their ways, defied the chuckle, dared to seem funny. If so, more honor to him. As he tells it: "The bird was a prisoner. Yet the flame of life burned up to a sharp point in the cock, so that it eyed askance and haughtily the man who had died. And the man smiled and held the bird dear, and he said to it: 'Surely thou art risen to the Father, among birds.' And the young cock, answering, crowed." Another passage edges on the ludicrous through Christ's use of colloquial speech to Mary Magdalen: "You took more than you gave. . . . I gave more than I took, and that also is woe and vanity. So Pilate and the high priests saved me from my own excessive salvation. Don't run to excess now in living, Madeleine." I could only think of Christ's alleged visit to Mrs. Ballard, head of the I Am cult, and their discussion of Germain, the cult's newly developed patron saint, whose portrait on I Am platforms equals in size that of Jesus. Mrs. Ballard is reported to have told her Visitor that she had been warned He would be jealous of St. Germain, and Jesus is said to have replied, "How perfectly ridiculous!" You respect Lawrence's returned Christ for saying, "My reach ends in my fingertips, and my stride is no longer than the ends of my toes. Yet I would embrace multitudes, I who have never truly embraced even one," and then, for unbelievable contrast, you have to read the passage: "He crouched to her, and he felt the blaze of his manhood and his power rise up in his loins, magnificent. 'I am risen!'" This symbol of the resurrection is, after all, almost as quaint as Longfellow's terming stars the "forget-me-nots of the angels."

It is odd that simple laughter did not always grow in Lawrence, as bubbles from a spring, considering the childlike nature with which he enjoyed ordinary daily living, the touch of homely toil and of the earth. Anna Brangwen spoke for him in *The Rainbow:* "What did she want, herself? She answered that she wanted to be happy, to be natural, like the sunlight and the busy day." Who else can embrace the goodness of life quite so simply close as that? "No task," records Jessie Chambers, "seemed dull or monotonous to him. He brought such vitality to the doing that he transformed it into something creative. He was proud of his small hands, extremely clever hands they were, equally deft at arranging sweet peas in a vase or at sowing the seed." Mrs. Carswell remembers that "once he bought a gauze shawl of Paisley pattern for Frieda—cheaply because it had the moth in it—and set himself to make it whole without delay by mending it himself. It took him two entire days, working well into the night and allowing only the shortest intervals for meals." I recall his adroitly instructive patching of the Mexican blanket he brought me at the hospital in Guadalajara. And Idella Purnell writes of the Chapala days: "I remember how he enjoyed baking, lovely crisp loaves of white bread; and he liked to mend things, and sew. He enjoyed designing blankets which the weavers at Jocotepec would make for you or for himself. We seldom went to Chapala without being asked to rejoice over a new blanket." Brett adds, of the Del Monte days: "I watch you, far away in the field, in your blue shirt and white corduroys and big straw hat. You love the irrigating; you love leading the water over the field, letting it run over your feet."

In these simple doings Frieda was ever, from the days of his knapsack and her "kitchenino" in Sardinia to the Mexican days and beyond, his comfortably busy mate. Mrs. Carswell instances "someone trying to commiserate with her over the nuisance of housework and other homely duties. 'But what else is there to do?' asked Frieda blithely. For her, as for Lawrence, life was richly in the everyday things." Out of our own time together in Chapala, Frieda was writing Knud Merrild as early as June of that 1923 summer, "If we see a place we really like, we will have it and plant bananas—I am already very tired of not doing my own work." But she was not tired of laughing with people; while Lorenzo, when lighthearted people drew him from his occupation, not his writing but his housework or tinkering, would often see nothing to laugh about and turn away crossly.

The character, Kangaroo, in the book of that name, says to Lovatt, who is Lawrence: "You are like a child. I know that is part of the charm of your nature, that you are naive like a child, but sometimes you are childish rather than childlike. A perverse child!" Oftener than he admitted, Lawrence knew himself.

I had often remembered him in Chapala; how I had there thought him on the edge of derangement when I saw the perversity completely swamp the child, when I watched his quick and exaggerated shifts of emotion or mood: dark hatred, bright passion, mild interest or dull indifference, alternating and impinging upon one another as they may readily do in any disordered and self-indulgent egotist. The following year, 1924, he wrote Mabel Lujan from the ranch: "Perhaps the only thing that will really help one through a great change is discipline, one's own deep, self-discovered discipline, the first 'angel with a sword.'" And Brett quotes him: "People don't discipline themselves enough." He believed in discipline for everyone but himself. But how could there be discipline for such intensity as his?—such contemptuous and yet hopeful intensity. In the two short stories, *Glad Ghosts* and *A Modern Lover,* he says first, "I did care about one passionate vision which, I could feel, lay imbedded in the half-dead body of this life . . . the unborn body of life hidden within the body of this half-death which we call life," and then, "Life is beautiful, so long as it is consuming you. When it is rushing through you, destroying you, life is glorious. . . . It's when you burn a slow fire and save fuel that life's not worth having." He had acknowledged to Jessie Chambers: "At times I am afflicted by a perversity amounting to minor insanity." Elsewhere he said: "Sometimes I think I should like to slip into an insane asylum and live in a mad world of my own creation, instead of in this mad world created by others."

As shown in his letters, however, he needed people and inclined to them generously in many directions. He was lavish with his interest and advice when people brought him their troubles, with answers when they asked him questions, with patience when women pestered him, and with money when friends needed it. His money sense was simple, almost like that of the Mexican Indian. He was happy when there was enough for the day's needs. If there was more, as Merrild, Aldington, and others testify, he was glad to share it in the same spirit which welcomed financial help when he was himself hard pressed, as when Amy Lowell and Rupert Brooke assisted him or friends lent him houses. If he could, as in the case of Mabel Lujan, he would make refund, and he was glad when such assistance as he himself gave could be refunded. Though he was angry when British censorship cut off his home income, he was more puzzled than angry when Seltzer, his American publisher, collapsed, owing him substantial funds upon which he had depended, or when Mitchell Kennerley, after publishing *The Widowing of Mrs. Holroyd* and *Sons and Lovers* in the United States, sent him a twenty-pound check which proved to be worthless. Perhaps he knew that Kennerley—who published among others, Lawrence, Millay, and me, our first books, and paid us nothing—spoke near and far his faith in us and sent uncounted copies of our work to helpful persons in many directions, all the while as troubled by his bookkeeping as we were and as wishful as we were that he might, financially, be doing better by us.

Yes, Lawrence was generous, more than generous. But he could not rid his mind of the theory that he did not love people and did not want people to love him. As Aaron says, in *Aaron's Rod:* "'I don't want kindness or love. I don't believe in harmony or people loving one another. I believe in the fight and nothing else. And if it is a question of women, I believe in the fight of love, even if it blinds me. And if it is a question of the world, I believe in fighting it and having it hate me, even though it breaks my legs. . . . For of all things love is the most deadly to me and especially from such a repulsive world as I think this is.'" Murry comments: "He will love, and hate himself for loving; he will hate and love himself for hating."

Lawrence could not untangle the idea of brotherly love from that of physical love and goes so far as to say, in *Fantasia of the Unconscious:* "Incest is the logical conclusion of our ideals, when these ideals have to be carried into passional effect." He goes even further, in considering loving-kindness, as apart from sexual love, and makes homicidal intent its logical conclusion. When he writes, in *The Lost Girl*, that Alvina and her mother loved each other in "an almost after-death love," his meaning is not so filial as it sounds. For instance there is Miss Frost, a fine woman who has come into the household to serve it tenderly and has won the girl's utmost affection. Alvina "loved her darling. She would love her through eternity . . . her darling, her beloved Miss Frost. . . . And yet. . . . Purity and high-mindedness—the beautiful but unbearable tyranny, the beautiful, unbearable tyranny of Miss Frost! It was time now for Miss Frost to die. It was time now for that perfected flower to be gathered to immortality. . . . She, Alvina, who loved her as no one else would ever love her, with that love which goes to the core of the universe, knew that it was time for her darling to be folded, oh, so gently and softly, into immortality." It was not that Miss Frost was sick but that Alvina loved her to death. Several times in his novels and in the guise of this or that character, Lawrence has wanted excellent people dead, that he may love them on his own terms. He had liked Fred Leighton but been through with him, dismissed him, "Go die!"

In *Son of Woman*, after Lawrence's own death, Murry said of him: "Theoretically, he had no use for the Christian virtues, but since in fact he possessed most of them in abundance, he was difficult to satisfy. His mind and heart were hopelessly at odds with one another. . . . He was tender, sympathetic, loving to an extreme degree. But mentally he was in a condition of violent reaction against these 'spiritual' virtues; he wanted to be 'a hardy and indomitable male,' and was always trying to dream himself into the part." And again: "Unless he will make himself a whole, he will never find the whole of which he can be a part."

In Lawrence's theories about the contrary forces of life, out of war would come peace, out of peace would come war. His ideological kinsman, Dostoyevsky, had said: "Lasting peace always generates cruelty, cowardice and coarse, fat egotism." Lawrence, through Cipriano in *The Plumed Serpent*, puts it more mildly: "Peace is only the rest after war. So it is not more natural than fighting; perhaps not so natural." Teresa, in the same novel, says to Lawrence, as represented by Kate: "You would fight with yourself, if you were alone in the world."

Says Emerson: "The moment we indulge our affections, the earth is metamorphosed: there is no winter, no night: all tragedies, all ennuies vanish, all duties even, and nothing fills the proceeding eternity but the forms all radiant of beloved persons." Lawrence never saw forms thus transfigured, nor wished to; but his hatred of affectionate love as an idea left him full of tragic ennui and of everlasting duty toward he knew not what. He hated pity too: he did not choose to pity even himself. What he thought he required of an associate was the intelligent response of a human being, whom at the same time he could control as he would a dependent animal. And yet with animals—as with human beings—he muffed that control, as shown in his pathetic stormings at Pipsy, his dog, and at Susan, his cow, and his slaughter of Smoky, his hen.

His three short stories in *The Ladybird* volume are all on the one theme of male mastery over women: I snap the whip—you trot or crouch where I say. In each instance—in *The Fox* and in *The Captain's Doll,* as well as in the title story—he does his old trick; he starts drawing an actual, credible man who is not at the outset Lawrence, and then destroys the character by pushing himself into it and imposing martial law—or marital law, they become the same—on a poor female. And in each case he cannot help showing the female's pathetic but helpless dislike of being bullied into subjection. They are all "lost girls." And in his own various guises, he himself does not seem any too pleased. He was far better pleased finally in life than in any of the paper roles he played, because Frieda refused to be a lost girl—except in fiction.

Of the purging elements in tragedy, Stephen Daedalus asserts, in James Joyce's *Portrait of the Artist as a Young Man:* "Aristotle has not defined pity and terror. I have, I say. . . . Pity is the feeling which arrests the mind in the presence of whatsoever is grave and constant in human sufferings and unites it with the human sufferer. Terror is the feeling which arrests the mind in the presence of whatsoever is grave and constant in human sufferings and unites it with the secret cause." Lawrence, by his own admission or boast, felt pity less often than terror, united his mind less often with the human sufferer than he tried to unite himself with the secret cause. He would never have chosen the childlike dance step of Robert Frost:

> We dance around in a ring and suppose,
> But the secret sits in the middle and knows.

Lawrence would have plunged into the middle and ripped the leaf off the secret. For him the tree of knowledge was the fig tree, not the tree of Judas but the tree of Adam; and while he felt that its "secret cause" was rooted in "dark" earth, yet he kept lifting and lifting fig leaves to find, revealed, the vital, pure, and seed-containing fruit. His little flutter of doggerel called *Nettles,* published in 1930, when his paintings, largely of nudes, had been exhibited in London, gaped at by crowds and then seized by the authorities as obscene, contains these lines:

> Thirteen thousand people came to see
>   my pictures, eager as the honey-bee. . . .
> And they stared and they stared, the half-witted lot
>   at the spot where the fig-leaf just was not! . . .
> Can it be they've been trimmed, so they've never seen
>   the innocent member that a fig-leaf will screen?

While Lawrence thought that instinct, intuition, directed his quest into human nature, it was mental determination trying to be instinct. Constantly he condemned probings by the intellect and constantly indulged in them. The truth was that he could never get out of his head what his abdomen was doing. A simple sweet woman told me recently that she did not read books. "Why read?" she said. "It's only what somebody else thinks." If Lawrence had meant what he wrote about the intellect, his conclusion should have been hers. He should, logically, neither have read nor written. He should have let school out, like Karl Shapiro, and felt relief:

> Then the clock strikes and I erase the board,
> Clearing the cosmos with a sweep of felt,
> Voiding my mind as well.

At one point, after his return to England from the Americas, he wrote, for Johnson's *Laughing Horse:* "I've been a fool saying: Europe is finished for me—it wasn't Europe at all, it was myself keeping a stranglehold on myself. And that stranglehold I carried over to America."

That stranglehold was his intellect, and he could never stop talking about how to undo it. He had early written Ernest Collings: "I'm like Carlyle, who, they say, wrote 50 volumes on the value of silence." Similar comment had been made, centuries before, concerning Laotzu who, however, bequeathed but one slim sheaf. Perhaps silence is better understood through being but slightly broken.

Rousseau had said that he "understood nothing and felt everything." Lawrence, in spite of himself, tried to feel everything and understand it, too. Well he might have agreed with what Margaret Fuller set down in her *Journal:* "With the intellect, I always have, always shall, overcome; but that is not the half of the work. The life, the life! Oh, my God! shall the life never be sweet?"

Lawrence, I summarize from earlier chapters, tries to douse the intellect and sweeten life by importing from the reaches of the dark earth a mystic power of animal being. He even goes so far, in his short story, *The Rocking-Horse Winner,* as to let a wooden animal impart second sight to the child who rides it. With their mystic, symbolic association, the boy rides the rocking horse in a madly hopeful and partly successful frenzy culminating in death. By such tokens Lawrence struggles to join man and animal into a centaur who shall trample all doubt away, into a Pegasus who shall take off from a rainbow, when what their author, their groom, would prefer all the while would be the quiver of a real horse's flank, the sough of a pine, the curl of a wave, the lift of the wing of any bird, the eye of an owl, the cold flight of a fish, the warm pouch of a kangaroo. He dreamed that he was happily betraying the foul human race by preferring to be a fine animal, when all he was doing was to intellectualize mankind's usual practice of enjoying its animal nature. Meantime he tried to believe, like many before him, that misty messages from the past might save him from answering the direct question of the present. He dodged the present, both in time and place. If he could have taken the people who were present around him as he took the wind and the waves, the wombats and the weasels which were present, if he could have granted people their love and not wished to space them apart from one another in all but body, he might have rested more easily. But he was not a groom for people. His currycombs, his martingales, and spurs were made for rocking horses and nightmares.

It was because he did not know how to blend. He could not blend past and future into the present. He could not blend intellect and emotion, pity and terror, freedom and control, any of the opposites. He could not let positive and negative make light. One of them must make light and the other make darkness, with no twilight and no dawn. Yet his haunting impulse was to slink back or rush forward into the womb of earth, where male and female are blended before they become separate; nor did he know whether his wistful hope of being enfolded there meant into the past or into the future, surrender to the unbornness of the old life or to the unknownness of the new. So he made of the womb a joining rainbow and crept softly under it. It was his way of self-appointed dying before his necessary time.

Rebecca West has said of him, too easily perhaps, that he "had the earnestness of the artistic writers" and "like them could know no peace till he had discovered what made men lust after death." It was not that. In *Glad Ghosts* he said: "The dead must be somewhere; there's no such place as nowhere"; and the woman in *The Woman Who Rode Away* said: "I am dead already. What difference does it make, the transition from the dead I am to the dead I shall be, very soon!" On the other hand, his poem, "Snap-Dragon," states for him: "And death, I know, is better than not-to-be;" and Jack Grant of *The Boy in the Bush* vaunts for him: ". . . 'when I die I shall not drop like a carrion on the earth's earth. I shall be a lord of death, and sway the destinies of life to come.'" Then again in *Kangaroo* he says: "If a man wants to make a fool of himself, it is well to let him," and "a man must even know how to give up his own earnestness when its hour is over, and not to bother about anything more, when he's bothered enough."

But for Lawrence at the end this was not a sadness. In his late essay, *On Human Destiny,* he writes: "I love the little sprout and the weak little seedling. I love the thin sapling, and the first fruit, and the falling of the first fruit. I love the great tree in its splendour. And I am glad that at last, at the very last, the great tree will go hollow, and fall on its side with a crash, and the little ants will run through it, and it will disappear like a ghost back into the humus. It is the cycle of all things created, thank God. Because, given courage, it saves even eternity from staleness."

I must compare to Lawrence a slightly later contemporary who may interestingly be differentiated from him: T. S. Eliot, who has achieved importance by being correct for his time, by anticipating its mood and its style. Certainly he has had enormous influence and may even be correct for later times. Lawrence could not have been correct for any time but was always alive, always an originator and, though I was thinking him in Chapala a "death-worm," was always, I know now, a breath-giver. He remained to the end a child, with the vision of a child, like Laotzu a "venerable child." In spite or perhaps because of his poutings and foot stampings, his semitragic impatience with burdens pettier than those of Atlas, despite the fact that he was born without divine laughter and could never attain it, what a good time he finally had, on a beautiful earth, in an eternity not stale!

44. The Artist in Spite
of Himself

ALDOUS HUXLEY, in his introduction to the collected letters, notes that "Lawrence was in a real sense possessed by his creative genius. . . . Like Blake, like any man possessed of great special talents, he was predestined by his gifts."

In spite of Huxley's considerable evidence to the contrary, I cannot help feeling that Lawrence was not too cordial toward his aesthetic gifts, that he set himself with resolution against being primarily the artist: that he wished primarily to be the preacher, to tell the world what ailed it, and how he thought it might recover. This dedication of himself not to his art but to his fellows, whom he mostly pretended not to care about, was a giveaway of his character, as distinct from his perverse nature, was a constant revelation of the evangelism at his root. Through being evangel to the individual in himself and making art its servant—"I always say, my motto is 'Art for my sake'"—he would also be evangel to the race.

All his life he had enjoyed keen fun with brush and colors. Now and then he had made a design of his own; but the activity had consisted mainly in copying. During his last few years he began painting his own inventions and he took great delight in them. He believed that paintings should be enjoyed for a while and then destroyed; and I think he would have advanced the same judgment as to the art of words if words might be as easily destroyed as canvases. Although his finest genius lay in use of words which flocked like birds, his conviction is evident that it lay, rather, in words of evangelical use. He says in his essay, *Pictures on the Walls:* "As a tree puts beauty into a flower that will fade, so all the hosts of minor artists, one way and another, put beauty and delight into their pictures, that likewise will not last beyond their rhythmic season." In another essay, *Making Pic-*

tures, he says: "All my life I have from time to time gone back to paint, because it gave me a form of delight that words can never give. Perhaps the joy in words goes deeper and is for that reason more unconscious. The *conscious* delight is certainly stronger in paint." It is certain that his own conscious pleasure in paint gave others no such important results as his unconscious pleasure in words; and it is likely that his very unawareness of how well he was doing with words is a contributing element in his fine use of them. Here was his instinct faring, as he would have had it do, better than his purpose.

Yet this believer in instinct and in the natural gestures of life, persisted in believing his intellectualized doctrines more important than his sheer responses to life and his expression of those responses. As he said himself in *Etruscan Places,* "before Buddha or Jesus spoke the nightingale sang, and long after the words of Jesus and Buddha are gone into oblivion the nightingale will still sing." His doctrines as to economics, as to sex, as to dark gods will fade away, as all doctrines do, except when they pare down to the barest clarity, simplicity, and straightness in a man's consciousness of life and thence in his living and thinking and speaking. The theories, the intellectual structures, the creeds, and the dogmas are flimsy alongside the sheer quickness of a man's connection with life, the joy of it, and his impulse to share that connection with others, through his own living and, when he is able, through record of his experience, through his use of words.

A man to whom temperament or experience or contemplation of life brings only sadness can, through exact expression of his sadness, give others and probably himself a kind of joy. Even scientists, finding an exactness with which the world creates and destroys itself, are compensated by the aesthetic quality of finding and using exactness. It is the artist in man whose seven-day week is all good, whose six days are creative and whose seventh is not needed for rest, since creation and rest are at one.

Lawrence felt this but did not like to know it. Forces in his background and upbringing had convinced him that art in itself is not service. If the missionary speaks well, he had been informed by his elders, so much the better; but the mission in itself is the vital office. He should have known that, beyond a man's living what he preaches, there is no use in his having a mission except in his speaking it well. Every message worth carrying is already implicitly known to every man; but often for connection, for joint joy, speaking it well is of service. Who, better than Lawrence, should have known that the world has paid too much attention to its teachers and not enough to its artists, its true seers, who, by merely seeing and recording, can teach better than the teachers? To share seeing the world and then die, is about all we can do, except for seeing it well. To explain it is, apparently, not our business.

I am myself being didactic about this artist who, in his boyhood, told Jessie Chambers that he felt he had something to say but that he thought it would be didactic. "Here was his sense of fate," she comments, "against his instinctive intent." Unfortunately she was right: the didacticism increased as he turned from the lyrically human impulses of his youth and obeyed the maturing dictates of his mind.

He said to me in Chapala, "You will like *The Lost Girl* best of all my novels." He may have been sorry for me when he said that; but I do not wholly think so. I had not read *The Lost Girl* then; but I have read it now and I like it best of all his novels. Granting that it may seem at first to be imitatively of a traditional school—George Eliot, Dickens, Hardy, Bennett, Butler, even Meredith whose writing is called by a figure in Lawrence's short story, *Witch à la Mode,* "very healthy"—I find this book authentic in Lawrence's own idiom and vivid with the life of people who are more interestingly differentiated than are his later variants of himself and Frieda. Apart from the egregiously silly and aforementioned passages about his Red Indian troupe, it is, as I have said before, a moving story of real people; and the entry of his own emotions and Frieda's, at the end in Italy, for once artistically identifies them with the emotions of his characters, is as real as the rest of the narrative and unforgettably beautiful. It is a sad book; but it is honestly sad; and the author does not squirm away from its sadness and its reality into a tangle of physical mysticism or a mire of intellectual jargon. Little by little, through the book, the girl is "lost" into a limbo of bodily love intellectually incomprehensible but physically inevitable. Stripped here of the intellectual trappings he imposes on it in later books, this bodily love was Lawrence's main theme; and here it stands clear, presented not by a doctrinist but by an artist. *Sons and Lovers* had been written for him by his own life and the life of his family and neighbors. *The Lost Girl,* too, contains elements of his early experience and his escape from England with Frieda; but here he has wrought the parts together, less as autobiography than as creative and notable fiction. Katherine Mansfield wrote

Murry of the book: "Lawrence denies his humanity. He denies the power of the imagination. He denies Life—I mean human life. . . . There is not one memorable word." This is obvious nonsense and, though it may have been prompted by some warrantable personal irritation, still goes to show to what vitiating, unjust attack Lawrence was being subjected by the supposedly friendly literary circle he met in London, as well as by the treadmill critics. No wonder he learned to ignore criticism from any circle. He was fond of Katherine Mansfield; and I doubt if sight of this stricture against his book would have in the least affected his fondness for her personally or his sense of the value of her work. I am sure that there was no meanness in his gesture after her death when, according to Mrs. Carswell, he warned Murry not to write of Mrs. Murry in *The Adelphi* that she was a genius: "She had a charming gift, and a finely cultivated one. But no more. And to try, as you do, to make it more, is no true service."

It would have been easy to condone Katherine Mansfield's losing her temper over later books like *Women in Love* and *Aaron's Rod* with their endless thrusts and parryings of dialogue in duels which, after the final pages, are still flashing inconsequentially. Thomas Campbell, the English poet, said in his century: "The mind becomes fatigued by constant flashes of wit, which dazzle rather than delight, and we grow weary of a conversation where there is nothing solid to gratify the understanding, and where the incessant poignancy almost sets the teeth on edge." Without granting that the Lawrence wit dazzled, she might well have agreed otherwise with the applicability of Campbell's paragraph to these other books; but it is not easy to comprehend her total denial of the genius which delineated, in *The Lost Girl,* the minor figures, James Houghton, Miss Frost, Miss Pinnegar, Dr. Mitchell, Madame Rochard, Mr. May, Mrs. Tuke, and Pancarazio, besides Alvina herself and her Italian lover. It remains of interest, in these continuing mechanistic days, to hear Madame Rochard, the vaudeville actress, say of movies: "The pictures are cheap, and they are easy, and they cost the audience nothing, no feeling of the heart, no appreciation of the spirit. And so they like them, and they don't like us, because they must *feel* the things we do, from the heart, and appreciate them from the spirit. There! . . . They want it all through the eye, and finished—so! Just curiosity, impertinent curiosity. That's all." Lawrence thought so too, but he made his thought this time sound like the voice of Madame Rochard.

"You see," Lawrence had said to Jessie Chambers, "it was really George Eliot who started it all. . . . It was she who started putting all the action inside. Before, you know, with Fielding and the others, it had been outside. Now I wonder which was right? . . . You know, I can't help thinking there ought to be a bit of both." Years later, in *Kangaroo,* he wrote: ". . . a novel is supposed to be a mere record of emotion—adventures, flounderings in feelings. We insist that a novel is, or should be, also a thought-adventure, if it is to be anything at all complete." On the other side, he had written Lady Ottoline Morrell in 1915: "Most puerile is this clabbing of geometric figures behind one another, just to prove that the artist is being abstract, that he is not attempting representation of the object."

From any point of view, his best writing in *The Rainbow* had been "outside" writing: the attempts of the child, Anna, to keep her mother away from the new father, the wedding of Anna Lensky and Tom Brangwen, the drowning of Tom Brangwen. Similarly in *The Lost Girl* one remembers vivid narrative of happenings among simple people, Calladine falling off the ladder and hurting his leg—real happenings, real talk, as against Lawrence's later method: the governed motion and dictated chatter of puppets who are all one person. The artist is best who so draws his characters that others will draw the conclusions he wishes drawn.

Lawrence said to Brett, "I never know when I sit down, just what I am going to write. I make no plan; it just comes, and I don't know where it comes from. Of course I have a general sort of outline of what I want to write about, but when I go out in the mornings, I have no idea what I will write. It just comes." This was not quite true. He was still consciously applying what he thought to be the George Eliot method, instead of doing, with Henry Fielding, what he could do best. As he said again to Brett, "Why do all the painters have to sit in front of what they paint? . . . It's because they feel nothing inside them, so they must have it before their eyes. It's all wrong and stupid: it should all be brought from inside oneself." Here, as he perversely would not do, he should have known the Chinese. The Chinese painter has always sat in front of what he painted; but he has sat without painting and has sat and sat there again. Afterward, away from the scene, when his actual eye is full and true, he has rearranged the scene with his inner seeing, recollected his emotion in tranquillity, but he has not denied what he saw, he has not imposed only an inner scene, like an author denying his characters and imposing himself.

The reason why Lawrence could not in his later books write lifelike dialogue was because he could not finally hear any voice but his own. "Self-exploration," Norman Douglas calls it. Kate, leaving the bull-fight, is audibly Lawrence. His later novels contain variety in his notations of setting and of animal life, or in fluctuations of philosophy, but not much change in his gallery of people, who have now become for the most part portraits of himself and his wife, taken from different angles. Their contact, interplay, and dialogue are, I repeat, the action and speech of a one-man puppet show, the movements and voices of a single person—and his wife. Men or women, they are all forced into facets of the Lawrences. Aldington tells of their playing charades: "How he bossed us about as if we were children and insisted on having the most important part himself!" Aldington might have added that, in playing fiction, Lawrence eventually took all the parts himself. Their discussions are inside himself and with himself. The dialogue becomes monologue. Even Frieda becomes a side of himself, absorbed into oppositional identity. It all becomes reflective soliloquy, not only the expositional passages but the dialogue. He does not give a damn for exchange between actual personalities but only between personalities inside one man. That is why the sole character he has fully created in a novel, after the family portraits in *Sons and Lovers* and the few outsiders in *The Rainbow* and *The Lost Girl*, the one character who looms large and alive, apart from glimpses of Frieda, is David Herbert Lawrence, burning himself, through all the books, with hotter flame than the natural sun. For me, as I have indicated, he is a less able because a less objective artist in the later novels than in the earlier. In the short stories and sketches, outer persons often remain alive because his jaw and maw lack time to masticate and digest them into himself. In sustained novels he enwinds characters, as a spider its victims, into a fine, strangling web from his entrails, his dark center, till the life goes numb in them and they become dead meals. But what a spider when he gets busy! The adroit spinning and winding, the quick-legged action of his prose!

Edgar Allan Poe distinguished between "two great classes of fiction: a popular and widely circulated class read with pleasure, but without admiration in which the author is lost or forgotten ... and then a class, not so popular, in which . . . arises a distinctive and highly pleasurable interest, springing from our perception . . . of the genius evinced in the composition. After perusal of the one class, we think solely of the book —after reading the other, chiefly of the author. The former class leads to popularity—the latter to fame." What might Poe have thought of Lawrence? Certainly no one, in the case of this author, thinks solely of the book. We think rather of the writer, because, in spite of himself, he could not quench his genius, although he often and at length interrupted it.

His favored hero, the irresistibly virile commoner, can have no more important a claim for respect than the oppositely snobbish favored heroine of Jane Austen. She likes her class, he likes his. England abides, for her, by exclusion of his class from established society. England for him is restored by the intrusion of his class into established society. Each author is a snob—she in favor of what has been, he in favor of what shall be. As Tindall says of Lawrence's steadily recurrent theme: "Husbands, fathers, mine-owners, and vicars generally serve in these allegories as representatives of the mind and the machine, from which their wives or daughters are freed by the aid of grooms, gamekeepers, gypsies, crooners, or horses." It is not his theme which gives him distinction. Any democracy could have afforded him his theme. Nor is it his characters. After his early writing, none of his characters come to the fore, nor is there a great personage among them anywhere— apart, as I have granted, from himself and his wife. In one of his later short stories, *Glad Ghosts,* he appears for a bit to be creating people. Through thirty of its pages real people live, recorded with genius, and then, as regrettably as in other tales, Lawrence's own character intrudes upon their reality and kills them off, one by one, into a heap of rhetorical ego. At the outset you see him satirizing with acute sense the spiritualistic nonsense of such of his own stories as *The Border Line, The Last Laugh,* and *Smile,* and then he weakens and yields to the ectoplasmic miasma which taints much of his writing. He still vacillates. First he almost believes that the dead return as ghosts with physical powers and creep under the sheets; then he makes their powers due to the fact that the living have not shot them full enough of straight, bodily juice, so that the ghosts return for more. Immortality is only physical. Wings sprout in the loins. Wonderful for the actors if he can manage it! But the genius of the author dies in the attempt to solve the problem of the universe.

A passage from a 1920 Taormina letter quoted by Norman Douglas records the occupation of the theorist as only a notable artist could tell it: "The dawn is so lovely from this house. I open my eyes at 5.0, and say Coming; at 5.30, and say yellow; at 6.0, and say pink and smoke blue; at 6.15 and see a lovely orange flare and then the liquid sunlight winking straight in my eye. Then I know it's time to get up. So I dodge the sunlight with a corner of the blanket, and consider the problem of the universe: this I count my sweetest luxury, to consider the problem of the universe while I dodge the dawned sun behind a corner of the sheet; so warm, so first-kiss warm. . . ."

E. M. Forster, in *Aspects of the Novel,* calls Lawrence "the only living novelist in whom the song predominates, who has the rapt, bardic quality, and whom it is idle to criticize . . . what is valuable about him cannot be put into words; it is colour, gesture and outline in people and things, the usual stock-in-trade of the novelist, but evolved by such a different process that they belong to a new world."

And so we come to Lawrence, the artist—the turn of phrase, the building of paragraphs, the way he wrote, the language of his heart. His genius did not consist fundamentally in what he had to say or in the way his characters said it for him but in the way he said it himself when he was most himself. He wrote Mrs. Lujan: "You may take it as a fair test, that what didn't bore you to write, won't bore the reader to read." Alvina, in *The Lost Girl,* had said of a figure in the book: "He did not think about what he was feeling, and he did not feel what he was thinking about. And therefore she hardly heard what he said. Yet she believed he was clever." Lawrence was clever, but cleverness was not Lawrence. He thought about what he was feeling and he felt what he was thinking about. He began and ended with sincerity. So, in response to the man himself we listen and are not bored. But we could not listen long even to sincere repetition unless he repeated himself well. His redundancy, after all, is sincerity trying to speak true.

A stylistic trick soon noticeable in his writing is actual verbal repetition. He said to Knud Merrild concerning the Dane's jacket design for *Kangaroo:* "I don't like the repetition of lines around the design," and Frieda cut in, "What would you do without repetition in your work?" Lawrence's repetitions are like the effective turnings of an awl. Aldington takes him to task for them; but I feel in them often a fine force, as in this passage from *The Lost Girl,* concerning Alvina and

Cicio: "She locked the door and kneeled down on the floor, bowing down her head to her knees in a paroxysm on the floor. In a paroxysm —because she loved him. She doubled herself up in a paroxysm on her knees on the floor—because she loved him. It was far more like pain, like agony, than like joy. She swayed herself to and fro in a paroxysm of unbearable sensation, because she loved him." Gertrude Stein might have studied this passage to advantage and learned that one may be repetitive and still mean something. Here is another passage from the same book, the repetitions succeeding one another more closely than in the original, because I have crowded them, but giving still—though perhaps too quickly here—the growing forceful effect of drum beats. Alvina is leaving England with Cicio: "So they turned to walk to the stern of the boat. And Alvina's heart suddenly contracted. . . . For there behind, behind all the sunshine, was England. England, beyond the water, rising with ash-grey, corpse-grey cliffs, and streaks of snow on the downs above. England, like a long ash-grey coffin slowly submerging. . . . It seemed to repudiate the sunshine, to remain unilluminated, long and ash-grey and dead, with streaks of snow like cerements. That was England! Her thoughts flew to Woodhouse, the grey centre of it all. Home! . . . Cicio at her side was as nothing, as spell-bound she watched, away off, behind all the sunshine and the sea, the grey, snow-streaked substance of England slowly receding and sinking, submerging. . . . It was like looking at something else. What? It was like a long ash-grey coffin, winter, slowly submerging in the sea." And then in his short story, *The Captain's Doll,* when he describes the lower reaches of the glacier near Kaprun in the Tyrol, he makes magical repetition of the meaning and sound of the word "down": "the zig-zag of snow-stripes and ice-roots descending, and then rivers, streams and rivers rushing from many points downwards, down out of the ice-roots and the snow-dagger-points, waters rushing in newly-liberated frenzy downwards, down in waterfalls and cascades and threads, down into the wide, shallow bed of the valley."

The music of his repetition is like Saul's lamentation in the Old Testament: "O my son Absalom, my son, my son Absalom! would God I had died for thee, O Absalom, my son, my son!"

Underlying such effective idiosyncrasy in literary style were Lawrence's natural gifts (when he was not clouded by ideology) of clarity, ease, and force. He would say flatly of a schoolteacher: "She could keep order and inflict knowledge on a class with remarkable efficiency." He would say: "Why is a woman lovely, if ever, in her twenties? It is the time when sex rises softly to her face, as a rose to the top of a rose-bush." He would say: "The sea seemed to heave like the serpent of chaos that has lived forever," or he would find it "this rippling rich fire." His speech would be as true about a person as about an element. In his short story, *The Last Laugh,* he unmistakably describes his friend Dorothy Brett: "Her odd, bright-eyed, deaf nymph's face lifted with blank listening." Ivor Brown has remarked that Lawrence was "able to see things with incomparable freshness, he could write about them as though they had never happened before."

He is right; and Lawrence especially felt this freshness when writing about the natural earth. As Tindall has said, "he loved the earth as he hated the world," and yet the observation should have acknowledged Lawrence's haunting hope that in simple people, in peasants, some-where, the world must be good. In *Sea and Sardinia* he images peasant nature, in contrast to his own sophistication, when he describes the Sardinian mountain Gennargento: "How different it is from Etna, that lonely, self-conscious wonder of Sicily! This is much more human and knowable, with a deep breast and massive limbs, a powerful mountain-body. It is like the peasants." But the natural earth was always his final refuge—even from peasants. The heart of an English poet would have been close to the heart of a Spanish poet if Lawrence could have heard Lorca say: "The life of an apple from the time when it is a delicate flower to the moment when, golden russet, it drops from the tree into the grass is as mysterious and as great as the per-petual rhythm of the tides. And a poet," continues Lorca, "must know this." Acknowledging "hints" from Fraser's *Golden Bough* and from Freud and Frobenius, Lawrence says in *Fantasia of the Unconscious:* "I only remember hints—and I proceed by intuition." *Reflections on the Death of a Porcupine* contains this "hint": "In the great ages man had vital relation . . . with the cow, the lion, the bull, the cat, the eagle, the beetle, the serpent. And beyond these, with narcissus and anemone, mistletoe and oak-tree."

Only once or twice have I known Lawrence's sense of humor to turn full play on a member of the animal kingdom. He did address a mosquito, in one of his poems: "Away with your paean of derision, you winged blood-drop!" And he appears to have been amused by the anecdote about a French poet (related in the short story, *Mr. Noon*) who was seen slowly leading a lobster by a blue ribbon along one of the boulevards of Paris and when asked why, "replied wistfully: 'You see, they don't bark.'" But for the most part he entered the animal kingdom tenderly and felt himself at home there. Lovatt says in *Kangaroo:* "I love nobody and I like nobody, and there's the end of it, as far as I'm concerned." Yet when Lovatt went over to the Zoo and saw the animals, "the tenderness came back." The creator in whose image Lovatt was made had written early in Jessie Chambers' French diary: *"Quant à moi je suis grand animal,"* and he spent his whole life trying to believe it. "Most people," he said in *Glad Ghosts,* "are just another species to me. They might as well be turkeys." He was weasel, adder, bull, but preferably not man. He would touch where he liked in men's haunts but himself be untouchable.

At least he was enough of an animal to describe his chosen kind incomparably. While man and woman made Lawrence squeamish or irascible, the beasts and birds always drew his tenderness. He had written the Murrys in 1915 about lambs: "They stand and cock their heads at one, then skip into the air in little explosions."

In *The Plumed Serpent,* elaborating from this, he describes a new-born burro: "The ink-black ass-foal did not understand standing up. It rocked on its four loose legs and wondered. Then it hobbled a few steps, to smell at some green, growing maize. It smelled and smelled and smelled, as if all the dark aeons were stirring awake in its nostrils. Then it turned, and looked with its bushy-velvet face straight at Kate, and put out a pink tongue at her. She laughed aloud. It stood wondering, dazed. Then it put out its tongue again. She laughed at it. It gave an awkward little skip, which surprised its own self very much. Then it ventured forward again, and all unexpectedly even to itself, exploded into another little skip." In the same novel, he pictures a turkey: "Below her window, in the bricks and fallen rubble of unfinished masonry, a huge white turkey-cock, dim-white, strutted with his brown hens. And sometimes he stretched out his pink wattles and gave vent to fierce, powerful turkey-yelps, like some strong dog yelping; or else he ruffled all his feathers like a great soiled white peony, and chuffed, hissing here and there, raging the metal of his plumage."

In *Sea and Sardinia* there had been "three delicate, beautiful merino sheep which stared at us with their prominent gold-curious eyes." *Etruscan Places* tells of his visiting Tarquinian tombs where he sees, even in paintings, "two spotted lionesses swing their bell-like udders" and "flights of birds flying through the haze, with the draught of life still in their wings." Only Ralph Hodgson, in modern English, can write like this of the animal world, as in his great poems, "Eve" and "The Bull."

Then comes Lawrence's direct comparison of animal with animal, and it works: "little black dolphins that run about like little black pigs"; attribution of human quality to birds: "on the fence the hawks sat motionless, like dark fists clenched under heaven, ignoring man and his ways"; and the strange, apparently unrelated imagery of sky and field and animal: "Siegmund sat watching the last morning blowing in across the mown darkness, till the whole field of the world was exposed, till the moon was like a dead mouse which floats on water."

Lawrence liked seeing people in the shapes and with the attributes of animals. It began with "the snake-frequenting Eve." Maurice Magnus was "a sparrow painted to resemble a tom-tit." Or again of Magnus, "he stuck his front out tubbily, like a bird, and his legs seemed to perch behind him, as a bird's do." In the short story, *Mother and Daughter,* a visitor was "fat, and he sat, with short thighs, like a toad, as if seated for a toad's eternity"; in *The Lovely Lady,* "her aunt, once a definite thrust of condemnation had penetrated her beautiful armour, had just collapsed squirming inside her shell," and in the same story, "He was a marvellous lover, soft as a flower yet piercing as a humming-bird"; in *The Lost Girl,* "Madame Rochard's pallid, waxy countenance, in which her black eyes were like twin swift extraneous creatures: oddly like two little bright dark animals in the snow." Then he has Count Dionys, in his short story *The Ladybird,* tell Lady Daphne: "You are a wild-cat with open eyes, half-dreaming on a bough, in a lonely place. . . . The wild-cat has wonderful green eyes that she closes with memory like a screen." Best of all, he describes Lady Lathkill in *Glad Ghosts,* beginning with comparison to a bird: "She murmured something to me, staring at me fixedly for a long time, but as a bird does, with shrewd, cold, far-distant sight. As a hawk, perhaps, looks shrewdly far down, in his search." After this he uses again what had been a tentative image for describing Madame Rochard and applies it to Lady Lathkill, one of his outstanding portraits of a person in animal terms. We trace it at intervals, with cumulative effect: "Lady Lathkill . . . looking half round after us with her ferret's blue eyes . . . under the crest of icily white hair. . . . The dowager peered across at me occasionally, like a white ermine out of the snow. . . . Lady Lathkill's voice [came] across at me, as if a white ermine had barked. . . . Lady Lathkill ate in silence, like an ermine in the snow, feeding on his prey. . . . Lady Lathkill . . . had stolen the authority that goes with the hostess, and she hung on to it grimly, like a white ermine sucking a rabbit."

Often he saw physical aspects of people in earthy terms as when Daphne, looking at Dionys, sees "the flesh through his beard, as water through reeds," or in terms of flowers, as when Dionys sees Daphne as "a flower behind a rock, near an icy water." In *Etruscan Places* he says of a peasant whom he sees, "His face is a faun face, not deadened by morals," but remarks, "They can't survive, the faun-faced men, with their pure outlines and their strange non-moral calm. Only the deflowered faces survive." And he speaks of the Etruscan cities "vanished as completely as flowers."

Human flesh and its doings, when he did not see them in animal or earthy terms, either frightened or frayed his nerves and drove him back for comfort to the actual birds, beasts, and flowers. His Alvina in *The Lost Girl* says: "Whatever life may be, and whatever horror men have made of it, the world is a lovely place, a magic place, something to marvel over." And he marvels over its blossoming: "the tiny irises, only one finger tall, growing in dry places, frail as crocuses, and much tinier, and blue, blue as the eye of the morning heaven, which was a morning earlier, more pristine than ours." In the same book, telling of crocuses, his imagery connects, as it often does, flower and animal: "She came again to them in the morning, when the sky was gray, and they were closed, sharp clubs, wonderfully fragile on their stems of sap, among leaves and old grass and wild periwinkle. They had wonderful dark stripes running up their cheeks, the crocuses, like the clear proud stripes on a badger's face, or on some proud cat." Then again he pictures birds in terms of flowers: "the yellow canaries like faded daffodils." He even dignifies the sea with his animal touch: "Dark-blue water, ruffled like mole-fur, and flicked all over with froth as with bits of feather-fluff," when to Longfellow, "fleecy waves looked soft as carded wool." This latter imagery made the sea stand still, whereas Lawrence's made it move. *Etruscan Places* contains one most memorable image of men and the ocean, in terms again of the flower world: ". . . in Homeric days a restlessness seems to have possessed the Mediterranean basin, and ancient races began shaking ships like seeds over the sea."

Stephen Spender has said of Lawrence, in his commentary, *The Life of Literature,* which appeared in the *Partisan Review:* "He does not want to make nature into a human spiritual possession, a philosophy, a consolation, as Wordsworth does, nor into a field of symbols which present man with opportunities of identifying his own mental states with them, as the symbolists do." Norman Douglas agrees: "He touched upon the common things of earth with tenderness and grace, like some butterfly poised over a flower. . . . No intervening medium, no mirage, hovered between Lawrence and what his eyes beheld. These things lay before him clear-cut, in their primordial candour, devoid of any veil of suggestion or association." On the other hand Richard Aldington attributes to Lawrence "a power of using countries and landscapes and animals to interpret the human mind and its moods and tragedies," and has edited a volume called *The Spirit of Place* in which he salvages, from the ideological murk blocking many Lawrence pages in novels and short stories, a cherishable group of sections dealing with the "magic place," the natural world. And here Lawrence survives his theories, helplessly the artist. He had to survive, he could not prevent himself from being the artist. Now and again, among his sermons, his nature had to sing. And his hymns are not those reflections of churchly upbringing which Mrs. Carswell has noticed in the formal chants of *The Plumed Serpent.* His hymns are the easy, natural, inevitable responses which he could not help giving to the natural world when church was over; and even during service his eye and heart could not keep from wandering through door or window. A crumb from the wafer in his ritual of deity or sex would fall to the altar floor—for a Holy Ghost of a mouse. As Count Dionys, he says in *The Ladybird:* " 'A white sea-hawk makes a nest on a high stone, and sometimes looks out with her white head over the edge of the rocks. It is not only a world of men, Lady Daphne.' 'Not by any means,' said she. 'Else it were a sorry place,' " he concludes.

His verse volume and its title, *Birds, Beasts and Flowers,* are obvious evidence that he was aware of his natural lyrical leaning toward the physical earth and its inarticulate breeds. But when he wrote verse, he stiffened.

A great deal of his verse is, to my ear, a collection of notes which resolved elsewhere into better music as prose, verse not being the born beat of his heart, as it was of Whitman's or Hodgson's. He has set down carefully, mathematically—in one of his letters, I think—the way his ear and voice heard and spoke prosody; but for me his calculations seldom resulted in a natural song or chanting—there was seldom the rounding flow of the chords of Whitman, which he took for a model but could not match. Said Whitman:

> Do I contradict myself?
> Very well then I contradict myself,
> (I am large, I contain multitudes.)

Lawrence, who later pitied Jesus because he who had "never truly embraced even one" yet "would embrace multitudes," snaps in his own turn:

> You tell me I am wrong.
> Who are you, who is anybody to tell me I am wrong?
> I am not wrong.

Here, aloud, from two poems, are the accents of calm on the one hand and of petulance on the other—the flow and ebb of a wave and a faucet sputter. The difference is not only in the content but in the sound. Music happens constantly in Lawrence's prose but less often in his verse. When he turns to verse he continually becomes self-conscious, forsakes native cadence and substitutes mannered artifice. He lames the rhythm, to make it more noticeable; he ends a line or a stanza with an ugly or weak word, in order not to sound obvious. The result is that in verse he speaks less naturally, less rhythmically, and less well than in prose. While his verse is rigid with prose, his prose is firm with poetry. Too often when he composes verse, he decomposes prose. I doubt if in prose he was ever very conscious of his medium. Here is an instance where he uses the same material in both forms of writing. In his poem, "The Greeks Are Coming," from the volume *Last Poems,*

> . . . an ocean liner, going east, like a small beetle
>   walking the edge
> is leaving a long thread of dark smoke
> like a bad smell.

Earlier, in the prose of *Kangaroo,* he had seen "on the sea's horizon . . . a steamer like a beetle walking slowly along." He had written to Edward Marsh, as early as 1913: "I think more of a bird with broad wings flying and lapsing through the air, than anything, when I think of metre." Why then, did not his own ear feel the difference between the two passages about the beetle? The passage he presents as meter walks like a hurt dog, whereas in the prose a bird with broad wings is flying.

Leonora Speyer has called to my notice a rhymed poem of Lawrence's, "Piano," which, not much liking his use of rhyme, I had overlooked:

> Softly, in the dusk, a woman is singing to me;
> Taking me back down the vista of years, till I see
> A child sitting under the piano, in the boom of the tingling
>   strings
> And pressing the small, poised feet of a mother who smiles as
>   she sings.
>
> In spite of myself, the insidious mastery of song
> Betrays me back, till the heart of me weeps to belong
> To the old Sunday evenings at home, with winter outside
> And hymns in the cosy parlour, the tinkling piano our guide.
>
> So now it is vain for the singer to burst into clamour
> With the great black piano appassionato. The glamour
> Of childish days is upon me, my manhood is cast
> Down in the flood of remembrance, I weep like a child for
>   the past.

With Mrs. Speyer and others I find these lines moving; but, studying them, I am convinced that their poignant human content is what moves one and that the same memory and emotion, if he had set them down in prose, when they were flooding him, would, in his more natural medium, have contained even more of his heart's rhythm.

He did write early a few dialect poems in ballad form, like "The Collier's Wife," which carried through effectively; and, at the end, his written and rewritten "Ship of Death" has, especially in its transcript form, a grave, fine beauty. It is interesting to note, in *Etruscan Places,* his surmise at Cerveteri that alongside the buried Lucumo in one of the tombs, among "sacred treasures of the dead," was laid "the little bronze ship of death that should bear him over to the other world." This image stayed with him to his final days when he wrought and rewrought the poem. His "Invocation to the Moon" has beauty too —peculiar, haunting beauty—and so have other poems, especially if

one is lucky enough to hear them spoken in the rich, tender, understanding modulations of Frieda's voice—the moon itself with shadows
crossing it.

But let us look at "Glory of Darkness," which I prefer to its later
version, the much admired "Bavarian Gentians":

> . . . .
> it is dark
> and the door is open
> to the depths
>
> It is so blue, it is so dark
> and the dark doorway
> and the way is open
> to Hades.
>
> Oh, I know.
> Persephone has just gone back
> down the thickening thickening gloom
> of dark-blue gentians to Pluto
> to her bridegroom in the dark
> and all the dead
> and all the dark great ones of the underworld
> down there, down there
> down the blue depths of mountain gentian flowers
> cold cold
> down the dark blue path
>
> What a dark-blue gloom
> of gentians here in the sunny room!

And now let us compare the poem with a passage of prose in *The
Man Who Died,* with another symbolic flower ritual: "The lotus, as
you know, will not answer to all the bright heat of the sun. But she
curves her dark, hidden head in the depths, and stirs not. Till, in the
night, one of these rare, invisible suns that have been killed and shine
no more, rises among the stars in unseen purple, and like the violet,
sends its rare, purple rays out into the night. To these the lotus stirs
as to a caress, and rises upwards through the flood, and lifts up her
bent head, and opens with an expansion such as no other flower
knows, and spreads her sharp rays of bliss, and offers her soft gold

depths such as no other flower possesses, to the penetration of the flooding violet-dark sun that has died and risen and makes no show."

Yes, Lawrence was a poet—in his own medium.

He would have shrugged those lean shoulders of his, lifted those querulous brows and then perhaps sunk the shielding beard a moment, if I had known enough to say to him in the days when I knew him, as I should be moved to say now: You will live among men, Lorenzo, because you have been given an extraordinary voice. Plenty of us know plenty of people who are convinced that plenty of animals are preferable to plenty of people. Animals have no minds. Animals have instincts, intuition. Animals have all the sex in the world, and they do not have to answer for it to God or society. Their eyes are clear. Their fur is beautiful. There is no such beauty in mankind and no such heavenly dumbness. But, even though you are a man, Lorenzo, there is a reed beside you for celebrating Eden, your colony, and its animals, even Adam and Eve. Pluck it, take it up, notch it with your teeth, breathe into it, make music, because for love of Eden, of the natural world, for use of the voice of the reed grown in that world, you were created, even with occasional crying need of mate or of comrade.

"Lawrence is a good writer," says Stephen Spender in his commentary, *The Life of Literature,* "but the enormous debt of gratitude which a whole generation owes him because he has helped them to make for themselves a more hopeful attitude towards life, does not make him a better writer than those great talents which have devoted their lives to producing an effect of profound spiritual and physical discouragement. One cannot complain that the greatest talents are those which are most bound up with the values of a civilization which is falling to pieces."

Standing by Lawrence, I incline to caution Spender against coming under the spell of an apparently dawnless dusk and therefore exaggerating the music in the voice of Cassandra and passing by poor Pan.

Lawrence wrote Mrs. Carswell in 1917: "One can only gather the single flower of one's own intrinsic happiness, apart and separate. It is the only faithful fulfillment."

He was partially right.

Even at dusk a cock can crow, though the barnyard may not like it.

45. Letters

NARRATION of my personal touch with the Lawrences has given way, in the preceding chapters, to my extended reflections concerning the writer after we unintentionally separated in 1924.

In late 1925 my volume, *Caravan,* was published and at once I sent Lawrence a copy. This was the first time he had seen the longer poem about him on which I had been working at Chapala and later:

D. H. Lawrence

I

Prowling in a corridor,
Coming upon a mirror,
You lay back your torn ear,
You arch your bony spine,
You spit at your own image;
And the image follows, swifter than a sunflower,
Your native superiority.

And when the housekeeper strokes your torn ear,
And thinks benignly of the alley and the night and you,
You purr awhile in the very lap you loathe
And, twenty-one inches superior to that foul image,
You forget to move your claws
And slowly, luxuriously, fall asleep.

II

Now and then your mute-footed being leaves you;
Your beard lies back again where it belongs

And your blue eyes relax in their slits—
And then wilderness again,
A hollow glare in the eyeball!

Do you see that the moon is on its back for you?
And has turned up the white fur of its belly
And put out a silver-haired paw?

III

After wondering a long time, I know now
That you are no man at all.

The whiteness of your flanks and loins and belly and thin
  neck
Frightens you, affronts you,
A whiteness to be sloughed off, to be left behind you like ashes,
Forgotten by the new body, by the new mind,
By the new conforming surfaces.

Women have chosen you, in your white arms.
But what have you to do with women?
Only your seeming is theirs and the falsehood of your skin.
You would lengthen your finger-nails and your teeth
To mangle these women, these people;
You would drop them behind you with your cast-off skin;
You would wonder at the glaze of their eyes;
And your new pelt would contract and would tremble down
  your spine
Before it settled into place;
And you would steal away, solitary,
To try in the wind the vibrancies of a new voice.

Only your reddish hair is you
And those narrowing eyes,
Eyes hostile to the flesh of people and to all their motions,
Eyes penetrating their thoughts to the old marrow of the beast,
Eyes wanting a mate and the starlight,
A mate to be snarled at and covered
And stars to be known and not named.

Some day, if you are left alone
Beyond the roads, in a tough tangle of wilderness,

You will be held and torn and known to your own innermost
    marrow,
Will be stripped of the skin that cumbers you,
Given over from the bondage of manhood,
And will be found at last,
With the blood of marriage in your teeth.

  But if you are never left alone,
Are constrained in a country of houses,
You will always be smouldering against men;
And, after yielding slowly
The nine lives of a domestic cat,
You will be worshipped by the Egyptians.

IV

The world is full again of centaurs and sphynxes;
But it is the horse-head now and the lion-head
On the bodies of men who are tired of being men
And of women who are tired of being women.
It is these who turn with you and follow you
To the hillsides that prick their flanks,
To the jungles that tear at their breasts;
It is these who forget with you
That the instep is not a galloping hoof,
That the finger-nail can not enter and climb the bark of a tree
Nor tear deep shreds
To be fed with,
And that the night can not last forever as a lordly dream
But must let in, finally, pointed barbs of light
To prick this hinge of the neck
Between what you are and what you would be,
Whether you are a man wishing to be an animal
Or an animal wishing to be a man.

When these lines were written I had not yet found in *The Plumed
Serpent* Lawrence's own description of himself, through the person
of Kate: "Suddenly she saw herself as men often saw her: the great
cat, with its spasms of voluptuousness and its lifelong lustful enjoyment of its own isolated, isolated individuality."
From The Villa Bernarda at Spotorno, early in 1926, arrived his

response to the book: "*Caravan* came today, and I have read it already, and I like it very much. Surely you don't think me an enemy of life? *My single constancy is love of life!*" He was quoting from one of the poems in my book and went on: "Caro, caro, is it *quite* true? But it's the only thing to be constant to, I'm with you entirely there; and against the old. But don't you go out and get old just now. Do you see me merely as a cat? Sometimes a cat, anyhow. I like these the best of your poems, that I know. They are more really you. Even serving happiness is no joke! I hope you won't mind the little sketch of you in *The Plumed Serpent*. I don't think it's unsympathetic—it only dislikes your spurious sort of happiness—the spurious side of it. Happiness is a subtle and aristocratic thing, and you mixed it up with the mob a bit. Believe me, I'm not the enemy of your happiness: only of the false money with which you sometimes sought to buy happiness. You must know what I mean: these poems are very sincere and really deep in life, so you do know. I hope, one day, when I've shed my fur and claws, and you've acknowledged your own fur and claws, we may be two men, and two friends truly. I don't know if I shall come back to America this year: it's a strain. I might go to Russia. Would you like to go with me? I've even learned my Russian A.B.C. Frieda sends her greetings—hope everything goes well with you."

I still hoped that the Lawrences would be returning to New Mexico. In any event Lorenzo would have been too ill for a Russian trip. This impulse of his to visit still another country seems to me now to have sprung from his obsessive hope that in some land on earth he might find the worthy human species he was looking for. I had realized by this time that though he was always "walking away from something," he was also always walking toward something. Dostoyevsky had insistently proclaimed superior natural worth in the Russian peasant; and I believe that the later novelist was drawn to Russia in hopes of seeing there what the earlier had seen. It might have been the last Lawrencian quest. And yet, almost in the same breath with laudation, the Russian novelist acknowledged his peasant to be a cruel, disappointing lout. Lawrence may have more than suspected by now that mankind is pretty much the same, the world over. His report on the Slavs might have been his best book; but he never went to Russia.

His second report on the Mexicans, after his second and third trips below the border, appeared in 1927, entitled *Mornings in Mexico*. At the risk of repeating myself, I append my contemporary and continu-

ing judgment of it, a review contributed to *The New Republic* in
October of that year:

"A person with a pen," he calls himself in the first of these eight
essays. D. H. Lawrence is always a "person." Whatever he may be
saying comes from the mind or the middle of an acutely sensitive
individual; and it's a pity that he lets his pen record too many of
his sensibilities, not distinguishing apparently between the trivial
and the significant, between the pettily personal and the deeply·per-
sonal emotions. His pen is so subject to his exaggerated moods, that
it can often make a pin-prick read like a lightning-bolt. In this
book, happily enough, person and pen are in better proportioned
accord than usual. To anyone who has read *The Plumed Serpent,*
with its incomparably fine descriptions of Mexican places and people . . . it is a disappointment to come upon them again seen, in
the first three essays of this book, with a tired squint and infirmly
told about. Even the dog and the parrot in the first essay have no
sharpness of life. You cannot hear them stir and breathe as you have
heard Lawrence's other birds and beasts. . . . In fact the first essay
is dispiriting to a reader who expects of Lawrence miraculously
intuitive writing about animals or else, through his attention to
them, some arresting revelation of himself. When Lawrence writes
of people, you remember none of them, but only Lawrence pared
into contradictory parts. He is forever fighting with himself or pat-
ting himself on the back in the guise of this man or that woman
in his books. If it be an objective group, in motion of some sort,
he will describe and narrate in vivider, closer-fitting terms than
those of any other living writer: but as soon as the impersonal becomes personal he either wrangles his wit into a temper or mud-
dles his ganglion into pseudomystical ecstasy. If only the unspoilt
artist in him might oftener discipline the spoilt child! Heretofore
he has at times been able to exorcize his disturbed spirit into the
spirit of some animal and be at peace awhile as a creature. Never
heretofore has he been able to enter intuitively into other persons
without injecting his own fret. At last, in this book, he has entered
without fear or favor into the beings of North American Indians.
His title is pardonably misleading. Only the first weaker half of
his book deals with Old Mexico. And in Old Mexico Lawrence is
for some reason never outside his fretful self. He is so intensely

personal: he is by turns timorous, querulous, resentful, wistful, superstitious. In New Mexico, on the contrary, the peak of the volcano has been snow-cooled. He is a different mountain. He says of Pueblo Indians, as they sing about a bear-hunt: "The man coming home from the bear-hunt is any man, all men, the bear is any bear, every bear, all bear. There is no individual, isolated experience. It is the hunting, tired, triumphant demon of mankind which has won against the squint-eyed demon of all bears. The experience is generic, non-individual. It is an experience of the human bloodstream, not of the mind or spirit. Hence the subtle, incessant, insistent rhythm of the drum, which is pulsated like the heart, and soulless, and unescapable. Hence the strange blind unanimity of the Indian men's voices. The experience is one experience, tribal, of the blood-stream." Later, to be sure, telling of the Hopi snake-dance and the Indians' "animistic religion," he thinks that "there is no oneness, no sympathetic identifying oneself with the rest. The law of isolation is heavy on every creature." However, Lawrence more nearly escapes the heaviness of the law of isolation, more nearly identifies himself with these Indians of the Southwest, than he has been able to identify himself with persons of any other race. He is "any Pueblo, all Pueblos," and the result is, as always when his feeling for actual life-happenings overcomes his intellectual insistences, he is a master describer, describes Indian ceremonies with a greater degree of essential truth than has been done by any other writer I know, whether or not that writer may have been technically more accurate or better informed. *The Dance of the Sprouting Corn* is one of Lawrence's masterpieces: which means that in its kind no one can better it.

I forget whether or not Lawrence ever saw the notice. It would have mattered little to him as a published review, though he might have been interested in it as the judgment of a friend. I have mentioned earlier my envy of his indifference to literary praise or dispraise, an indifference which used to seem to me sometimes his only calm. Bennett Cerf recounts an amusing instance of it reported to him by Edith Sitwell. She had told Lawrence that she thought his poetry "soft, woolly and hot like a Jaeger sweater," and says, "I thought Lawrence would have a fit but he didn't. The Jaegers, however, did. They informed me indignantly that their sweaters were indeed soft and woolly, but never hot, due to their 'special system of slow conductivity.' "

In any event, I am sure that, remembering our Chapala debate as to "journals of opinion," Lawrence would have grinned over the fact that four years after our discussion at Chapala of the Japanese play I was then reviewing for a journal of opinion, I was still contributing reviews to *The New Republic.*

Idella's *Palms* was still going too. She had married and had moved her magazine from California to the state of Washington. Lawrence wrote her on November 11, 1927, from Florence: "Your letter today—imagine you married and moved far off to Aberdeen, Wash! And will *Palms* grow in such a northern climate, to produce real crops of nuts? I've not written a poem hardly, these last three years and more—not a jingle in me. Instead I paint pictures, here—which seems the right thing to do, in Tuscany of the painters. And I'll see if I can't warble some little lay for *Palms.* We may come to America in the spring—though whether we'd ever reach your far edge, I don't know. . . . How is your father? Is he still safe and sound in Guadalajara? What a long time it seems since Chapala!" A month later, December 11, he continued: "I had your letter two days ago—of course it found me in bed, and feeling limp. If I can rouse up during this week I'll do you a little article and get it off: but don't count on me, for anything more uninspired and uninspiring than myself just now I wouldn't want you to see. If the Lord sends me a flicker, I'll send you one. It's the best I can promise."

At last, at the end of 1927, I screwed up my courage to give Lawrence a careful little sermon about *The Plumed Serpent:* the only one of my letters to him of which I have a copy. Why the communication was quite so belated I do not know. Perhaps I had hesitated to be presumptuous but finally realized that, after all, I was his elder by four whole years and therefore, had a right to speak. All I had said to him previously was that I did not mind his delineation of me as Owen, although I think I did mind. After all, he had made Owen a bit of a prig or a booby. And so off to Italy went my epistolary sermon: "Not wishing to dictate what I had to say about *The Plumed Serpent,* I waited. And now's a chance on this leisurely motor trip to California. You must know, without my saying so, that I think the first half of it a consummate piece of noticing and writing. You are much better about Mexico there than you are in *Mornings.* But, after that, I'm ready to quarrel with you. It's a fundamental quarrel. You are forever hunting out in mankind some superior being (sometimes yourself) and attributing to him mystical or semi-mystical qualities of godly leadership. In this way you try to justify man's ways to God, or to yourself. There is always a physical tinge in it—an animal admiration—and often, arising out of that, a blur of spiritual admiration. . . . You carry over, from Egypt or from England, a need of religion: or of authority. Touching on it, you become vague and feminine. Fair enough. . . . Distrusting your gesture toward religion, I see well how you must detest mine. For years, I have innerly believed that no man, not even the authoritative or prophetic leader, has any importance at all except as he foresees and furthers the ultimate amalgamation of all life into one total, completed consciousness which will somehow fulfill these imperfect and vain fragments of the totality, these individualities which we jealously, restrict when, for right and happy growth, we should be enlarging them toward that final merged realization of the only self. Your way of thought for us seems to me to make man not more but less; and I don't doubt that my religious groping has the same effect on you.

"Apart from this fundamental difference between us (a difference of similarity), I resented, with perhaps too personal or perhaps sufficiently reasonable irritation, the intrusion into your book of an outside influence—a presence of weakness, after your own presence had been strong. . . .

"You emerged and shone your clear self in the narratives about destroying the Roman images and that unforgettable fight at the hacienda; but the rest of your finish sounded like Mabel. I could feel her suave presence imposing Orage, or something of the sort, on the gullible. It wasn't you. She missed your person, old boy; but she caught your book—or part of it. Now flay me!"

With this letter I had sent him a sheaf of my verse issued in a series called *The Pamphlet Poets* and with it a few Chapala poems, one of the latter, to which he refers in his acknowledgment, called "Calendar":

> Why should I know or care what month it is?
> An Aztec calendar was made long since.
> What year was it? What century? What matter?
> A piece of stone became symmetrical.

If I watch the time, some of my friends will die,
If I watch the time, I shall surely die myself.
Let me, then, gather all my friends about me
And carve an endless moment out of stone.

From Switzerland, he answered me on January 31, 1928. My initial sorry feeling, when I had finished reading his reply, was that he was offended. But it was a temperate reply:

"Your letter, and the poems came today—and I haven't read the 'Pamphlet' ones yet, only the little Chapalan slip, which I think have poignancy, and I like them. It's a fact, it doesn't matter what year it is. Time is where one is and with whom. And I do think it's about now when one should be back in New Mexico under the turquoise.

"But I've had a paltry time, being ill—since last June. I never got right—cough, bronchials very bad. So we came up here to see if it would do me good—the altitude—only about 3500, but fairly high for Europe—and the snow and the sun. We've been here about ten days, and I'm no worse, anyhow. But I do wish I could get really better. I'm only half myself. That's why I never sent you *David:* I felt so limp and dragged. But I'm getting a copy now and will write in it and send it.

"I feel about as you do about Europe. It isn't really there. I'd rather be at the ranch. But I've got to be well enough to take that journey. And Frieda doesn't much want to come: Brett and Mabel in her way: it's a weariness, and I wish I could get a sort of lift out, else I'm stuck. But I'll really see if we can't come, end of April: and yours was the first New Mexican hospitality, so I should like to come to you for a day or two. After all, as men we get on right enough. I don't care a bit what you say of me—no doubt it's all true. But it's not really saying that matters, it's some sort of lingering feeling, as one likes the blue of turquoise. For the rest, I don't give a damn. Even if someone gave me a knock on the head with a lump of turquoise, I'd still like the blueness of the stone.

"When will you really get your Chinese book out? Probably I shall like the Chapalesque better—but we'll see. I've been collecting my poems together—Secker wants to do a Collected Poems of me. But what a job! I feel like an autumn morning, a perfect maze of gossamer of rhythms and rhymes and loose lines floating in the air. I did a novel too, which perhaps I'll publish privately in Florence—and then castrate for the public. I have most obviously left the balls in—and not even circumcised.

"I don't know how long we'll stay here—perhaps till March—then go back to the Villa Mirenda, and clear up there. I'm giving it up, definitely. Enough of Italy this spell. Hope we'll get out to New Mex. So *au revoir.*"

I should have known better than to think Lawrence offended by my homily. Six weeks later, on March 13, 1928, he wrote again, from Florence. He had thought me over, and I was touched by his gentle conclusion, by the generous candor with which he modified his stand in our long debate over the divine right of the few. Although Tindall believes, from *Apocalypse,* the final work, that Lawrence "found comfort again in thoughts of leadership, ecclesiastical polity, and power," I incline to believe that the following paragraphs which he wrote me held good for him, at least that he tried to make himself think they did:

"I sniffed the red herring in your last letter a long time: then at last decided it's a live sprat. I mean about *The Plumed Serpent* and the 'hero.' On the whole, I think you're right. The hero is obsolete, and the leader of men is a back number. After all, at the back of the hero is the militant ideal: and the militant ideal, or the ideal militant seems to me also a cold egg. We're sort of sick of all forms of militarism and militantism, and *Miles* is a name no more, for a man. On the whole I agree with you, the leader-cum-follower relationship is a bore. And the new relationship will be some sort of tenderness, sensitive, between men and men and men and women, and not the one up one down, lead I follow, *ich dien* sort of business. So you see I'm becoming a lamb at last, and you'll even find it hard to take umbrage at me. Do you think?

"But still, *in a way,* one has to fight. But not in the O Glory! sort of way. I feel one still has to fight for the phallic reality, as against the non-phallic cerebration unrealities. I suppose the phallic consciousness is part of the whole consciousness which is your aim. To me it's a vital part.

"So I wrote my novel, which I want to call *John Thomas and Lady Jane.* But that I have to submerge into a subtitle and call it *Lady Chatterley's Lover.* But I am printing here in Florence an unexpurgated edition of this tender and phallic novel, far too good for the public. The expurgated will come in the autumn. But this, the full fine flower with pistil and stamens standing, I hope to have ready by May 15th, 1000 copies, of which 500 for America, at ten dollars a copy. I shall send you a few little order-forms and *do* please send a few out for me, to the right people. You can reach a lot of the right sort of people in the Universities. I shall mail direct from Florence, as soon as the book is ready: a good book. And why should the red flower have its pistil nipped out, before it is allowed to appear? So I shall trust you in this.

"We are in this house till May 6th, then I don't know where. I want to come to New Mexico—perhaps even earn a little money this way to come with. Tante belle cose!"

Mexico, New Mexico, still drew him.

46. Illness

IN 1926 I had published a play called *Cake,* some aspects of which were said to be a satire on Mabel Lujan. The slant was sportive but not, I thought, malicious and, since I had visited several times at her house in Taos, I inscribed the copy I sent her: "Cast your bread upon Witter and it shall return to you as Cake." I have heard that she was not amused. Why the play was not sent at the same time to the Lawrences I do not know; but apparently a copy did not reach them until two years later. From the Villa Mirenda in Florence Lawrence acknowledged it, April 13, 1928: "I got *Cake* and read it with a good deal of amusement. It is often very witty, and in parts really funny. It's not particularly 'Mabel'—rather a type than a specific person—so she needn't 'get her hair off' about it. Its fault is perhaps in scattering the scenes over the earth, so destroying some of the unity, maybe. But it remains very amusing—and at last just spiteful, which of course tickles me. But you notice the chief mischief of Mabel in your letter—her effect on the ——s. I don't mind her passion for cake—it's her passion for breaking other people's eggs and making a mess instead of an omelette, which is really dangerous. She seems to hate anybody to care for anybody—even for herself—and if anybody does care for anybody, she must upset it—even if she falls herself out of the applecart. Do write a play about that—the helpless way a woman *must* upset any applecart that's got two apples in it: just for the fun.

"My health's a good bit better—and if I can sell my novel, and have some money, I want to start off sailing round the world with Frieda in the autumn—there's a grand cheap way, by the Messageries Maritimes—and land in San Francisco—and come on. And then really I think—Frieda certainly thinks—it would be better to stay in Santa Fe for some time till we could go to the ranch. It would be fun. And perhaps one could have friends among one instead of *ces femmes.* It would be nice to feel something stable. I begin to feel a bit battered, one way and another. . . .

"You'll help me what you can with my novel, won't you? It seems to be rousing already a lot of gratuitous hostility. Povero me!

"Well, *pazienza!* don't be irritated by me—I'm really more good natured than most people.

"We leave the Mirenda for good at the end of this month. . . . And I'm looking forward to a proper reunion, really.

"I think it's very silly of——and——to be at outs and made mischief by. People who have lived together had best stick together. You can only change for the worse."

A letter from Frieda followed, April 22: "We read *Cake* and it was amusing. . . . When Mabel wrote: 'in a book where I come in, it mentions that I have had 9 lovers'. I wrote back: 'Don't worry, my dear, alas, alas, not one!' She has made a myth and a golden calf of herself and is so strong that dancing round that golden calf, she can persuade others to do so as well—but I like *much* about her and you ought to try her from a new angle—try again and don't be taken in and you'll like her. Lawrence is not well enough yet to risk the journey. Why aren't you a real nice Hal and come and see us here? Bring us some of your hospitable, generous spirit and a breath of New Mexico—it would do us both good in our souls. We have had a thin time and the worst, but it was no joke trying to keep his body and soul together— you might enjoy Europe for a little while—you know that I always think of you as a *real* friend. I didn't tell Lawrence I wrote this letter but I know he would *like* to see you."

Later that same month Frieda wrote again, from Baden-Baden: "Your letter to L came just as I was reading the 'Bullfight of the Plumed Serpent' in French, a simple translation. It took me back so vividly. You are right the end is muffed, the religious part isn't religious, but desiccated swelled head—I am glad you think of us (I include myself) with fondness. Some of L's horridness to you was the green-eyed monster and sickness, he is very frail, but much less nervy and cantacarous! [*sic*] Indeed I'm scared of the 'heavenly Twins' Brett and Mabel in Taos. If I come it will be to ignore them, to have done with them—Brett's last letter to L that I was responsible for his sickness!! So *vile,* but I suppose mosquitos must bite and bitches bark! Mabel is I, I, I spreading herself on the face of the earth in houses and self. But you exaggerate her importance. The real living place, where a woman can help to make new things live and flourish does not know her, there she doesn't exist. And one does so *long* for a little delicate warmth and good will and understanding, I am just unspeakably sick of this eternal spite and assertion and intellectual bunk. We have been in Switzerland, L is better, but *always* it's scaring, his health. How I would love to stay in your house and get the breakfast! And you have made it bigger! I always wear a white chain you gave me and the other day it fell down the W.C. in Diablerets but after being sad about it I got it *back,* wasn't that a good omen! So all good things to you." And then a little later, on Easter Monday, with a reference to my poem, "D. H. Lawrence": "You know it hurt me when you called me the 'housekeeper' in that poem, but alas you were right; but I am not by nature the 'housekeeper' and 'nous avons changé tout cela!' . . . Why do you never come? You know there is a cousinship between us!! . . . It's the most adorable Tuscan spring and something in me just insists on being blissfully happy! My daughter Barbara is here. I wish I could make her as happy as myself, but then she is so young! Lawrence paints and has written a novel! . . . We'll come to Santa Fe some day again! But you pay us a visit!—and we would wander a bit once more!"

Letters through the following months were either scarce or have disappeared. My hope of joining the Lawrences was not realized that year nor the next. In 1929 the obstacle was my own ill health, and Frieda wrote from the Hotel Beau Rivage in Vence: "Well, it's sad to know you aren't really fit, but we were glad of your letter. Lawrence is much better, we're by the sea in a comfortable hotel—we need comfort too, what with the great fuss of Lady C., it would take several days to tell you, and some 'Pansies' Lawrence has written, pansies indeed, they are very revolutionary and will mean trouble again!! What with his health and all this, it's a fierce life—still we live quietly enough day by day. There is the sun to shine on you and flowers on your path and there is a fine bird but it's rather like a wild chicken, and there's a moon in one of your poems! . . . Our Taos turtle doves are in New York—Mabel being 'psyched' as Spud calls it. 'Gurjeffing!' Leo Stein, Orage—a boredom infinite and worse!—I hear that Mabel thinks she is the heroine in the Plumed Serpent!! But, the Owen is not *all* of you, Hal. Also there's something else that isn't you. I am flourishing, better looking in my old age, I think, except my hair is no longer an unmixed color. I shall have to dye it. Lawrence is still the Saint Francis. The Huxleys have just been here. . . . Why do you never come over the ocean to see us? Let's have a cocktail!"

Then, in answer to word from me that I should like to dedicate to him my *Indian Earth,* containing the Chapala poems, and that I was attempting a novel, came the last letter I was to receive from Lawrence, and it was an echo of a passage he had written in *The Ladybird* about Lady Daphne and her malady, "It was nothing but frustration and anger which made her ill, and made the doctors fear consumption":

"I meant to answer you long ago," he wrote from France, "but the flesh is very weak. My health is *very* tiresome, and I don't feel like doing a thing: unusual for me. But I do believe the root of all my sickness is a sort of rage. I realize now. Europe gets me into an inward rage, that keeps my bronchials hellish inflamed. I believe I'd get better in no time in New Mexico, because I'm really not weak. But I can't digest my inward spleen in Europe—that's what ails me. And in New Mexico I can. Now I have really come to this conclusion, I shall try all my might to arrange getting back, in the New Year. I wish there weren't all these passport difficulties. And if we can come we should probably try to take some little furnished place in Santa Fe for the first month or so, to get used to the altitude—and also to look round for a winter house near Santa Fe, and just summer at the ranch. That is what *Frieda* wants.

"No, I'm sure I'm flattered if you dedicate your poems to me: but you haven't sent me the poems. And I am all agog to hear of you writing a novel. I hope by now it's done. What a great lark, a novel after all! And I was sorry to hear of you so ill. But illness seems to be one's portion nowadays. I feel I'm a chastened bird—but perhaps I'm not.

"We have got this little house on the sea near Marseille until end of March—then I really wish we could come west. . . . I don't quite know whether I'm *persona grata* in U.S.A. just now—after Lady C. etc. But I don't suppose anybody really cares. It's the emigration question which is most difficult—and so silly. Frieda is prepared to come back: but warily.

"I do really and firmly believe, though, that it's Europe that has made me so ill. One gets so innerly angry with the dull sort of hopelessness and deadness there is over here. Anyhow in New Mexico the sun and the air are alive, let man be what he may. But here they've killed the very sun, the very air. . . .

"Well—I'm really quite an amiable person underneath, even if I'm as catty as you say. But cats are really very easy animals. I feel a rather bedraggled one at present—wish a few people would stroke my fur the right way and make me purr. Perhaps when we come to Santa Fe. So *au revoir.*"

47. Death

"AU revoir," he had written, but I was certain that I should not see
him again. Over the page of his letter, as over the face of a
stricken person, I had felt the cast of dissolution. The spirit
of the phoenix was still there; but, despite his yearnings for return to
New Mexico, his promise of return must have been known in his heart
as a mirage. His body was caught in the Europe he had abjured. I
should not be seeing him.

So I began still again to remember the man. I remembered him that
first night at my house when he split the painted piece of Sicilian cart
and flew into a rage. I remembered him genial at the corner table in
the Monte Carlo; silhouetted slim and active on a pyramid at Teotihuacan; crisping the station platform at Orizaba with his dark heat;
striking at the bullfight with his fist, at Frieda with his forked tongue,
at Leighton with his icy eye, at me through the orphans in Chapala.

I could not remember his clothes, whereas Frieda's were always hung
like solid fleecy clouds around her, almost as though she were carrying
a lamb; but I could remember, under whatever he wore, the bony
white body which I once saw bobbing in the water of the inlet near his
Chapala house. I remembered his kind keen fingers in the yarn of
the serape at the hospital and the little silver tokens he had given me
to string. And the letters afterward, impatient against all deadness:
manly, alert, fired with final fairness and decency, the cold loneness
relenting into friendship. I remembered his going back twice to Mexico,
toward which he had been like a dog hurt without knowing why.
Mexico had punished him; and yet he was a Pipsy drawn back to
Mexico, wondering with hurt eyes. But New Mexico was different.
"Anyhow in New Mexico, the sun and the air are alive, let man be
what he may." The sun and the air were alive still, and perhaps that

341

was enough for him to know, even though he alive could not quite reach them. Perhaps he had done enough for man. Man might now shift for himself.

While I remembered, from our days in Mexico, each trivial petulance, each whale of a whim, each self-importance, each flaming intolerant outbreak, I remembered also the lost-child look, the wistful wandering, the earnest hope, the quest, the quickening fire, the essential fundamental generosity toward both the individual and mankind. He would not have berated too much, if he had not expected too much and cared too much; and as often as not he was castigating, in the image of another, himself. My distaste for his doctrinal balancing of love with hate, of peace with war, of faultless hero with blind adherent, was melted into understanding of his fundamental, ultimate zeal to find some explanation of life—an explanation which would not be aerated philosophy, or idealization away from facts, but would meet facts head on, would face both the animal in man and the man in animal, would face them with intrepid determination to wring out of life and death everything good and true that he could find in them. In the depth of him, he would not sentimentalize, he would not falsify or avoid, he would not fabricate or fancify, he would find out all he could by observation, by contemplation, by practice, by honesty of body and spirit; and, though in the end the struggle might be unavailing and death conquer him, his fate would be the fate of good men before and after him, and he would have had all he could have of integrity. Meantime if there were any course in thought or emotion by which death might be explained as an intelligible part of life, he would find that course. I began to feel that his lifelong fleeing from place to place, from person to person, from emotion to emotion, from idea to idea, had been in reality a perpetual flight from death itself. He had long known that he was ill, with a likelihood of short span ahead. Had he always been haunted by death? Was that why he had worked at such a high-fever pitch? Was death what he had been trying to hide from when he fled over sea and land, hoping for a while that death might not follow? In *The Man Who Died,* he wrote of the tired Christ, seeing life again with the eyes of death: "It was fear, the ultimate fear of death that made men mad. So always if he stayed, his neighbors wound the strangling of their *fear* and bullying round him." Was that why Lawrence wandered? Or had he been fleeing his own fear of death? Or had he been hunting to find death and its meaning before death should stop him? Had he been less a fugitive than a hunter? Whatever the case, I discovered myself—as I felt his image sitting under the willow tree on the beach, near the burros or walking a hill in the dusk—more and more at peace with him.

And now in Vence, what was he thinking as to the death that approached him? For him no established creed or philosophy had solved existence and apparent nonexistence. Our churches in the Occident try to animate death with a lure of heaven and a menace of hell. Oriental philosophy tries to recommend it with a notion of open-eyed sleep. People the world over try to ease it with fond images of reunion after separation. Death stops them all.

I had thought earlier that, though his persistent purpose was to take death as naturally as he took life, yet he could not rationalize or instinctualize himself into accepting it, was always at bay against it. But now I thought otherwise. It had been enough for him to do as well as he could by life and to trust that, after this, death would do as well as it could by him. Did he feel now that he had enjoyed the life-and-death chase and had been proudly making himself worthy of the kill?

"We've all got to die," he had written in one of his *Studies in Classic American Literature* ". . . and disintegrate while we still live . . . Only, we know this much. Death is not the *goal*. And Love, and merging, are now only part of the death-process. Comradeship—part of the death-process. Democracy—part of the death-process . . . One identity—death itself . . . It is Finished. Consummatum est."

He had meant, then, to understand death by merging it with life. As Edgar Allan Poe had written in *The Premature Burial:* "The boundaries which divide Life and Death are at best shadowy and vague. Who shall say where the one ends, and where the other begins?" In Eugene O'Neill's *Mourning Becomes Electra,* Christine Mannon asks, "Why are you talking of death?" and Ezra Mannon answers, "That's always been the Mannons' way of thinking. They went to the white meetinghouse on Sabbaths and meditated on death. Life was a dying. Being born was starting to die. Death was being born. How in hell people ever got such notions!" Lawrence, in such notions, could not keep away from the white meetinghouse. Its pulpit still held him, also, in other notions, though he tried to vary his diction from that of the Christian preacher. I went back to *Fantasia of the Unconscious,* the book I had mainly disliked before ever we met, and there I found three memorable statements: "When I say to myself: 'I am wrong,' knowing with sudden insight that I *am* wrong, then that is the whole self speaking, the Holy Ghost. . . ." "Conscience is the being's consciousness, when the individual is conscious in toto, when he knows in full. . . ." "Real goodness brings us into a deeper life-flow; evil is that which impairs the life-flow." To the quick, Lawrence had always felt the sense of honor of a true individual and its connection with cosmic flow, and what better might carry on through the dead of him? However his body may smart and be restless, I reflected, he knows that he has always tried to reach his own summit. And that's enough.

Frieda's letter of March 13, 1930, came from Vence: "You will know that Lorenzo is dead. Right up to the last he was *alive* and we both made the best of our days, then he faced the end so splendidly, so like a *man* and I could help him through, thank God. Dead he looked proud and at peace and fulfilled. We had a simple cheap funeral, he would have liked it cheap, wouldn't he? Now I have one desire to take him to the ranch and make a lovely place for him there. He wanted so much to go. . . . There is very little money for me; he didn't make a will, according to English law I only get the *interest* on the £4000 that there are but I hope the pictures and manuscripts are mine. I have enough I hope for my few wants. . . . Do you remember our glamorous time in Mexico? Yes, you do, we read the poems together and he loved the one you wrote about him. How it took us back to Chapala, they *are* good—the world is changed for me. . . . Write to me, there was something vital between him and you. . . . Aldous Huxley editing his letters with little impressions by different people, would you do one? With love and sorrow—Frieda."

Richard Aldington speaks of being told by "the doctor who attended Lawrence in his last illness" that "although the lungs were badly scarred, there was still plenty of resistance, and he would have survived even then but for the psychological defeat which had destroyed his will to live." Murry implies, or more than implies, a similar judgment. To me the judgment seems mistaken, I should say that Lorenzo himself, and Frieda, knew better than they. What he wanted of life he could no longer have. It was not just bodily exercise or fulfillment, it was bodily rightness, upon which, for him, depended all psychology. And his body was not right for living, nor ever would be again, even with "plenty of resistance." It was the final physiological defeat which had destroyed his will to live. The psyche would still pulse, undefeated if it could, with other dark gods in his heavenly Hades.

Four months later, July 23, 1930, Frieda sent a letter from London: "Yes, I knew you would write as you have written and that you haven't forgotten him or me. But your letter was even *better* than I thought and lovelier. When you didn't write I read your 'Indian Earth' again and I could almost *smell* Chapala. How good these poems are. I still feel as if for years I had looked into a terribly strong light and now I'm dazed. He grows bigger and clearer for me and his death was so marvelous in its simplicity and control and belief in life—and now his bones are in the earth and he has become of the elements again and I feel everything more alive because he is a part of it. I do admire him so, you know, the way he managed his frail body and life little and big and he saw so far and so deep, through and round the world— and my pride is that I saw him right through and you know it was diabolically *hard* at times. In every way—you know! I want to bring him to the ranch, yes. . . . I shan't be *poor,* but for all that I would *love* it if his friends and admirers paid for his transport to the ranch, the Americans—the English have treated him so badly. . . . I want to make a life at the ranch—am a bit scared of Mabel and Brett. Mabel wrote a book, Lorenzo in Taos, and dear! O dear! Anyhow I have the satisfaction of knowing that we were *all* nicer, even she, than she makes out. . . ."

Frieda did return to the ranch and she brought Lawrence with her, not only the ashes but the man. Still where she goes, he goes. And now there is less wandering.

48. Legends

MABEL LUJAN had sent Lawrence when he was in England a typescript of some of her memoirs and he had showed it to Mrs. Carswell. "It was so full of personalities and so unreserved," records the latter, "that it struck me as unfit for publication for many years to come. When I told this to Lawrence, he agreed. 'But I don't care,' he added with a grin, 'so long as she dies before she gets to Frieda and me.'" But he died first, and Mrs. Lujan's *Lorenzo in Taos* appeared in 1932. It is a vivid and in many ways a courageous book, since it does not spare the author any more than it spares other figures appearing in it; but it bothered Frieda, with whom I agreed that it exceeded bounds here and there. She wrote me from Vence, May 15, 1932: "Yes, you were quite right—I implored Mabel, write that book again, it's not doing Lawrence justice, it's small beer! But she wouldn't, then I thought, all right, give yourself away!"

Presently Frieda went back to Europe on what, like other friends in the States, I thought a fool's errand. Lawrence had huffed often at his wife's faculty for losing things. Small objects were always disappearing, even jewelry. If he had known that his will was among the losses, he would have, naturally, made provision again. Years before in England he, Richard Aldington, and Middleton Murry had made their wills in concert, each thereby stirring the others into a needful but annoying action which human beings are apt to defer. After Lawrence's death, Frieda's sanguine idea was that, if she could assemble these friends to testify, she could establish in an English court her right to the principle of Lawrence's small estate. We advised her against the trip, fearing that it would but consume what little she had; but she was resolute. Writing her in England to wish her well, I had told her that I was setting out for Chapala again, which had now become for me a

346

habitual retreat, with the now married, twenty-six-year-old Ysidoro Pulido, the bootblack of earlier days, always ready to be my *mozo* and usually serving friends of mine in my absence; and I had deplored the fact that I could not be sharing the village and the lake again, as in 1923, with the Lawrences.

Her letter from Vence goes on: "We should have been so happy in Chapala, don't make me think about it. I am kind of fighting for Lawrence all the time. I am having a case to prove that there was a *will* leaving all to me. Pray for me to all the decent gods you know. I told you, I wanted you to write about him—but I fear the letters are nearly out; in print: I read them and thought them marvelous, his book of letters will be great, but couldn't you use them *again?* Any permission of mine you have. . . . I want to come back; O, this Europe! I think they'd like to treat me like the Lindbergh baby! Your letter made me happy! We know each other in all friendliness, don't we? I am going to London for the will business."

Murry and Aldington testified that they had been present when Lawrence drew his will leaving everything to Frieda and that they had signed it as witnesses. Even at that, her chance in the intestacy case appeared, from the austere expression of the probate judge and the atmosphere of the courtroom, to be weak. And then came what is now legend. Mrs. Lawrence's attorney made his final plea, his summing-up, drew an eloquent picture of the long years of poverty, of the couple's unfailing devotion to each other, of their idyllic life together with never a quarrel, at which his client, unable to contain herself longer, fountained to her feet protesting, "Oh, but no! That's not true! We fought like hell!" After a moment of shock the room burst into laughter, with Frieda finally joining. Laughter, as usual with her, was a following wave of her heated sincerity. The wig of the judge bent forward, while his hand hid his lips. Then, recovering, he solemnly announced himself to be persuaded of the plaintiff's "obvious honesty" and decided in her favor.

Richard Aldington has pointed out the ironic fact that the judge's mention of Lawrence as "a distinguished man" was the first deference given him from a public source in England. Until almost a decade after his death the British Broadcasting Company would not allow his name to be mentioned. It might be writ in water but not in the air. Even airy habitation was too much monument. William Cullen Bryant had said, in declining to be present when Mrs. Clemm's body was to be buried alongside that of her son-in-law, Edgar Allan Poe: "There should be some decided element of goodness in the character of those to whose example a public monument directs the attention of the world." In England, Lawrence's goodness was not decided.

Though funds had been pledged to bring his body from the temporary grave in Vence to his hill in New Mexico, Frieda now resolved, with the suit ended in her favor, that she would bear expenses and that cremation would be more feasible and fitting. Ashes were truer to the phoenix symbol than a coffined body would have been. So, returning from Europe herself, she arranged to have their Italian friend, Captain Ravagli, attend to details and follow with the urn.

The sequel may be, in part, another legend. Sometimes legends, though not quite accurate, are truer than the truth. Being in Chapala at the time, I was told the tale by letter. When Frieda and some companions met the train at Lamy, the junction which connects with Santa Fe by bus, they were so cordial in greeting the Captain and he— speaking only Italian—was so confused, that not till they had almost reached town nineteen miles away were they aware of having left on the station platform the urn containing Lawrence's ashes! Back they went, recovered it and took it safely to Del Monte, where a tiny chapel was built for it under tall pines on a rise behind the ranch house.

The ashes were to be sealed in a concrete altar. Another legend grows. It is said that Mrs. Lujan and the Honorable Dorothy Brett, sure that Lawrence would have abhorred such enshrinement of his ashes, conspired to prevent it; that Mrs. Lujan would have liked to be his midwife and deliver him to infinity by scattering the ashes; that a female emissary, sent to visit Frieda, was instructed, when next her hostess should be absent, to filch the urn but that the woman broke down and confessed, so that the ashes, as well as anyone. knows, rest safe and sound in their sealed repository, surrounded with frescoes of sunflowers and phoenixes. Brett's brush had contributed, on the outside doors of the shrine, a pair of prancing horses which, after her supposed share in the plot that failed, were erased.

"*Ces femmes!*" he had written.

But peace has been established, both inside the shrine and outside. Lawrence's cowboy hat which was on the altar and a guestbook which was at one side of the chancel have both been partly chewed away by chipmunks with "wonderful dark stripes running up their cheeks." Frieda has come down from Del Monte to a less isolated house in the valley, nearer Taos, where she can stay, if she likes, through the winters as well as through the summers; and American friends, or English friends like the Aldous Huxleys, Aldington, and Stephen Spender often use the ranch for withdrawal and work. In the mild months, also, many pilgrims make the climb and stand on the high spot where Lawrence's longing to return to New Mexico has been quietly granted, under pines and stars.

As to Old Mexico, when news came of his death, I wrote it to Ysidoro in Chapala. Unable to read even Spanish, he carried the letter to his cousin, Alfredo Padilla, who knows English; and Alfredo informed me: "Ysidoro was at the Post Office at the time the mail arrived and immediately ran to my house to take your message. And as soon as I started to read the letter he was ostensibly influenced with your words." Ysidoro, the young bootblack who, at Lawrence's summary insistence, had first been ordered from the terrace of the hotel and later jailed with all the orphans, had forgiven long since.

49. Frieda

FRIEDA, if one knows her, answers with her presence almost all questions. She sits now in mountainous Taos as one of its crags, as naturally there as they are. How a mountain could have wandered around the world and over oceans—with her Mahomet still in tow—only she could answer. She did answer me a while ago on this edge of the second half of the twentieth Christian century: "Think of the millions of people who have taken themselves as seriously as we have and they've all disappeared." But she looked cheery when she said it. How could Lawrence have had better support, even though it chafed him? Where was that dark self of his if she was right? And yet he knew that she had always been right and always would be. So she had to persevere, replacing him on his balance when he fell off it and saving him from his neighbors, some of whom occasionally tried to assist with his unbalancing. She never meant that we must always accept the air into which we happen, she only meant that we must not arrogate too much against it.

And so when the Lawrences were in Taos, where friends could sometimes become fiends, Frieda strengthened her love of him, her love of life, and her extraordinary balance between the two. I can see that from the outset, this balanced love of hers was intended by neighbors to be a target. Mrs. Lujan appeared from her own accounts to care less for anybody's love than for her own will. By resultant complications Frieda was fundamentally bored. And soon enough so was Lawrence. But there was an interval of unrest. And the period blends into the second year when Dorothy Brett, the one disciple who would have followed Lawrence to the ends of the sky, did follow him to the extremes of Taos. The period is recorded in books by both women friends and the book by Knud Merrild, *A Poet and Two Painters*. It was a bothered period for the Lawrences. In the short story, *Two Blue Birds*, Lawrence, reflecting Frieda's situation, gives a vivid line: "His halo was like a bucket over her head." When Mrs. Lujan proposed writing a novel with Lawrence, Frieda said, "I did not want this. I had always regarded Lawrence's genius as given to me. I felt deeply responsible for what he wrote. . . . I was thoroughly roused and said, 'Try it then yourself, living with a genius, see what it is like and how easy it is, take him if you can!'" Knud Merrild records, "More than once I remember her saying, 'It's not so easy to live with a genius,'" and the painter adds, on his own account, "Don't I know it, hadn't I seen it?"

And yet Mrs. Lawrence not only lived with a genius, she powerfully directed the genius. Again and again, from many sources, it is clear that she showed her phoenix the nest that flamed with new birth. Dorothy Brett reports saying to Lawrence about *The Boy in the Bush*: "'I don't like the end. He should have died. A man like that could never have gone on living; he could never have settled down to an ordered life; the only way out was for him to die,'" and Lawrence's answering, "'I know. That is how I wrote it first; I made him die— only Frieda made me change it.'" And then "Frieda looks up from her embroidery. 'Yes,' she booms, 'I made him change it. I couldn't stand the superiority of the man, always the same self-importance. Let him become ordinary, I said. Always this superiority and death.'" And there in a few words is the "unordinary" Frieda, candid, fearless, direct. I wonder if her husband realized how often she saved him from false heroism and false escape. It is probably too much to say of Frieda and Lawrence that she did to him what Anna Lensky did to Will Brangwen in *The Rainbow*, "forced him to the spirit of her laws, while leaving him the letter of his own"; but I am sure that Lawrence as well as Brangwen "knew with shame, how her father had been a man without arrogating any authority." I can hear Frieda saying to him, as Harriet says in *Kangaroo* (can hear her physical accent as well as her sense) when he revolts against people and despairs of them and she protests, in Australia, as she had doubtless done elsewhere: "'Yet like a dog to his vomit you always turn back. And it will be the same old game here as everywhere else.' . . . He was silent. He heard all that she had to say: and he knew that as far as the past went, it was all quite true. He had started off on his fiery courses: always, as she said, to fall rather the worse for the attempt, on her. She had no use at all for fiery courses and efforts with the world of men. Let all that rubbish go.' " He persists: " 'I want to do something with living people, somehow, somewhere, while I live on the earth. I write, but I write alone. And I live alone. Without any connection whatever with the rest of men.' 'Don't swank,' " was her rejoinder, " 'you don't live alone. You've got me there safe enough, to support you. . . . I know how much alone you are, with me always there keeping you together.' ". . . " 'Him, a lord and master!' " The novel then echoes what Frieda was thinking and probably saying: "If he had been naturally a master of men . . . with thousands of men under him—then, yes, she could have acknowledged the *master* part of the bargain if not the lord. . . . Whereas, he had absolutely nothing but her. And that was why, presumably, he wanted to establish this ascendancy over her, assume this arrogance." And so said Frieda, through Harriet: " 'Of course, you lonely phoenix, you are the bird and the ashes and the flames all by yourself! . . . I don't exist.' 'Yes,' he said, 'you are the nest.' 'I'll watch it!' she cried. 'Then you shall sleep on thorns, Mister.'. . . 'Believe in *me,*' he said desperately. 'I know you too well,' she replied, and went on thinking: He *wanted* to be male and unique, like a freak of a phoenix. And then go prancing into connections with men like Jack Calcott and Kangaroo, and saving the world. She could *not* stand these world-saviours. And she, she must be safely there, as a nest for him, when he came home with his feathers pecked . . . he had preached at her, like a dog barking, barking senselessly. And oh, how it had annoyed her."

It was not that she disrelished his interest in other men's lives. Her pride is more than once recorded as helpmate of a man who wanted to give the world better health than he found in it. She believed, however, that this health-giving lay not in social or religious organization but in the integrity and simplest wisdom of a man's own being and living. Toward this realization, for both herself and him, through whatever temporary distraction or disturbance, her aim remained true and her fortitude deep.

Mrs. Carswell has noted, through the Lawrences' early years of hardship, Frieda's "simple animal stoicism in the face of pain and discomfort"; but she concludes with this accolade: "Sometimes it seemed to us that he had chosen rather a force of nature—a female force—than an individual woman. . . . At times she hated Lawrence and he her. There were things she jeered at in him and things in her that maddened him—things that neither would consent to subdue. But partly for that very reason—how he admired her! . . . In Frieda, Lawrence found a magnificent female probity of being, as well as of physical well-being. She could bear the pressure of his male probity—his 'demon'—as no other woman could have borne it. Sure in herself, she could accept anything and recover from anything. She was the 'freest' woman he had ever met. . . . For myself, I find that in her own very different way Frieda is a person as remarkable as Lawrence, and that Lawrence knew it."

In 1912 Lawrence had written David Garnett of Frieda in straight terms that she was "perfectly unconventional, but really good—in the best sense." In 1926 Mrs. Lawrence wrote Mrs. Lujan, with a candor which should have been respected: "Why do you all think my life is a desperate struggle to hang on to Lawrence? It really does make me appear such a poor thing! I am jolly glad to be alone sometimes, so is he, but we are both glad to come together again, very glad! Our lives, Lawrence's and mine, are so easy, if nobody makes any mischief!"

Mabel Lujan and Dorothy Brett, in their own accounts of Taos and New Mexican life with Lawrence, give Frieda bountiful reason for any irritation she may have felt or expressed toward them for their fussing round her husband. Though she had said, "Why don't you go to it and really see what it's like?" she grew tired, at the ranch, of having an outsider on hand all the time and at last suggested that Brett's presence there be not more than three times a week. When Brett found a pretext for a fourth day, Frieda cried out, " 'I won't *have* you up here every day!' " to which Brett, by her own account, replied airily, " 'Oh, go to hell, I won't be bossed by you!' " Lawrence, as the would-be aristocrat, must have been amused by such spirited interchange, between the daughter of the Baron von Richthofen and the daughter of Viscount Esher.

Brett reports further: "Frieda is walking about with her head down, always a bad sign," or again, "Frieda is nervous, her eyes darting about, looking nowhere and at no one," or still again, as often, "Frieda lies on her bed, smoking." Brett refused to recognize a smoking volcano. Brett was the placid village, threatened but never quite doomed.

Let me remember for myself Frieda's husky-voiced remonstrances, with a bewildered look half-assumed, when she knew that assertions by her husband were false or doubtful or theatrical. Or when she felt that he and the whole roomful in some of our Chapala discussions were right, let me remember her hearty gurgles of mirth, her *"ja"* gushing out with keen agreement. Let me remember and cherish the usual straight look under that eagle-sure profile. It is exciting when a profile can turn full on you and still be seen from outside and from inside and from broadside, looking full on you as hers does, the straight look which passes by the superficial or the make-believe. I remember too her look when disagreement was not worth while, her place set at the table but the guest not there.

In the summer of 1923, when for a brief interval cleavage had come between the Lawrences, because Frieda insisted upon seeing her children and sailed alone to England, and when Lawrence joined the Danes in Los Angeles and Merrild wrote, "Without Frieda he was restless and in lonely mood," he himself wrote, "The four walls are a blanket I wrap around myself in timelessness and nowhere, to go to sleep."

No wonder he had earlier written to Ernest Collings: "I daren't sit in the world without a woman behind me." It was Frieda who was behind the husband—except that she wouldn't let him stay sitting in prejudice, in malice, in pretense. If she had, there might have been from him but the brilliant fretful record of an invalid. Frieda contained always what he craved and lacked—an absolute animal sense of security. "Whatever may happen elsewise," was what one knew Frieda was thinking, "this is mine. And I like it. It is enough." That was the doctrine Lawrence wanted, denounced, hailed, glorified, and vicariously achieved. It was the consistent Frieda who lived the life he wanted, with no need of outside help from bearded Druids, Etruscan nobles, Egyptian priests, Aztec gods—or even other women. While from the width of the world, and from dark gods stirring in its depths and seas like Chinese dragons, the real Lawrence sought refuge in actual violets under mossy stones and in the motion and markings of small animals, Frieda faced boldly and happily the warmth and the wind of the world; and in the human world she quickly distinguished the warm truth from the cold mistakes.

The match was between a good man and a sure woman. Her detractors were wooden ships against Gibraltar.

Was ever anything simpler than her record in the book she wrote, *Not I but the Wind:* "I will not stay in your husband's house while he is away," said Lawrence, "but you must tell him the truth and we will go away together, because I love you." That was his declaration; and later he wrote: "I shall love you all my life." Though she loved her children, she had not loved her professor husband. The Lawrence flight was no Bohemian caprice. It was no escapade of passion. It was no conquest of a woman by a man's callous will. Lawrence was on a spiritual rack; and before resurrective decision, he communed deep with all that was good in him and found the answer, which was as sure in Frieda as it was in himself.

In 1914 he wrote Middleton Murry: "There isn't a soul cares for me, except Frieda—and it's rough to have all the burden put on her." He might have thought of that oftener—but he did think of it oftener than he admitted. There was not a soul who cared for him except Frieda—in the way he wanted to be cared for. He wrote to Mrs. S. A. Hopkins on a Christmas Day: "Once you've known what love *can* be, there's no disappointment any more, and no despair. If the skies tumble down like a smashed saucer, it couldn't break what's between Frieda and me. . . . I'll do my life work sticking up for the love between man and woman." At the end of his life, he said to Frieda, "Why, oh, why did we quarrel so much?" But she answered, "Such as we were, violent creatures, how could we help it?" I remember an early sly jab at his aristocratic Frieda, before he thoroughly knew her, when in *The Lost Girl* he wrote of Alvina: "She was ladylike, she was not vehement at all."

Their differences, the snarling spats, the wrangles, the pitched battles were harder for her to take than they were for him, since she felt far less reliance than he thought he did on psychological explanations. All was not fair for her in love and war when war and love appeared to be the same. In the end, though, she agreed with the poems he had written earlier: "Look, we have come through!"

Ruth Laughlin Alexander has recalled meeting the Lawrences one afternoon at my house in Santa Fe, after which we all went to some restaurant for the evening meal. "The waitress was slow," she says, "and when food came it was cold, whereupon Lawrence reared, exploding first at the waitress and then, for no reason, at Frieda. We all sat back in terror of what would come next. He was an exhibit, his wife was the whipping-girl." Mrs. Alexander added: "Creative fulfillment was what he was always writing about, while in her simpler, ampler way his wife did the fulfilling." I agree. Frieda took her husband's life doctrine naturally, with understanding that when his time should be done, she would still face life to the last flicker. She would poke an ember and see.

Roark Bradford, of *Green Pastures,* told me once of meeting Mrs. Lawrence in a group, without noting who she was. In the course of talk, the novelist's name came up.

"Those women in Taos ruined him," said Bradford.

"*Ja,*" said Frieda.

"Including his wife," said Bradford.

"*Ja,*" said Frieda.

And then he asked, "I didn't catch your name?"

"I'm Mrs. Lawrence," she beamed.

"I guess I'm in the wrong place," laughed Bradford. "I'd better get out of here. I'm lost."

"No, please don't," laughed Mrs. Lawrence. "I'm the one that's lost. I lose everything."

Everything but her direction.

One night in my Santa Fe library she read from manuscript the final chapter of *Not I but the Wind.* Before she finished, four of us saw her glasses clouded so thickly that she could not have read the words. She did not need to read them. The reality of her husband comes through in her own words about him: "I certainly found him more delicately and sensitively aware of me than I ever imagined anybody would be. To be so enveloped in tenderness was a miracle in itself to me." Her own reality has been recorded in a line of Lawrence's *Look We Have Come Through,* as to her companionship with him or with life, and it never changed: ". . . let me be myself, not a river or tree." I can hear her saying it and can see the river slip aside and the tree give way. Lawrence answers in the same book, and with unchanging love:

> So I hope I shall spend eternity
> With my face down buried between her breasts:
> And my still heart full of security
> And my still hands full of her breasts.

Index